THE COMPLEAT OPTION PLAYER

Winning Strategy and Tactics in the New Options Game

By KENNETH R. TRESTER

ISBN: 0-9604914-0-6

To Merle

She helped make an impossible dream possible.

Also By Kenneth R. Trester
The Option Player's Advanced Guidebook

CONTENTS

PART I — THE NEW OPTIONS GAME

Chapter 1   The Only Game in Town 3
Chapter 2   The Name of the Game 8
Chapter 3   The Rules of the Game 16
Chapter 4   The Incredible Shrinking Option 25
Chapter 5   The Psychiatric Guide
             to Options Behavior 37
Chapter 6   How to Get Started on Small Capital 51
Chapter 7   The Art of Buying Options 55
Chapter 8   The Playable Stock 64
Chapter 9   The Playable Option 70
Chapter 10   The Game Plan 79

PART II — WINNING THROUGH OPTION WRITING STRATEGIES

Chapter 11   Taking the Bets Rather
             Than Making the Bets 86
Chapter 12   The Secrets of Exercise 93
Chapter 13   The Secrets of Strategy Design 99
Chapter 14   The Business of Option Writing 103
Chapter 15   Play It Naked .121
Chapter 16   The Secrets of Naked Option Writing 132
Chapter 17   The Road to Riches -
             The Naked Spread 143
Chapter 18   Molding Innovative Strategies 158
Chapter 19   The Spread Game 167

PART III — SECRETS OF THE PROFESSIONAL OPTION TRADER

Chapter 20   The Compleat Option Trader 180
Chapter 21   Professional Trading Tactics 184
Chapter 22   The Ten Commandments of
             Option Trading .199
Chapter 23   Danger! Beware of Commissions 208
Chapter 24   Winning the Margin Game 221
Chapter 25   Selecting Your Options Team 241
Chapter 26   Tools Needed for Professional Play 251
Chapter 27   The Tax Game .263
Chapter 28   A Look Into the Future 265

THE APPENDIX

Normal Value Option Tables 274
The Normal Value Listed Call Option Tables
The Normal Value Listed Put Option Tables

PART I

THE NEW

OPTIONS GAME

THE ONLY GAME IN TOWN

Chapter 1

THE ONLY GAME IN TOWN

A WINNING INVESTMENT SYSTEM:
FANTASY OR FACT?

Consider an investment game where you have no risk and a high probability of reward. Consider an investment game where you win if your investments go up a little, down a little, down a lot, or don't move at all. Then consider the results of the following system:

"1. The system gained more than 25% per year for seventeen years.

2. From September, 1929 to June, 1930, the system could have doubled an investment.

3. The system showed a real five year track record generating average returns of 25% per year.

4. The system actually doubled $100,000 in four years."[1]

Could such a game, or such a system truly exist? To answer this question, let's turn the clock back several years. During the 1960's, two university professors, using computer technology, took on the challenge of the stock market. These

[1] Edward O. Thorp, Sheen T. Kassouf, *BEAT THE MARKET,* Random House, Inc., New York, 1967.

two pioneers were Edward O. Thorp and Sheen T. Kassouf, and their goal was to *beat the market scientifically.* Using the computer, Thorp had already beaten the casinos of Las Vegas, forcing them to change their rules for blackjack.

Now he had taken on a far more formidable challenge: design a system to beat the stock market. After extensive experimentation, Thorp arrived at one major conclusion — the stock market is unpredictable. Stock prices move in an unforeseeable manner, and profits are as difficult to anticipate as profits at the gaming tables in Las Vegas. In other words, anyone who buys or sells stocks is taking a random walk down Wall Street.

Having made these findings, Dr. Thorp began to investigate possible stock market methods that would not require the prediction of stock price behavior. Finally he discovered a system utilizing a special hedging strategy in convertible securities. The key element of the system was *to sell warrants short.* (Warrants are securities issued by companies giving the right to buy their common stock at a set price during a given period.) The results of this system are demonstrated in the four points above. The only problem was the limited number of investment opportunities available to the game player.

NEW CONVERTIBLE SECURITY CREATED

In 1973, a revolutionary new convertible security was born — the "listed call option." The new entity traded on the first options exchange, the Chicago Board Options Exchange, (CBOE), which began operations on April 26, 1973. The new listed option, along with the recently formed CBOE, opened a whole spectrum of opportunities for the use of Thorp's stock market system, for this new Exchange gave his system the spark that was needed and had been lacking in the warrant and convertible securities market.

ADVANCES IN THE THORP SYSTEM CREATED

The new listed options are a close relative of both the warrant and the old over-the-counter (OTC) option, meaning that any systems or investment techniques which were successful with the old vehicles for investment would also be directly applicable to this new medium. Being a strong advocate and user of Thorp's warrant system, I was extremely enthusiastic about the birth of the unique Options Exchange. Thus when the Exchange opened and began operations, I altered Thorp's basic system and applied it to the new Options Exchange. The results far surpassed my greatest expectations. I documented these results in a two-year market letter, which showed an annualized return of over 40%.

Using Thorp's work as a base, I began to develop new types of strategies, such as: ratio calendar spreads; ratio vertical spreads; and unique naked option writing strategies. Sound like some kind of pornographic game? Well, believe it or not, the results of this game are far more interesting.

PROFESSIONALS TAKE UP THE STRATEGIES

My success was not rare; other professionals began to discover these new exciting strategies. Normally, these options traders came out of the old OTC options market, where their past experience would give them a clear picture of the profit potential of the new listed option.

One of the first institutional money managers to enter this market was Jerry M. Traver, of the small Bank of Commerce in Fort Worth, Texas. Traver boasted an excellent four year track record using the OTC options market. The strategy he employed was called "covered option writing," the most well known and also the most conservative option strategy. Using this technique, Traver raised the accounts held by his bank by approximately 4% in 1969, 15% in 1970, 18% in 1971, and 20% in 1972. Then with the birth of the CBOE, Mr. Traver immediately moved into this new market, and from May, 1973 through April, 1974, the Bank's average option writing account rose 12.6%. In comparison, it is interesting to note that during this period, the Dow was off almost 10%, the Standard & Poor's 500 fell 15%, and the New York Stock Exchange Composite declined 15%.

Another professional who entered this new game was actually our pioneer of options strategies — Ed Thorp. Thorp and Kassouf's unique warrant system attracted many investors to Ed Thorp's door. An investment pool (using variations of his warrant system), which he began managing in 1969, has since grown to about 20 million dollars, and has out-performed all but one of the more than four hundred mutual funds tracked by Standard & Poor's Mutual Fund Guide. Exact performance figures are not available. However, reliable brokerage house sources close to the funds say that they have averaged better than 20% a year in net asset growth since 1969, an enviable record considering the general market decline during this period.[2]

Thorp, of course, became an active member of the new options market, where a gold mine of systems opportunities is available. His performance results demonstrate the success of options strategies, and the potential of the new options market.

Given these results, the new *listed call option* has been proven to be an investment vehicle which:

1. Can be used to reduce risk to almost zero
2. Can promise consistent and high profit return, without the need to predict action in the market
3. Can be a trading medium that, if applied properly, will provide the consistent return described at the beginning of this chapter.

THE LISTED PUT OPTION

And now, a new dimension has been added to the options market — the *"listed put option."* The advent of this new option, the counterpart to the listed call option, has opened

[2]J.R. Laing, *"Computer Formulas are One Man's Secret to Success in Market"* Reprinted with permission of the Wall Street Journal, Dow Jones & Co., Inc. 1974. All rights reserved.

up still another new realm of investment opportunities to the individual investor. The ability to trade in listed put options adds tremendous flexibility and firing power to options strategies. The evidence presented in this chapter has demonstrated the outstanding attributes of listed call options. In later chapters, we will look more closely at the new listed put option, and prove that by integrating the use of *listed put options* with *listed calls,* you can develop an investment vehicle that will far surpass the results attained in any other investment media.

IS THE OPTIONS MARKET FOR EVERYONE?

You may wonder then, if this new fangled options market is so great — why isn't everybody using it?

The average investor fears the complicated or the novel investment. The new listed options are very complex and difficult to visualize and comprehend, and the introduction of the new listed put option has greatly added to this confusion. Numerous amateurs have entered this game uneducated, unskilled, and unprepared for the fast and diverse action of the options market. They have been introduced to the game by inexperienced brokers who suddenly call themselves "options specialists." Consequently, these investors have been burned — receiving a very expensive education. This book is dedicated to those who wish to avoid paying such a high tuition, to those who wish to come prepared to play the game.

In conclusion, the new options market is the best investment media the author has experienced, finally giving the small investor an advantage. The small investor now has a weapon to counter the institutions; he can take his turn at being the house, rather than being a pawn to be pushed and shoved by the big boys.

However, the road to riches offered by this new game is not an easy one. Don't throw caution to the wind; to succeed in this new market requires you to do your homework and acquire some specialized knowledge and trading skills. You must become a COMPLEAT OPTION PLAYER; an options player well prepared for the unusual action of the new options markets.

Chapter 2

THE NAME OF THE GAME

BECOMING A COMPLEAT OPTION PLAYER

To become a COMPLEAT OPTION PLAYER, you must gain a complete understanding of the focal point of this game — *the listed option.* You must be able to easily visualize the listed option from every angle, and then become an options psychologist, totally familiar with the behavior of these unique and unpredictable artificial beings. The option player who fails to clearly see, touch, taste and feel the listed option will never reach the winner's circle.

Now let us unravel some of the mysteries of the listed option. A look at an example will help us begin our discussion:

XEROX   Jul   60

What is described above is a listed call option, listed or available on the new Chicago Board Options Exchange (CBOE). You will notice that there are three parts to the option.

Part I: "XEROX" — This represents the fact that this option is the <u>right</u> to buy 100 shares of Xerox Corporation common stock.

Part II: "JUL" — This represents the *time* when your right expires. This entity is termed the "expiration date", which falls on the Saturday immediately following the third Friday of the expiration month. In this case, it is in the month of July.

Part III: "60" — This represents the *exercise price* at which the Xerox stock can be purchased. This price is also referred to as the "striking price".

Now, let's add to our example one more item:

XEROX   Jul   60   (at)   3

Part IV: "(at) 3" — This refers to the price at which this option was bought or sold on the last transaction, with one qualifying point. The 3 represents $3, the price to buy the option of one share of stock. All listed options carry the right to buy or sell 100 shares of stock. Therefore, always multiply the price by 100 to get the true price of the option. In this case, the true price is $300.
($3 x 100 = $300)

A listed option then has four major segments:

I. The RIGHT — to buy or sell 100 shares of a specific stock.

II. The EXPIRATION DATE — The date that your right ends or expires.

III. The EXERCISE PRICE — The price at which you can buy or sell.

IV. The OPTION PRICE — The price you paid for the right to buy or sell 100 shares at an exercise price until an expiration date.

Let's look at a few more examples of listed call options.

> **EXAMPLE I:** IBM Oct 270 at 12
> This listed option is: the right to buy 100 shares of IBM, which expires in the month of October, on the Saturday immediately following the third Friday of the month. The price of this option is $1200, and the option gives you the right to purchase 100 shares of IBM stock at a price of $270 a share, which is the exercise, or striking price.

> **EXAMPLE II:** G.D. SEARLE Nov 15 at 3/16
> This listed option gives you the right to buy 100 shares of SEARLE at a price of $15 a share, which ends in the month of November, again on the Saturday immediately following the third Friday of that month. The price of this option is 3/16, which converts to $18.75.

Now that you have a clear idea of what a listed option looks like, and which parts compose it, let's see if we can properly define this entity.

LISTED OPTION DEFINED

A listed option is a stock option. An option is simply a contract, one that gives you the right to buy or sell, (in this case), 100 shares of stock at a specific price, for a specific period of time. While stock options have been with us for many years, the brilliant idea of creating a *listed option* has opened up a whole new investment media.

Further, listed options are stock options which are liquid, standardized, and are continually created at the changing price levels of the common stock. When we say a listed option is liquid, we mean that it can be bought and sold at any time in an auction market, similar to the New York Stock Exchange.

Formerly in the old over-the-counter (OTC) market, stock options could be purchased, if you could find a seller. But, in order to have taken your profits from that option, you would have had to *exercise* the option, actually buying the 100 shares of the stock that you had the right to purchase. Now, with the new options exchanges, this costly process of actually buying the stock, or selling the stock is not necessary. All you have to do is to go back to the Exchange, and sell your option, just as you would sell shares of common stock. And, even better, commissions are lower, and the profits are fatter with listed options than with the old type of option.

Thus, we can see that the listed option has several clear advantages — you can buy and sell very freely; there is a continuous market in each specific class of options; and, when necessary, a new class of options can be established by the Exchange.

HOW THE LISTED OPTION WORKS

To demonstrate how the listed option works, let's look at our second example of the G.D. SEARLE Nov 15 option. Let's say that you, as an investor, went into the market and purchased that option for a price of 3/16, which is $18.75. Then, one hour later, you find that the stock has moved upward, which means that your option has also moved up in price on the Exchange. Now this listed option is priced at $50, rather than $18.75, and you decide that you wish to sell it. All you have to do is to call your broker, and have him put in an order to sell your option at $50. Within one brief hour, you have bought and sold the same stock option. This never would have been possible in the old OTC options market, but with the new, exciting options exchanges, the game has been totally changed. In the course of one day, you can buy and sell the same option many times.

TWO CATEGORIES OF LISTED OPTIONS DEFINED

At this point, you understand the listed option, and researching it more carefully, you discover that there are two types, the listed "call" option, and the listed "put" option. Since the advent of the CBOE in 1973, the only type of option that had been traded in these new markets had been the listed "call" option, which is simply *the right to buy stock.* When you purchase a call, you are betting that the underlying stock price will move *up.*

But there is another listed option which has come upon the horizon, called the listed "put" option, which is *the right to sell stock.* When you purchase a put, (a put is very similar to selling short the stock without the extensive risk) you are betting that the underlying stock price will move *down.* With the addition of the put option to the market, we have another revolutionary new tool with which to work in the listed options field.

A BET TO WIN AND A BET TO LOSE

Another way to describe the difference between a "put"

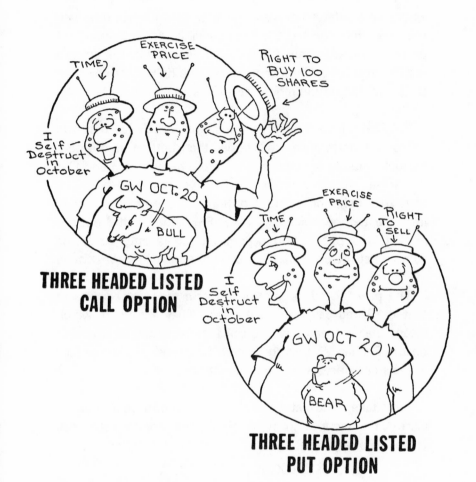

THREE HEADED LISTED CALL OPTION

THREE HEADED LISTED PUT OPTION

and a "call" is to use an analogy. Let's say that you have gone to the race track, and have placed a bet on a horse to win the race. The bet you've placed on the horse to win would be similar to a "call" option. If the horse does win the race, then the bet becomes valuable. Just as your bet becomes valuable only if the horse wins, so in the options market, the call option becomes valuable only if the common stock that the option represents moves *up*.

Now let's take the opposite example. Let's say that you go to the horse race, and rather than betting at the pari-mutuel windows on a horse to win, you bet with a friend that the horse will come in *dead last*. This bet would be analogous to purchasing a "put" option. If the horse comes in last, the bet becomes valuable. Similarly, in the options market, the put option becomes valuable only when the common stock price that the option represents moves *down*.

The new "listed put options" retain the same advantages that the listed call options possess. They are liquid, which means that you can buy and sell them as freely as you wish on the Exchange; they are standardized; and puts are created as the stock prices move to different price levels.

Let's take a look at a sample listed put option, in order to clarify the manner in which it differs from a listed call option. For example:

XEROX   Jul   60   (at)   2

Here we have a listed put option, which looks just like a listed call. But the difference is that this option is *not* the right to *buy* 100 shares of stock, it is the right to *sell* 100 shares of stock, at a price of $60 a share. The price of this option is $200.

Now let us say that after intense analysis, you have decided that the Xerox Corp.'s stock price will decline significantly in the next two weeks. Hypothetically, let's say that the Xerox stock price at the present time is $65, and you feel it will move down to $58 a share. Now, how can you place a side bet on your belief that Xerox will move *down* in this market? You can do this very easily, by purchasing the put option we have just discussed — a Xerox Jul 60 — at the present price of $200 an option. So, you pull $200 out of your coffers and buy one Xerox Jul 60 put.

Watch — as you had predicted, the stock moves down the next day from $65 a share to $60 a share. This kind of a move in a stock, of course, greatly increased the value of your put option. The value of the put option now moves up to 4½ ($450) in the market. Immediately, not being greedy, you move in and sell your put option on the Exchange for $450. You have made a nice easy $250 profit within one day by buying a put option. What you have done is purchased a side bet, betting that the Xerox stock price would move down.

Now, if you had believed that the Xerox stock price was going to move up, then you would have wanted to buy a listed *call option,* which would be a side bet that the stock price would move *up.*

Thus far, you have a better feel for listed options, understand what they represent, and comprehend the difference between a listed put and a listed call. You are ready to move on to the next chapter. In it, we will discuss the arena in which these listed options are traded, and the rules by which you can buy and sell listed options.

Chapter 3

THE RULES OF THE GAME

HOW LISTED PUT OPTIONS AND
LISTED CALL OPTIONS ARE TRADED

Having had some exposure to listed options in your early training, you're ready to talk about the ball park in which these listed put and call options are traded. This ball park is called an "Options Exchange". An options exchange, like a stock exchange, is an auction market, where buyers and sellers gather to trade securities. In this case, the security is a listed option.

The first of these exchanges, the Chicago Board Options Exchange (CBOE), was established in April of 1973, and it is probably the one best structured to handle the job. Since then several other exchanges have been established, including the American Options Exchange, the Philadelphia-Baltimore-Washington Options Exchange, the Pacific Coast Options Exchange, and the Midwest Options Exchange; these all jumped into the game after they had seen the tremendous success which came from the trading of listed options.

THE LISTED OPTION EXCHANGE IS AN AUCTION MARKET FOR STANDARDIZED OPTIONS

Each exchange operates under very similar rules, and each uses the same clearing corporation, which means that they all carry out the same kind of bookkeeping activities. However, the CBOE has a more unique type of trading setup, being far more sophisticated, and experienced than the other exchanges. As we move through this material, we will continually be referring back to these arenas of action whenever we discuss the Options Exchange.

Now let's take a closer look at the option transactions that occur in these options markets. There are two parties to every listed option. If you're the buyer, you may be wondering, "who is the seller?". The seller is a new man on the scene, often called an "option writer." An option writer is analogous to the casino operator who backs your bet at the gaming tables –– he will pay off if you win. (This is a very simplistic presentation of an option writer, but it will suffice for now.) Later on, you will discover that with this new Options Exchange, you, the small investor, actually have the opportunity to become an option writer, a person who backs bets, rather than simply the person who makes bets. It's a very exciting position to be in, and there is tremendous profit potential in option writing.

A listed option, as you have just learned, is similar to a side bet on the price action of a specific common stock. The stocks which are selected to have options listed on the options exchanges must meet a set of very strict criteria. These criteria are available from your brokerage house. After reading through all the legal jargon, you will find that only common stocks of the highest quality can meet the tough standards for options listed on the exchanges. Even with these limitations, there are over 400 different common stocks which have had options listed on the different options exchanges.

LISTED OPTIONS AVAILABLE

Each individual stock must have at least three different options listed on the Exchange, but can have many more. Each common stock has listed options with expiration dates occurring in four different months, but only three expiration dates are available to the option player at any one time. Options can be traded with expiration dates up to nine months in the future.

For example, IBM has listed options which expire in January, April, July, and October. However, in the month of June, options with only three of these expiration dates would be available. These would include July, October, and January. The option player never has more than three expiration dates available to him within each family of options.

EXAMPLES OF LISTED OPTIONS AVAILABLE

A glance at the CBOE prices published in most daily newspapers and in the Wall Street Journal (an example is also presented in Figure I), will quickly show some of the listed options that are available.

For the call options quotations for Feb. 9, 1977, you will find that Polaroid has options showing different exercise prices, ranging from 30 to 45. You will also notice that options are available at these exercise prices with three different expiration months (April, July, October). Add all these options together, and you get twelve different listed call options available to the option trader on Polaroid common stock.

Further, you will find that the "Volume", or the number of listed options traded on Feb. 9, is listed for each specific option. If you look at the Polaroid (PRD) Apr 40 option,

FIGURE I

CBOE Prices published in the Wall Street Journal

Chicago Board

Option &	price	Feb Vol.	Feb Last	May Vol.	May Last	Aug Vol.	Aug Last	N.Y. Close
A E P	..20	12	4⅛	1	4¾	3	4¼	24¼
A E P	..25	283	1-16	50	7-16	98	⅝	24¼
Am Hos	25	b	b	14	2 5-16	22	2¾	26
Am Hos	30	70	1-16	103	7-16	71	1	26
Am Hos	35	a	a	22	1-16	a	a	26
A M P	. 25	a	a	1	2	14	3⅛	25¾
A M P	. 30	a	a	8	⅜	11	1	25¾
Baxter	. 35	66	3-16	42	1 11-16	17	2⅝	33⅞
Baxter	..40	a	a	37	½	3	1¼	33⅞
Baxter	. 45	4	1-16	27	⅛	3	½	33⅞
Blk Dk	15	8	2⅜	10	3¼	14	3⅝	17⅝
Blk Dk	20	6	1-16	38	½	54	1	17⅝
Blk Dk	. 25	a	a	5	⅛	b	b	17⅝
Boeing	. 35	23	5⅛	19	5¾	3	6⅛	40
Boeing	40	189	11-16	117	2¾	13	3⅞	40
Boeing	. 45	7	1-16	293	13-16	26	1⅝	40
Bois C	..25	37	4	19	4⅜	1	5⅝	29
Bois C	..30	267	3-16	207	1⅜	135	2¼	29
Bois C	..35	a	a	64	5-16	66	15-16	29
C B S	.. 50	29	6	5	6¾	a	a	55⅝
C B S	.. 60	35	1-16	25	1 3-16	a	a	55⅝
Coke	... 70	19	5	17	6½	1	8	75¼
Coke	... 80	75	1-16	85	1 7-16	47	2¾	75¼
Coke	... 90	a	a	20	3-16	b	b	75¼
Colgat	..25	18	3-16	58	1⅛	81	1¾	24¾
Colgat	..30	a	a	8	⅛	7	⅜	24¾
Cmw Ed	30	54	⅛	9	⅝	6	15-16	29⅝
C Data	20	103	3½	75	4⅜	31	5	23½
C Data	25	1271	⅛	430	1¼	168	2	23½
Gn Dyn	.45	1	13	8	13½	b	b	58⅛
Gn Dyn	50	128	7¾	80	9½	35	12	58⅛
Gn Dyn	60	890	⅜	407	3⅜	168	4¾	58⅛
GE Ut	46⅛	17	4⅝	8	5⅝	a	a	b
GE Ut	53⅞	33	1-16	7	1⅜	12	2⅝	b
Gen Fd	25	2	6⅞	a	a	a	a	32¼
Gen Fd	.30	163	2¼	11	2	10	2⅜	32¼
Gen Fd	.35	a	a	8	⅜	8	9-16	32¼
Hewlet	..70	b	b	57	5⅛	12	7¼	71
Hewlet	. 80	7	1-16	46	1¾	63	3⅛	71
Hewlet	..90	a	a	21	5-16	29	1⅛	71
Hewlet	.100	a	a	a	a	8	⅜	71
H Inns	. 10	109	1 15-16	15	2 5-16	127	2⅝	11⅞
H Inns	. 15	29	1-16	122	¼	103	7-16	11⅞
Honwll	..40	83	4¾	44	5⅞	a	a	44¾
Honwll	. 45	836	⅝	334	2⅝	144	3¾	44¾
Honwll	. 50	26	1-16	376	13-16	105	1 11-16	44¾
In Flv	..20	29	1-16	32	15-16	30	1⅝	18⅞
In Flv	..25	3	1-16	15	¼	19	½	18⅞
J Manv	25	17	4⅜	2	4½	10	5¼	29½
J Manv	30	109	3-16	137	1 5-16	84	2	29½
J Manv	35	1	1-16	4	5-16	10	9-16	29½
MGIC	...15	a	a	7	3¼	a	a	17⅝
MGIC	...20	a	a	22	11-16	5	1¼	17⅝
Mobil	.. 55	93	10⅝	54	10½	b	b	65⅞
Mobil	...60	62	5⅝	92	5¾	76	6⅝	65⅞
Mobil	.. 65	b	b	41	2¾	54	3¾	65⅞
Mobil	.. 70	b	b	111	¾	55	1½	65⅞
N Semi	20	b	b	1039	1¾	500	2 9-16	19⅛
N Semi	.25	16	1-16	688	7-16	435	1 1-16	19⅛
N Semi	.30	27	1-16	113	¼	72	7-16	19⅛
N Semi	35	10	1-16	7	⅛	b	b	19⅛
N Semi	40	a	a	221	1-16	b	b	19⅛
Occi	... 15	36	9½	20	9¼	a	a	24½
Occi	... 20	363	4½	58	4⅞	158	5⅝	24½
Occi	... 25	418	⅜	458	1½	299	2⅜	24½
Raythn	. 50	35	7⅜	3	8¼	a	a	57
Raythn	60	120	1-16	62	1 9-16	14	2⅞	57
Raythn	. 70	a	a	51	⅛	b	b	57
Rynlds	. 60	21	3⅝	3	4⅜	20	5½	63½
Rynlds	..70	a	a	24	7-16	21	⅞	63½

Listed Options Quotations

Wednesday, February 9, 1977

Closing prices of all options. Sales unit usually is 100 shares. Security description includes exercise price. Stock close is New York Stock Exchange final price.

Option &	price	Apr Vol.	Apr Last	Jul Vol.	Jul Last	Oct Vol.	Oct Last	N.Y. Close
In Pap	. 60	244	15-16	81	2 1-16	2	3⅛	54⅝
In Pap	. 70	6	⅛	9	½	b	b	54⅝
I T T	.. 25	47	8⅞	b	b	b	b	34
I T T	...30	153	4	22	4⅛	21	4¾	34
I T T	...35	495	9-16	201	1 3-16	159	1 13-16	34
John J	. 70	130	2	5	3½	13	5	67½
John J	..80	276	⅛	30	⅝	a	a	67½
Kenn C	.25	48	3¾	22	4⅝	6	5⅛	27¾
Kenn C	.30	105	¾	110	1⅝	66	2⅜	27¾
Kenn C	.35	26	⅛	227	½	169	⅞	27¾
Kerr M	.70	203	2 11-16	53	4¾	5	6	69⅝
Kerr M	.80	280	7-16	185	1⅜	49	2⅝	69⅝
Kresge	. 35	239	1¾	173	2¾	29	3⅝	34⅝
Kresge	. 40	480	⅜	126	15-16	30	1½	34⅝
Kresge	. 45	28	1-16	3	⅜	b	b	34⅝
Loews	.. 25	9	8⅜	24	9	b	b	33
Loews	.. 30	181	4⅛	104	4⅞	b	b	33
Loews	..35	509	1¼	172	2⅜	75	3	33
Loews	..40	196	¼	117	11-16	93	1¼	33
Mc Don	50	482	1⅛	476	2 5-16	220	3⅜	46¼
Mc Don	60	134	⅛	13	½	b	b	46¼
Mc Don	45	464	3½	104	4¾	39	5¾	46¼
Merck	..60	88	2¼	22	4	10	5¼	59¼
Merck	..70	4	3-16	93	13-16	12	1⅝	59¼
Merck	.. 80	1	1-16	a	a	b	b	59¼
M M M	50	91	2	37	3¼	64	4¼	49⅝
M M M	60	120	3-16	84	9-16	55	1¼	49⅝
Monsan	.80	30	2¼	51	3¾	4	5½	78⅛
Monsan	.90	11	3-16	44	15-16	24	1¾	78⅛
N C R	..30	34	7	6	7½	b	b	36⅞
N C R	..35	167	2⅞	25	4	a	a	36⅞
N C R	..40	167	⅝	35	1 7-16	115	2⅛	36⅞
Nw Air	25	62	2	7	3	a	a	25⅞
Nw Air	.30	93	7-16	61	1	10	1½	25⅞
Pennz	...25	5	10	a	a	b	b	34⅜
Pennz	.. 30	52	4⅝	18	5⅝	3	6⅛	34⅜
Pennz	.. 35	363	1¼	141	2⅛	93	2¾	34⅜
Pepsi	... 70	a	a	5	5⅞	a	a	72½
Pepsi	...80	18	½	5	1⅞	6	2¾	72½
Polar	...30	249	5	46	5¾	53	6⅞	34
Polar	...35	846	1¾	447	2 15-16	245	3¾	34
Polar	...40	900	7-16	502	1⅛	192	1 13-16	34
Polar	... 45	23	⅛	b	b	b	b	34
R C A	..20	2	8⅛	a	a	b	b	28¼
R C A	..25	529	3½	38	4	13	4⅜	28¼
R C A	..30	654	⅜	526	1 3-16	231	1 11-16	28¼
Sears	...60	309	4⅛	85	5¾	41	7	62⅝
Sears	...70	364	7-16	326	1 7-16	96	2½	62⅝
Sperry	..35	5	5¼	9	6⅛	a	a	39¼
Sperry	..40	117	1⅝	63	2⅝	5	3⅜	39¼
Sperry	..45	51	⅜	56	15-16	b	b	39¼
Syntex	..20	107	2 1-16	49	2⅞	31	3½	21¼

you will find that 900 PRD Apr 40's were traded on Feb. 9. This volume figure is very important to the option trader and will be expanded upon later.

In addition, the letter "a" in the Volume column indicates there were no trades for that listed option during that day. The letter "b" indicates that no option exists at the indicated exercise price and expiration month.

WHY OPTIONS VARY

You are probably wondering why some stocks have more options, and more exercise prices than others. When options for a stock are first listed on the Exchange, options with one or two exercise prices will become available. According to the rules, each will have three expiration months. Therefore, we start with three to six listed options for a specific stock. Then, if there is a significant change in the market price of the underlying common stock, new options with new exercise prices then become available. Normally, options with new exercise prices are established at 5 point intervals for stocks trading below 50, or at 10 point intervals for stock trading above 50.

A look at an example may help (refer to Figure I.)

American Electric Power (AEP) options listed:

AEP	Feb	20	at	4 1/8
AEP	May	20	at	4 3/4
AEP	Aug	20	at	4 1/4
AEP	Feb	25	at	1/16
AEP	May	25	at	7/16
AEP	Aug	25	at	5/8

AEP common stock is trading at 24¼. If the AEP stock rises to at least 27½, (halfway to the next 5 point interval), a new set of options with an exercise price of 30 will be listed. If AEP stock falls to 17½, a new set of options with an exercise price of 15 will then become available. You should also be able to identify, from your training in the previous chapter, that the last option price paid for each option is also presented in CBOE quotations.

One more discovery that you will make as you glance over the options quotations is the fact that each specific option — such as the AEP May 25 — is not just one option, but a whole class of options, all with the same standardized characteristics. As a buyer and a seller settle on an option price for the AEP May 25, another AEP May 25 option contract is created. Consequently, you create the volume figure presented. If you buy an AEP May 25 one day, you have created an option contract. If you sell that same option the next day, you theoretically dissolve that contract. As we move along through this book, many of these subtleties will become much clearer.

Now that you're aware of the rules by which listed options are established, let's go to the next chapter, in which we will take an even more specific look at the listed option.

Chapter 4

THE INCREDIBLE
SHRINKING OPTION

In this chapter, we will take the listed option, put it under a microscope, and look even more closely at the option price. The *price,* you will discover, is the most important element of a listed option. The price of an option is valued on the Options Exchange according to two different values:

1. THE INTRINSIC VALUE
2. THE TIME VALUE

INTRINSIC AND TIME VALUE DEFINED

The "intrinsic" value is defined as the *real* value of the option. This means that if you were to exercise your call option contract, (which you will normally never do in the new options market), you would purchase 100 shares of stock at a price lower than the current market value of the common stock. Thus, the option has some *real* value. If you were to exercise a put option contract with intrinsic value, you would sell 100 shares of stock at a higher price than the current market value of the common stock -- the put option would then have real value.

How does this differ from "time" value? Remember, that an option is a right you have for a period of time. You must pay for that right, and the amount of money that you pay is referred to as *time value.* As time passes, the time value of an option decreases, and as a result, (if we disregard the intrinsic value) the price of that option will decrease. The time value is the most important entity that we work with. In many cases, most of the options you will buy will be options which only have time value, and no intrinsic value.

EXAMPLES OF INTRINSIC AND TIME VALUE

Let's take two examples to help clarify the two types of values which make up the option price, first looking at a call option:

				Gulf & Western (GW) Common Stock
GW 25	JUL	OCT	JAN	PRICE
(Call)	2	2¾	3¼	26

Look closely at the GW Jul 25 listed call option, which, as you can see is priced at 2 ($200), with three months remaining before July expiration. The current market value of Gulf & Western at 26 is higher than the exercise price (25). This option is then called an "in-the-money" option, which means that it *does* have *intrinsic value.*

CURRENT MARKET PRICE OF STOCK	26
LESS EXERCISE PRICE OF LISTED CALL OPTION ON STOCK	−25
= INTRINSIC VALUE	1

The intrinsic value, as you can see, is $100. Now, if you will refer to the example above, the price of the GW Jul 25 is 2.

OPTION PRICE	2
LESS INTRINSIC VALUE	− 1
= TIME VALUE	1

The remaining value of the option price is *time value.*

Now let's look at the same GW Jul 25 option price on the day in July when the option will expire, and let us assume that the stock price has not moved.

GW 25	JUL	OCT	JAN	GW COMMON STOCK
	1	2	2¾	26

Again the GW 25 has 1 point of intrinsic value because the stock price is 1 point in-the-money.

But, on this date there is no more time left in the life of the July option, and consequently, there is no time value remaining.

GW Jul 25 Option Price	1
Less Intrinsic Value	−1
= Time Value	0

You will also notice that the GW Oct 25 and the GW Jan 25 have also lost some of their time value. The GW Oct 25 has lost $75 of value, and the GW Jan 25 has lost $50 of time value.

CONCLUSION: The option price is made up of two values: *Intrinsic Value and Time Value.* Based on these facts, the following formula can be developed.

INTRINSIC VALUE + TIME VALUE = OPTION PRICE

To clarify this further, let's take another example using a listed put option instead of the call option we just used. Our second example has three months remaining before it expires in April:

TIME VALUE IS WHAT THE MARKET THINKS THE INTRINSIC VALUE OF AN OPTION WILL BE IN THE FUTURE

				POLAROID
				(PRD)
				Common Stock
PRD 35	APR	JUL	OCT	PRICE
(Put)	2	3	4¼	37

Remembering that a *put* is the right to *sell* not to buy, you will notice the PRD 35 options do not have any intrinsic value. Look closely at the PRD Apr 35:

Exercise Price of PRD Apr 35	35
Current Market Price of PRD (out-of-the-money)	37
Intrinsic Value	0

Intrinsic Value + Time Value = Option Price

$$0 \quad + \quad 2 \quad = \quad 2$$

Here the *full price* of the PRD Apr 35 is *time value.* You have an "out-of-the-money" option, which means that it has *no intrinsic value,* (real value) — it has only time value. You are paying for time, enough time, you hope, for the Polaroid stock price to move below $35 a share.

Time passes . . . and now let's look at the same option on that day in April when the PRD Apr 35 expires — again assuming the Polaroid stock price is unchanged at 37.

				STOCK
				PRICE
PRD 35	APR	JUL	OCT	
(Put)	1/16	2	3	37

With the Polaroid stock price unchanged, there still is no *intrinsic value* in the PRD 35 options. Look at the PRD Apr 35 —— the option price is down to 1/16, because there is no more time left in the option. Therefore:

Intrinsic Value + Time Value = Option Price
      0   +   1/16   =   1/16

You will discover as you move through this book that the experienced player, whether he is a buyer or a writer, will spend most of his time with out-of-the-money options — options that only have *time* value.

Table I presents more good examples of listed puts and calls breaking down their intrinsic and time values. Looking at this table will help you to remove any lingering confusion.

Tables 2 and 3 show how changes in the underlying stock price will effect the time value and the intrinsic value of a specific listed option.

Tables 4 and 5 show time value declines with a constant stock price for both a listed put and a listed call as these options approach their expiration.

SHRINKING OPTIONS AND THE BUYER

You may be wondering why the author has named this chapter, THE INCREDIBLE SHRINKING OPTION. You should have seen by now that an option is a depreciating asset which shrinks in value as time elapses; therefore, when the life of an option ends, it has "zero" value. To the option buyer and seller this is a super critical concept, which should always be a *top priority* consideration. If you purchase an option with a two month life remaining, every day that you hold that option, its value is declining, even if the underlying stock price is moving in the correct direction. To the option buyer, this price behavior is his major handicap; to the option writer, it is his major advantage.

It is of great importance that you brand this rule into your mind:

THE TIME VALUE OF AN OPTION CONTINUALLY DECLINES TO "O" AS TIME PASSES AND THE OPTION REACHES THE END OF ITS LIFE.

TABLE I

DISSECTING THE LISTED OPTION

Listed Call Options	Stock Price	Option Price	Intrinsic Value	Time Value	Out-of-the Money	In-the-Money
Boeing May 20	18	1½	0	1½	X	
CBS Aug 50	52	4	2	2		X
Mobil Oil Feb 70	65	4-5/8	0	4-5/8	X	
Am Tel Apr 60	55	3	0	3	X	
Avon Jul 45	47	3¼	2	1¼		X
Bank Am Oct 25	26	2½	1	1½		X
Texas Instr. Apr 100	80	¾	0	¾	X	
Pepsi Apr 80	85	6-1/8	5	1-1/8		X
IBM July 280	275	13¾	0	13¾	X	
Tiger Int Feb 10	11	1¾	1	¾		X
Rockwell June 35	34	1	0	1	X	
ASA May 15	20	5½	5	½		X
Searle Aug 10	12	4	2	2		X
Listed Put Options						
Gen Food May 35	30	6	5	1		X
Texas Instr. Apr 80	75	8	5	3		X
Upjohn Oct 40	38	3½	2	1½		X
Syntex Oct 20	22	1-1/8	0	1-1/8	X	
N Semi May 25	19	7¼	6	1¼		X
MGIC Aug 20	22	1½	0	1½	X	
Sears Oct 60	63	2¾	0	2¾	X	
MMM July 50	44	8¼	6	2¼		X
NCR Apr 30	29	2½	1	1½		X
NWA July 25	30	1¼	0	1¼	X	
Monsanto Oct 90	87	5½	3	2½		X
IBM Apr 260	270	10	0	10	X	
Coke May 80	75	9	5	4		X

TABLE 2

LISTED CALL OPTION BEHAVIOR

XEROX July 60 Call Option

Value of Option	Common Stock Price	Option Price	Time Value	Intrinsic Value
In-the-Money	70	10-7/8	7/8	10
In-the-Money	68	9	1	8
In-the-Money	66	7-1/4	1-1/4	6
In-the-Money	64	6	2	4
In-the-Money	62	5-5/8	3-5/8	2
ON-THE-MONEY	60	4-3/8	4-3/8	0
Out-of-the-Money	58	3-1/2	3-1/2	0
Out-of-the-Money	56	2-3/4	2-3/4	0
Out-of-the-Money	54	2	2	0
Out-of-the-Money	52	1-1/8	1-1/8	0
Out-of-the-Money	50	1/2	1/2	0

TABLE 3

LISTED PUT OPTION BEHAVIOR

CONTROL DATA   February 30 Put Option

Value of Option	Common Stock Price	Option Price	Time Value	Intrinsic Value
Out-of-the-Money	40	1/4	1/4	0
Out-of-the-Money	38	1/2	1/2	0
Out-of-the-Money	36	1	1	0
Out-of-the-Money	34	1-3/8	1-3/8	0
Out-of-the-Money	32	1-7/8	1-7/8	0
ON-THE-MONEY	30	2-5/8	2-5/8	0
In-the-Money	28	4-1/8	2-1/8	2
In-the-Money	26	5-3/4	1-3/4	4
In-the-Money	24	7	1	6
In-the-Money	22	8-3/4	3/4	8
In-the-Money	20	10-1/8	1/8	10

TABLE 4
THE OPTION LIFE CYCLE

DUPONT Oct 150 (Put)

Time Remaining Before Expiration	4 Months	3 Months	2 Months	1 Month	2 Weeks	Expiration Day
Dupont Stock Price	155	155	155	155	155	155
Option Price	5	4	3	1-1/2	1	1/16
Intrinsic Value	0	0	0	0	0	0
Time Value	5	4	3	1-1/2	1	1/16

TABLE 5
THE OPTION LIFE CYCLE

BOEING Nov 30 (Call)

Time Remaining Before Expiration	4 Months	3 Months	2 Months	1 Month	2 Weeks	Expiration Day
Boeing Stock Price	29	29	29	29	29	29
Option Price	3-1/2	2-3/4	1-3/4	1	1/2	1/16
Intrinsic Value	0	0	0	0	0	0
Time Value	3-1/2	2-3/4	1-3/4	1	1/2	1/16

From the author's experience, the major error of the option buyer is his disregard for this law when he plays the game. In the options game, "time is money." Those who use this concept to their benefit will reach the winner's circle; those who ignore the law of time value will fall by the wayside.

For the option buyer: TAKE HEED — make sure that you buy plenty of time in your options — don't stick your options in a closet and forget about them, for as time passes, your options will also pass away.

As we move on to study other aspects of listed options, keep in mind that the option price is determined by adding *intrinsic value* to time value. Intrinsic value is the *real* value of the option. The time value is the value that you place on the possibility that the option will attain some intrinsic value by having the stock price move through the exercise price and into-the-money.

PRACTICE OPTIONS PSYCHOLOGY

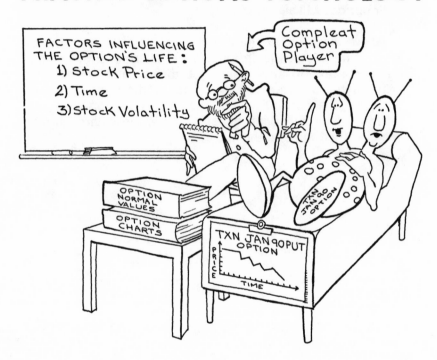

Chapter 5

THE PSYCHIATRIC GUIDE TO OPTIONS BEHAVIOR

Welcome to your first introduction to OPTIONS PSYCHO-LOGY. In this chapter you will encounter a brief training course in the study of *option price behavior.* The astute option player must become an expert in predicting and understanding listed option price behavior as a prerequisite to success. As you study and analyze listed price behavior, you will discover that it can be very erratic, especially when we work with out-of-the-money options, which have no intrinsic value. The whole price of that option is determined by time value, which is also referred to as PREMIUM.

Time value is a value based on opinion. How do you place value on two days in the market, or on two weeks or six months in the market? Every investor will place a different value on that period of time, and he will inject numerous variables in coming up with those values. Place these out-of-the-money listed options in an auction market, and the results can be very amazing at times.

TEN FACTORS INFLUENCING
OPTION PRICE BEHAVIOR

To gain a complete understanding of option price behavior, let's take a close look at the ten factors listed below which have the greatest influence on this behavior.

1. THE PRICE AND MOVEMENT OF THE UNDER-LYING COMMON STOCK

2. THE TIME LEFT IN THE LIFE OF THE OPTION

3. THE VOLATILITY OF THE UNDERLYING COMMON STOCK

4. MARKET RALLIES, AND MARKET DECLINES

5. THE PSYCHOLOGY AND MOOD IN THE MARKET

6. SUPPLY AND DEMAND

7. INSTITUTIONS

8. THE LIQUIDITY OF THE OPTION IN THE MARKET

9. THE NUMBER AND TYPE OF LISTED OPTIONS AVAILABLE FOR THE UNDERLYING COMMON STOCK

10. THE YIELD OF THE UNDERLYING COMMON STOCK

CHIEF FACTORS

Out of this list of influencing factors, two of them have a very significant effect on the price of a listed option. In fact, these elements constitute from 50% to 80% of the price of the listed option. They include the *price* of the underlying common stock, and the *time* left in the life of the option.

Since an option is the right to purchase or sell 100 shares of a specific stock at a specified price, the price of that common stock will be a very great determiner of the price of the option. Because of the critical nature of time value, when you purchase an option, the time left in the option will have a very strong bearing on the price you pay for that option. Time value thus becomes extremely significant as the option nears its expiration.

Another element that controls the price of a listed option is the price volatility of the underlying common stock. A common stock price which has high volatility normally moves in very wide ranges over a period of time. A volatile stock may move from 40% to 60% of its base price annually. Such wide price movements give it a much greater probability of moving through the exercise price of a listed option, and as a result, that listed option will take on more premium (time value).

On the other hand, a stock with low volatility normally trades within a very narrow range, not moving very far in any one direction. This will have a negative effect on the option price, because the probability of the stock price moving through the exercise price is greatly diminished.

Understanding stock volatility in the options market can be very tricky. In some cases, a common stock that has been historically quite volatile may reach periods in which it is somewhat dormant, and conversely, stocks which are normally quite low in price volatility will suddenly move dramatically in one direction or another. These shifts in price behavior will alter the influence of this factor on the listed option.

As we move through this text, we will continually refer to volatility, and will study this very important component much more closely. Many option players place *far too much* importance on the volatility of a specific stock, and will overvalue or undervalue the options which are associated with that stock.

In summary, the three major factors which will influence option behavior include, (1) the price of the underlying stock, (2) the time left in the life of the options, and (3) the volatility of the underlying stock. These three factors will probably constitute up to 90% of the price of the listed option.

RALLIES AND DECLINES
– HOW TO HANDLE CALL OPTIONS & PUT OPTIONS –

There are other influences which, in some cases, have very marked effects on the price behavior of the listed option. Two of the most important influences are market rallies and market declines. Option prices can have significant moves without much of a movement in their underlying stock during a market rally or a market decline. Optimism rises during a market rally, large amounts of money flow into listed call options, and their prices become over-inflated, in some cases regardless of the price movement of the underlying stock. In addition, during a market rally, some investors have visions of grandeur, whereby the investor sees the market climbing another 100 or 200 points on the Dow. These visions are totally unrealistic, but they do have a strong bearing on the prices of the listed options.

Conversely, during market declines there is extreme pessimism, which overflows into the options market. Call option prices become extremely depressed, even though the underlying stock prices may not be moving in any direction. As the market declines, the investor has visions that disaster is near – he believes that the world will fall apart, and therefore, the prices of the listed call options follow suit and begin to fall apart.

The option player must use these market rallies and declines to execute his strategies, and to do his buying and selling at these optimum points in time. *Market rallies are the best time to sell call options.* The price of the option is over-inflated at this time, as the market makers and option traders attempt to cover their short positions in these listed options. *At the depth of market declines, in some cases, it is best to buy call options,* or to cover option writing positions (short positions).

The ability to use these market rallies and declines to benefit your strategies is an important skill that you, as an option player, must develop. Unfortunately, this skill counters your natural impulses, because during market rallies, not only will everyone else be overflowing with optimism, but you will also be overflowing with optimism. However, you must counter this impulse, and do your selling during these optimistic periods of time. Conversely, you should do your buying at the depths of a market decline.

Note that if you are working with listed *puts,* you would do exactly the opposite from what you do with calls. At the peak of market rallies, you wish to be buying puts, and in the later stages of market declines, you would be selling puts.

MARKET MOOD & PSYCHOLOGY

Another factor very closely related to market rallies and declines which has an important effect on option price behavior, is the market mood and psychology. Although you may not be in the midst of a market rally, or in a desperate decline, there is normally some kind of mood and psychology to the market, and this will have an influence on the price behavior of your options. At certain times, there is a total lack of interest in the market. Stocks move nowhere, investors are on vacation, or there is definite indecision on the part of investors whether the market will be moving upward or downward. Normally at these times, option prices decline.

A stock market which has been drifting for several months will have a very damaging effect on the prices of all listed options, both puts and calls. For either a listed put or a listed call to have a healthy premium, that option requires that the common stock price maintain "active" price action, and that the overall market also maintain active price action. When stock prices in the overall market move in a very slow and sideways motion, this has a surprisingly negative effect on most options.

SUPPLY, DEMAND,
AND THE INSTITUTIONAL INVESTOR

Another element which the option player must consider when attempting to predict option price behavior is the old supply and demand factor. How many buyers are out there, and how many sellers? This, of course, will have a definite effect on the price of an option.

Add to this the new influence in the options market of *institutions,* and we have a very interesting scenario. New changes in the tax laws have greatly encouraged institutions to enter the options game. They have seen the tremendous success that investment managers have had in this new game, and attempting to improve the disappointing performance of their portfolios, the institutions are lining up in droves to move into this new market. Their entry into the options market will have a very significant effect on the supply and demand for listed options. We will look at these factors throughout this text, and because of the tremendous impact of institutions, we will attempt to demonstrate strategies which will take advantage of the participation of institutions.

The influence that institutional investors have on the price behavior of the listed option centers in the area of listed call options. Up to this point, these options have been the easiest to understand, and they have been accepted by the institutional community as effective income producers. Therefore, the institutions have chiefly been *option writers,* not *option buyers.* As option writers, they have driven down the prices of many classes of listed call options. This fact provides an advantage to the option buyer, who will now get far better prices for the options he wishes to purchase. The institutional investors are one of the most important factors in the stock market today, and they will probably become one of the most important factors in the options market in the future. So, option players, BEWARE of the institutional influence.

Other supply and demand considerations regarding the price action of options come into play during market rallies and market declines. During market rallies, we normally have significant *volume* in the market, and this volume also carries over to the options market. Consequently, there is a much greater demand during market rallies for the purchase of listed call options. During market declines, normally the volume in the stock market dries up — one of the reasons why the decline occurs — and there is a lack of buying interest in the market.

Next, this lack of buying interest in the stock market carries over to the options market, where the same lack of demand ensues. As the market declines, puts become more attractive, but because of the low volume factor, the amount of demand is not as great for puts during a decline as for calls during market advances. Therefore, as you will discover, puts may not have as high a price as calls in the market. As a result, they may be a more attractive ploy for the option buyer.

LIQUIDITY

Another factor which has a powerful indirect influence on option price behavior, is the amount of *liquidity* that exists in a specific listed option. Liquidity refers to trading volume, or to the ability to move in and out of an option position easily. Liquidity requires that plenty of buyers and sellers be available to ensure such transactions. Options which do not have liquidity may trap you into a position, or prevent you from taking a large enough position to make the transaction worthwhile. Liquidity in the options market can be measured by the number of specific listed options that are traded every day.

For example, how many Xerox Jul 60 calls are traded on the average day? Calculating this average would give you an idea of the degree of liquidity that the Xerox Jul 60 has at present. Note that liquidity changes throughout the life of a specific option. The Xerox Jul 60 may have no liquidity at all when the stock is at 90, because the option is so far "in-the-money" that no one is interested in that option. Or, it may not have any liquidity at all if the stock is at 30, because now the option is so far "out-of-the-money" that it hardly has any value at all. In fact, it may be restricted according to the Options Exchange rules.

Also, if there are nine months left in that Xerox Jul 60, its price may be so high that it will lack the necessary liquidity to be an effective trading vehicle. In fact, options which usually have very long lives of seven, eight, or nine months normally do not have the liquidity that an option of two or three months would maintain. This again is an important consideration when you design strategies, and decide when and where to take certain positions.

CLASSES OF OPTIONS AVAILABLE AND STOCK YIELD

Still another factor that the astute option player looks at when predicting option price behavior is the number of classes of options that are presently available for a common stock. If only a few standardized options are available, all the demand for the options of that stock is channeled into these few options. This becomes an important consideration when a stock that has been dormant for an extended period of time begins to attract some price action. Suddenly there is a demand to purchase the common stock's listed options. Of course, there are only a few options to choose from, and the result is inflated option prices.

A final key factor to consider would be the yield of the stock. High yielding stocks become very attractive covered option writing vehicles, and we will discuss this later in the text. *Covered writing* indicates that people will purchase the stock, and write or sell an option against it. When institutions and individuals carry out these writing activities extensively, the option premiums will decrease. Therefore, stocks with high yields normally will have options with low premiums (prices), as compared to the average listed option.

THE LIFE AND TIMES OF THE LISTED OPTION

Now that you have a more extensive knowledge for determining what effect various factors will have on option price behavior, we are ready to look at the overall "life and times of a listed option." In other words, let's look at the life cycle of a listed option, and see what changes occur in that option, as it moves from its birth, when it has nine months of life remaining, to its death at its date of expiration.

Options will take on many changes in their price behavior as they move through this nine month period of time. They will move from a very inactive period of price action, to a very active period. Surprisingly, the most active period in the life of an option normally begins when it has three months left. From this point in time, it becomes more and more active until it approaches its expiration. In many cases, when the underlying stock price is still very close to the exercise price as the option approaches expiration, the option becomes feverishly active. At this time, every movement in the underlying stock, whether it is a quarter or a half a point, causes significant movement in the option price.

Table 6 draws out the complete life of a Xerox Jul 60 call option, showing what the theoretical values of the option would be at each point in its life, and at each possible stock price. You can also look in the back of the book at the Appendix where we determine the normal value of each option, at each point in its life, and again, at each underlying stock price.

By looking at all these examples, you will note that during the first three months of the life of a listed option, the value of that option depreciates at a very slow rate. In the second three months of the listed option, the price depreciates at a more accelerated rate, but it has not yet reached its peak rate of depreciation. In the fourth month of the life of an option, it normally has the highest time value it will have per the amount of time left in the life of the option. If you were buying an option at that time, you would generally pay the highest percentage rate possible on that option. (We are holding all other variables constant, so that we can see what occurs to the price, and the price alone, as time passes through the option's life.)

As the option passes into its last three months of life, its depreciation begins to accelerate. But when the option approaches the very last month of its life, the depreciation speeds up, and in the last month, there is a very accelerated depreciation of value, ending up at the end of this period with no time value at all. The last month of an option's life

TABLE 6
THE LIFE AND TIMES OF A LISTED CALL OPTION
THE XEROX July 60

Months Left in Option Life	Xerox Price	52	54	56	58	60	62	64	68
9 Months	Option Price	3-1/2	4-3/8	5-1/8	5-1/8	6-3/4	7-3/4	8-3/8	11
	Time Value	3-1/2	4-3/4	5-1/8	5-7/8	6-3/4	5-3/4	4-3/8	3
	Intrinsic Value	0	0	0	0	0	2	4	8
6 Months	Option Price	2-3/4	3-1/2	4-1/4	5	5-1/8	6-3/4	7-1/2	10-3/4
	Time Value	2-3/4	3-1/2	4-1/4	5	5-7/8	4-3/4	3-1/2	2¾
	Intrinsic Value	0	0	0	0	0	2	4	8
4 Months	Option Price	1-1/2	2-1/4	3	3-3/4	4-3/4	5-1/2	6-1/4	9¾
	Time Value	1-1/2	2-1/4	3	3-3/4	4-3/4	3-1/2	2-1/4	1¾
	Intrinsic Value	0	0	0	0	0	2	4	8
3 Months	Option Price	-3/4	1-3/8	2-1/4	3	4	4-7/8	5-1/2	9¼
	Time Value	-3/4	1-3/8	2-1/4	3	4	2-5/8	1-3/8	1¼
	Intrinsic Value	0	0	0	0	0	2	4	8
2 Months	Option Price	-1/4	-7/8	1-3/4	2-3/8	3-1/4	4	5	8¾
	Time Value	-1/4	-7/8	1-3/4	2-3/8	3-1/4	2	1	¾
	Intrinsic Value	0	0	0	0	0	2	4	8
1 Month	Option Price	-1/16	-1/4	-5/8	1-3/8	2-1/4	2-7/8	4-1/2	8¼
	Time Value	-1/16	-1/4	-5/8	1-3/8	2-1/4	-7/8	-1/2	¼
	Intrinsic Value	0	0	0	0	0	2	4	8
2 Weeks	Option Price	-1/16	-1/16	-1/16	-3/4	1-5/8	2-1/2	4-1/4	81/8
	Time Value	-1/16	-1/16	-1/16	-3/4	1-5/8	-1/2	-1/4	1/8
	Intrinsic Value	0	0	0	0	0	2	4	8
The Expiration Date	Option Price	0	0	0	0	0	2	4	8
	Time Value	0	0	0	0	0	0	0	0
	Intrinsic Value	0	0	0	0	0	2	4	8

normally causes the greatest damage to the option price and all option traders should consider this fact carefully.

OPTION PRICES & COMMON STOCK PRICES

How does the declining option price described above relate to the price of the underlying common stock? Holding all other variables constant, when the stock price is right at the exercise price of the listed option, the listed option will have its maximum possible time value.

For example, if we are looking at the Xerox Jul 60 option, and Xerox is priced exactly at 60, the Xerox Jul 60 will hold its maximum time value in this option (will have its highest price), taking into consideration the amount of time left in that option. This is a very important point to the option trader. Buying options when the stock is at exercise, whether you are covering a position, or taking a new position, normally results in your paying the highest possible time value for that option.

When the stock price moves away from the exercise price (out-of-the-money), the amount of option premium will decrease at a constant rate. Thus, as it moves from 20% to 30% out-of-the-money, the option will lose most of its time value, and, according to Options Exchange rules,[5] will eventually be restricted from trading on the options exchanges. If the stock price moves into the exercise price (in-the-money), again, the premium (the time value) that is built into the price of that option will decrease, and will continue to decrease as the stock moves further and further into-the-money.

Let's take an example — let's look at the Xerox Jul 60 call, with three months left in the option. The Xerox stock is priced at 60; the option is priced, as you can see from Table 6 at 4. All four points are time value.

[5] Rule changes in 1980 removed restrictions to trading out-of-the-money options.

Let's say that the stock moves from 60 to 64. Presently the option is worth 5½, but the time value of that option has decreased from 4 to 1½.

Now let's say that the Xerox stock moves from 64 to 68; looking at the Xerox July 60's price, it is currently 9½. Our time value has now decreased to 1¼.

Next, let's move in the other direction. Let's say that the Xerox stock has moved from 60 to 56. At 56, the Xerox Jul 60 is priced at 2¼, so the option has moved from a time value of 4 to a premium of 2¼. At 52, the Xerox Jul 60 is worth ¾; so now the time value has moved from 4 to less than 1. There is almost the same type of decrease in time value whether the stock moves up or whether the stock moves down.

Unfortunately, option players often forget the principle that you just observed. Yet this is a very important principle for you to consider when you design strategies, and when you attempt to alter or change your strategies. It is also a very important principle for the option buyer who is attempting to pay a bargain basement price. As you can see, there are times in the life cycle when you should be buying the option, and times when you should not, all depending on the location of the stock price, and the number of months left in that option.

EFFECTS OF STOCK PRICES ON OPTIONS

During the many phases in the life cycle of a listed option, probably one of the greatest combined effects on the option price will be the trend of the stock price in one direction or the other, and the speed of that trend. Suppose we are working with a listed call option. If the stock price trend is upward, and if the speed of that trend is very accelerated, then the option premium accelerates in value very quickly, and shows far more time value than would normally be expected. On the other hand, if the trend is upward, but the movement of that trend is very slow, the effect on the option price would be very small, but positive. Finally, the opposite result would occur if we had a downtrend in the stock price and the movement was either accelerated, or very slow.

Note that when we are working with listed put options, the exact opposite of the effects described above would be true. A very fast moving downtrend in the stock price would greatly increase the price of the listed put option, and vice versa.

To summarize, in this chapter, we have introduced a large number of factors which effect the price behavior of listed options. We have briefly looked at the life cycle of the listed option, and have demonstrated the effect of both stock prices and time on both the listed call and put options.

Should "Options Psychology" continue to bewilder you, I suggest that you re-read this chapter, study the tables very closely, look over your newspaper each morning, and attempt to secure a feel for the pricing behavior of an option.

One technique for practicing options psychology is to collect a series of listed options, then follow them closely each day and attempt to estimate their value at the end of each closing day before you look at their actual quotations. In the beginning, you will probably be a little frustrated, but eventually you will develop the skill which will allow you to be able to measure exactly what the value of an option should be at any one point in time.

These last few chapters have provided you with many of the basics. You probably are a little perplexed in certain areas, and this is to be expected. In succeeding chapters, we are going to move into some of the applications of all this theory, and as we work through different examples, and cover new material, the basics already covered will become more familiar. You will be well on your way to acquiring the knowledge and skills of the COMPLEAT OPTION PLAYER.

Chapter 6

HOW TO GET STARTED
ON SMALL CAPITAL

HOW MUCH CAPITAL DO YOU NEED TO START
A SUCCESSFUL VENTURE INTO
THE OPTIONS MARKET?

That is a question that can be answered in a thousand different ways, but for the speculator, the exact amount isn't great, provided that you have all the other prerequisites that you need to beat the game. This chapter is aimed at the speculator who wishes to enter this new, exciting game with a minimal amount of capital, or who only has a very small amount of pure risk capital. If an investor is going to move into this market with small capital, the risks will be very great, but the possible rewards may be even greater.

One rule that you, as a speculator, must follow, is to be sure that you are financially able to handle the possible loss of the capital that you are investing. It should not be borrowed or distressed money, or money taken out of the necessary living expenses that should be provided for your family. When you work with such capital, it places too much pressure on your mind; you become too emotional, and you lose the key factor of success in the options market, which is *rationality*. You must be able to make quick, rational decisions without having outside factors influence you. As soon as the money becomes more important than playing chips on a table, your factor of success decreases tremendously.

As a speculator entering this game with a limited amount of risk capital, there is only one road that you can follow, and that is to *buy options.* (The opposite of *buying* options is *writing* options, which will be introduced further on in this text. In the case of the latter, the more capital you have, the more effectively you should be able to operate.)

Later you will discover that there are many more profitable strategies available in this new market than buying options, but they require minimum investments of at least $2,000. However, beginning with a small investment can be a definite asset rather than a detriment, as the successful purchase and sale of options requires effective bargain hunting, effective use of specialized knowledge, and extreme patience. A small amount of capital will force you into some of these successful behavioral patterns.

One very special feature of the options market is the outstanding leverage that you can obtain by buying options. For the modest amount of $6.25 you can control over $25,000 worth of stock. Under the proper conditions, and with the appropriate moves in that stock, your investment may multiply a hundredfold. This is the pot of gold of the new options game, and it is available to the small speculator. Of course, to succeed in this endeavor requires some very important knowledge, skills, and patience.

Many of the prodigious number of books available on the new options game have stated that this low capital buyer's game is a loser's game, or a sucker's game. This kind of statement shows the amount of ignorance prevalent among the "self proclaimed" authorities on the subject. For the arguments which will be presented in this text will show that buying options can be as profitable as many other strategies available to the player. In fact, with new tax law changes, more and more institutions are entering the options game, and they are option writers, not option buyers. As a result, the law of supply and demand will create more and more bargains for option buyers, especially during periods when there is extreme bearishness or extreme bullishness. At these times, puts or calls will become unbelievable buys, and the option buyer with a small amount of capital then will have a definite advantage, making it easy for him to enter and win this game.

CAPITAL NEEDED TO START PLAYING

The exact dollar figure is very hard to pin down, but normally $200 would be a minimum starting figure for the novice. Setting a $200 or $300 limit on your losses will force you to take, at the maximum, only two or three positions. One important consideration is that commission costs will constitute a large portion of your purchase price at this level, and should be incorporated into your risk-reward analysis. Of course, you incur these costs in any game that you enter, be it a visit to Las Vegas, or a visit to one of your local racetracks. In these situations you have transportation costs, entrance fees, program costs, and the other additional expenses that are incurred when traveling to and from your local gaming activity. The stock market has these same costs. Your options trading skill must pay for these costs and add a profit on to your investment. Remember, starting with small capital forces you to take on very high commission costs.

THE SMALLEST AMOUNT OF CAPITAL PER STRATEGY YOU SHOULD INVEST IN THE OPTIONS MARKET

As mentioned before, an option can be purchased for as little as $6.25, giving you the right to profit from the price move of 100 shares of a specific common stock, for a specific period of time. Add to that your commission costs, which may run from $15 to $20, and you have a pretty accurate figure of what a minimum investment can be. But that gives you only one very long shot in this game, and the commission costs will eat up some of your potential profit.

Therefore, a rule for the investor with small capital to follow would state:

> **BRING ENOUGH CAPITAL TO BE ABLE TO TAKE AT LEAST TWO OR THREE POSITIONS, WITH EACH POSITION CONTAINING AT LEAST FIVE OPTIONS.**

Following such a rule will force you to diversify by not putting all your eggs in one basket, and will reduce commission costs per option, giving you a chance to stay and profit in this new game.

Chapter 7

THE ART OF BUYING OPTIONS

PLAYING THE GAME

Are you tired of the basics? Then, let's begin playing the game. The easiest way to play this game is to buy options. If you are betting that the market is going up, then you buy call options; if you are betting that the market is going down, then you buy listed put options. If you believe the market is going to fluctuate violently, then you can buy straddles, strips, or straps. Although buying options may seem to be a strategy specifically designed for the small investor, it is a very viable investment tool for all investment managers, even those who manage millions of dollars of institutional funds.

ADVANTAGES OF BUYING OPTIONS

Buying options has three very distinct advantages. These include:
1. LEVERAGE
2. LIMITED RISK
3. SMALL CAPITAL REQUIREMENT

In the previous chapter, we have already discussed the advantages of entering this buying game with very small capital. *Leverage* gives the option buyer the ability to control thousands of dollars worth of price action on the Stock Exchange for pennies. In the previous chapter, you discovered that for $6.25 you could control and participate in the price action of up to $25,000 or more of stock. Normally, by paying from $50 to $200, you can control the price action on a $5,000 or a $10,000 round lot of common stock. If the stock price goes up 10, 15, or 20 points, you can cash in your $100 or $200 option, and collect up to $2,000. That could be the exact amount that you would have gained if you had owned the actual stock itself. In other words, an option gives you a chance for the action and excitement of owning 100 shares of stock without having to put down all the money and taking all the risk incurred in owning that stock. The only risk is the $200, or whatever price you pay for that option. If the price action of the stock is not positive, then you may lose a portion of that risk capital, but you will not lose $5,000 or $10,000, which would be possible if you owned the stock.

So, when you buy options, you gain tremendous leverage in the market by controlling a large amount of money for a very small investment, and here is where the *limited risk* factor comes into play.

The new Options Exchange helps you to reduce the risk of buying options because of its liquidity, which provides tremendous flexibility for the option buyer. If you purchase an option, and the next day, decide that that was an incorrect move, you can immediately go back into the market, and sell that option. As the option buyer, you can also take advantage of very small movements in that 100 shares of stock that you are controlling, by moving in and out of your option positions as the stock moves up and down. In some cases, the stock price may not have to move at all for you to make a slight profit on your options. The market itself, in many cases, will generate premiums in options even when the stock price of a specific option is not moving.

For example, let's look at the flexibility of the options market in the following case. Let us assume that you have been closely following the Ford Motor Co. stock, and have decided that at its present price of 52, it will move down to

45 in the next three weeks. To take advantage of this price action, you decide to purchase one Ford Jan 50 put option at a price of 2 ($200). You purchase this one put, and sit back to watch the price action of the stock. After one week's time, the stock price rises from 52 to 55. Your prediction of the stock price movement is incorrect. Therefore, you immediately move into the market, and sell your Ford Jan 50 put, now priced on the Exchange at 1-1/8. You receive proceeds of $112.50, having reduced your loss on that option to $87.50, plus the commissions of moving in and out of that position.

So, even if your predictions are incorrect regarding the price actions of a stock, you can salvage much of the value of that option if you act quickly and move out of that option position immediately.

OPTION BUYING AND THE INVESTMENT MANAGER

Though this chapter is aimed at the speculator, buying options can also be a very sophisticated investment tool for the investment manager. There are numerous ways in which an investment manager can buy options — for insurance, for hedging, or to take advantage of other stock and option positions. For example, the astute investment manager who handles $100,000 in cash for a client (which must be protected and cannot be exposed to any risk), will invest the cash in 91 day Treasury bills at $100,000 face value. Such a purchase will cost approximately $98,500 (depending on prevailing interest rates), leaving $1500 cash for further investment.

Instead of leaving this cash sitting in the account, he will purchase "bargain priced" listed puts and calls. Now the client can participate in big moves in the stock market without risking any of his *principal.*

SOME DISADVANTAGES OF OPTION BUYING

Now let's take a look at the disadvantages of buying options. Our whole discussion in talking about the "cons" of buying options focuses around one thing, — *time.* The purchaser of 100 shares of stock may not have the leverage or the limited risk that the option buyer has, but he can hang on to that stock for five, ten or twenty years, and wait for it to reach his price objective. Normally, the option buyer will only have from one or two days up to nine months in which to attain his price objectives. Also, common stocks generally will not depreciate in value as you hold them, but options will. Therefore, as you hold onto options, waiting for the underlying stock price to increase, the option price is continually depreciating. This factor of time and depreciation is the major obstacle that has been the downfall of the majority of option buyers.

To beat the option buying game, you have to beat the clock, a sometimes difficult task. In the next section of this chapter, we will spell out a set of guidelines that will give you a chance to beat the game, and we hope that you will follow them. To become a successful option buyer, you must become shrewd, patient and be a quick decision maker. With these tactics, excellent profits will flow your way.

To begin your further training in the art of option buying, the author has developed the following "ten commandments of option buying." Read these commandments, memorize them, and follow them.

THE TEN COMMANDMENTS OF OPTION BUYING

    I.   BE PATIENT
   II.   PLAY ONLY VOLATILE STOCKS
  III.   BUY "OUT-OF-THE-MONEY" OPTIONS
  IV.   PLAN BEFORE YOU PLAY
   V.   PLAY ONLY UNDERVALUED OPTIONS
  VI.   DIVERSIFY
 VII.   MAXIMIZE YOUR LEVERAGE
VIII.   MINIMIZE YOUR RISK
  IX.   DON'T BE GREEDY
   X.   BE PATIENT

The first and last commandments are : *Be Patient,* because it is the most important commandment of option buying. You must wait for option opportunities and you must wait until your playable options become extremely underpriced. If you require action every day, this chapter is not for you; possibly this book is not for you. Without patience, you might as well disregard the rest of these commandments, because they will not help you. The only way to beat the option game from the buyer's position is to be very selective in picking your spots, and to be able to wait until you can get your price.

Play Only Volatile Stocks — Remember, you only have a limited amount of time to work with when you own an option. You are betting on price action; therefore, play stocks that are big on price action, that move around very frequently, and move within wide ranges of their base value.

Buy Out-of-the-Money Options — Options which are normally "in-the-money" are far too fat for the option buyer, and although they may have intrinsic value, they also have far more risk. Out-of-the-money options normally will have much lower prices, and as a result, will have far less risk.

Plan Before You Play — This commandment is critical to your success. Even though you are buying options, you must have a game plan which maps out exactly what you will do at every point while you own an option. You must set a time parameter for the length of time that you will hold the option, and decide when you will take your profits. If you do not have a plan of action through each stage of your purchase of each option, you are doomed.

Play Only Undervalued Options — The successful option buyer is a very meticulous bargain hunter. When making decisions, wait for your price, pay no more than the price you demand, and make sure that price is far below the true value of that option. The Appendix at the end of this book displays the normal value of all options under all price and time conditions. Use these tables as a guide to determine which options are underpriced, and which are overpriced.

THE SUCCESSFUL OPTION BUYER IS A DEDICATED BARGAIN HUNTER

Diversify — In order to improve the probability of profit in the game, do not put all of your eggs in one basket. Take at least two or three option positions, and try to maintain at least five options in each position to reduce your commission costs. Four is the ideal number of option positions you should hold at any one time. If you can get to this level, you will be well diversified.

Maximize Your Leverage — Attempt to select an option which will increase in value at least 200% if there is a 10% move in the stock price. Attempt to derive at least a 3-1 risk-reward ratio for any option that you purchase. If you do this, the long term odds will be in your favor.

Minimize Your Risk — The best way to minimize your risk is to pay as little as possible for each of your options. A rule I like to follow is that I rarely pay more than $100 for an option. I will attempt to find very positive risk-reward plays where I only have to invest from $50 to $100 per option. By doing this, I normally attain outstanding leverage, and of course, have a very limited risk. All I can lose is the small amount that I paid for that option.

Don't Be Greedy — The downfall of 90% of all investors, especially in the options market, is greed. They wait for that next move in the stock, wait for another week to get another point or two out of that option. To avoid this natural tendency toward greed, make sure that you follow your game plan to a T. Place your limit orders when you take the position, and leave those limit orders in, regardless of what factors develop. As soon as you rely on your emotions, rather than on your game plan, your portfolio will become a disaster area.

Be Patient — Again, we see the most important commandment, and the one that you will have the roughest time following. Wait for your spots, wait for your plays, wait for your price, and pay no more than the price you demand.

In the next chapters, we will demonstrate how these Ten Commandments can be applied in the selection of options, and we will cover some of the finer points to be followed in successful option buying.

THE 4 S's
– TO BE USED BY THE EXPERIENCED BUYER ONLY

But, before we move on to the finer points of option buying, you should be aware of some of the other option merchandise available to the option purchaser. We mentioned that the option buyer can buy a listed put or a listed call. Now he can also purchase:

- A *Straddle* – which is actually a set of options, both a put and a call, both at the same exercise price, with the same underlying stock.

- A *Strap* – which is the purchase of two calls, and a put, again at the same exercise price.

- A *Strip* – which is the purchase of two puts and one call, both with the same exercise price.

- A *Spread* – where he purchases a put and a call with different exercise prices.

You need to be careful with these, for sometimes this wide array of merchandise simply confuses option buyers, and may lead you astray in making your critical buy decisions. Another problem with these fancy buy strategies involves *commission costs*. They can run very high with these types of strategies and will cut deeply into your potential profits.

The time to use these types of buy strategies occurs when you are working with an extremely volatile stock, which has a high probability of making some very voluminous fluctuations.

In entering such strategies, make sure that you get the right price for both legs of the strategy, a sometimes impossible task.

Because of the difficulties involved, the author suggests that you stay away from such strategies unless you have extensive experience and sophistication in the art of option buying. These strategies may have a look of glamour, but they are very expensive and can inhibit the *necessary* bargain hunting behavior of the successful option buyer.

Chapter 8

THE PLAYABLE STOCK

Having looked at the "art of buying options," and at the guidelines that will put you on the road to success in this challenging game, it is time for you to put these guidelines into action. In the process of making the key decision regarding which options you should purchase, and determining the all important *time* when you should purchase them, you will discover that there is a tremendous amount of homework that must be completed in preparation for this difficult task. If you pass over this homework, and do not prepare yourself for playing this game, you are doomed to failure.

SELECTING THE RIGHT STOCKS — TIME & TRENDS

The first step that the successful option buyer must take before he makes his key purchase decisions, is to decide which common stocks are playable in this option buying market. A common stock must meet some special prerequisites before it can be classified as a playable stock by the sophisticated option buyer. The first requirement, and the most crucial, regards the *trend* of the stock price. If you are planning on buying *call* options, or developing bullish buy strategies, the underlying stock *must* be in an *uptrend*. When buying call options, never buy options on a stock that is in a downtrend, or moving in a neutral pattern.

The exact opposite would be true when purchasing listed

put options; never purchase a put option unless its underlying stock is moving in a downward direction and maintains a declining trend channel.

Time is a factor so valuable in the option buying game that
you cannot afford to wait for a stock to change its trend of
price action. Nor can you wait for a stock to move out of a
neutral trading range. There is not time to hope or pray that
a stock will reverse trend, or that it will move from a dormant position to an active upward or downward position.
Even if the listed options available on that stock are at bargain basement prices, never purchase these options unless
there are signs that the correct trend is developing. Bargain
basement prices will do you little good if the stock is moving
in the wrong direction.

THE "FUNDAMENTAL APPROACH" OUTDATED

In the evaluation of the trend and the future behavior of
a stock price, the "fundamental approach" to stock analysis
is a waste of time. This approach to stock evaluation measures the true value of a stock, assuming that eventually the
stock will adjust to this true value. Since we don't have time
to wait for that adjustment in the options market, the option
buyer is not concerned with the long term value of a stock.
He is concerned with the price action of that stock *today,*
not in six months, or in five years. We must have that price
action *now.* Therefore, the fundamental approach, and any
other approach that requires a lag time of any type should
not be considered in evaluating the stock price action.

ANALYZING
MARKET TRENDS AND INDUSTRY TRENDS

Another trend that you must be very concerned about as
you go about selecting the playable stock is the *trend of the
market* and the trend of the industry that your stock is in.
These two trends must be congruent, must move along with
the trend in your stock. If the market is going in an adverse
direction to your stock's trend, it will definitely have an

adverse effect on the value of the options you have purchased. Any delay in the price movement of your stock will begin to destroy the value of the options you hold. Therefore, make sure if you are purchasing call options, that the trend of your stock is up, and the trend of the market is up. Conversely, if you are purchasing put options, make sure that the trend of your stock is down, and the market is down.

Another suggestion —— when measuring the trend of a stock price, avoid looking at all the statistics and advice that stock brokers and brokerage houses throw your way. Look at only one thing: *the stock price.* Look at the past action of that stock price. Chart the price action of that stock. Then, to determine the strength of an upward or downward move in the stock, look at the volume it attracts as it moves. This will indicate the strength of a price move, and will determine how authentic the uptrend or the downtrend really is.

For example, if a stock price is moving in an upward direction, and is receiving above average volume as it carries out this price move, that would be a very bullish sign. If the stock move is in an upward direction, and there is a below average dose of volume moving into the stock, this would be a sign that you should proceed with caution. Possibly this price move is artificial, and a decline is pending.

If a stock price is moving in a downward declining trend channel, and the stock is receiving significant volume, this would be a bearish sign. On the other hand, if this declining stock was receiving below average volume, again there is a possible sign of caution, although low volume on declining moves in stock prices can be a very deceptive signal for both a bullish or a bearish move.

NEED FOR VOLATILE PRICE ACTION

The playable stock must also meet another very important prerequisite — it must have very *volatile price action.* We mentioned before that measuring the volatility of stock can be very difficult. Volatility in some cases is quite unpredictable, but you must make the best attempt that you can at measuring past and future volatility.

To aid you in this process, we are presenting here a formula which does a good job of measuring past volatility:[4]

$$\text{VOLATILITY} = \frac{\text{12 MONTH STOCK PRICE RANGE}}{\text{Average 12 Month Stock Price}}$$

or, in algebraic terms:

$$\text{VOLATILITY} = \frac{\text{STOCK HIGH} - \text{STOCK LOW}}{(\text{Stock High} + \text{Stock Low})/2}$$

Stock High = The Stock's 12 Month High
Stock Low = The Stock's 12 Month Low

Example: Xerox high and low for 1975 was 86 and 46.

$$\text{VOLATILITY} = \frac{86 - 46}{(86 + 46)/2}$$

$$\text{VOLATILITY} = \frac{40}{66}$$

Xerox Volatility = 60.6%

This volatility formula measures the percentage move that a stock is likely to have above or below its average price for a one year period of time. In this case, Xerox, trading at an average price of 50, is likely to move as high as 80, or as low as 20. This formula of volatility can also be used to measure volatility in a stock price for shorter periods of time.

This information may be more helpful for the option player who is concerned with volatility for one or two months rather

---

[4] Reprinted from *Strategies and Rational Decisions in the Securities Options Market* by Burton G. Malkiel and Richard E. Quandt, by permission of The MIT Press, 1969, Cambridge, Massachusetts.

than a full year. By plotting the volatility for each quarter during the past thirty months, you may get a very accurate picture of the price range of the stock for the next three months. Such homework can provide exceptional information in predicting the future price action of a specific stock. One guideline that we suggest that you follow when using this volatility formula, is to select only stocks which have at least a 20% volatility record over a twelve month period of time. The higher the volatility for a common stock, the more playable that common stock becomes with regard to a stock option purchase.

NEED FOR ACTION

Another more subjective method of evaluating a common stock price's volatility is to look at its daily, weekly, and monthly price ranges and to study the cyclical action of the stock over the past few months. The wider the trading range of the stock, the more attractive it becomes. The perfect playable stock is one that moves in deep and rapid wave formations; the more violent the fluctuations, the better. Stocks which have wide trading ranges, receive good volume, and are moving in an upward trend are excellent candidates for the purchase of call options. Stocks which have wide trading ranges, good cyclical patterns, and are moving in a declining channel, are excellent candidates for the purchase of listed put options.

MONITORING YOUR STOCKS

Once you have identified a series of stocks that meet the volatility requirements we have discussed, and have the necessary action, you are ready to closely monitor these stocks, and begin to identify playable options associated with them. Normally, it is wise to monitor from one to ten different common stocks. By spending your time in a selective group of stocks, you will get a better feel for the price action of these stocks, become far more familiar with them, and of course, you will have much greater success in predicting their future price action. If you attempt to follow too many stocks, you lose the price sensitivity which is very important to the option buyer.

In the process of monitoring these stocks, attempt to chart the price action — the influx of volume into these stocks. Once you have a total familiarity with the stocks you are monitoring, then you are ready to begin monitoring their *playable options,* and can wait for the proper price and time to make your very first purchase of playable options.

Chapter 9

THE PLAYABLE OPTION

PRICE AND TIMING

Having carefully selected and monitored your stocks, you are ready to select the playable options. In the process of selecting the playable option, there are two factors that should have priority over all others, and the first is: *the option price.* Regardless of whether or not the options you are considering buying meet all other requirements, they must be properly priced before you can take any action on that option. They must meet the price that you demand that they meet. If you cannot purchase an option at your price, then either forget it, or continue to monitor that option until it reaches your price.

The second important factor to consider as you hunt, compare and attempt to identify the playable option, is *timing;* the timing of your purchase of the winning option. Remember, you are continually working against the clock. Every minute that passes chips a piece of the value out of the options that you own.

OTHER FACTORS

When comparing the attributes of candidates as possible

playable options, the following characteristics also must be a part of the makeup of such options:

1. The exercise price of the options that you plan to purchase should be as close as possible to the stock price. Normally, as a rule of thumb, you should avoid buying options that have exercise prices that are further than 15% to 20% away from the stock price.

2. Attempt to select options which have as long a life as possible. Remember the rule we discussed before: "as the option approaches expiration, it depreciates at a faster rate."

3. Select options which are extremely undervalued. Option value can be measured by using the Appendix of this text, which displays the true value of listed puts and listed calls at all possible exercise prices, for all possible stages in the option's life cycle.

One important plus you will have when owning an undervalued option is the possibility that the time value of the option will return to a more normal evaluation during the time that you hold the option. This will provide an additional source of profit for your portfolio.

RISK — REWARD ANALYSIS

To repeat, the playable option must have the right price; a price that minimizes your risk and maximizes your leverage and reward. The exact price that you pay for an option should be determined by your risk-reward analysis. Normally, as a rule of thumb, attempt to avoid paying more than $200 for any one option, unless there is a definite risk-reward advantage in taking this step. If you only pay $50 or $100 for an option, you can lose no more than that amount. For the beginner, this can be a very big advantage.

We have discussed risk-reward analysis, and some of you may be confused by this investment concept. Actually, risk-reward analysis is just a way of comparing the *potential return on your investment,* to the *risk of your investment.*

USING THE PLAYABLE OPTION COMPARISON CHART PREDICTION & PROJECTIONS

In order to aid you in comparing and selecting the playable option, and determining the return on investment, we have developed the PLAYABLE OPTION COMPARISON CHART. This chart will greatly aid you in the selection of ideal listed option purchases. The Comparison Chart forces the option buyer to put down in black and white all the key factors to be considered in making the selection decision. This type of an approach to option selection will remove much of the emotionality that interferes with your decision making process.

You will notice as you go over this invaluable chart, that it also requests that you, the option buyer, *predict* where you believe the *stock* price will move, *predict* where you believe the *option* price will move, and *predict how long* it will take the stock price and the option price to move to the target areas. Your ability to predict the price action of the common stock in the future will be an important determinant of your success as an option buyer.

Predicting the future option price is a far easier task than predicting the stock price. First, determine the target date of your option price move, the date that your stock price will reach its goal. Then go back to your option tables in the Appendix at the back of this book, and you can easily determine what the normal value of that listed option will be at that point in time. With this projected option price, you can determine your expected return on investment. This will give you a very important guide in the option selection process.

Our goal in using the Comparison Chart is to determine the probable return on investment if your stock price predictions are correct. Next, to measure risk, you must write-off the amount you invest in your option purchase, even though you may salvage some of the value of the option

PLAYABLE OPTION COMPARISON CHART

	1	2	3	4	5	6	7	8
Option (Call or Put)	Stock Price	% Distance Stock Price From Exercise Price	Stock Target Price	Time Stock Price Will Take To Reach Target	% Stock Price Move To Reach Target	Option Price	Normal Value of Option	Option Target Price
NSM Aug 50 Call	43	16%	50	9 weeks	16%	1 3/8	7/8	2 3/4
Xerox Oct 70 Call	55	27%	65	9 weeks	17%	1/2	3/8	3
Texas Inst. Oct 100 Call	83	20%	95	9 weeks	9.6%	1	2 1/2	5 1/2
ASA Nov 20 Put	25	20%	20	13 weeks	20%	1/4	0	1
Eastman Kodak Oct 70 Put	80	12.5%	72	4 weeks	10%	1 1/2	2 3/8	4 1/2
Digital Equip. July 45 Put	50	10%	46	4 weeks	8%	1/4	7/8	1 3/4

PLAYABLE OPTION COMPARISON CHART (CONTINUED)

	9	10	11	12	13	14
Option (Call or Put)	Stock Trend	Market Trend	Time Left in Option Life	Stock Volatility	Risk Reward Ratio	Return on Investment
NSM Aug 50 Call	UP	UP	17 weeks	136%	1–1	100%
Xerox Oct 70 Call	UP	UP	26 weeks	61%	5–1	500%
Texas Inst. Oct. 100 Call	UP	UP	26 weeks	64%	4.5–1	450%
ASA Nov 20 Put	DOWN	DOWN	21 weeks	57%	3–1	300%
Eastman Kodak Oct 70 Put	DOWN	DOWN	26 weeks	66%	2–1	200%
Digital Equip. July 45 Put	DOWN	DOWN	13 weeks	103%	6–1	600%

when your predictions go astray.

Don't worry if you find prediction tricky. The best stock traders in the business are only "right" 50% of the time, for stock price prediction is a very difficult game. Some authorities believe the stock market is a random world, and it is impossible to accurately predict stock price action. Even the astute technical analysts will admit that it is very difficult to predict when and where a stock price will move. Many say they can tell you where a stock will move, but indicate timing this move is a totally different matter. In order to profit in the option buying game, you *must* determine where a stock will move and the maximum amount of time it will take to make this move. If you have done your homework, you will probably be successful at this feat 35% of the time, depending on your experience; 65% of the time your predictions will be off target. Therefore, your projected return on investment for any option buying strategy should be at least 200% to generate a profit in the long run.

To determine the return on investment figures, complete the Comparison Chart for each playable option you are considering.

Now let's look closely at some of the variables on the chart.

— (2)   To identify the percentage distance that the stock price must move to reach the exercise price, look at the National SemiConductor (NSM) example. NSM is 43, 7 points from the exercise price. Dividing 7 by 43 will give us .16, or 16%.

— (3)   Identifying the stock target price is one of the most difficult tasks of the option buyer. The stock target price is your projection of the future price of the underlying stock.

— (4)   Once you have identified the stock target price, you must project how long it will take to reach your price objective, another difficult endeavor.

— (5)   Then by looking at our target price objective for

our common stock, we can determine the distance it must move to reach the target. In our Xerox example, our target price is 65 and the present price is 55, a 10 point move. We can find the percentage move by dividing 10 by 55, and multiplying by 100.

$$10 \div 55 = .181 \times 100 = 18.1\%$$

— (7) The present normal value of the option candidates is readily available in the Appendix. Use these guidelines to identify bargain options.

— (8) The option target price can be easily identified by going to the Appendix and by using the information from (3) and (4). We can then identify the normal value of the option if your projections are correct.

— (12) Stock volatility can be determined for a year or for a shorter, more revealing time frame.

— (13) The risk-reward ratio is determined by comparing the potential reward to the potential risk. In the ASA Nov put example, if all target prices were reached, the profit or reward would be $75 per option. ($100 less $25, the initial price of the option). The potential risk is the maximum you can lose which is $25, the initial price of the ASA Nov 20 put. Therefore, the risk-reward ratio is $75 to $25 or 3 to 1.

— (14) Once we know our risk-reward ratio, we can then determine our potential return on investment in the case of the ASA Nov put. A 3 to 1 risk-reward ratio is the same as a 300% return on investment.

The examples we have used should provide some insight into how to complete the Comparison Chart and to use the variables as a means of comparison in the selection process.

PUTS ARE CHEAPER

One comment should be made as you carry out the option

selection process. Listed puts are far better priced than listed calls. Normally, puts will be priced from 10% to 50% lower than calls. Consequently, playing with puts may be much wiser than playing with calls. The typical investor has a difficult time betting that the market will go down. THE COMPLEAT OPTION PLAYER has no difficulty at all.

OTHER HINTS

A few additional guidelines to help you to eliminate stiff (loser) options should also be mentioned here:

—— Never require more than a 15% move from the common stock in order for it to reach its target price.

—— Never select an option which generates a potential profit of less than 100% return on an investment.

—— Avoid buying options whose exercise price is more than 20% away from the stock price.

—— Make sure there are at least three months left in the life of the option that you select.

—— Never buy options on stocks with a volatility of less than 20% annually.

Finally, as we conclude our discussion of the playable option, remember the "Golden Rule" of the successful option buyer — "WAIT FOR A PRICE THAT WILL GIVE YOU A HIGH RETURN ON INVESTMENT — A HIGH RISK-REWARD RATIO." To do this requires a lot of patience, and a lot of maturity in the options market. The greatest problem the option player encounters is enthusiasm for a possible common stock. After extensive study, he will see a stock preparing for a big move, and jump into the options market, playing an option with a relatively poor risk-reward ratio.

The unsuccessful option player will not wait for an acceptable price, nor will he be willing to skip the stock's action if he can't get that price. In fact, most option players will have a difficult time walking away from a very attractive opportunity on which they have spent a lot of time, even though they cannot get the "right" price. Using every emotional defense mechanism in the book, they will talk themselves into taking an undesirable option price. Remember — before you buy any option, *all* systems must be go; *all* factors must be right before the purchase can be made. THE COMPLEAT OPTION PLAYER will have this discipline. The unsuccessful option player will not.

Chapter 10

THE GAME PLAN

At last you have made your decision. You have selected an option with an excellent potential return, an option which meets the guidelines that we have established; your homework has disclosed a potential rally in the market and in your common stock. ALL SYSTEMS ARE GO. You move into the option market and get "your" price. You are now the proud owner of a listed call option. Now you can relax. WRONG!

This is exactly the point at which most option buyers go wrong. Remember - as every minute passes, your option is slowly depreciating away. You should be watching your option, the underlying stock, and the market like a hawk. In fact, before you buy any option, you must have a "game plan".

VARIABLES IN YOUR GAME PLAN

Table 7 presents the format the author suggests for this game plan. Variables from your Playable Option Comparison Chart are used in this table to map out the action points you have established in your preliminary plans. This game plan

TABLE 7
THE GAME PLAN

Date ___4* 30*___

Option	Stock Price	Stock Target Price	Option Target Price	Time to Reach Target Price	Maximum Time to Liquidate or Hold Option	Anticipated Return on Investment	Time Before Option Expires
Texas Inst. Oct 100 Call at 1	83	95	5 1/2	2 months	2 1/2 months on June 16,	450%	6 months
Digital Equip July 45 Put at 1/4	50	46	1 3/4	1 month	5 weeks on June 4,	600%	3 months

should display the underlying common stock's target price that you have established, the target price for your option, and the time you have predicted it will take these prices to reach their objectives.

Another important variable that you have added to this game plan is the maximum time that you plan to hold your option. You must set this time parameter and follow it. The most frequent mistake that an option buyer will make is to hold on to an option too long, either because of greed or desperation. To avoid this emotional impulse, set a *point of no return* and sell out your option positions, when the maximum amount of time you allot the option has passed. In determining the maximum hold period, avoid retaining options in the last month of their life. At this point in time, the option depreciates at its fastest rate and only the most sophisticated day trader can handle such action.

A side comment is appropriate here - buying and selling options during the last month of their life is a very exciting and action filled game, but it is full of dangers and only the most experienced and skilled option player can handle these dangers.

MONITORING YOUR OPTION GAME PLAN

Now that you have a game plan, it is important that you closely monitor the price action of your option, the underlying stock, and the market, to identify any changes in trend or trading activity. If the underlying stock price doesn't move according to your game plan, you should immediately abort your mission and sell out your option positions. To paraphrase the old saying, "He who retreats today can return to fight another day". Take heed and follow these famous words.

Too many option players are in the class of the hopers and the prayers; they have lost control of their destiny. The common stock buyer can afford to wait for his stock price to come back, the option player cannot. As soon as the COMPLEAT OPTION PLAYER feels "uncomfortable" with his option positions, he sells them. As soon as his stock price

predictions go astray, he salvages what he can from his option position and moves on to new opportunities.

When you are planning to buy options, PATIENCE is the key to success. But now that you *own* options, QUICK, DECISIVE ACTION is the key to success.

PART II

WINNING THROUGH

OPTION

WRITING STRATEGIES

THE OPTION WRITER IS ANALOGOUS TO A CASINO OPERATOR

Chapter 11

TAKING THE BETS, RATHER
THAN MAKING THE BETS

OPTION WRITERS DEFINED

In our early discussion of the option buying game, we've indicated that option buying is analogous to a side bet on the price action of a specific stock. The backer of that side bet is referred to as the *option writer.* He takes the bets of the option buyer, and in a sense, he pays off when the option buyer is a winner, and pockets the option proceeds when the option buyer is a loser. Option buying has been with us for many years.

However, option writing, "as it is today", is a creation of the new options exchanges. Option writing, for those who are market players, is very similar to selling short a stock, or in this case, selling short an option. Actually, what you are doing is *selling* an option, rather than buying an option. The option seller, or the option writer, has a huge advantage over the option buyer. While time works *against* the option buyer, time works *for* the option seller. As time passes, the value of an option depreciates, and this depreciation, this value, slips into the pocket of the option writer.

Let's take an example. Let's say that you purchase a call

option - a Gulf & Western October 25. Let's say that there are three months left in the life of that option, and you pay a price of $300, plus commissions. At the same time that you are buying that option, someone unknown to you, on the other side of the Options Exchange, is selling (writing) that option, and is receiving your $300. This money will go into his account; so, in a sense, you have just put $300 into the pocket of the option writer. Now, he has certain obligations. If you request 100 shares of Gulf & Western by exercising your option, he must deliver to you 100 shares of Gulf & Western stock at a price of 25.

Let's assume that the Gulf & Western price is now at 23, which means we are working with an "out-of-the-money" option. One month passes, and the stock has moved from 23 to 24. The GW Oct 25 has depreciated in value from $300 to $200, even though the stock has moved upward. The option writer now has a paper profit of $100, less commissions. If he wishes, he can go back into the Options Exchange, and buy that option back for $200, and take his profits. Or, if he feels that Gulf & Western is going to stay where it is, or not move any further than 26 or 27 on the upside, he can hang on to that option and wait for it to continue to depreciate to zero. If you, the option buyer, hold on to the option, you will continue to see it depreciate in value, unless the stock moves up suddenly in a very strong and positive direction.

So, the option writer has a huge advantage. While he is backing your bet, that bet, that option is depreciating; while the option buyer is holding that bet, he is losing money.

Let's look at this example in a different context. The call option writer will be a winner if the stock moves up a little, does not move at all, moves down a little, or moves down a lot. The option buyer will be the winner, will profit from an option purchase, *only* if the stock moves up a great deal. Another way of putting it is to say that the option seller (writer) has, in a sense, an 80% chance of winning, while the option buyer has only a 20% chance of winning. Here is the advantage of option writing. Of course, if the option buyer pays a very small amount for that option, his risk-reward ratio can be very significant, and he can afford to take that 20% chance of winning.

The option writer, then has the odds in his favor. As time passes, that option depreciates, and the depreciation slips right into his pocket. This is the reason why the options game has become so popular, why the institutions are jumping onto this bandwagon, attempting to take advantage of the lucrative profits that are made by the option writer. The new listed put option now creates many more option writing opportunities for the option player, and we will go on in later chapters to explain how you can use these options to develop a very high-powered, profit-making portfolio.

THE TYPES OF OPTION WRITERS

There are two types of option writers: there are the option writers that go *covered,* and there are the option writers that go *uncovered,* or "naked". The *covered* option writer is in a very conservative position; the *uncovered* option writer is in a very speculative position.

Covered option writing refers to a situation in which the option writer protects himself in case of a possible exercise of his option, or an increase in the value of that option. At the same time that he writes (sells) an option, he buys 100 shares of the stock on which he wrote the option. In this way, he receives *premium* (time value) from the option; yet if the stock moves upward, he still profits from the move in the stock offsetting any possible losses from the option that he has just written (sold). This kind of strategy is the most popular today; it is the one that most institutions are moving into. It is simple to understand; it generates a very reasonable return on investment; and it has low risk. This strategy will be covered extensively in a later chapter.

On the other hand, the *uncovered* writer, rather than buying 100 shares of stock, to protect the option that he has written, decides to take the gamble, and write the option without any type of hedge, or protection. He is referred to as a *naked writer.* Now this type of a position does have some risk. There is unlimited risk to the naked call writer and extensive risk to

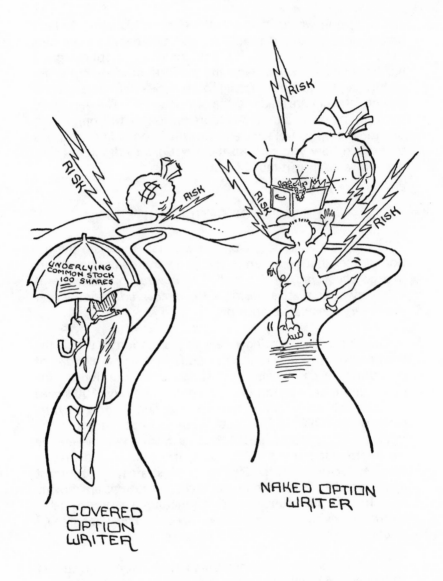

COVERED OPTION WRITER

NAKED OPTION WRITER

the naked put writer. But, you must remember that this is only a theoretical risk; it is not an actual risk in many cases, for the sophisticated option writer knows when the risk is very great, and when it is minimal.

To guarantee to both the options buyer, and to the Options Exchange, that the naked writer will make good on the option that he writes, he must put up cash and/or collateral to back up his naked option writing position. Naked option writing, because of its very speculative nature, is limited to individual investors, market makers, and other option traders, and is normally not entered into by institutions.

Yet, naked option writing is probably the most revolutionary new investment medium which has come out of this new exciting options market. Naked option writing is an unbelievable investment tool which can provide tremendous flexibility and protection to almost any stock or bond portfolio. The numerous strategies which can be designed from naked option writing positions would take many volumes of text to describe, but the author will present what he feels are the most profitable means of using naked option writing, and will identify strategies which have proven to be very successful in the past.

THE MECHANICS OF OPTION WRITING

Many an investor who is still fuzzy about what option writing is all about will discover that it is as easy as buying stock, or buying options, as long as you put up the necessary cash or collateral in your account, and therefore the ease of writing options creates its greatest danger to the novice investor. The investor can so easily write many options, that he will, in many cases, abuse this investment medium and build extensive dangers into his portfolio.

The only difference between buying and writing options lies in the order in which you carry out the process. The option writer sells an option to *open* a position, and buys an option to *close* that position. This process releases him from the responsibilities which are part of his option obligations.

Conversely, the option buyer buys an option to *open* a position, and sells an option to *close* the position, an act which relinquishes the rights which he purchased with that option.

The option writer, like the option buyer in the options market, has the advantage of liquidity. At one moment, he can write an option, and at the next moment, he can close that position out on the Exchange by buying back that option. In this way, the shrewd option writer can avoid being exercised by the option buyer, or opening himself up to the potential dangers of option writing.

THE RISKS OF OPTION WRITING

A discussion of the option writer's risks is appropriate at this time. The writer of a call option, like the individual who sells short 100 shares of stock, has unlimited risk on the upside. If you write an option, and the stock goes up 50 points while you hold the position, you would lose up to $5,000 - $100 for each point that the stock rose above the exercise price. This is the possible risk, the unlimited risk, a rise in the stock price can create. This factor alone scares many an option player.

The writer of a put option, on the other hand, has limited risk. For example, if you were to write a GW Jan 25 put option, when the stock price was right at 25, your risk can be easily determined. When you write a put, you are backing the side bet of the option buyer, a side bet that the stock will fall below the exercise price of the option, which in this case is 25.

How far can that stock fall? Theoretically, it can fall to zero. For each point that it falls, the option buyer *makes* $100, and you, the option writer *lose* $100. Consequently, with the GW Jan 25 put, your maximum risk, less the premium you received from the option buyer, is $2500. Therefore, theoretically, the writing of puts has less risk than the writing of calls. But practically speaking, the risk for writing both puts and calls is actually about the same, and we will be covering this point again later when we discuss option writing strategies involving both put and call options.

The second risk to the option writer is the risk of exercise, and the real danger does not lie in being exercised, it lies in the *cost* of exercise. The cost of the exercise is a roundtrip commission on 100 shares of stock that you will have to buy and then deliver to the option buyer. This cost can run over $150, depending on the commission schedule of the brokerage firm which holds your account. In the next chapter, we will be discussing the problems of exercise at length, and the secrets of avoiding the exercise of options you have written. In Chapter 12 we will dispel some of the old wives tales which have filtered through the market regarding the mystical dangers of exercise.

THE SECRETS OF EXERCISE

The first major secret of exercise is: TO AVOID EXER-CISE.

The second major secret of exercise is: IT IS EASY TO AVOID EXERCISE.

EXERCISE DEFINED

What is this game of exercise all about? When you buy an option, whether it is a put or a call, you are buying a right to exercise. When we say exercise, with regard to a call option, we mean to "call" from the writer (backer) of the option, the 100 shares of stock as specified in the option, at the specified option exercise price. The writer is required to deliver that 100 shares of stock at the specified exercise price to the buyer, if the option is exercised by the buyer.

With regard to a put option, we mean to "put" (sell) to the writer of the option, the 100 shares of stock as specified in the option, at the specified option exercise price. The writer is required to buy that 100 shares of stock at the specified

THE ART OF EXERCISE

exercise price from the option buyer, if the option is exercised by the buyer.

In practical terms, the new options market has been designed to avoid the use of exercise. It is constituted so that rather than exercising if you are a buyer, under most circumstances, you can sell your option position on the Options Exchange, and avoid this costly process. To the seller, it means that rather than being exercised, you can go back into the options market and just buy back your option, paying the prevailing option market price to discontinue your obligation to the option buyer.

EXERCISE AND MARKET SPECIALISTS

As you can see, the options market has been designed to avoid this matter of exercise in most cases. Sometimes the problem of exercise does occur, although probably less than 10% of all options are ever exercised. Many of these are exercised by specialists and market makers on the floor of the options exchanges. These market makers and specialists are taking advantage of what is referred to as a "discount" in the price of the option. In this situation, there is normally no time value at all, or there is actually a negative time value; the price of the option is less than the intrinsic value of that option. But the average investor cannot take advantage of this negative price because the cost of exercise is so high. On the other hand, the specialist or market maker on the floor, because he is able to avoid paying commissions, can take advantage of these negative premiums, and usually does this by exercising the options that he purchases.

DANGERS IN EXERCISE

The real danger to the option buyer who is forced to exercise, or to the option writer whose option is called, or exercised, lies in the cost of exercise - in the commission costs. That cost is the only real concern that the option buyer or the option seller should have with exercise. To the option writer, an exercise of an option may put him in jeopardy if it removes an element in his option strategy. All the other mechanics of the process will be taken care of neatly by the internal mechanisms of the options market, and your brokerage firm.

WHY OPTIONS ARE EXERCISED

Although options are rarely exercised, there are reasons why they would be exercised, and these should be well known to the option player:

1. The first, and most important reason for exercise relates to the time value of the option. Options which have little or no time value are ripe for exercise. Options included in this class would be options which are "deep-in-the-money", referring to the fact that the stock has moved far beyond the exercise price of the option.

   For example, by looking at Table 8, three options are displayed which have no time value, and therefore, would be open to exercise.

2. Options with a negative premium, or what is referred to as a discount on their price, would also be extremely ripe for exercise. Normally, this situation would only exist when there is very little time left in the option.

   Table 8 provides three examples of options which have a negative premium, or time value.

There are other incidental reasons why options could possibly be exercised, but normally they all relate back to the fact that there is little or no more time value in that option. An option exercised with time value would create a loss for the option buyer. He would in a sense be throwing away the time value of the option which is still built into the option price. Consequently, this type of an option would rarely be exercised, and if it were, it would provide a cushion of profit to protect the option writer from the commission costs which will be incurred by the exercise.

TABLE 8
OPTIONS RIPE FOR EXERCISE

Option	Option Price	Stock Price	Time Value	Intrinsic Value
Disney Jan 35 Call	3	38	0	3
Loews Jan 30 Put	1	29	0	1
Charmin Dec 25 Put	5 1/8	20 1/8	0	5 1/8
Xerox Jan 50 Call	7 3/4	58	−1/4 Negative	8
Alcoa Jan 60 Put	5 7/8	54	−1/8 Negative	6
ITT Jan 30 Call	6 5/8	37	−3/8 Negative	7

HOW TO AVOID EXERCISE

Now that we know the root cause of your option being exercised, we will show that it is quite easy to take steps to avoid this costly experience.

Whenever an option writer holds an option which has a price which is approaching zero time value, or zero premium, he should immediately buy back that option, and write another option which still maintains some time value. This action will have two benefits:

1. It will avoid possible exercise

2   It will place you into an option which has time value, which of course works to the benefit of the option writer, because time value depreciates as time passes.

As you enter the option writing game, you will discover that in some cases, you forget about options. They are not monitored closely enough, and once in a while, an option writing position will be sitting there in your hands without any time value to protect you from exercise, and then there is that chance that exercise will come. In this case, your only real danger is the cost, and that will probably run no more than $150 per 100 shares.

So, to summarize, the greatest concern of most beginners in this new options game is exercise, but exercise is only a minor concern of most professionals in this game.

Chapter 13

THE SECRETS
OF STRATEGY DESIGN

THREE MAGIC WORDS

Three words will expose the secrets of strategy design. These three magic words that all option players should be totally familiar with are: STRATEGY, DISCIPLINE, and DEFENSE.

The first hidden secret of strategy design is a very simple prescription - make sure that you always have a well defined *strategy* - a well defined plan of attack. The new options market has generated a very high powered method of making money, but with this high powered potential, we also have a very high powered risk. The game player requires a very carefully planned out strategy to control that risk. With such a strategy, the limitless risks which are continually present to the option writer can be carefully controlled, creating a very safe environment for investment. The game player who enjoys the glamour and glory of flying by the seat of his pants will surely crash land when he enters the options game.

The second key word of strategy design is *discipline.* Discipline relates to your ability to *follow* your game plan. You may consider this secret to be very elementary, but it is

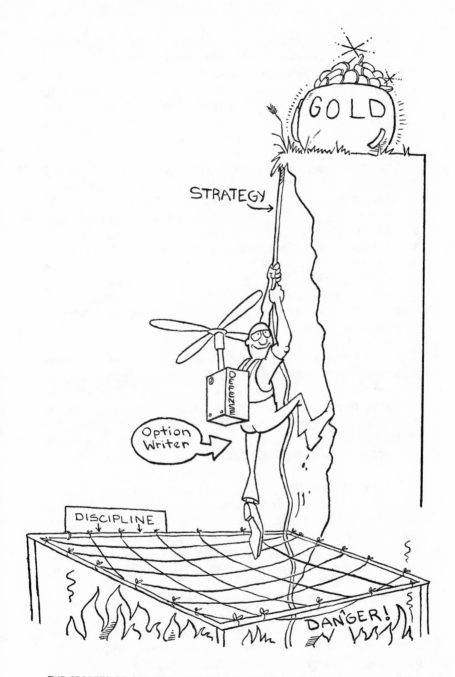

THE SECRETS OF STRATEGY DESIGN — STRATEGY, DISCIPLINE AND DEFENSE

usually totally ignored by the option player. The greatest enemy of any option player is his own emotions. As you begin to play with your own personal money, the most powerful elements of your emotions come into play attempting to coax you off of your plan of action. Once you have lost your rationality in the options game, you have lost the options game.

You must have the discipline to follow your well defined strategy to the letter, not breaking one rule or parameter that you have set. True, this may result in some inflexibility, but in the long run, discipline will provide for a far more consistent return, and a far safer, more successful venture into the extremely volatile options market. Remember, the options market attracts the most brilliant game players in the world; the COMPLEAT OPTION PLAYER must be cool, calculating, and totally disciplined, able to disregard past losses with ease, without disturbing his present strategies and tactics.

If you have ever watched a college football team, you have seen many teams that will let it all hang out. Hook or crook, they will put all their offense on the line, trying to win big, throwing numerous passes, trying out exotic plays, taking every risk in the book in order to win the game. Many of these teams falter in the dust, because of the numerous errors that occur from such a wide open offensive stance.

Then we look at the professional football team which plays a much duller game. They have good offense, but their defense is where all the action lies; a defense that creates openings for the team, prevents any damage from occurring, and that generates a far more consistent win record than teams with a wide open offense.

In the options market, *defense* is the name of the game. As we grow older and wiser, we discover that it is far more practical and there is a far better return if we conserve and protect our capital, and aim for a consistent return rather than laying everything on the line and going for that one super victory, using all of our resources in one burst of energy.

The options market has been beautifully designed to aid the investor in building a very powerful defense. The wise option player uses these investment tools to create strategies which provide a very high degree of safety and a very high and consistent return, not strategies which will live or die on the price action of the stock market. The wise option player paces himself, follows his strategies very carefully to avoid any type of costly error, and shows tremendous maturity in using his offense. He continually conserves his resources, using his offense only when the time is ripe, patiently waiting for the best opportunities to develop, and then striking hard; leaving enough in reserve to be able to return another day.

Option strategies then, have tremendous potential if you remember the three key words to success: STRATEGY, DISCIPLINE, and DEFENSE. If you do not heed these words, there are numerous risks, and tremendous disappointments that will face you in this new options market.

Chapter 14

THE BUSINESS
OF OPTION WRITING

The number of different option writing strategies available
to the option player is almost limitless. To provide proper
treatment for each type of strategy would require several
volumes of text. Therefore, the author will present a select
few of the most powerful and successful option strategies.
We will be looking at option strategies which have a sound
theoretical and academic foundation, proven track records,
and the potential to generate surprisingly high returns on investments over a long period of time.

This chapter presents you with the most elementary and
conservative of all option writing strategies, the one that
contains a good dose of safety and consistency. If you have any
knowledge of the options market, you have already guessed
what this strategy is all about. Of course, it is COVERED
WRITING, probably the most popular option writing strategy
today. This is the most understandable option writing strategy
available to the public. Therefore, many brokers and money
managers have jumped on the bandwagon, and are touting
this money making system.

THE BUSINESS OF COVERED OPTION WRITING

The best way to introduce you to covered option writing

is to look at this approach to the options market as a *business*, not a strategy, or a game, or an investment. Covered option writing is a business, just like running a book store or a supermarket. When you enter the business of option writing, the merchandise or inventory that will be on your shelves will be common stocks (which have options listed on the Options Exchange).

The objective of your business will be the same as any other business - to generate a cash flow, and to generate a flow of income. You will generate income, cash flow, and capital gains from your merchandise - your common stock, by writing options against it.

In the past, the investor purchased a common stock with the *hope* that it would appreciate in value through an increase in price in the marketplace. However, the new Options Exchange has greatly changed that picture, and with covered option writing, we are not involved in such a "hoping" and "praying" game. The business manager who is running a covered option writing program is not concerned with significant stock price increases. But he is concerned with generating a high flow of cash, and capital gains, not from movements in the common stock price, but from the continual writing of options against that common stock, against that merchandise he has on the shelves.

Covered option writing is a rational and rewarding approach to the market. If you own common stock, you should be involved in the business of option writing, generating a cash flow and income from that stock. If you are not, you are letting that common stock go to waste. You are allowing your inventory to sit on the shelves, not opening the store for business. When you own rental property, you rent it, or when you run a book store, you sell books; you don't lock the doors and hope the books will increase in value over the years. The same analogy applies to the stock market.

The business of option writing has a far better track record than most other businesses that we see today, consistently generating a potential 10% to 40% return on investment each year over a very long period of time. Compare this record to

COVERED OPTION WRITING IS SIMILAR TO OPERATING A BUSINESS

your own track record up to this time, not for just one year, but for all the years that you have been in the market, or have been making investments. The record of covered option writing is overwhelmingly better than the track records displayed by the best institutional money managers in the country.

Now that you have seen the attractiveness of the business of covered option writing, let's discuss some of the advantages and disadvantages, and look at some of the risks that are involved in this business.

THE PROS AND CONS OF COVERED OPTION WRITING

The major advantage to the investor is that the business of covered option writing is far safer than the straightforward ownership of common stock and most other securities. For example:

An investor owns 100 shares of Skyline, presently priced at 19-3/4. His risk in holding these shares is $1975, the total value of the 100 shares of stock. Now if he were to write a Skyline Nov 20 call option at 2 in July, he would receive a cash refund, or discount on that stock of $200. For that $200, he has traded the right to deliver the stock to the buyer of the option at a price of 20, any time before the expiration date in November. If the 100 shares of Skyline are exercised (called) by the option buyer, the option writer would have a locked-in profit of $225, less commissions. However, if the stock moves down in price, the stock will never be exercised, (remember we are working with an "out-of-the-money" option, it has no real value).

The investor, by writing the option, has bought an insurance policy with $200 worth of downside protection. If the stock price has not changed by the end of November, the investor has generated a cash return of 10% for a four-month period of time. (30% return per annum). In each case, the investor comes out a winner - unless the stock price drops more than 2 points during that period of time.

On the other side of the coin, if Skyline went from 19-3/4

to 26, the investor would not be able to participate in the total price move of the stock. All he would receive would be the $225 worth of locked in profit.

The above example, then, brings up some of the disadvantages of covered option writing:

1. The downside risk in ownership of the stock is not eliminated, only reduced.

2. The limited profit or opportunity loss if the stock price makes a significant upward move.

Thus, the covered option writer only partially reduces his risk of stock ownership and cannot take total advantage of good moves in the stock price.

On the other hand, counter arguments can be presented to offset these disadvantages. If a stock price falls, we can buy back the option that we have written for a lower price, then write another option against our stock with a lower exercise price and different expiration date.

Referring back to our last example:

Suppose that Skyline now falls from 19-3/4 to 16. The Skyline Nov 20 call option is now priced at 3/8. We buy back the Skyline Nov 20 at 3/8, making a profit of $162.50, less commissions. Now there is also a Skyline Feb 15 option available on the Exchange priced at 3½. If we write this option, we will receive $350 in additional cash to protect our position and add to our gross profits of $162.50. As Skyline continues to fall, we can buy back options and continue writing options in order to provide additional insurance and cash flow to our portfolio. In this way, we can reduce the downside risk of our stock position.

Though this situation may look like a super deal for the covered option writer, sometimes the stock price will drop at too rapid a rate to enable the writer to roll over into a new option, or the call option premiums for new options may be too low to make them a worthwhile ploy.

To counter the argument that the option writer is unable to reap the profits of a significant move in his stock, we should look closely at the volatility of each stock on the Exchange. If you were to study the volatility formula that we presented at the beginning of Chapter 8, and checked on the glamour issues as well as other historically volatile stocks for the last five years, you would discover that their volatility is not as high as you thought; most stocks have volatility factors which are less than 20% a year. Consequently, as an investor, you should not expect a stock with such volatility to move much more than 20% in a positive direction.

The covered option writer now becomes a very wise investor. He has taken a guaranteed 10% return on investment for a four month period. After a year has passed, he has probably received option premiums equal to 30% of the value of his stock, a comfortable return on investment.

Conversely, the typical investor does not write covered options; he holds on to his stock and hopes to reap high profits if the stock rises significantly during the same period of time. When the stock price does rise significantly, rarely does the investor take the cream off the top or profit from the move. Over a year's period of time, the stock investor might get lucky and get a 20% rise in the value of his stock. On the other hand, the stock may have fallen in price, or may be right where it was when he started a year ago. He has not received any insurance whatsoever, or any return on his investment.

PRINCIPLES OF COVERED OPTION WRITING

Now that we have looked at the pros and cons of covered option writing, let's start looking at the process of option writing itself -- how do you run this business? The examples we have presented demonstrate that covered option writing involves the purchase of stock, and the writing of one option against each 100 shares of stock. In this way, the option writer is totally covered. He has no upside risk. If the stock goes up in value, the profits he gains from the stock will cover the losses he incurs from writing the option against the stock. If the stock goes down in price, the premiums (cash) that he receives from the sale of the options will cover some of the loss and decline of the stock price. Therefore, the investor who buys and writes one option against each 100 shares of stock is referred to as a "covered option writer".

It may be helpful to look at an actual example which the author recommended on Dec. 21, 1973, using International Harvester (HR) common stock.

```
Buy 100 shares of HR at 25 ...........$2500
Sell 1 HR Apr 25 call option at 3 ... less   300 (proceeds
                                              received)
              Total Investment    $2200
```

If Int'l Harvester is purchased on margin, the required investment would be $1,325.00.

The profit-loss table is presented below:

HR Price at the end of April	Gross Profit	Loss
20		(200)
21		(100)
22	0	0
23	$100	
24	$200	
25 or higher	$300	

Using this covered option writing strategy, if Int'l Harvester is 25 or greater at the end of April, a gross profit return of 22% for the four month period will be generated, which also works out to a 66% gross return on an annualized basis. This is true when the Int'l Harvester is purchased on margin. Commissions and interest costs plus dividends received are not included in the example.

The results of this covered option writing strategy actually showed a gross profit of $300 before commissions when the HR Apr 25 expired at the end of April. Int'l Harvester was then priced at 25-1/8 at the close on April 27, 1973.

OBJECTIVES IN THE OPTION WRITING BUSINESS

Option writing is not as easy as it sounds. There are many decisions that the investor must make before he jumps into this business. Just like any other business, it requires some training in order to give you a better chance of succeeding.

To open up shop, and begin our option writing business, we should have some very specific objectives to guide us, and the two which the author feels are the most important to the covered option writer are the following:

1. To maximize the flow of income per month.

2. To minimize the risk to the portfolio.

In order to maximize the flow of income from this covered option writing business, the covered option writer should attempt to extract at least a 30% annual return on the value of each 100 shares of stock that he holds in his portfolio.

The second objective is to continually gather enough option premium to reduce the downside risk of holding common stock, and to sell off stock positions which become unattractive because of changes in their inherent price trend.

With these objectives in mind, we must make some very important decisions in choosing which stocks we will purchase for the purpose of option writing. Many investors are in the unfortunate position of already owning a portfolio of common stock, which they definitely plan to keep for tax reasons, or other considerations. These stock positions will greatly influence their flexibility and profits because they will not be able to take the proper corrective actions when necessary, or have the freedom to select proper stocks for option writing.

GUIDELINES FOR STOCK SELECTION

In the search for the correct stocks for covered option writing, you should use the following guidelines very closely to aid you in attaining the objectives that we have set:

1. Select Stocks with a High Volatility

There are conflicting arguments over this point. Many option players believe that stocks with a low volatility are far easier to handle, are exercised less often, and require less surveillance. But stocks that maintain a low volatility normally have very poor premiums, and it would be impossible to use these types of stock in your portfolio and attain the goals we have set for operating our business.

On the other hand, you will find as you get into this new business, that stocks with a high volatility have much higher premiums in their listed options. These stocks normally have better liquidity, as do their listed options. Normally, stocks with high volatility also act in a much healthier and predictable manner. Further, volatile stocks will create a good income flow -- one that can generate up to a 30% to a 40% return per year.

2. Select Stocks Which are in an Uptrend - Sell Any Stocks Which Show a Reversal of Trend.

In covered option writing, we buy stock, and sell call options against each 100 shares of stock. We don't work with puts in this business, nor do we play the bearish side of the market in any other manner. Therefore, it is important for the reduction of risk to insure that the stocks that you do purchase and place in your inventory are in an uptrend.

In a bear market, you cannot write options fast enough to protect your behind; if the stock is moving down at a rapid pace, you are going to take a loss. Volatile stocks provide good premiums, and normally you can write fast enough to protect some of that downside risk, although it is very difficult to protect all of it. Therefore, you should only stock your shelves with common stocks that are in a bullish trend, and when that stock price changes its trend, you should divest yourself of those positions.

Investors locked into a situation where they cannot afford

to divest themselves of stock positions must, of course, take their losses during the periods when their stock is moving down significantly. But it is far better to be writing options during this period than to be sitting on your stocks praying for the next bull market.

A final comment regarding this guideline - during bear markets, you should be out of the covered option writing business. You should sell most of your merchandise, except those stocks which are running counter to the overall market trend, and you should be moving into other options strategies which work well during bearish markets. In addition, you might want to know that there are other alternative strategies which are almost as safe as covered option writing. These strategies can provide tremendous protection during a bear market, and they will be discussed later in this text.

3. Diversify Your Inventory of Common Stocks - Hold at Least Four Different Common Stocks, in Different Industries.

The wise covered option writer will always have a good range of common stocks in his portfolio. This diversity greatly diminishes risk. If you have only one position, and the stock dives downward in price, your performance will suffer, as you would not be able to write options fast enough to protect the total downside risk. To smooth out the peaks and troughs of the stock values which are being held in your portfolio, attempt to hold at least four positions; this number has been academically proven to provide good diversity.

4. Favor Low-Priced Stocks Over High-Priced Ones.

Low-priced stocks, such as $10, $15, or $20 a share, have a tendency to have higher premiums per the value of that stock as compared to stocks that are running at $100 or $200 a share.

Commissions are another area in which the writer of low-priced stocks has an advantage. If you use your funds to purchase 1,000 shares of Skyline at 20, rather than 100 shares of

Eastman Kodak at 100, you can reduce the commission costs of writing options, because you now can work with ten options, rather than one option.

Later, when we talk about the tools and tactics of trading, you will find that commissions are a real obstacle in this game. The covered option writer who carefully watches and measures his commission costs, and takes every opportunity he can to reduce these costs, will show a far better annual return than the covered writer who ignores this important consideration.

5. Purchase Stocks on Margin - Fill Your Stores as Full as Possible With Merchandise

When you begin your option writing business, set aside a lump sum which you will use to purchase your merchandise, the common stock that you will be writing options against. You should attempt to get the maximum leverage from your investment. If you have $20,000 to invest in covered option writing, you should be purchasing as much stock as you possibly can with that money, even if you have to buy stock on margin (borrow money from the brokerage firm to buy stock). The going interest rate for borrowing money to buy stock normally runs from 8½% to 10%. But by following the guidelines we have provided, you will generate better than a 10% return from writing options, making marginable stock profitable. Thus, the wise option writer will buy as much stock, or merchandise, as he can on margin.

Another great advantage of covered option writing is that when you write options, you receive the premium from that option back immediately in the form of cash, which goes directly into your account, and can help to finance the purchase of more stock. Then as you continue to generate more and more premium from your option writing business, this premium should be used to re-invest and attract more and more stock, and at the same time, make more margin available to purchase additional merchandise. By holding a philosophy of expansion, you will obtain a very attractive return on your investments and see your portfolio grow rapidly.

6. Select Stocks Which Have the Highest Yield

A final consideration in the selection of which playable stocks should fill the shelves of your portfolio is the yield of that stock. Again, remember, our objective -- to maximize the flow of income per month. Dividends, of course, would be part of that flow of income. Therefore, the option writer should look not only at what kind of a premium he is going to attract from writing options against 100 shares of stock, but also at the dividend of that stock, adding the dividend to the return which he will receive from his other option writing premiums.

GUIDELINES FOR OPTIONS SELECTION

Now that you have the key steps to follow in selecting the merchandise (stocks) to put on the shelves of your portfolio, you have come to another important decision in the operation of your covered option writing business -- which option should you write for each 100 shares of stock that you own? The Options Exchange is like a supermarket - each stock has several options with different exercise prices, and different expiration dates available to the option writer, and the option buyer. As the option writer, you must select the option that will do the best job for you.

Remembering our objectives, high return and low risk, let's look at the following, as we move now to select the best options:

1. Select Options Which Show the Maximum Income Flow Per Month

This first guideline is the most critical - the selection of options which will provide the greatest cash flow and income on a per month basis. In measuring the income generated by an option, the only thing that we can consider is the time value, or the premium value of that option. The intrinsic value of the option should not be considered in this analysis. You should only consider the intrinsic value of an option when you are attempting to provide some downside protection, but are not looking for actual income generation from that portion of the option.

Table 9 shows how to break down the option price to determine the income flow per month. Let's go back to our example of the Skyline Nov 20 call. We received $200 for a four month period of time. The whole value of the call is time value, as indicated in the table. Thus on a per month basis, we receive $50 of time value for each month. Now let's compare that to the Nov 15 Skyline at 6. In this case we receive $600 of cash flow. We obtain $600 from the option, but only 1¼ points of that option price is true time value. The other part of that option price is intrinsic value; in other words, the option is in-the-money. In this case, the true return is the time value, which is 1¼ points. This is broken down over a four-month period to approximately $31 per month. The formula for determining the per month flow is presented as follows:

$$\text{INCOME PER MONTH} = \text{TIME VALUE} \div \text{NUMBER OF MONTHS TO EXPIRATION}$$

As you can see from Table 9, the Skyline Feb 20 option generates a monthly income of $41, as compared to the $50 you would receive on a monthly basis from the Skyline Nov 20. Therefore, we find the Skyline Nov 20 option to be the most attractive.

Having determined which option produces the most income per month, you need to look at another factor -- how important is it to reduce your downside risk? If you believe that the stock is ready for a short downtrend, then possibly you should be more concerned about the total price of the option, because that provides the total cash flow, and you should be writing in-the-money options such as the Nov 15 at 6. Remember, if the trend of the stock turns bearish, you should sell that stock, should not continue to write options against it. But, if you are unable to do this, or if you feel the downtrend is only a short-term move, then possibly writing an option which is in-the-money might be a wiser move at

TABLE 9
COVERED OPTION COMPARISON TABLE

(Skyline at 19 3/4 on July 15)

OPTION	PRICE	INTRINSIC VALUE	TIME VALUE	NO. OF MONTHS TO EXPIRATION	INCOME PER MONTH
Skyline Nov 20	2	0	2	4	$50
Skyline Nov 15	6	4 3/4	1 1/4	4	$31
Skyline Feb 20	2 7/8	0	2 7/8	7	$41

this time, rather than strictly considering the amount of income which the option produces.

2. Generally Avoid Deep-in-the-Money Options Which Show Little Time Value

The example we have just examined would be the one exception to this rule. When you are hunting for reduction of downside risk, then in-the-money options can be attractive, because they do provide more of a cash flow to protect a downside move of the stock.

But note that such options as we viewed in the preceding example, and other deep-in-the-money options normally provide very little income, because there is very little time value in them; consequently, they are always in danger of exercise. Therefore, *avoid* getting involved with deep-in-the-money options, unless you are forced to protect a downside risk.

3. Maintain a Policy of Continuous Option Writing - Roll Over Into New Options When Old Options Lose Their Time Value.

There are two ways in which the covered option writer can run his business. The first is to write options against his stock positions, and either wait for the options to expire, or for the stock to be exercised. This method requires less surveillance by the option writer, but it also generates less premium.

In contrast, another more sophisticated technique, one that takes far more time and surveillance, is called CONTINUOUS OPTION WRITING. Of particular advantage to this approach is that it actually will reduce downside risk if a stock falls at a fast rate.

The procedure involved in "continuous option writing" is to "roll over" into new options when old ones lose their time value. What does this mean? It means that when an option loses almost all its premium, even though there may be a lot more time left in the life of that option, the option businessman goes in and buys the option back and writes a new option which is fat in time value. Now this may occur when the stock drops, or when it declines away from the exercise price, or it may occur when the stock moves deep-in-the-money, far over the exercise price. Under these circumstances, the option writer will buy back the option, and roll over into another option with a different exercise price or a different expiration date. In this way, he can generate a much greater amount of premium over a period of time, thereby providing far more protection from downside risk.

Such a procedure will also avoid exercise, and will create a much more active portfolio - a much more active business. Continuous option writing, then, takes more time and more surveillance, but it generates far more premium and provides much more protection for your portfolio of common stock.

4. Beware of the Danger of Commissions.

As mentioned before, commissions are your greatest obstacle in the option writing game. Not only will you have to pay the commissions from purchasing common stock, but you will also have to pay commissions created by buying and selling options on a very periodic basis. If you "roll over" into new options every month or two, the commissions can mount up drastically. So, as you decide on which options to write, always consider the question of commissions.

In many cases, it is far wiser to write an option which has a more distant expiration date, even though the income per month may be lower, because such a transaction only requires *one* commission. If you write an option with a much shorter life, you may have to write another option, which requires a duplication of commissions. In other words, when determining which option to write, always consider the *total* commission costs that will be involved over the same period of time. If you are comparing writing a three month option to writing a six month option, the six month option may have a better per month flow of income, after you subtract the additional commission costs of writing two three-month options as opposed to the cost of writing only one six-month option.

5. Do Not Write Undervalued Options.

At the back of this text, we have provided you with a set of tables which you can use to determine when an option is overvalued, and when it is undervalued. Always use these tables in measuring the options premiums that are available for writing. The options which are overvalued are the ones which should be the prime targets for option writing; the undervalued ones should be avoided. In the end, writing undervalued options will definitely affect your return on investment.

If you follow these guidelines closely, your probability of generating a 30% to a 40% return annually will greatly increase. The business of covered option writing, like any business, requires some experience, so your first year or two in this activity may be a little rocky. But do your homework, follow your guidelines, and direct all your attention towards attaining your objectives. Your rewards will be handsome.

THE FUTURE

Having read this chapter, you probably now are turned on by the business of covered option writing. But before you jump on the bandwagon, let's look at the future for a moment. Covered option writing is gaining enormous popularity. Whenever a money-making operation such as this becomes popular, it ceases to be a money maker. Eventually, this may be the case with covered option writing. New changes in tax laws, and the outstanding success of the new Options Exchange have created an environment in which droves of individuals, money managers, and institutions are entering the covered option writing business. The participation of these institutional money managers will have a definite effect on the operation of this business.

There are some advantages for the average investor as the institutions enter into this market. Having seen the outstanding profits that have been generated under covered option writing over the past several years, the institutions will now drop from their portfolios stocks that do not have options listed on the Exchange, and purchase stocks that are on the Options Exchange, usually carrying out continuous option writing programs. This will create a bullish tinge to the stocks that have options listed on the Exchange. The institutions will have a much greater tendency to hold on to these stocks, rather than jumping in and out of such positions. This situation will create excellent price stability for the common stocks that have action on the Options Exchange, helping all investors who are holding these stocks. Eventually, any respectable institution will make sure that they have 90% of their portfolio full of optionable stocks.

A disadvantage to the entrance of the institutions into covered option writing is that institutional investors will drive call option prices down. Options which are ideal for covered writing will lose much of their value, and will become far less attractive as an option writing vehicle. As a result, the cash flow and the capital gains opportunities in this business will greatly diminish, decreasing the attractiveness of this conservative and popular game. The astute option player should be aware of this trend, and when he finds it difficult to get the right option premiums on his common stocks, he should move on to the many other option strategies that are available in this market. Many of these other option strategies are difficult for the institutional investor to enter.

Chapter 15

PLAY IT NAKED

You have received your first application of option writing with a very conservative, defensive strategy, covered option writing. Now let's pull out some of the stops and play a far more exciting game. Let's PLAY IT NAKED.

Up to this point, we have been discussing the position of the covered option writer, who *covers* his option writing risk by owning the underlying common stock. He gains only part of the benefit of option writing by playing it safe and maintaining a very conservative defense; he cannot reap all the various profits available to the option writer.

In contrast, "playing it naked" is a method which reaps *all* of the benefits and potential profit of the sport of option writing. The naked option writer writes options *without the common stock covering his position.*

Although there are some substantial risks in this game, which we will explore later, let us first look at some of the important benefits to be gained by playing this exciting game.

ADVANTAGES OF NAKED OPTION WRITING

1. The Potential Rewards Are Outstanding

To the professional option player, naked option writing is the Cadillac division of the new options market. If you have the discipline, patience, knowledge and the skill, this is the game that you should be playing. The profit potentials here are greater than in any other segment of the options market. The skilled and disciplined naked option writer can generate from a 50% to a 100% return annually on his investment, and normally can do this consistently over a long period of time. The advent of the new listed put options provides even more flexibility to the naked writer's repertoire of opportunities. Now he can become a "man for all seasons," confronting numerous opportunities, both in bull, bear, and nomad market conditions.

2. The Odds Of Winning Are Strongly In The Writer's Favor

You will discover, if you decide to participate in this Grand Prix of the options market, that when you run a naked option writing portfolio, a high percentage of your positions will be winners. By following the rules that we will set out in Chapter 16, 80% of your positions are likely to come out profitable, and only 20% will be losers. In other words, the odds are stacked heavily in your favor. Naked option writing is probably the only game in town where the investor truly has a strong advantage over the rest of the market. Consider this analogy:

The casino operator who offers roulette, craps, and blackjack to patrons who visit his casino is similar to the option writer. The casino operator backs the bets of the gaming customers — he pays off when the customers are big winners; on the other hand, he takes in the profits if they are losers. The casino operator has a slight advantage working for him in each game. In the game of roulette, for instance, he has approximately a 5% advantage over the gaming customer.

The option writer is in a similar position, but his advantage is even better than 5%. The academic studies and research that have been done so far have indicated that the option writer (seller) actually has approximately a 10% to 20% advantage over the *option buyer* (if he does not write undervalued options). The option writer, like the casino owner, provides the option buyer with a market in which to speculate, in which to gamble. For this service the option writer receives a 10% to 20% advantage in the options game.

In other words, if you were blindly and randomly to select overvalued options for a naked option writing program, were to maintain a large enough portfolio with enough diversification, and were to run your program over a long period of time, you would come out with a profit probably running between 10% and 20% year in and year out, under present market conditions. Carrying out the same procedure in the stock market by buying common stocks would create a totally different picture.

The major advantage that is always working for the naked option writer, that gives him this percentage edge, is TIME. The option buyer bets that the stock will go up significantly when he buys a call. But unlike the option buyer, the option writer wins under all other stock price conditions. The call option writer is a winner even if the stock moves up too slowly, because as time passes, the premium that the option writer receives from the option buyer for backing his bet depreciates, therefore moving into the pocket of the option writer.

So, the option writer has two important factors in his favor:
  A. He does not require the underlying stock price to move to make a profit.
  B. As time passes, he is continually making a profit, as the option that he has written shrinks in value.

The naked option writer who writes strictly naked options, with no hedges, no stock, and no long options to cover his naked positions is attempting to maximize these advantages.

For example:

An option buyer purchases an Upjohn Jan 40 call option at 3, with three months to run. The stock price is at 37 — there is actually no real value in that option at the time the option buyer purchases the option. The only value the option holds is time value. The $300 option price goes to the option writer.

In order for that option to take on any real value at all, the stock price must move above 40. For the option buyer to break even at the end of that three month period, the stock price must be at 43. If the Upjohn stock price is below 40 at the end of the three month period, the option will expire, worthless. The writer will have made $300 less commissions, and the buyer will have lost $300.

Therefore, the profit parameters for the option writer would read — by the end of January, if the stock price is *below* 43, he wins. Conversely, if the stock price is *above* 43, the option buyer wins. However, the option writer starts with the advantage, because when the option was purchased, the stock was 6 points below the breakeven point for the buyer. Actually, the option writer starts with a profit — he has $300 and 6 points to work with before the time period begins.

3. Success Does Not Depend On Predicting Stock Price Behavior

The option writer, unlike the option buyer, is not required to predict the exact extent of a stock price move. By the fact that the option writer begins the game with the odds stacked in his favor, he can afford a wide margin of error in measuring and predicting what a stock price will do in the future.

In fact, there are many theorists who believe that it is impossible to predict the price action of a stock in the future. They consider the stock market a random walk down Wall Street. As you operate your naked option writing portfolio, although you should not ignore the trend of the market, or the trend of a stock, you can partially adopt a random walk theory in operating your portfolio. Even if you should write an option, and the stock should move in the wrong direction, if that move is slow enough, or is not far enough, you can still come out ahead.

Remember that in our scenario regarding the price action of a specific stock, a stock can move up significantly, can move up a little, can stay where it is, can move down a little, or can move down a lot. Thus when you are writing calls, the only time that you will lose is if the stock moves up significantly during the period that you back that contract. If you are writing puts, the only time that you will lose is if the stock moves down significantly.

4. The Theoretical And Academic Arguments Supporting Naked Option Writing Are Excellent

Before the existence of the new options markets, naked option writing was practiced by a select few in the old over-the-counter (OTC) market, and was a far more dangerous game than writing listed options today. The OTC option writer faced numerous obstacles which made it unfeasible for most investors to enter that game. Yet, even with these dangerous pitfalls, studies of the old OTC market show encouraging results, which support the more advantageous position of the option writer today. The opinions of the OTC option experts indicate that almost 65% of all options in the OTC market were never exercised (expired without value).

In the old OTC market, when an option was written, or sold, the stock price was right at the exercise price. (However, this is not true today; now you can write options which are a great distance from the exercise price. We refer to these as either *out-of-the-money* options, or *in-the-money-options.*) In the old OTC market, normally the only type of option that was written was an *on-the-money* option, an option in which the exercise price and the stock price were identical.

Even in the OTC options market, and even when options

were on-the-money, evidently the writer had a slight advantage in the fact that only 35% of all options were exercised. These performance claims are backed by a considerable body of research. In the book, STRATEGIES AND RATIONAL DECISIONS IN THE SECURITIES OPTIONS MARKET, the authors, Burton G. Malkiel, and Richard E. Quandt, reported that their research conducted from 1960-1964 proved that writing OTC options on a random basis, without any judgements or safeguards was indeed a profitable game in all cases.[6]

In contrast, those who *bought* during that period, regardless of what strategy was used, always ended up with a negative result. Therefore they discovered that the writing of *naked* call options was one of the optimum strategies available in the options market, generating over a 10% annual return. With such encouraging results on a random basis, imagine what the returns would be if a little skill, a little knowledge and the proper timing were added to this investment mode!

Another study which indicated the feasibility of option writing came from the book, BEAT THE MARKET by Sheen Kassouf and Ed Thorp. The results of their strategy, based on the shorting of warrants on the Stock Exchange, (which is almost the same process as writing call options on the Options Exchange) were presented at the beginning of this text in Chapter 1. These results are very impressive, and will be discussed further in a later chapter. Kassouf and Thorp proved, through the use of track records and through some very sound theoretical and academic studies, that the short selling of warrants can provide a very high and consistent profit when the investor also uses a hedging strategy. Though they did not discuss writing warrants without any type of hedge, the maximum flow of profit came from this technique.

Finally, documentation verifies that in the first year and a half of operation of the new CBOE, only 10% of all options in the new options markets had any real value when their lives expired.

[6] Reprinted from Strategies and Rational Decisions in the Securities Options Market by Burton G. Malkiel and Richard E. Quandt, by permission of The MIT Press, 1969, Cambridge, Massachusetts.

DISADVANTAGES OF NAKED OPTION WRITING

When we look at the disadvantages of naked option writing, one disadvantage stands out clearly above all others——RISK. There is unlimited risk when writing naked call options, and extensive risk when writing naked puts——the risk that the underlying stock price will move through and far above or below the option exercise price. This highly publicized risk scares many investors away from the naked option writing game, and many who have played in this unusual game have been wiped out by the volatility and action of naked options.

Regulatory agencies, brokers, and many option players cringe when you talk about naked options; there is probably more fear floating around about naked options than about any other investment vehicle available today. But although a definite risk does exist in the naked option writing market, this risk has been greatly exaggerated.

To show why this is true, let us examine these possible risks of naked option writing in detail, and decide which actions to take to guard against them.

1. The Risk of Not Being Covered by Common Stock

We have already mentioned the unlimited risk that the option writer has when he is not covered by the common stock. For example:

If you were to write five call options on Upjohn with an exercise price of 40, and Upjohn were to move through the 40 exercise price in an upward direction, you would be responsible for delivering 500 shares of Upjohn to the buyer, if he at any time chose to exercise his options. Your risk for each point that Upjohn moves above 40 will be $100 per option position that you hold. In the case of the five Upjohn calls, you would have $500 of risk for each point that Upjohn moved above the exercise price of 40. If Upjohn were to move from a price of 40 to 45, your actual loss would be $500 per option for the 5 points that the stock moved, which comes out to $2,500.

2. Negative Risk-Reward Ratio

A second related risk that scares many a player away is the possibility of a negative risk-reward ratio. In our first example of Upjohn, we mentioned the fact that the maximum amount that the option writer could gain by writing an Upjohn Jan 40 at 3 was $300 in profit. The option writer can make no more than $300 on that position.

On the other hand, his counterpart, the option buyer, has unlimited profit potential from that option position. If the Upjohn price were to move from 37 to 60, within a short period of time, the option buyer would generate a profit of $1700, less commissions on his $300 investment. The option writer, who only had $300 to gain, would lose $1700 on that naked option writing position. Consequently, the risk-reward ratio in this example does not look very attractive to the naked option writer.

However, there are two counter-arguments in favor of the naked option writer regarding this risk.

1. The probability that Upjohn or any stock would make such a large move within a short period of time is extremely small. The likelihood that the buyer will be a winner in his option positions is normally very minimal. It is important for you to consider the probabilities with any stock, in order to reduce the negative risk-reward scenario which can occur to the naked option writer.

2. The shrewd naked option writer will never own an option which has become so fat as to provide a big reward for the option buyer. He will never allow such a negative risk-reward scenario to develop. The professional naked option writer will have left that option position long before this occurs. One of the beauties of the new options markets is the ability to close out a transaction at any time. Here the all-important quality of DISCIPLINE comes into play. When the stock moves in the wrong direction, moves through his parameters (which he must *always* set before entering a position), the naked option writer *must* immediately extricate himself from that position by buying back the option.

A professional option writer cannot afford to write an option at $300, and buy back, or pay off to the buyer that same option at $1,000 or $2,000. That is one risk the naked option writer cannot afford to take if he plans to stay in this game very long.

So, despite these risks we have discussed, there are counter-measures which can provide strong safeguards for the disciplined naked option writer. If you use these tools, (to be discussed further in a future chapter) the naked option writing game can lead you to a large pot of gold rather than a dangerous pit of fire.

MARGIN REQUIREMENTS FOR NAKED OPTION WRITING

The naked option writer, unlike the covered option writer, must put up a certain amount of cash or other form of collateral for each option position that he establishes. This cash or collateral (referred to as a margin requirement) guarantees to the Exchange and the brokerage house that the writer will make good on his contract if the underlying stock suddenly moves in the wrong direction.

There are many firms who continue to live in ignorance, and thus set up ridiculous margin requirements for naked option writers, requiring an initial deposit running from $25,000 to $50,000. There are, however, brokerage houses that are far more reasonable, which provide minimal margin requirements and initial deposits to enter this exciting game. These are the types of firms you must seek out if you wish to take on the supreme challenge of the new options market.

During the first two years of the existence of the new Options Exchange, the margin requirements were minimal in many CBOE member firms, giving the naked option writer significant leverage, and therefore, significant return on investment during that bear market period. Portfolios multiplied within weeks; gains of 1,000% to 2,000% were not unusual. Unfortunately, pressure from the SEC and the

New York Stock Exchange has forced margin rules upward to a point where now, in order to write a naked option, you must put up, in the form of cash or collateral, 30% of the value of the underlying common stock. For example:

If you were to write an option on Xerox when Xerox was selling for $60 a share, you would have to put up a deposit of 30% of the value of the 100 shares of Xerox stock, which comes out to $1800 (less the value of the XRX option). This $1800 margin requirement would be increased or decreased, depending on how far the stock price was from the exercise price of the option you have written.

A major obstacle that the professional option writer faces is his ability to get a high enough return on investment for each position he enters. The margin requirements will be the greatest hurdle that he encounters in meeting this challenge, so he must continually attempt to identify naked options which require a minimum amount of margin. We will cover margin requirements in greater depth in a later chapter.

USING NAKED OPTIONS AS A DEFENSE

You will discover in future chapters that naked option writing, besides being a method of maximizing leverage and reward, can be used as an excellent investment tool. Naked options are ideal vehicles for use in building high-powered *defenses* for your portfolio. The more you use naked options, the healthier that defense will be, and the more protection you will receive. Naked options, combined with common stock, fixed securities, convertible bonds, or long option purchases provide outstanding protection and consistent returns. Some money managers are beginning to discover this fact, and use naked option writing to cushion their portfolios from the uncertainty of the stock market. For example:

A money manager with a portfolio consisting of common stock, or fixed securities, might consider taking 10% of his portfolio, and just writing naked options with that portion of the portfolio. Writing naked puts and calls will provide a cushion against risk in both bull and bear markets and provide excellent results in nomad markets. Over all this approach to the market is very defensive providing a lot of protection to such a portfolio.

Future chapters will discuss in depth different ways of using naked writing techniques as an investment tool to build a defense, and as an income producer for your portfolio.

The next chapter will move into the keys to success in operating a portfolio in which you *only* write naked options.

In conclusion, when you write naked options, if you are careful, and if you follow the guidelines and the safeguards we have developed, your rewards will be far more handsome than in any other strategy presented in this text, or available in the investment markets today.

Chapter 16

THE SECRETS OF
NAKED OPTION WRITING

As we disclose more of the secrets of the mysterious art of naked option writing, you will learn that they are based on simple and concrete principles. In Chapter 13, we discussed the secrets of strategy design, and found that a solid strategy, a good defense, and the discipline to follow them are critical to the success of the option player. The secrets that we will disclose regarding naked option writing follow this scene very closely.

The naked option writer must develop and adhere to a solid strategy which has a very simple but solid defense built in to protect and control the numerous risks that surround him as he plays the game of naked option writing. You must have the discipline to follow the controls that you set up, you must follow your strategy, you must follow your defense. Most important of all, you must be able to "pull the trigger" and take a loss gracefully.

Only by using the following guidelines will you protect yourself from the numerous risks that scare many brokers, brokerage houses, and many option players away from this game. But if you do follow these guidelines, you will reap the outstanding rewards that this game offers.

Let's begin by looking closely at THE ELEVEN SECRETS OF NAKED OPTION WRITING:

1. Set a Bail-Out Point and Use It.

A bail-out point is the price, or the point in your strategy at which you wish to buy back your naked positions in order to limit your losses. This stock price, or option price, at which you wish to bail out of your position, is the most important segment of your naked option writing strategy. With naked options, you *must* have a set of safeguards as a defense to limit your losses and control the tremendous risks You must have a point at which you will bite the bullet if your naked options go astray.

As you remember, the outstanding feature of the new options markets is the right that you have, as an option writer, to go into the market at any time and buy back your naked options, thereby limiting all possible future losses. Setting a bail-out point is a way of insuring that you will use this right when the price hits the parameters that you have set.

How do you bail out of a position?

There are actually two approaches that you can take to limit your losses in a naked option position:

The first requires an option player of very strong mind and body, an option player with nerves of steel, and with outstanding discipline.   This type of an option player can afford to have the perogative of voluntarily moving into the market when the underlying stock price touches his bail-out parameter, and buying back his options at his own discretion.

One point which should always be kept uppermost in the option player's mind when he carries out this process, is that if he does not bail out at this point, there is a chance that he will lose everything. When you are running a naked option writing portfolio, your overall goal should be to stay in the game, and the only way you will ever stay in the game eventually to participate in the outstanding profits of this game is by bailing out whenever your loss parameters are touched.

A second approach to bailing out of an option position has been designed for the option player who is not as experienced, or feels that he doesn't want to rely totally on his own discipline. This method requires the use of a "stop-loss" order. Just think of jumping out of an airplane as analogous to taking a loss in a naked option position. If you feel that you can easily parachute out of that airplane every time, without getting a push, then you may have the discipline necessary to voluntarily move out of your option positions. On the other hand, if it might be easier for you to receive a little push when you jump out of that plane, then possibly the use of a *stop-loss order* to bail you out of your option positions would probably be the wiser alternative.

Remember, it might be easy now to say, "Yes, I'll voluntarily cover my naked shorts, and buy my options back when the underlying stock hits my loss parameters." But when you actually get into the midst of the battle, investors have a hell of a time making decisions which involve taking losses. They will not bite the bullet; they would rather wait and hope that the stock will change direction. Their emotions take over; they have illusions which are totally unrealistic; they start to build stories around why their stock will not move any further. All these factors can come into play, and the investor must win over these emotions, or else in most cases he will lose. Therefore, in some cases, the stop-loss order might be a much wiser alternative than attempting to jump out of that plane voluntarily.

What is a "stop-loss order"? A stop-loss order is a special order placed on the Options Exchange whereby your naked option position will be covered (bought back) under one of two conditions:

    a. If the underlying stock price reaches a certain price, which you have set as your bail out price.
    b. If the option price reaches a certain price.

The author strongly suggests that you use the first of

USE STOP-LOSS ORDERS TO GIVE YOU A LITTLE PUSH WHEN YOUR STRATEGIES TOUCH THEIR BAIL-OUT POINTS

these. Attempt to set the point at which you have decided to limit your loss by using the stock price's action, rather than by using the option price. Option prices move in erratic patterns, and in many cases, they may become extremely inflated, even though the stock price has not moved accordingly. Your major concern as a naked option writer is— where is the stock price going to end up? Consequently, you should select a stop-loss order which is contingent upon the stock price if possible.

For example:

Let's say that you wrote a Xerox Jan 60 call option when the stock was at 50, and you set your bail-out point at 58. This order would indicate that if the Xerox price reached 58, your option would immediately be bought back, and your position would be closed out. The order to buy back your option would be a market order.

The market order feature of a stop-loss order is the only real disadvantage to using stop-loss orders in the options market. Market orders in the stock market work out quite well in most cases, but on the Options Exchange, a market order can be dangerous. Some options trade in very thin markets — in other words, they have a very low liquidity, and market orders in thin markets can be a costly experience. On the floor of the exchange, market makers love to take advantage of market orders when there are few buyers and sellers around.

2. Write Naked Call Options in Bear Markets;
Write Naked Put Options in Bull Markets

This secret of naked option writing is quite self-explanatory. To improve your probability of winning this game, it is far wiser to write calls when the stock prices in general are moving down, and to write puts when stock prices are moving up. This strategy puts the odds in your favor; although

NOTE: Several options exchanges and brokerage houses do not accept option stop-loss orders.

naked call options during bull markets can be profitable, and naked put writing during bear markets can be profitable, because of the inherent advantage the naked option writer holds. By following these rules, you will improve your probability of winning the game, and reduce some of the risk.

3. **Write Naked Calls on Underlying Stocks That are in a Major Downtrend;**

   Write Naked Puts on Underlying Stocks That are in a Major Uptrend

Your profits will be much greater in the naked option writing game if you write calls when the underlying stock is moving downward, and if you write puts when the underlying stock is moving upward. The best way to project this type of price behavior is to look at the underlying trend of each of the optionable stocks.

4. **Select Stock Candidates with a Low Price Volatility**

While the option buyer always hunts and pecks for options on stocks which are extremely volatile, the option writer loves stocks that don't move anywhere. He wants stocks that move very slowly, and ones that move in a narrow range, because the option writer always has time working in his favor. The slower a stock price moves, the more money he makes. Options with slow moving underlying stocks will depreciate to zero before the stock ever reaches a bail-out point. Unfortunately, the stocks with the highest volatility maintain the highest and fattest premiums for option writing, and so the option writer must attempt to find options with low volatility, and correspondingly high premiums (time values) when possible.

5. **Diversify — Maintain at Least Four Different Option Positions with Different Underlying Stock**

You've heard this before in previous chapters. Naked option writing, with its extreme risks, requires diversity. Remember, one of your overall goals is to stay in the game, and the best way to do that is to avoid betting all your money on one horse. Although the odds are heavily in your favor — one loser can put you out of the game, if everything you have is bet on that one position.

6. Write Puts and Calls Which are at Least 15% Out-of-the-Money

The author feels that when you are carrying out a naked option writing program, the only options you should ever consider as writing candidates are those that have no real (intrinsic) value, that are not in-the-money. Use only those options that are out-of-the-money, which have only *time* value. Select options which are *significantly* out-of-the-money, so that it will take a strong move in the stock, (a move that normally would not occur in a two or three month time period) to hit your bail-out parameters. These *out-of-the-money* options, which require a major move in the stock to take on any value at all, have a low probability of ever being exercised, or of ever having any real value, and this low probability is a strong advantage to the naked writer. In other words, in selecting your option positions, select those options which have the highest probability of expiring before the stock price ever gets close to the exercise price. It is your ability to carry out this patient selection process, and to wait for those opportunities to develop that will determine the degree of your success.

7. Write Naked Options with No More than Four Months Left in Their Life

Remember that as an option approaches expiration, its rate of depreciation normally increases. Consequently, these are the times to write naked options. You will receive a higher rate of premium in the last three or four months of the option than at any other time in its life. Write naked options during the months that they depreciate at the highest rate.

8. Write Options Which are at Least 25% Overpriced According to Their Normal Value

One of the most important secrets to successful naked option writing is to write only options which have been *overpriced* by the market, options which the buyer is paying too much for. This will add insurance to your profit potential, and is an important key to successful option writing. The Appendix again provides the normal values of all options. Make sure that the options you plan to write are at least 25% over the normal value presented in these tables.

9. Write Options Against Treasury Bills

We've mentioned before that when writing options, you must put up a margin requirement. That margin requirement can be in the form of cash, or it can be in the form of securities. It can also be in the form of *Treasury bills.* If it is in the form of securities, you can only use the loan value of the securities, which means that you will pay an interest charge each month.

However, if you use Treasury bills, you don't have to borrow. The Treasury bills are treated just like cash, and this is one major advantage of using them. Treasury bills will generate from 4% to 10% annually, depending on the money market, and this will be an added dividend to your option writing portfolio. Not only will you generate the profit from option writing, but you will also generate the return each year from your Treasury bills. If the brokerage house that services your account does not accept them, then find one that does, because it is an important advantage.

10. Maintain a Strict Stock/Option Surveillance Program

Watch your stock and option prices like a hawk. Monitor every move that the stock and option prices make during the periods of time that you are holding these naked option positions. The professional naked option writer will keep a close eye on the price action of the underlying stock, and will cover a position, bail out of a position, or buy back a position if there is a change in the trend of the underlying stock.

He will also take profits early, when the option shrinks in

value quickly because of an advantageous stock price move, or he may take action when the options become extremely undervalued, according to the value of the stock price. The closer you carry out a surveillance program, the better your profits will be, and the smaller your losses will be.

This surveillance program should also contain a continuous writing feature which is best described as a method of re-investing funds into new naked option writing positions as profits are taken. This process is similar to compounding interest in your bank account, although in a naked option writing account, the profits that are being compounded are much greater. By continually re-investing in new investment positions, and by actively taking profits when they develop, your portfolio will grow at a far faster rate than is possible if you maintain a static program of waiting until options expire.

There is a tremendous difference between an active naked option writing program, and a static one, where no action occurs until the expiration date arrives. The compounding of profits in a naked option writing portfolio can be an extremely significant factor in providing outstanding returns.

11. Set a Bail-Out Point and Use It

Yes, you've heard this one before, and you will hear it again, many times. This is the most important safeguard of your naked option writing program. Make sure that you use it. Make sure that you *set a bail-out point,* a price at which you will always, regardless of any other circumstances, buy out your position, and bail out. The best way to insure this action is to use a stop-loss order. The author cannot over-emphasize the importance of this secret of naked option writing. Fortunes can be made or lost by the manner in which you pull the trigger to take your losses. As the saying has it, "He who hesitates is lost."

Now let's take all of these important rules of naked option writing and map out a game plan. Table 10 displays all the many pieces of information needed by the professional naked writer in order to select, and then later monitor, his

TABLE 10
NAKED OPTION WRITING STRATEGY CHART

Date _7* 20*_

Option Candidate	Option Price	Under-lying Stock Price	% Distance Stock Price from Exercise Price	Bail-Out Stock Price	Stock Vola-tility	Normal Value of Option	% Option Price over Normal Value	Margin Require-ment	Time Left in Option	Anti-cipated Return on Invest-ment (Annual)	Trend of Stock	Anti-cipated Commis-sion Costs (In and Out)
Houston Oil & Mineral HOI Oct 60 Call	4	52	13.2%	64	200%	1 1/2	260%	$490	18 weeks	240%	Down	$50
Eastman Kodak EK Jan 50 Put	2	60	16.6%	48	40%	1 1/4	60%	$600	30 weeks	58%	Up	$50
Teledyne Tdy Oct 70 Call	3 1/2	60	16.6%	73 1/2	118%	1 1/4	200%	$450	18 weeks	224%	Down	$50
ASA Nov 15 Put	1/2	20	25%	14 1/2	90%	1/16	700%	$250*	22 weeks	47%	Up	$40

* $250 is the minimum margin requirement for any naked option writing position.

naked option positions. This strategy format will be indispensable to the naked writer in planning and building his naked option writing portfolio.

A WARNING is appropriate here: make sure that you always have your naked option positions mapped out in the manner demonstrated in Table 10 before you enter them. Attempting to design and implement strategies which are not displayed on paper, in black and white, is a dangerous game, especially with naked options.

Chapter 17

THE ROAD TO RICHES -
THE NAKED SPREAD

You have seen the many rewards and advantages of naked option writing, and have been exposed to a totally naked option writing portfolio. Now let us look at a new variation of the naked option writing strategy, one which will reduce your margin requirement by 50%, will improve your leverage, and will reduce the highly publicized risk of naked option writing. This is a strategy with an extremely solid theoretical foundation that will double your return on investment.

The author refers to this strategy as the supreme strategy. From his research and experience, there is no other investment opportunity as powerful and profitable as the NAKED SPREAD, which is actually a very close relative to a typical naked option writing program. The naked spread involves using only naked options as its base; we don't work with common stock, or with long options.

The major difference between this strategy and the one that we presented in the previous chapter relates to the *selection* of naked options; they are not selected strictly on market timing, or on the bear or bull of the market. Naked options for this strategy are chosen based on the criterion of margin requirements, in order to minimize the use of margin. By doing this, we are able to increase the return on investment by up to 100% over straight naked option writing. This new strategy also factors out some of the risk by the manner in which the naked options are selected. The track record of such strategies has been very successful even in the old over-the-counter (OTC) market.

NAKED SPREAD DEFINED

To get into the thick of things, let's first define a naked spread. A *naked spread* combines the writing of a naked call and a naked put, both with the same underlying common stock, and the same expiration date, but with *different* exercise prices.

For example:

Write (sell)   1 Sperry Rand Apr 45 call option
Write   1 Sperry Rand Apr 35 put option

Writing both of these options at the same time would create a naked spread.

Of course, within the definition of a naked spread, we can have in-the-money spreads, partially-in-the-money spreads, and out-of-the-money spreads. As an experienced option player, you have discovered that the skilled option writer always writes out-of-the-money naked options. Therefore, when designing a portfolio full of naked spreads, both the put and the call should be out-of-the-money.

For example:

Write   1 McDonald's Jul 50 call option
Write   1 McDonald's Jul 45 put option

McDonald's common stock price is 47. Therefore, both the naked put and the naked call are out-of-the-money.

If a naked spread is designed properly, the option writer can actually reduce his risk tremendously, because the profit and loss scenario is very much to his advantage.

In Table II we have mapped out the profit picture for a naked spread in order to demonstrate the advantages of this sophisticated strategy. The naked spread in Table II entails the writing of:

(1) One Xerox Jul 70 call at 4
(2) One Xerox Jul 60 put at 3

By writing these two options, we generate premiums of $700, which goes into our account. At the time that we carry out this position in May, the price of the Xerox stock is 65.

Now let us look at this picture in July when the options expire: if Xerox is anywhere between 70 and 60, we will make a full profit of $700 on this strategy. If the stock is anywhere between 53 and 77, we will definitely have some profit. In other words, we have placed a tent, or a canvas of profit over the movement of the Xerox stock.

Of course, if during the life of the option, the price hits the parameter of 77, or the parameter of 53 (our bail out points), we should immediately buy back both options, and close out the strategy. Be sure to move out of both options; do not hang on to your opposing option when an outside parameter is hit. If you do not carry out this action, the win/breakeven feature of this strategy is destroyed.

If this event occurs late in the option period, we will come very close to breaking even before commission costs, because our bail-out points are so far in-the-money for each of the options we have written, that there will be very little time value left in the options.

For example: If the Xerox stock price hits 53 (our break-out parameter) a few weeks before the options expire in July, the following picture would hold true —
Price of the XRX Jul 70 = 1/16
Price of the XRX Jul 60 = 7 1/8

We would have already received $700 in cash when we initiated the strategy. That will cover all but 1/8 of the cost to buy back the Xerox Jul 60. The cost to close out the XRX Jul 70 is only 1/16. Total cost less commissions to exit the strategy is only 3/16 ($18.75). The same picture would develop in reverse if Xerox hit 77 rather than 53.

TABLE 11
THE NAKED SPREAD

| Sell | 1 | Xerox | Jul | 70 | Call | at 4 |
| Sell | 1 | Xerox | Jul | 60 | Put | at 3 |

The Xerox common stock price is 65 at the time of entry on May 1 for this theoretical strategy.

The Initial Margin Requirement would be $750.

The Profit-Loss Table is presented below.

XEROX Price at the End of July	Gross Profit	Loss
80		($300)
79		(200)
78		(100)
77 Bail-out Point 0		
76	100	
75	200	
74	300	
73	400	
72	500	
71	600	
70	700	
69	700	
68	700	
67	700	
66	700	
65 Present Price	700	
64	700	
63	700	
62	700	
61	700	
60	700	
59	600	
58	500	
57	400	
56	300	
55	200	
54	100	
53 Bail-out Point 0		
52		(100)
51		(200)
50		(300)

Profit Zone

With this strategy, if the Xerox price is between 53 and 77 at the end of July when the options expire, a gross profit will be realized. If the Xerox stock price moves to 77 or 53 before, we should bail out of both naked options to minimize potential losses. Commission costs are not included in this profit-loss scenario.

TABLE 11A

In order to demonstrate how we come up with the profit-loss scenario presented in Table 11, we have generated another table below, mapping out the same strategy in a different manner, again looking at the profit-loss picture at the end of July.

XRX Stock Price at End of July	Value Of Put	Value Of Call	Profit or (Loss) From Call	Profit or (Loss) From Put	Gross Profit or Loss
80	0	$1,000	($600)	$300	($300)
79	0	900	(500)	300	(200)
78	0	800	(400)	300	(100)
77	0	700	(300)	300	0
76	0	600	(200)	300	100
75	0	500	(100)	300	200
74	0	400	0	300	300
73	0	300	100	300	400
72	0	200	200	300	500
71	0	100	300	300	600
70	0	0	400	300	700
69	0	0	400	300	700
68	0	0	400	300	700
67	0	0	400	300	700
65	0	0	400	300	700
64	0	0	400	300	700
63	0	0	400	300	700
62	0	0	400	300	700
61	0	0	400	300	700
60	0	0	400	300	700
59	$100	0	400	200	600
58	200	0	400	100	500
57	300	0	400	0	400
56	400	0	400	(100)	300
55	500	0	400	(200)	200
54	600	0	400	(300)	100
53	700	0	400	(400)	0
52	800	0	400	(500)	(100)
51	900	0	400	(600)	(200)
50	1000	0	400	(700)	(300)

In this strategy, it is hard to lose money, because if the stock moves to your outer parameters, you probably will break even, or take a very slight loss, and if it stays within the parameters of the strategy, you will have a profit.

As we have seen, if Xerox is between 60 and 70 at the end of July, your profit will be $700. The amount of margin you must put up to attain that $700 is $1700, which means that you would generate more than a 40% return over a three month period. That is, of course, an excellent return compared to similar conventional strategies with limited downside risk. A 40% return works out to be an annual return of 160%. You can now see the outstanding value of this kind of strategy.

Of course, the potential of your naked spread will all depend on the prices you receive for writing your put and your call, and the volatility of the stock that you are working with.

SELECTING STOCKS WITH LIMITED VOLATILITY

Unlike other types of strategies which depend on market timing and market moves for their success, the naked spread does not require this kind of prognostication. In fact a stock market that is moving nowhere is excellent for the naked spread writer. The naked spread is ideal for those who believe that the stock market is a random walk scenario, where it is impossible to predict stock price behavior.

Through a study of stock volatility tables you will discover that even the most volatile stocks do not move very dramatically. The lack of volatility in the movement of a stock is very important to the naked spread writer. You are betting that a stock will not move outside of a wide trading range when you write a naked spread, and if it stays within that range, you are a winner. If it hits the outside parameters, you will break even or take a small loss.

The name of the game is to build naked spreads which have a wide enough trading range so that the stock price has a very low probability of touching your parameters. In

Table II a 40% trading range was developed for the Xerox naked spread. Normally, a high percentage of all stocks will rarely move more than 20% in any direction, especially within a three or four month period. As a result, such a naked spread has a high probability of coming out a winner.

To conclude, the most important principle in naked spread writing is to map out the naked spread, ensuring that the range of profit that you develop for that naked spread is wider than the price movements of the underlying stock price during the life of the strategy. Tables 12 and 13 demonstrate another naked spread and map out the manner in which profits and outside parameters are developed. You should study these tables very closely and follow this format in designing and mapping out your own naked spread strategies.

THE SELECTION AND DESIGN OF NAKED SPREADS

Selecting naked spreads, unlike selecting other option strategies, is more of an art than a science. Going back to our Xerox example — if Xerox rarely moves more than 20% in either direction during a three-month period, that would be an excellent strategy, because there is little likelihood of your profit parameters being violated. When there is a low probability of this occurring, you have a high quality naked spread strategy.

In order to come up with ideal naked spreads, the following guidelines should be followed:

1. Know Your Stocks

In order to determine whether or not a naked spread will be successful, you must have a thorough understanding of the price movement of the underlying stock, and that understanding should lie basically in the area of its volatility. Use our suggested volatility formula, plotting out what the three-month volatility has been for the past three to five years. Doing this will give you a good feeling for projecting the maximum possible move in that stock. With this knowledge, you can then begin to seek out and compare naked

TABLE 12
ANOTHER NAKED SPREAD

June 21, 19

| Sell | 1 | Digital Equip. | Oct | 45 | Call | at 1 1/2 |
| Sell | 1 | Digital Equip. | Oct | 35 | Put | at 1 |

Digital Equipment common stock price is 40. The position is theoretically taken on August 1.

The Initial Margin Requirement would be $450.

The Maximum Margin Requirement would be $1360.

The Profit-Loss picture is presented below.

Table 13 shows how we generate this profit picture using our custom worksheet.

Digital Equip. Price at Expiration Date in Oct.	Gross Profit	Loss
49		($150)
48		(50)
47 Breakeven Point	50	
46	150	
45	250	
44	250	
43	250	
42	250	
41	250	
40 Present Price	250	
39	250	
38	250	
37	250	
36	250	
35	250	
34	150	
33 Breakeven Point	50	
32		(50)
31		(150)
30		(250)

TABLE 13
THE NAKED SPREAD WORKSHEET

Date June 21, 19

WRITE 1 Digital Equip. Oct. 45   CALL at 1 1/2   PROCEEDS = $ 150
(SELL)

WRITE 1 Digital Equip. Oct. 35   PUT at 1   PROCEEDS = $ 100
(SELL)

Digital Equip. STOCK PRICE 40   TOTAL PROCEEDS
INITIAL MARGIN REQUIREMENT $ 450   RECEIVED $ 250

MAXIMUM MARGIN REQUIREMENT $1360   PROJECTED
                                                          COMMISSION COSTS $ 75

Digital Eq. PRICE EXPIRATION DATE IN October	(1) PROCEEDS FROM CALL	(2) VALUE OF CALL	(3) PROFIT OR (LOSS) FROM CALL	(4) PROCEEDS FROM PUT	(5) VALUE OF PUT	(6) PROFIT OR (LOSS) FROM PUT	(7) GROSS PROFIT OR (LOSS) (3) + (6) = (7)
49	$150	$400	($250)	$100	0	$100	($150)
48	150	300	(150)	100	0	100	(50)
47 Bail-out Point	150	200	(50)	100	0	100	50
46	150	100	50	100	0	100	150
45	150	0	150	100	0	100	250
44	150	0	150	100	0	100	250
43	150	0	150	100	0	100	250
42	150	0	150	100	0	100	250
41	150	0	150	100	0	100	250
40	150	0	150	100	0	100	250
39	150	0	150	100	0	100	250
38	150	0	150	100	0	100	250
37	150	0	150	100	0	100	250
36	150	0	150	100	0	100	250
35	150	0	150	100	0	100	250
34	150	0	150	100	100	0	150
33 Bail-out Point	150	0	150	100	200	(100)	50
32	150	0	150	100	300	(200)	(50)
31	150	0	150	100	400	(300)	(150)
30	150	0	150	100	500	(400)	(250)

spread strategies.

2. Select Option Candidates Which are Over-Priced

You should always attempt to write options which are over-valued by the market, as this will give you much more premium to work with and will also provide an additional bonus for your strategy. With naked spreads, your goal is to get as much cash (premium) as possible from each option that you write, to provide a wider profit range within which the common stock price can fluctuate.

3. Carefully Map Out Each Potential Strategy

This is the only way to compare the profitability of different spread strategies. You must determine what the profit range is for each naked spread that you are considering, and what percentage move in the stock would be required to violate that range. By following this procedure, you can determine what the probability is that each strategy will be profitable.

4. Beware of Commissions

Commissions are always a critical consideration. They have not been included in our tables and examples in this chapter, because we do not want to confuse the issue at this time. However, they are of critical importance, and we will spend a full chapter discussing the use of commissions and how to select strategies which will reduce your commission costs. You will discover that naked option writing strategies contain far fewer commissions than any of the other elaborate strategies that can be designed with options.

THE NAKED STRADDLE

The *naked straddle* is another sophisticated strategy, similar to the naked spread, with many of the same benefits. The author will not cover this area very extensively, because the naked straddle contains many of the same elements as the naked spread. However, the naked straddle is more market sensitive than the naked spread, the volatility of the underlying stock is more critical, and the chances of being forced out of your strategy are greater.

A "naked straddle" is a situation where you write a put and a call, with the same underlying common stock, the same expiration date, and in this case, the *same exercise price.*

Tables 14 and 15 map out a naked straddle and show the profit parameters and breakeven points for the straddle. Using the Xerox Jul 70 put and call, the profit parameters for the Xerox naked straddle run from 60 to 80. Again we have what is referred to as a win or breakeven scenario, which is greatly to the advantage of the naked writer, and reduces the risk of naked option writing. The profit range is smaller for this strategy, as are the profits at each level compared to the naked spread. Consequently,there is a better possibility of being forced out of a strategy. On the other hand, this strategy has many of the same advantages as naked spreading, and should be considered as a very viable strategy.

In their book, STRATEGIES AND RATIONAL DECISIONS IN THE SECURITIES OPTIONS MARKET, authors Malkiel and Quandt studied the options market between 1960 and 1964, and compared the naked straddle to all of the other naked option buying and writing strategies. The results were outstanding. They found that the return on investment was much higher than the very favorable return for writing naked call options. In their research, the writing of naked straddles showed a 28½% annual return. This return again was based on a random approach to the selection of straddles, with no judgment, timing, or other rational considerations involved.[7]

You have an excellent arsenal of investment weapons to choose from if you plan to become a naked option writer. You can write naked puts or calls, or you can combine these

[7] Strategies and Rational Decisions in the Securities Options Market, B.G. Malkiel and R. E. Quandt, MIT Press, Cambridge, Mass. 1969.

TABLE 14
A NAKED STRADDLE

Theoretical Date —
May 1, 19

| WRITE (Sell) | 1 | Xerox | Jul | 70 | Call | at 5 |
| WRITE (Sell) | 1 | Xerox | Jul | 70 | Put | at 4½ |

The Xerox common stock is 70 at the time of entry into this theoretical strategy.

The profit-loss table is presented below. With this strategy, if the Xerox price is between 79 and 61 at the expiration date in July, a gross profit will be realized. If Xerox moves to 79 or 61 before that time, you must bail out of both sides of the strategy.

Table 15 presents a worksheet which demonstrates how the profit-loss table is developed.

Xerox Price at Expiration Date in July	Gross Profit	Loss
81		(150)
80		(50)
79 Bail-out Point 50		
78	150	
77	250	
76	350	
75	450	
74	550	
73	650	
72	750	
71	850	
70	950	
69	850	
68	750	
67	650	
66	550	
65	450	
64	350	
63	250	
62	150	
61 Bail-out Point 50		
60		(50)
59		(150)
58		(250)

Profit
Zone

-154-

TABLE 15
THE NAKED STRADDLE
WORKSHEET

WRITE (SELL) __XRX Jul 70__   CALL at __5__   Date __May 1, 19__   PROCEEDS = $ __500__

WRITE (SELL) __XRX Jul 70__   PUT at __4 1/2__   PROCEEDS = $ __450__

__XRX__ STOCK PRICE __70__

INITIAL MARGIN REQUIREMENT $ __1150__

MAXIMUM MARGIN REQUIREMENT $ __2320__

TOTAL PROCEEDS RECEIVED $ __950__

PROJECTED COMMISSION COST $ __75__

Xerox PRICE EXPIRATION DATE IN July	(1) PROCEEDS FROM CALL	(2) VALUE OF CALL In July	(3) PROFIT OR (LOSS) FROM CALL	(4) PROCEEDS FROM PUT	(5) VALUE OF PUT In July	(6) PROFIT OR (LOSS) FROM PUT	(7) GROSS PROFIT OR (LOSS) (3) + (6) = (7)
81	$500	$1100	($600)	$450	0	$450	($150)
80	500	1000	(500)	450	0	450	(50)
79 Bail-out Point	500	900	(400)	450	0	450	50
78	500	800	(300)	450	0	450	150
77	500	700	(200)	450	0	450	250
76	500	600	(100)	450	0	450	350
75	500	500	0	450	0	450	450
74	500	400	100	450	0	450	550
73	500	300	200	450	0	450	650
72	500	200	300	450	0	450	750
71	500	100	400	450	0	450	850
70	500	0	500	450	0	450	950
69	500	0	500	450	100	350	850
68	500	0	500	450	200	250	750
67	500	0	500	450	300	150	650
66	500	0	500	450	400	50	550
65	500	0	500	450	500	(50)	450
64	500	0	500	450	600	(150)	350
63	500	0	500	450	700	(250)	250
62	500	0	500	450	800	(350)	150
61 Bail-out Point	500	0	500	450	900	(450)	50
60	500	0	500	450	1000	(550)	(50)
59	500	0	500	450	1100	(650)	(150)
58	500	0	500	450	1200	(750)	(250)

two types of options, and write naked spreads, or naked straddles. Naked spreads and naked straddles improve your return on investment, because they greatly reduce your margin requirement, and actually reduce your risk, creating what is referred to as a win or breakeven profit-loss scenario. If you follow the rules that we have brought out in the last three chapters, you will be engaged in a lucrative adventure.

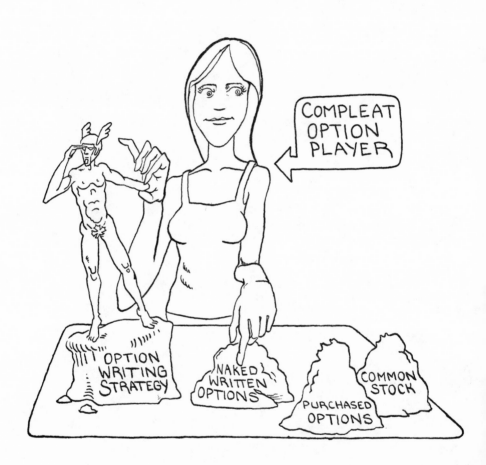

MOLDING INNOVATIVE STRATEGIES

Chapter 18

MOLDING
INNOVATIVE STRATEGIES

By now you have discovered the rewards of naked option writing. We have demonstrated how naked option writing can be used as a strategy in and of itself, how to alter it to reduce the inherent risk, and how to improve profits.

Up to this point, we have discussed naked option writing strategies which involve the writing of naked options exclusively. Now we are going to look at some new approaches which utilize not only naked options, but also other investment vehicles as well. As we did in Chapter 17, we are going to mold strategies which have a very small possibility of incurring any loss. If a loss is incurred, it will be very slight.

THE RATIO HEDGE

The major strategy we will study is referred to as the ratio hedge, or the variable hedge. The foundation of a ratio hedge strategy is 100 shares of common stock, similar to that of a covered option writing strategy. In the case of a ratio hedge, we take several naked call options, and wrap them around the 100 shares of underlying stock. We take the benefits of naked option writing, the high probability of reward, and use it to protect a common stock position. At the same time that we are protecting the 100 shares of stock, the 100 shares of stock is shielding the naked option writing positions from a severe loss. As the stock price moves up, the common stock will appreciate in value, countering potential losses from the naked options, which will also expand in value. If the stock moves down, you will take a loss in the stock, but you will profit from the depreciation in the price of the naked options.

The ratio hedge was practiced long before the new Options Exchange was established. In fact, the ratio hedge is the heart of the Thorp and Kassouf system, which they present in their book, BEAT THE MARKET. The authors provide a tremendous amount of documentation to support their findings, and the results are impressive. We presented these findings at the beginning of this text, and will present them again so that we may look at them more closely. Their research shows:

"1. The system, using a ratio hedge as its base, showed a gain of more than 25% per year for 17 years.
2. From Sept., 1929 to June, 1930, the system could have doubled an investment.
3. The system showed a real five-year track record, generating average annual returns of 25%.
4. The system actually doubled $100,000 in four years."[8]

These results should prove the viability of ratio hedge strategies. The work of Thorp and Kassouf in this area used warrants rather than naked options, which were not readily available at that time. They shorted warrants, and used these vehicles as a means of providing a canvas of protection over the common stock. The short sale of a warrant is a very close relative to the writing of a listed call option. Therefore, the material we present in this chapter can be seen as an outgrowth of the work that Thorp and Kassouf completed in their book.

The major objective of the ratio hedge is to create a

[8]Edward O. Thorp, Sheen T. Kassouf, *Beat The Market,* Random House, Inc., New York, 1967.

strategy which is not market dependent, which does not require the proper prediction of where stock prices will move in the future, or the proper timing to take advantage of market moves. This strategy is designed assuming that the market moves in a random fashion. Your goal is to move into positions and wait until the options expire and then move out; or to wait until the stock price breaks one of your outside parameters.

In this strategy, you will want to design a profit pattern in which the underlying common stock price fluctuates *within* the parameters of the strategy, in a manner similar to the design of the naked spread. This strategy is designed so that the stock price can move in a wide range, and if it stays within that range, it will generate a profit, when either the options expire, or shrink in value.

Let us take a close look at a ratio hedge strategy. Tables 16 and 17 map out a ratio hedge strategy using 100 shares of National Semiconductor (NSM) as the base. We have used as our molding material, three NSM Nov 45 call options, which we will write to protect the common stock position. You will notice the wide profit range that has been created. If NSM stays within that range (which runs from 30 to 53) until the end of November, and does not break through our parameters before that time, a profit will be generated. If the NSM stock hits one of the outside parameters, the strategy requires that you remove yourself from the total position, including selling the stock and buying back all the options. When you bail out, there is a very high probability that there will be little time value left in your naked options, and therefore, you will probably break even (before commission costs are incurred).

THE ART OF RATIO HEDGE DESIGN

The designing of ratio hedges, like the designing of the naked spread, is probably as much an art as a science; yet through practice, you will gain more and more skill in mapping out these potential strategies. Table 18 presents

TABLE 16
A RATIO HEDGE

July 19, 1976

| Buy | 100 | NSM | Common Stock at 43 3/4 | Cost = $4375 |
| Write | 3 | NSM | Nov 45 Calls at 4 3/4 | Proceeds = $1425 |

The profit-loss table is presented below.

NSM Price at the end of November	Gross Profit	Gross Loss
55		(450)
54		(250)
53 Bail-out Parameter		(50)
52	$150	
51	350	
50	550	
49	750	
48	950	
47	1150	
46	1350	
45	1550	
44	1450	
43	1350	
42	1250	
41	1150	
40	1050	Profit
39	950	Zone
38	850	
37	750	
36	650	
35	550	
34	450	
33	350	
32	250	
31	150	
30 Bail-out Parameter	50	
29		(50)
28		(150)

TABLE 17
THE RATIO HEDGE
WORKSHEET

BUY __100 NSM Common__ at __43 3/4__ COST = $ __4375__

WRITE __3 NSM Nov 45 Calls__ at __4 3/4__ PROCEEDS = $ __1425__
(Sell)

INITIAL MARGIN REQUIREMENT $ 5800

MAXIMUM MARGIN REQUIREMENT $ 7620 at 52

PROJECTED COMMISSION COSTS $ 210

Date __July 19, 19__

NSM PRICE EXPIRATION DATE IN November	(1) VALUE OF STOCK	(2) COST OF STOCK	(3) PROFIT or (LOSS) from STOCK	(4) PROCEEDS FROM WRITTEN OPTIONS	(5) VALUE OF WRITTEN OPTIONS	(6) PROFIT OR (LOSS) FROM WRITTEN OPTIONS	(7) TOTAL GROSS PROFIT OR (LOSS) (3) + (6) = (7)
54	$5400	$4375	$1025	$1425	$2700	($1275)	($250)
53	5300	4375	925	1425	2400	(975)	(50)
52 Bail-out Point	5200	4375	825	1425	2100	(675)	150
51	5100	4375	725	1425	1800	(375)	350
50	5000	4375	625	1425	1500	(75)	550
49	4900	4375	525	1425	1200	225	750
48	4800	4375	425	1425	900	525	950
47	4700	4375	325	1425	600	825	1150
46	4600	4375	225	1425	300	1125	1350
45	4500	4375	125	1425	0	1425	1550
44	4400	4375	25	1425	0	1425	1450
43	4300	4375	(75)	1425	0	1425	1350
42	4200	4375	(175)	1425	0	1425	1250
41	4100	4375	(275)	1425	0	1425	1150
40	4000	4375	(375)	1425	0	1425	1050
39	3900	4375	(475)	1425	0	1425	950
38	3800	4375	(575)	1425	0	1425	850
37	3700	4375	(675)	1425	0	1425	750
36	3600	4375	(775)	1425	0	1425	650
35	3500	4375	(875)	1425	0	1425	550
34	3400	4375	(975)	1425	0	1425	450
33	3300	4375	(1075)	1425	0	1425	350
32	3200	4375	(1175)	1425	0	1425	250
31	3100	4375	(1275)	1425	0	1425	150
30 Bail-out Point	3000	4375	(1375)	1425	0	1425	50
29	2900	4375	(1475)	1425	0	1425	(50)
28	2800	4375	(1575)	1425	0	1425	(150)
27	2700	4375	(1675)	1425	0	1425	(250)

a form that the author highly recommends that you use to develop these strategies, and to map out the potential returns at each price level of the stock. This formula also identifies the breakout points at which the total strategy begins to lose money on the upside and on the downside.

The ratio hedge is an ideal strategy for an investor who does not have the time to watch his positions every minute of the day, or the time to develop a technical or a fundamental analysis of the market.

In order to design ratio hedge strategies properly, the following guidelines should be followed:

1. Three is a Lucky Number

The work of Thorp and Kassouf indicates that three options is the ideal number to write against each 100 shares of stock in a ratio hedge strategy. If you wish to input market direction into your strategy, then you could change this mix. But now you move away from a random walk approach to the market, and your market predictability will determine some of your profitability.

For example:

If you were bullish, and felt that the Sears stock price had a higher probability of moving up than moving down, you might wish to write only two options against each 100 shares of stock. On the other hand, if you are bearish regarding the price action of Sears, it might be wise to write four or five options against your 100 share stock position.

2. Select Over-Priced Options

An important element of any option writing system is to identify and select overpriced options. In the Appendix we provide this invaluable guideline and indicate whether or not an option is over or underpriced by comparing its normal value to its actual value. By using overpriced options, you will build a wide enough profit zone to provide a high probability of success with each strategy that you design.

TABLE 18

THE RATIO HEDGE
WORKSHEET

BUY _____ at _____ COST = $ _____ Date _____

WRITE _____ at _____ PROCEEDS = $ _____
(Sell)

INITIAL MARGIN REQUIREMENT $ _____ PROJECTED
COMMISSION
MAXIMUM MARGIN REQUIREMENT $ _____ COSTS $ _____

PRICE EXPIRATION DATE IN _____	(1) VALUE OF STOCK	(2) − COST OF STOCK	(3) = PROFIT or (LOSS) from STOCK	(4) PROCEEDS FROM WRITTEN OPTIONS	(5) − VALUE OF WRITTEN OPTIONS	(6) = PROFIT OR (LOSS) FROM WRITTEN OPTIONS	(7) TOTAL GROSS PROFIT OR (LOSS) (3) + (6) = (7)

-164-

3. Carefully Map Out Each Potential Strategy

It is important that you know what your profit will be at each price level of the underlying common stock. You must determine the bail out points for the stock so that you can compare stock volatility with the potential profit zone. This will prevent you from entering a strategy where there is a high probability that a stock will break out of that zone before the option expiration date arrives. The only way that you can really compare ratio hedge strategies is to compare the mapped out profit-loss scenario as demonstrated in Tables 16 and 17.

4. Follow Your Strategy — Use Your Bail Out Points

When these parameters are hit by the stock, move out of the positions. You may take a small loss, but that is better than hoping and praying as your stock continues to move strongly in the wrong direction, generating heavy losses. Remember, even with a ratio hedge, you still maintain two naked option positions (when you are using a 3 to 1 mix) and you should always be aware of the dangers of naked options.

5. Write Out-of-the-Money Options, On-the-Money Options, or Options that are Only Slightly In-the-Money

Normally, the ideal options for a ratio hedge strategy are those that are close to-the-money. They will usually provide the most premium, the most protection, and the maximum possible profit zones.

With these guidelines, you should now be able to design and compare ratio hedge strategies with considerable success. The best way to approach this unique type of strategy is to practice designing numerous strategies; try them out on paper before jumping into the market. Map them out and watch what occurs. Try to limit your strategies to a three or four month period. Although ratio hedge strategies can run for four, five, six, or even nine months, the longer the life of the strategy, the better the chance that the underlying stock price will move through its outside parameters, ejecting you from the strategy. Consider contingency stop-loss orders to help build the necessary discipline into your strategies.

Also make sure commissions are included in your strategy design considerations. Each strategy has two separate transactions, and as a result, commissions can build up very suddenly. We have not included a discussion of commissions in this chapter to avoid confusing you and to provide for more simplification, but as we have mentioned many times, they are a critically important consideration.

Although the strategies presented in this chapter are not as high powered as a straight naked option writing portfolio, or a naked spread strategy, they have less risk, and show a very solid track record. The author feels that this strategy is, in fact, more conservative than a covered option writing program, or than the ownership of common stock, because if handled properly, the investor will either win or break even most of the time.

In the next chapter, we will discuss variations of the ratio hedge, some of which are far more attractive, others which are less appealing, and many which have market timing and market direction built into their systems. We will be discussing hedges which, rather than using common stock, employ the purchase of stock options as a means of building a foundation for the system.

Chapter 19

THE SPREAD GAME

The spreading game is becoming one of the hottest games on Wall Street. Brokers who think they know a lot about options talk in terms of spreading, rather than covered writing, or other more conservative terms. The spreading game has some very unique features. We have already encountered spreads in our discussion of the novel and profitable naked spread. But the spreading that is popular on Wall Street is somewhat different.

ADVANTAGES AND DISADVANTAGES OF SPREADS

The basic element of the highly popular spread is the *purchase of an option.* We combine this purchase of an option with the sale (or the writing) of another option, both with the same underlying common stock.

The basic advantage of the spread is the minimum amount of cash outlay that is required for any one position. Actually a spread costs a lot less than buying an option by itself.

Listed below are the major advantages of spreads:

1. Stock ownership is not required.

2. Spreads require a very small amount of cash outlay.

3. There is limited risk.

4. The risk is clearly identified.

5. There is good leverage.

6. Your maximum profit is clearly spelled out.

The author feels that if given a choice, spreading is normally a better game than buying options. When spreading, you are able to reduce your risk.

To the average investor, spreading can have some drawbacks, such as commissions, which can get out of hand very quickly in this fast moving game. Trading skills are also needed to reap the rewards of spreading. For those without these skills, the spreading game can be a painful experience.

Listed below are the major disadvantages of spreads:

1. Spreads generate a lot of commissions.

2. Spreads are difficult to move into and out of.

3. Spreads contain some risk.

4. Spreads are normally market sensitive.

Furthermore, spreading is usually more market sensitive than other writing strategies. Therefore, timing and the study and knowledge of future market conditions are critical to success in the spreading game. Yet there are spreads which have advantageous profit-loss scenarios, and can be very successful in an uncertain market. Spreads can be designed for all types of market conditions, and can be altered to meet the moods and changes in the market. Thus they can be an excellent hedge, or the ideal offensive weapon for a portfolio.

In order to enter spreads, a $2,000 initial margin requirement is necessary for most brokerage houses. Such requirements are really needless, but ignorance on the part of the regulatory agencies has resulted in these unreasonable demands. If you have $2,000, a spreading vehicle is an excellent trading medium.

With a wide variety of options available for each underlying stock, there is an extremely wide range of spreads to choose from. There are what we call backspreads, vertical spreads, butterfly spreads — the list goes on and on. All these spreads do not have any naked options attached to them. They are similar to a covered option writing position, which was discussed in Chapter 14. Each long option position is covered by a short option position. Consequently, the investor does not have to handle the highly volatile naked option. A spread that does not have any naked options is referred to as a one-on-one spread.

Spreads can be a versatile investment tool if placed in the proper hands of an options specialist. In the hands of a novice, they can do as much damage as naked options.

The art of spreading is only touched on in this text. A chapter cannot do proper treatment to the spreading game. Once you have the basics down cold and have gathered some experience in the options market, then it may be time to take a graduate course in spreading. Once you get into the spreading game, you will find the opportunities limitless.

Now let's look at a few spreads. Table **19** presents examples of several different one-on-one spreads.

THE VARIABLE SPREAD

Using the one-on-one spread as a base, we can now develop a far more sophisticated spread, one which adds naked options to its makeup.

We already know the value of writing naked options. Therefore, in order to build more firing power into our strategies, we should consider writing naked options freely in molding spread strategies. Again when you use naked options,

TABLE 19
THE WORLD OF SPREADS

Given 6 listed options of ASA, here are just a few of the possible spreads that can be created:

ASA	May	25	call				
ASA	May	20	call		ASA	Aug 20	call
ASA	May	25	put				
ASA	May	20	put		ASA	Aug 20	put

The Bull Spread I (A Vertical Call Spread)

Buy 1 ASA May 20 call
Sell 1 ASA May 25 call

The Bull Spread II (A Vertical Put Spread)

Buy 1 ASA May 25 Put
Sell 1 ASA May 20 Put

The Bear Spread I (A Vertical Call Spread)

Buy 1 ASA May 25 call
Sell 1 ASA May 20 call

The Bear Spread II (A Vertical Put Spread)

Buy 1 ASA May 20 Put
Sell 1 ASA May 25 Put

The Calendar Call Spread

Buy 1 ASA Aug 20 call
Sell 1 ASA May 20 call

The Calendar Put Spread

Buy 1 ASA Aug 22 put
Sell 1 ASA May 20 put

you must be aware of the dangers and risks, but to be successful in this options market, you must be able to face and surmount them.

The *variable spread* is similar to the ratio hedge which we discussed in Chapter 18, with the exception that we do not purchase 100 shares of stock. The foundation of the variable spread is a one-on-one spread. Around this spread, we again mold a strategy writing naked options.

We found in Chapter 18 that the ideal number of options to write against each long position was *three*. The beauty of using an option instead of the common stock is that a stock has a tremendous amount of value that must be protected; an option does not.

SUB-CLASSIFICATION OF VARIABLE SPREADS

In Tables 20 and 21 we map out two different variable spreads. The first is a variable call spread, and the second is a variable put spread. You will notice that both sides of the spread have the same expiration date, with different exercise prices. This would be defined as a "vertical spread."

It is also possible to develop what are referred to as "calendar spreads." In Table 22 we show a variable calendar call spread, which is mapped out to demonstrate the profit parameters of such a strategy.

In all the strategies in the examples, you will notice that we write out-of-the-money options at all times, again following our rules regarding naked option writing.

One of the major advantages of using variable spreads is greatly increased flexibility. As demonstrated, you can use calendar spreads, which are spreads with different exercise prices, rather than different expiration dates. In addition, you can use vertical spreads, whereby you have the same expiration date, with different exercise prices, or you can use either puts or calls in designing your variable spreads. The spread which you do select will depend on your feel for the market.

TABLE 20
A VARIABLE CALL SPREAD

(An actual strategy recommended by the author on Oct. 22, 1973)

Buy 1 Polaroid Jan 110 Call at 11 3/4
Sell 3 Polaroid Jan 130 Calls at 4 3/4

Polaroid Price is 105 5/8

With this strategy, if the Polaroid stock is below 141 at the expiration date in January, a gross profit will be realized. If Polaroid moves above 141, you must bail out of the strategy.

The profit-loss table is presented below.

Table 20A shows how to map out the profit-loss picture using our suggested worksheet.

Polaroid Price at the end of January	Gross Profit	Loss
$145		($750)
142		(150)
141 Bail-out Point	$ 50	
140	250	
137	850	
135	1250	
132	1850	
130	2250	
127	1950	
125	1750	
122	1450	
120	1250	
118	1050	
116	850	
114	650	
112	450	
110 or Lower	250	

TABLE 20A
THE RATIO SPREAD WORKSHEET

Date Oct. 22, 1973

BUY __1 PRD Jan 110 Call__ at __11 3/4__   COST = $ __1175__

WRITE __3 PRD Jan 130 Calls__ at __4 3/4__   PROCEEDS = $ __1425__
(Sell)

PROJECTED COMMISSION COSTS $ __120__

INITIAL MARGIN REQUIREMENT $ __1113__

MAXIMUM MARGIN REQUIREMENT $ __5143__ at __41__

Polaroid PRICE EXPIRATION DATE IN January	(1) VALUE OF PURCHASED OPTION(S) In January	(2) COST OF OPTION(S)	(3) PROFIT OR (LOSS) FROM OPTIONS	(4) PROCEEDS FROM WRITTEN OPTIONS In January	(5) VALUE OF WRITTEN OPTIONS	(6) PROFIT OR (LOSS) FROM WRITTEN OPTIONS	(7) TOTAL GROSS PROFIT OR (LOSS) (3) + (6) = (7)
145	$ 3500	$ 1175	$ 2325	$ 1425	$ 4500	($3075)	($750)
142	3200	1175	2025	1425	3600	(2175)	(150)
141 Bail-out Point	3100	1175	1925	1425	3300	(1875)	50
140	3000	1175	1825	1425	3000	(1575)	250
137	2700	1175	1525	1425	2100	(675)	850
135	2500	1175	1325	1425	1500	(75)	1250
132	2200	1175	1025	1425	600	825	1850
130	2000	1175	825	1425	0	1425	2250
127	1700	1175	525	1425	0	1425	1950
125	1500	1175	325	1425	0	1425	1750
122	1200	1175	25	1425	0	1425	1450
120	1000	1175	(175)	1425	0	1425	1250
118	800	1175	(375)	1425	0	1425	1050
116	600	1175	(575)	1425	0	1425	850
114	400	1175	(775)	1425	0	1425	650
112	200	1175	(975)	1425	0	1425	450
110 or Lower	0	1175	(1175)	1425	0	1425	250

TABLE 21
A VERTICAL RATIO PUT SPREAD STRATEGY

Theoretical Date —
July 15, 19

Buy 1 Dupont Jan 130 Put at 8
Sell 2 Dupont Jan 120 Put at 4

Dupont's theoretical price at the time of the strategy is 125.

In this strategy, we use a 2 to 1 ratio rather than 3 to 1. When the proceeds from 2 of the out-of-the-money options equals or exceeds your option positions (as in this case), you normally have an excellent strategy.

The beauty of the ratio spread comes in the fact there usually is only one bail-out point. In this case, that bail-out point is on the downside at 110. On the upside, there is no risk except the commission costs.

The profit picture is presented below.

Table 21A shows how we determine these figures using our custom worksheet.

Dupont Price at the expiration date in January	Gross Profit	Loss
130 or higher	0	
129	$100	
128	200	
127	300	
126	400	
125	500	
124	600	
123	700	
122	800	
121	900	
120	1000	
119	900	
118	800	
117	700	
116	600	
115	500	
114	400	
113	300	
112	200	
110 Breakeven Point.	0	
109		(100)
108		(200)

-174-

TABLE 21A
THE RATIO SPREAD
WORKSHEET

BUY __1 Dupont Jan 130 Put__ at __8__

WRITE __2 Dupont Jan 120 Puts__ at __4__
(Sell)

Date July 15, 19_____

COST = $ __800__

PROCEEDS = $__800__

INITIAL MARGIN REQUIREMENT $ __2750__

MAXIMUM MARGIN REQUIREMENT $ __3800 at 110__

PROJECTED COMMISSION COSTS $ __100__

Dupont PRICE EXPIRATION DATE IN January	(1) VALUE OF PURCHASED OPTION(S) In January	(2) COST OF OPTION(S)	(3) PROFIT OR (LOSS) FROM OPTIONS	(4) PROCEEDS FROM WRITTEN OPTIONS	(5) VALUE OF WRITTEN OPTIONS In January	(6) PROFIT OR (LOSS) FROM WRITTEN OPTIONS	(7) TOTAL GROSS PROFIT OR (LOSS) (3) + (6) = (7)
130 or Higher	$ 0	$ 800	($800)	$ 800	$ 0	$ 800	$ 0
129	100	800	(700)	800	0	800	100
128	200	800	(600)	800	0	800	200
127	300	800	(500)	800	0	800	300
126	400	800	(400)	800	0	800	400
125 Present Price	500	800	(300)	800	0	800	500
124	600	800	(200)	800	0	800	600
123	700	800	(100)	800	0	800	700
122	800	800	0	800	0	800	800
121	900	800	100	800	0	800	900
120	1000	800	200	800	0	800	1000
119	1100	800	300	800	200	600	900
118	1200	800	400	800	400	400	800
117	1300	800	500	800	600	200	700
116	1400	800	600	800	800	0	600
115	1500	800	700	800	1000	(200)	500
114	1600	800	800	800	1200	(400)	400
113	1700	800	900	800	1400	(600)	300
112	1800	800	1000	800	1600	(800)	200
111	1900	800	1100	800	1800	(1000)	100
110 Bail-out Point	2000	800	1200	800	2000	(1200)	0
109	2100	800	1300	800	2200	(1400)	(100)
108	2200	800	1400	800	2400	(1600)	(200)

TABLE 22
A RATIO CALENDAR CALL SPREAD

Theoretical Date —
August 1, 19

Buy 1 EK Jan 70 call at 2
Sell 2 PK Oct 70 call at 1

Eastman Kodak theoretical price at the time of the strategy is 60.

With a ratio calendar spread, a 2 to 1 ratio is normally recommended. With this option writing strategy, the only risk lies on the upside. Using a ratio calendar put spread, the only risk would be incurred on the downside. With a ratio calendar spread, the bail-out point is located near the exercise price of both options; a key disadvantage, if you remember options psychology. The most premium will be incurred at the exercise price; therefore, it may be more expensive than normal to bail out of the strategy.

The estimated profit-loss picture is presented below. The strategy terminates when the October options expire. Then the profit picture will be dependent on the value of the January option in October.

Table 22A shows how we generate this picture using our custom worksheet.

EK Stock Price at the Expiration Date in October	Gross Profit	Loss
73		($25)
72 Bail-out Point	$ 125	
71	287.50	
70	450	
69	412.50	
68	375	
67	325	
66	287.50	
65	250	
64	212.50	
63	175	
62	125	
61	87.50	
60	62.50	
59	12.50	
58	0	
57	0	
56	0	
55	0	
54 or Lower	0	

TABLE 22A
THE RATIO SPREAD
WORKSHEET

Date August 1, 19

BUY 1 EK Jan 70 Call at 2 COST = $ 200 (2)

WRITE 2 EK Oct 70 Calls at 1 PROCEEDS = $200 (4)
(Sell)

INITIAL MARGIN REQUIREMENT $ 1900

MAXIMUM MARGIN REQUIREMENT $ 3200

PROJECTED COMMISSION COSTS $ 77.00

(1) EK PRICE EXPIRATION DATE IN October	VALUE OF PURCHASED OPTION(S) EK Jan 70	(2) COST OF OPTION(S)	(3) PROFIT OR (LOSS) FROM OPTIONS	(4) PROCEEDS FROM WRITTEN OPTIONS 2 EK Oct 70s	(5) VALUE OF WRITTEN OPTIONS In October	(6) PROFIT OR (LOSS) FROM WRITTEN OPTIONS	(7) TOTAL GROSS PROFIT OR (LOSS) (3) + (6) = (7)
73 Bail-out Point	$575.00	$200	$375.00	$200	$600	($400)	($25.00)
72	525.00	200	325.00	200	400	(200)	125.00
71	487.50	200	287.50	200	200	0	287.50
70	450.00	200	250.00	200	0	200	450.00
69	412.50	200	212.50	200	0	200	412.50
68	375.00	200	175.00	200	0	200	375.00
67	325.00	200	125.00	200	0	200	325.00
66	287.50	200	87.50	200	0	200	287.50
65	250.00	200	50.00	200	0	200	250.00
64	212.50	200	12.50	200	0	200	212.50
63	175.00	200	(25.00)	200	0	200	175.00
62	125.00	200	(75.00)	200	0	200	125.00
61	87.50	200	(112.50)	200	0	200	87.50
60 Present Price	62.50	200	(137.50)	200	0	200	62.50
59	12.50	200	(187.50)	200	0	200	12.50
58	0	200	(200.00)	200	0	200	0
57	0	200	(200.00)	200	0	200	0
56	0	200	(200.00)	200	0	200	0
55	0	200	(200.00)	200	0	200	0
54	0	200	(200.00)	200	0	200	0

(Obtained from normal value tables)

-177-

With the ratio hedge, your only alternative was to buy stock, and to write a number of *call* options against that stock. Now we have greatly expanded our horizon of opportunities, because we can move into a variable vertical put spread, a variable vertical call spread, a variable calendar put spread, a ratio vertical put spread, and many others. We are again using the premise of designing and molding naked options around a long option position, (purchased option), and designing and developing a defensive, but a powerful strategy, which has a win or breakeven profit-loss scenario.

The types of variations of ratio spreads and one-on-one spreads are almost unlimited. One-on-one spreads usually are far more market sensitive. Like option buying strategies, their success depends on your success in calling the market. Ratio spreads have the ability to generate a win or breakeven profit-loss picture, where your probability of incurring a loss is very low.

The spreading game is an unbelievable game, with an almost infinite number of opportunities for the creative player. Then, when you write naked options in developing these strategies, you add a tremendous amount of firing power to them, and develop profit scenarios which make the game very worthwhile.

Spreading, of course, is a very complex art. To the novice, it can be a very dangerous game. But to the professional, it is an outstanding investment tool.

PART III

SECRETS OF THE

PROFESSIONAL

OPTION TRADER

Chapter 20

THE COMPLEAT OPTION TRADER

You have now been introduced to the basics and the rules of the options game and have the resources necessary to become a skilled option strategist. We have covered a lot of information up to this point, but now we must break some important new ground. It is time to graduate from college, and to move into the real world. You have seen some outstanding strategies, and have been exposed to new and exciting ways of making money in the new options market.

You are now ready to reap the rewards that are available in the new options market, but this is not an easy task. Implementing the strategies we have presented, monitoring these strategies, making the right decisions at the right times, pulling the trigger when it needs to be pulled — these are all very critical skills that the COMPLEAT OPTION PLAYER must have. Therefore in the next few chapters, we will provide you with the secrets necessary to develop and to use these critical skills.

Once you have mapped out your strategies and are prepared to play the game, you come to the important area of strategy implementation and surveillance. In other words, getting these strategies off the ground and keeping them up in the air.

Many novice option players who have entered the options market fully knowledgeable in the use and design of option strategies, have been severely injured because of their inability to carry out these two important steps:

1. To implement strategies properly

2. To carry out a proper surveillance program

IMPLEMENTATION OF STRATEGIES

In the stock market, when you purchase stock, implementation of the order normally is quite an easy task. You simply make a call to your stock broker, and tell him that you want 100 shares of XYZ stock: you may tell him what price you would like, or you may just say, "go get it in the market." Either way, you will easily obtain 100 shares of stock.

The average investor then hangs on to that stock, in many cases for years, before he ever decides to sell it. Such an investment system, used by the majority of investors, requires a very small amount of time for implementation and surveillance.

But options are a different breed of cat. Unlike stock, they "self-destruct" after a short period of time. *Time* is the name of the game, and an option has a microscopic life, compared to the life of a stock. Options are extremely volatile instruments —— they can self-destruct, or explode in value, or they can expire very quietly. One option may have many violent moves in price over its very short life.

Options, because of their volatile nature, because of their tendency toward self-destruction, and because of their very short lives, require a tremendous amount of attention. The option player will move in and out of positions on a very rapid basis, if he closely follows the strategies he has mapped out. Therefore, the matter of executions and implementation is critical, and the skilled option player is a skilled option TRADER who knows how to get a good execution, and how to face the complexities of the options trading arena.

The option player must face many obstacles in handling, implementing and monitoring his options portfolio. These obstacles include: the need for simultaneous transactions to implement different types of strategies; the many complicated types of orders that can be utilized on the trading floor; the complexities of the trading floor; and the questionable liquidity of each separate class of options.

Another obstacle that the option player faces as he attempts to implement his strategies is the question of margins, which are very complicated in the options market. Even the most experienced options specialist may have questions regarding what margin is required for each type of option strategy.

Add to this obstacle, the problem of commissions. Commissions in the options market are far more important than they are in the stock market, because of the large amount of trading activity that you, as an option player, are forced to be involved in as you implement, monitor, and maintain your option strategies. You must keep a close watch on commissions which are tacked on to the numerous trades that you will make. As in any business, the option player must be extremely cost conscious, continually watching the pennies that must be paid into the commission coffers.

In summary, the COMPLEAT OPTION PLAYER must also be a Compleat Option *Trader.* He must be an expert in the use of option trading tactics, have a complete understanding of margin rules, and know how to use them properly. He must be extremely cost conscious, and he must be able to properly monitor and guide his options portfolio, in order to reap the profits that are possible in the new options market.

It will take time for you to acquire the proper trading tactics to implement your strategies and to reap the rewards of this options game. In order to help you with this process, the author will attempt to present to you the many secrets that he has discovered in the options market, and to dispel the old wives tales and false assumptions regarding options trading.

Remember, being an options strategist able to map out outstanding strategies is only half of the game — the other half is getting those strategies off the ground; and hence becoming a Compleat Option Trader.

SEEK A PROFESSIONAL

"I don't have the time to spend monitoring and altering my options positions every moment of every trading day."

This is a very familiar comment made by many potential options enthusiasts. However, the option player entering this investment game can greatly reduce the time involved in the trading activities of the game. He can do this through the use of special trading tactics (which will be introduced later), and through the selection of a *competent options specialist.*

To the beginner, just entering the game, the most important decision he will ever make will be his selection of an options specialist, who will help him implement and maintain his options portfolio. The options specialist will be an indispensable member of the option player's winning team. He will take much of the weight off your shoulders and save you a great deal of time and money. Therefore, we have dedicated a full chapter to the selection of the options specialist.

Chapter 21

PROFESSIONAL TRADING TACTICS

To be a winner in the options game, the option player must be a nimble trader. To handle the large volume of trans-actions that will occur in your options portfolio, you must be a compleat trader, becoming competent in the area of trading options.

When we talk about trading tactics, we are talking about *executions.* Good executions mean: getting into your options positions at the right price, being able to move out of options positions and options strategies with ease and with honor, and protecting the profits that you have built into your strategies.

THE TRADING ARENA

In order to learn these important trading tactics, you must first completely understand the arena in which options are traded, for several options markets trade listed options today, and some of these Exchanges trade options in a different manner. For our purposes, we will concentrate on the activity and the manner in which options are traded on the floor of the Chicago Board Options Exchange (CBOE). The CBOE was the first Exchange to enter and initiate this new game, and it is the one that uses the most sophisticated trading methods for listed options.

When you deal with the CBOE, you will want to be acquainted with three types of people. These are:

1. The Floor Broker
2. The Market Maker
3. The Board Broker

Let us take an example of an option order, and see how each of these individuals participates in the execution of that order.

Suppose that we wish to buy one Xerox (XRX) Jul 60 call option, and we want to put a limit order in at 2½ (we wish to pay no more than $250 for that option). We call our broker, and he takes our order. He then either places it on a teletype, or (if he has a direct line to the floor), calls it directly onto the floor of the Exchange.

When the order reaches the floor of the CBOE, the order is given to the *floor broker,* who works for our brokerage firm. Floor brokers are sometimes called $2 brokers, because in the past, they received $2 for each order that they executed on the Exchange. The floor broker takes our order to the Xerox pit, which is the trading area for the XRX Jul 60.

In that area, there are numerous *market makers* who are trading for their own account, and maintaining a market in the XRX Jul 60, very much like a specialist on the New York Stock Exchange (NYSE) does. The market maker's job is to maintain the market in that option, and of course, to profit from trading for their own account. On the NYSE there is just *one* market maker (specialist) who makes a market in a common stock; but on the CBOE many market makers compete against each other, which provides for a more honest and competitive option price.

The floor broker, holding our order to buy one XRX Jul 60 call option, calls out the order to the market makers, attempting to find an interested seller of a XRX Jul 60 at

THE LISTED OPTIONS TRADING ARENA

2½. If the market makers are not able to sell that option at that price, the floor broker then goes to the *board broker.*

Unlike the market maker, the board broker does not trade for his own account. He is an employee of the Exchange. His job is to list in his book for XRX Jul 60's, our order to buy one XRX Jul 60 at the limit order price of 2½. What does this mean? It means that when that order goes into the book, it has *top priority* over any other order, except those that precede it in the book. When the asked price of the XRX Jul 60 moves to 2½, our order will be executed immediately, and the market makers will not be able to see the book. (On the NYSE, the specialist *is* able to see and control the book.)

You should be aware that if the floor broker is required to put an order in the book, giving that order to the board broker, he does not receive any individual compensation for that order. Consequently, it is to his advantage to execute the order immediately, before it goes into the book. By doing this, he is able to attain $2, or whatever compensation he receives for executing that order.

These three individuals are important as we begin to look at the different types of orders that you can enter, and the different problems that are encountered in getting that execution.

GETTING THAT EXECUTION

The ability to "enter" and to "exit" different option positions effectively (i.e. to buy and sell options), is truly an art, and only through experience will you be able to carry out this trading activity with finesse. Let's look closely at the different types of orders that can be used to ENTER an option position, whether you are going to buy an option initially, or to write a naked option.

1. Market Orders

The first and the simplest order that can be utilized is called a *market order,* and it acts just like a market order for the purchase or sale of stock. The market order is the best way of making sure that you get an execution, whether you are buying or selling an option. The major problem with this type of order is that you are going into the market blind—you do not know what price you will get for the purchase or the sale of your option. The price will be whatever the market will bear.

This tactic can be dangerous in the options market when you attempt to buy or sell an option which has poor liquidity. (Poor liquidity means that there are not many options being traded in that market.) Because of the large number of different options available in the various option markets, poor liquidity can occur quite frequently, especially in deep-in-the-money options, or far-out-of-the-money options. There is a likelihood if you are buying an option that you will pay far more than you would have expected, or if you are selling an option, that you will sell your options for far less than you expected. In a sense, you will be paying for a night out on the town for the market maker, who takes advantage of the lack of liquidity in this market.

Of course, you have quotes available from your option broker to indicate current prices in the market. But those quotes can be very misleading. Price action in options moves so fast that a quote that you receive from your broker is probably five or ten minutes behind the real action in that market. At the time that you place your market order, the situation may have changed dramatically from the bid or the asked price that you were quoted. The bid or the asked may have disappeared, and only a money grubbing market maker is available to support that market. As a result, he may take as much as a point or two out of your option price.

So, when you enter a market order, make sure that a large number of options are continually trading in that option class. In this way, at least you will be moving into a market that has liquidity. Then a market maker cannot sneak in and rake you over by giving you a poor price on your option.

Market orders are also dangerous when you attempt to buy or sell too many options at one time. For example, let's say that you wish to buy 100 XRX Jul 60 call options. Well, the market may not be able to handle that number of options, but some market maker surely would move in there and charge you an outrageous price for the remaining options you requested. For all of these reasons, be very careful when you play with market orders.

2. The Limit Order

Another type of order that you can use to get an execution is called a *limit order.* This is a far safer order, but does not guarantee that you will get your execution. You are setting a limit on what price you will pay to buy an option, and also setting a minimum on what price you will receive for selling an option. In our example of the XRX Jul 60, we had set a limit order of 2½, which means we would pay *no* more than 2½, although we could pay less than 2½.

When you wish to buy options, or to write naked options, it is best to use a limit order if you have the time to wait for your price, rather than going blindly into the market, and impatiently using the market order.

However, when you are in the opposite position, and must *exit* a strategy because a stock price has hit one of your bail-out parameters, the limit order can be dangerous, because it does not guarantee that you will execute your trade. Again, we warn you not to rely on the quotes that you receive from your broker before you enter an order. Those quotes are behind the action, and can be almost worthless in a fast moving market.

In addition, whenever you place a limit order, make sure that you *always* instruct your broker, (if he is not already aware of the procedure) to place the order "in the book." Remember, orders that are on the books of the board broker have top priority over all other orders. In some cases, when you give a limit order to a broker, the floor broker will hang on to that order, will put it in his pocket, waiting for the right price, so that he can get the rewards from that execution. By doing this, he takes your order off the top priority list, and decreases your chances of an execution.

3. Limit Order With Discretion

The third type of an order that can be used when you are attempting to get an execution is referred to as a *limit order with discretion.* In this instance, you give your broker a limit order, but you also provide an extra eighth or a quarter point for the floor broker, to aid him in obtaining an execution. This type of order is actually identical to the previous limit order, except that you now put it into the hands of the floor broker, and give him a little incentive to get the execution. If he is unable to get the execution with his discretion, he will then place the order in the board broker's book.

The three types of orders we have discussed are the best alternatives available to the option player who plans to enter a new, single position, either to write or buy options.

EXECUTING STRATEGIES

Because of the outstanding profits that can be made in the area of strategy design, taking positions is not always simple for many option players. Many options strategies involve not just one option purchase or sale, but a simultaneous transaction in which you write some options and buy some other options, or write some options and buy stock, or a combination of the two. The need for simultaneous transactions makes trading in the options market a difficult task. Let us examine some of these simultaneous transactions.

1. The Spread Order

One of your needs might be to buy and sell options at the same time, either to enter or to leave a position. The *spread order* has been especially designed and custom-made for this type of transaction. The spread order is an order where you wish to buy one class of options, and sell another class of options at the same time. When you first hear about the spread order, you will be extremely turned on by it, but this type of order does have some deficiencies.

For example:

Say you wish to buy one XRX Jul 70 put and sell one XRX Jul 60 put, a good example of a vertical spread. You could enter that order as a spread order, requesting that your broker buy a 60, and sell the 70, either at market, which would be easily executed, or with a specific spread limit. In other words, if you wish to buy the 60 and sell the 70 with a maximum of two points difference between the two option prices, you can enter it in that manner, with a spread of 2.

The spread order then goes to the floor broker, and the floor broker is responsible for executing that spread, if he can. If he cannot, the spread order goes in the book of the board broker, where it receives top priority treatment.

On paper, the spread order looks great; in action, it does not pan out as well. Even though spread orders have top priority in the book of the board broker, they are still very difficult to execute. Before a spread order can be executed, the conditions regarding the bid or asked on both sides of the spread must be perfect.

Given this fact, in many cases, the best strategy to use in handling a spread order is to give the order to the floor broker, rather than to place it in the book. In this situation, a talented floor broker will be more aggressive in trying to find the perfect combination needed to execute a spread order. Of course, by putting your order in the hands of a floor broker, you have taken it out of the book where you have top priority status.

Whether or not you are able to execute spread orders will depend on the skill of your floor brokers (attached to your brokerage house), the amount of discretion you give the broker (the size of the spread between the two option prices), and the amount of time you are willing to wait for a potential spread execution.

Spread orders are an important trading tactic, but even professionals depend on other orders to insure faster and sometimes better executions; but executions that may contain far more risk.

In the future, spread orders will probably become a far more feasible trading instrument than they are now. Market makers and floor brokers are becoming far more sophisticated in the use of options strategies and are becoming far more proficient in the use of spread orders. Already, spread quotes are being utilized on the floor of the Exchanges. Eventually, spread quotes may be available on the quote machines in all brokerage houses. Then, the spread order will be the *key* tactic to get a good execution for an option strategy.

2. The Contingency Order

Another order used to implement simultaneous transactions between options and stock, or between options and options, is called a *contingency order.* With a contingency order, you place a limit order for one of your transactions, *and* either a market or a limit order for your other transaction. This second order will be put into play if the first transaction is completed first.

For example:

Let's say that you wish to buy 100 shares of Gulf & Western, (GW) and wish to write 3 GW Jan 25 calls against that position. Let's say hypothetically that the GW Jan 25's are trading in the range of 2 to 2½. The best way to approach this simultaneous transaction is to enter a contingency order with the purchase of the stock contingent upon the sale of the 3 GW Jan 25's.

Because the premium received from the options is the most important element of your strategy, you should set a limit order to implement the execution of a sale of the 3 GW Jan 25's. Let's say that we wish to sell the three options for 2½, so we will place a limit order in at 2½. Contingent upon the execution of these three options, we instruct the broker to buy 100 shares of GW at the market. Now we sit back and let the contingency order work for us. As soon as we get our price for the sale of the GW Jan 25 options, immediately, the stock will be purchased for us in the market.

Remember, we have used a market order to purchase our stock. It is very important when we enter a market order to ensure that the market which we are entering is quite liquid, in order to provide for a fair price. Market orders used in the purchase of stock, of course, are far safer than market orders which are used to buy or sell options, because of the very big question of liquidity in the options market.

Another type of contingency order is one that uses *two* limit orders — one to enter one position, and one to enter the other, once the first position has been executed. In our example of Gulf & Western, we would place a limit order to sell three GW Jan 25's at 2½, contingent upon that order being executed to buy 100 shares of GW at 25. When the three options were sold, the limit order would then be placed automatically to purchase 100 shares of GW at 25.

The dangerous problem with this type of contingency order is that you may not get the second leg of the order off; you may not purchase the 100 shares of GW at 25, because the price might be above your limit.

Consequently, if you wish to ensure a simultaneous transaction, half of your order must be a market order. Contingency orders are also used to exit an option strategy and this feature will be discussed in the following section.

3. Legging into a Position

The third type of trading technique for executing simultaneous transactions is one that the novice option player should not touch. Only those who are extremely skilled in option trading should consider this tactic. This method of execution is referred to in the business as *legging into a position*. This method has far more risk than either the contingency order, or the spread order. On the other hand, it has the advantage of being able to generate better executions and profits than the more conservative trading tactics. *Legging-in* refers to the taking of one side of your strategy first, and then the moving into the second phase of your strategy.

With our Gulf & Western example, you would first put a limit order in to sell your three GW options. When that order has been executed, you would then move in and attempt to get the price to execute your 100 shares of GW. In some cases, it might take the whole trading day to complete this simultaneous transaction.

The problem with this tactic is that when you enter one leg of your strategy, you become exposed to some risks. The option player who attempts to leg-in, in many cases, will fail to accomplish his total strategy because he becomes too greedy as he moves into the second leg. Or, equally disasterously, he will move into the wrong leg first, and then find that the market has moved in the wrong direction, before he has ever put on the second leg. The last pitfall is that the option player is far too dependent on the mood and whims of the market with this tactic.

The author, therefore, feels that the legging into and the legging out of option strategies should be left to the professional or to the options specialist. What should you do? Generally, it is far better to rely on a contingency or a spread order, where you are GUARANTEED both sides of a transaction.

PULLING THE TRIGGER

Up to this time, we have only discussed how to get executions to *enter* both option positions and option strategies which require simultaneous transactions. Now let's talk about methods to obtain executions to EXIT option strategies. I refer to this section as "Pulling the Trigger," because in many cases, the orders that you use to exit positions will force you to take a loss or to shave important profit from your option strategy.

Moving out of option positions is probably the most difficult task that the option player must face. It really separates the men from the boys. To guard against the inherent risks in the naked options used in many of the strategies we are discussing, you must extricate yourself from option strategies when the underlying common stock price touches your bail-out parameters. Often the option player must "pull the trigger" in the midst of a strategy in order to take a profit that has developed. The ability to exit a position with honor, in many cases is dependent on the type of execution orders that you use.

For the novice option player, the best way to approach this problem is to use *stop-loss orders.* By using stop-loss orders, the novice has removed the position from his own hands and put it in the hands of his brokerage house. These stop-loss orders normally should be put on as soon as he enters a strategy. In this way, he will greatly reduce the amount of time that he spends in monitoring and guiding his options portfolio. A stop-loss order is a market order, and as you already know the dangers of market orders, you have to be prepared to take some of the disadvantages that go with them.

Let's say that you purchased one Teledyne (TDY) Oct 80 put at 4, and you put a stop-loss order on the option at 2. If the option price goes down to 2 at any time during the life of that option, then you wish to move out of the position immediately, and your stop-loss order would automatically be activated. This means that the board broker would immediately sell your one option at whatever the market would bear. Remember that a stop-loss order is a market order, and you are not guaranteed a full price of 2, but at least you are assured of an execution. Further, you do not have to be there to activate that order, and this is the major advantage of a stop-loss order. At this writing, stop-loss orders on options are only accepted on the American Options Exchange.

THE CONTINGENCY ORDER

Because of the complicated nature of option strategies, you should consider a more sophisticated way of handling stop-loss orders. The more sophisticated approach is to integrate a stop-loss order with a contingency order. However, many brokerage houses will not handle these complicated contingency orders, and few if any will guarantee executions.

The contingency order that we are going to look at is one that is contingent upon the price level of the stock. Most of your option strategies will be strongly influenced by the price action in the common stock underlying your options. Therefore, it makes sense for you to understand and be able to use a contingency order which deals with the common stock price.

For example, with a ratio hedge, a ratio spread, or with a naked option writing position, you have breakeven or bailout parameters, and you must move out of the position if the stock price reaches a specific point, whether on the upside or the downside.

For example, if we moved into a ratio hedge centered around Gulf & Western common stock, and our upward breakeven point was $30 a share, then we would want to move out of our total position, and sell our stock at $30. We could ensure that this would be accomplished through a contingency (stop-loss) order, which would automatically detonate at 30, selling out our stock position, and covering our option positions immediately.

For the novice option player then, the contingency (stop-loss) order should be considered for all option strategies which involve naked options, or spreads. This contingency order would probably also be appropriate for the closing of single option positions. The major problem you face is finding a brokerage house that will handle the order.

OTHER TRADING TACTICS

Whenever you have time to act, and are not rushed or forced to move out of positions, it is wise to try to get your price. Then, of course, the use of *limit orders* is the best approach that you can take. When you enter a limit order always give your floor broker a little leeway to work with to ensure a high probability of execution. Remember, the quotes you received from your broker are old quotes, and they may not provide an accurate picture of what is happening on the floor. So, if you plan to write an option, or to sell a long position, set a limit which is a quarter or an eighth below the bid. Conversely, when you are planning to buy options, either to cover a short position (writing position), or to take a long position, set a limit which is a quarter or an eighth above the asked price. By doing this, you will ensure an execution 80% to 90% of the time.

Limit orders are safer; leave legging-out as a method of getting out of strategies to the braver souls. Remember, the toughest job you will ever have in this game is sticking to your strategies —— and you must stick to them to survive. Legging-out is useful only if you have the discipline to get out of your positions every time that your strategies call for it.

Unlike the less skilled players, option professionals some-times do rely on legging-out of their option strategies because their profit margins are often too thin to rely on a market order or a stop-loss order. Market orders and stop-loss orders will ensure that you get out of your strategies when you move into the loss zone — but they definitely will take chunks out of your profit picture. Also remember that the market makers on the floor of the Exchange make their living by attempting to cheat you out of an eighth or a quarter, or even half a point of profit for each option that you hold, and they love receiving market orders from the public.

In light of these facts, the author suggests that you leave riskier trading tactics to the professional, especially if you are playing with naked options. When you play with naked options, profits can be outstanding, but make just one mistake and the game may be over. Often that one mistake is to hesitate and not pull the trigger at once. The use of a stop-loss order will ensure that you do pull the trigger.

Chapter 22

THE TEN COMMANDMENTS
OF OPTION TRADING

By now you have discovered that option trading tactics are an important part of the option player's "bag of tricks." The author, through his experience, has developed ten major principles that you should follow if you wish to be a successful option trader. We have discussed some of these concepts before and they summarize many key points. These Ten Commandments relate to your ability to *implement* the strategies you have designed, and to *monitor* those strategies. These rules also should help you decide when and where to take profits, or how to exit the strategies, as happens should your options or stock touch a red alert zone. Now let us look briefly at these Ten Commandments, and then cover them in greater depth:

THE TEN COMMANDMENTS OF OPTION TRADING

I   DON'T BE GREEDY

II   LOOK BEFORE YOU LEAP

III   FOLLOW YOUR STRATEGY

IV   PULL THE TRIGGER

V   USE CONTINGENCY ORDERS

VI   BEWARE OF COMMISSIONS

VII   AVOID EXERCISE

VIII   BE PATIENT

IX   USE AN OPTIONS SPECIALIST

X   MANAGE YOUR MARGIN

I.   DON'T BE GREEDY

The first commandment of option trading is a very simple one, but it is probably the most important one. Don't be greedy. You may laugh, but this is probably the root cause of many an option player's failure to succeed in the options game. When we say "Don't be greedy," we just mean, "Do not be unrealistic when you take a position, or take profits, or move out of a position."

An old option trader with plenty of experience frequently states the following seasoned principle:
"You can buy the world for an eighth."
What he is referring to is simply an eighth of a point. Option players incur significant losses and lose significant opportunities because they do not give their broker enough room to execute new trades, or to execute and take profits properly. They spend their time looking for that extra eighth of a point profit whenever they conduct an option transaction, and unfortunately this prevents them either from taking advantage of many profitable opportunities, or from exiting a position when the danger zone has been reached. When you get too greedy in the options market, your portfolio will suffer the consequences; you may pay a very high price for an eighth of a point.

II.   LOOK BEFORE YOU LEAP

In the options game, like in any other game, it is critical that you have some kind of a plan, and that you carefully map out a detailed picture of what will occur in the future to that strategy. Because of the nature of options, strategies can be formulated in great detail. Right in front of you, you have the exact amount of time left in the life of each option. This can greatly help you map out clearly what will happen at every point in the life of your strategy. By doing this, you will have no surprises and you can build a defense against any unexpected contingencies into your strategy. Without a strategy in the options game, you are playing with dynamite, especially when you write naked options.

III. FOLLOW YOUR STRATEGY

You have now spent many hours mapping out several alternative strategies and you have selected the strategies you feel have the highest profit potential and the lowest possible risk. Now follow them. This may be easy to say, but in the heat of battle, your emotions may attempt to take command of your actions. Many an option player will fall by the roadside because he has been swayed by his emotions, rather than following the very detailed strategies he mapped out before he entered this action filled market.

IV. PULL THE TRIGGER

This recommendation may be the hardest one to follow. We have discussed this concept many times throughout the text. We have repeated it numerous times because it is so very important. You have been trained to build defense mechanisms into your strategies: danger points, breakeven points, parameters where you bail-out of your positions to avoid a potential loss. Because of the inherent dangers in the writing of naked options, it is critical that you take action when these points are reached, that you pull the trigger and immediately move out of all these positions. We've talked about ways of building this ejection system into your strategies through the use of contingency orders and stop-losses. Whether you use a stop-loss, or whether you rely on your own discretion to pull the trigger, it must be pulled. The only way you will open yourself up to financial disaster in the options market is to hesitate one time and not pull the trigger.

When we talk about pulling the trigger, we also refer to your ability to take profits *when they develop* in your strategies. The best comment we can make here is — never, never be afraid to take a profit. Then don't have any regrets because the strategy would later have become more profitable. Once you are out of a strategy, do not consider what happens to it in the future.

V.   USE CONTINGENCY ORDERS

We've talked about the many types of trading tactics that can be used in the options market. For the extremely experienced option player, legging-in and legging-out techniques might be considered — they provide the most profit and take advantage of market moods. But to the player who does not have the time or the inclination to monitor his positions closely on an hour by hour basis, or to spend large amounts of time moving into and out of strategies, or for the player who does not have that good intuitive feel for the market, the contingency order is the best type to use.

VI.   BEWARE OF COMMISSIONS

We have not, in our examples, clearly displayed the commission costs involved in different types of options transactions. In the next chapter, we will identify in depth the different possible commission costs involved in each type of option strategy, and discuss which ones can best minimize commission costs over an extended period of time. Being aware of commission costs is one of the Ten Commandments because commissions are so important in our options portfolio. Options are traded far more extensively than are stocks, and therefore, commission costs per dollar of investment are much greater. These commission costs, of course, should be offset by the many advantages of the options market, but they are there, and they must be watched closely and carefully controlled.

The use of options as a trading vehicle, where you move in and out of option positions on a daily basis, can be extremely dangerous unless you carefully watch the buildup of commission costs. Options have been highly touted as an excellent trading vehicle, but if you look closely at the amount of commission costs involved in such transactions, this method could become far less attractive. Only those who have commission advantages, where they receive heavy discounts, or where they have a seat on the Exchange can be viable *daily* option traders.

VII.   AVOID EXERCISE

We spent one full chapter talking about exercise, and dispelling some myths that are passed on about the dangers, uncertainties and the fears of exercise. Exercise is nothing to fear, but when you are exercised, there are additional costs.

There is a very simple prescription to guard against exercise. *To avoid exercise, never hold a short position (a writing position) in an option where the option has no time value, or a negligible time value.* This is a very easy principle to follow, and it will save you a lot of money if you follow this commandment.

VIII.   BE PATIENT

We have talked about being patient when you plan to buy options, because you are starting with a slight disadvantage, and therefore, you must get an excellent price. Only through a good price can your overall results be profitable, and consequently you may have to wait extensive periods of time until the market and the option price are ideal.

In strategy development, the same rules apply. Do not be overly impatient in attempting to find an interesting option strategy. Wait for the ideal strategies to develop, those which have very high profit potential and very low risk considerations. As you bide your time and continue to compare different strategy alternatives, trying to find the one that really turns you on, you can always have your money invested in Treasury bills. They are acceptable collateral when you are writing options, and therefore the time that you wait will not be wasted.

Because of the high commission costs of different strateggies, and the importance of executions, it is vital that you select the most powerful strategies that are available, and these strategies may not be present every day of the week; you may have to wait for them. The question of getting the right prices for that strategy is another story, and if you cannot, you then must pass, and move on to other strategies. There are over 200 stocks that have options on the new options exchanges, and there are over 1,500 different options available. So, there are plenty of strategies to pick from. Take your time and pick the best of the crop. Make sure you get the prices you need and the strategy that really turns you on before you make a move.

IX. USE AN OPTIONS SPECIALIST

Even though this is the ninth Commandment, this is probably one of the most important ones that the option player should be aware of. Because of the intricacies of the new options market, and the numerous strategies available, because of the complicated and complex problems involved in options trading, because of the need for effective option implementation and execution, and because of the need for day to day surveillance of all strategies, your broker is a very important member of your team.

A good competent options specialist (not a stock broker) who spends all of his time in the options market and has years of experience in that market can be an indispensable asset to your portfolio and to your performance. He will get you out of a lot of tough spots, get you into some good strategies, and obtain good executions for you.

He will solve many of the problems and guide you through many of the commandments that we have talked about. Equally important, he will provide you with the on-the-job experience and education that we cannot cover in this text. So, when you go out to select the broker you wish to use, find a good man, a good options specialist to guide you. It will be the best move you make toward winning the options game.

X.   MANAGE YOUR MARGIN

Another subject the option player must be concerned with is margin, the good faith deposit he will put up in order to initiate and maintain his naked option writing strategies and spreads.

The amount of margin required for an option position or strategy will have a significant effect on your return on investment. Maintenance margin calls may force you out of potentially profitable strategies and cause havoc to your portfolio. Therefore, managing margin requirements is a supremely important activity to the option trader. Your ability to select low margin strategies and to avoid margin calls will be a strong determinant in the profit picture of your portfolio. Chapter 24 is dedicated to winning the margin game.

Chapter 23

DANGER:
BEWARE OF COMMISSIONS

One of our Ten Commandments of option trading states: beware of option commissions. As in any other sport, there are admission fees and expenses that must be paid to play the game. In the options game, these expenses are high. A moderately active options portfolio will generate from 15% to 30% of the value of that portfolio in the form of commissions per annum. In other words, if you have a $10,000 options portfolio, at the end of your first year of trading, you will probably incur commission costs running from $1,500 to $3,000. So, if you do not *earn* more than $1,500 in that account, you will lose.

The options game, then, has a high cost of doing business. The option player should be wary of commissions, which should be carefully watched, mapped out, and avoided whenever possible. Of course, the stock market does have commission costs too. But by their very nature, (and especially because of their short life), options tend to be traded frequently. Therefore, an option account has a greater amount of trading inherent in its behavioral pattern than a stock account does. In fact, the major criticism of playing in the options game is that the investor must pay excessive commissions, because of the excessive trading options create.

However, you should be aware that there are ways to avoid and reduce high commission costs, and institute defenses to protect yourself against them.

Although commissions are high in the options game, they are high in many games that you play, and in many business activities. What you are looking for is the bottom line, the net profit margin at the end of the year. With option writing strategies that bottom line is very fat, even with the high commissions.

STRATEGY SELECTION

To control your commission costs, you should attempt to select strategies which incur the smallest commission costs per dollar invested. The most ideal strategies are the *simplest.*

1. Buying Options, Writing Naked Options

The buying of options, and the *writing of naked options* create the smallest amount of commission costs. Why? Because when you enter an option buying position, you are only required to pay one commission, and if and when you exit that position, there is only one commission charge, which nets out to two total commissions.

If you are absolutely wrong about the purchase, and the market goes in the opposite direction, you may never have to close out the position. It will be worthless before you can take any kind of constructive action. Therefore, the commission costs in buying options are low, especially when you are working with the simplest strategy, which is buying very cheap options, and hoping that they will appreciate.

In many cases, when you are writing naked options, especially if they are way out-of-the-money, you may not have to close out the position at all. The option simply expires, and when it does, there are no commissions involved in the closing of the transaction. So, the writing of naked options is probably the most ideal strategy if you wish to reduce commission costs.

When you write such out-of-the-money options, the chance that you will have to close out that option position may occur only 20% to 30% of the time; the other 70% of the time, the options that you write will expire with no exit commission costs.

2. Naked Spreads

The second most attractive strategy with regard to commissions is the writing of a naked spread, where both the naked call and the naked put are out-of-the-money. Here again, your only commission costs are your costs of moving into both positions. The odds are in your favor that one or both options will expire, and you will not be forced to close out your positions by buying back the options, thereby incurring additional commissions.

3. Covered Option Writing

The third ranking strategy with regard to commission costs per dollar invested is the conservative covered option writing program. We mentioned before that this approach is similar to operating a business, and this strategy normally will generate small commission costs. This is true especially if you hang on to your pivotal common stocks, and are not active in buying and selling common stocks to use as the merchandise in your covered option writing program. By avoiding excessive trading of both options and common stock under a covered option writing program, you will greatly reduce the commission costs per dollar of investment.

In a covered option writing program, you can also greatly reduce your commission costs by writing longer term options; options which have a six month, eight month, or even a nine month life. Activity in your account will be reduced, and the commission costs will be too.

4. The Ratio Hedge

Moving down the list, our commission costs rise at a much faster rate as we move into the more sophisticated, more complicated types of strategies. For instance, the ratio hedge accrues far more commission costs because you must make two simultaneous transactions to move into the position, and two simultaneous transactions to move out of the position, unless the options that you write against each 100 shares of stock expire. (The self-destructive nature of naked options is the one advantage you have going for you with a ratio hedge over some of the spreads that we have discussed.) You may, if forced out of your position, incur four different commission costs. Yet with the ratio hedge, because you are doing a lot of naked writing, you do have the odds in your favor, and this should offset some of the additional commission costs that are incurred with this fancier strategy.

5. The Ratio Spread

The next type of strategy, the ratio (variable) spread, again incurs two commissions when you move into the strategy, and two when you move out of it, unless some of your naked options, or long options expire. Thus normally, you must pay for four commissions — two roundtrips.

6. The One-On-One Spread

As a rule, the most expensive type of option strategy is the one-on-one spread, where you write one option, and buy one option against that option. Here again we have the problem of a roundtrip commission in the long side of the spread, and a roundtrip commission in the short side, which nets out to four different commission costs. This strategy is even more expensive than the ratio hedge, or the ratio spread, because normally the transaction requires more activity — you have to be much more active with this type of strategy, dropping and adding legs, and taking profits, as soon as they develop. Therefore, the commissions can be excessive. Further, in many cases, you do not have the advantage of writing out-of-the-money options with these spreads, and this also creates far more roundtrip commissions.

Sounds complicated, and it is. One-on-one spreads have been highly touted because of the tremendous leverage and the limited risk you can attain. But they have been touted by *brokers* because they are very lucrative for brokers — they generate a lot of commissions. Also, one-on-one spreads normally are created for the purpose of trading action, and this is something the option trader must be very careful with. You may have a lot of action with one-on-one spreads, but you surely are going to have a lot of commissions along with that action, and those commissions will cut deeply into your profits.

7. Bear Spreads

One example of a spread which is very expensive because of the kind of commission costs it creates is called a "bear spread," where you buy an out-of-the-money call option, and sell an in-the-money call option (using puts instead results in a back spread) in an attempt to gain leverage through the reduced margin that is required for this strategy. By the nature of the strategy, you will be very active during the life of that strategy. Usually you must move out of all positions before expiration, or you will be required to cover your short positions before they expire, in order to avoid a possible exercise. You also are writing an in-the-money option which may have very little time value, with the result that you then become a likely prospect for exercise — and don't forget our rules about avoiding exercise! Bear spreads can give you a lot of leverage, but they also incur a lot of costs, because you will normally always have four commissions and continually are in danger of exercise.

8. Butterfly Spreads

Probably the most expensive of all option strategies is the "butterfly spread." This is another strategy that is often touted by stock brokers because they want to greatly improve their own income. It sounds very fancy, and the profits look pretty good, but CAUTION: the butterfly spread has not *four* commissions, but *six* commissions. This spread requires three different option positions to establish and maintain the strategy, and that adds up to six different commissions incurred during the life of that strategy. At the bottom line, there is not enough profit to cover these commission costs. So, beware of the butterfly spread.

Only if you are a market maker on the floor of the Options Exchange, can you afford to play with butterfly spreads! If you are just a typical option player who works through a brokerage house and pays his bill of fare, you cannot afford to play with such fancy strategies.

In conclusion, the fancier the strategy gets, the more expensive it gets, and although it may show greatly reduced risk, the commissions will take such a toll that the strategy probably will not have been worth attempting.

THE DAY TRADER

One approach to the options market which we have not yet covered in this text is *daily* option trading. Options, because of their extreme leverage, limited risk, and their tremendous volatility, are ideal for the day to day trader, who can take a one hour move in a stock and play it in the options market. In many cases, the day trader will use spreads — bear spreads, bull spreads, butterfly spreads — every spread under the sun. He will employ naked writing, the buying of options or any technique which best plays on the moves of the most active common stocks. By doing this, he can profit from a one or two point move in a stock and from the volatility of the glamours.

This sounds like great fun; there is a lot of action involved, and there are some who are able to make a good living at this sport. However, the author does not recommend this course of action for the average investor, because of the tremendous commission costs he will incur. Many foolhardy novice players have attempted to be a day option trader and have found that within two or three weeks, their account has disappeared into the night. It has been dissipated, not by trading losses, but by commission costs. I have seen it happen many times — the more active you are, the more excessive your trading activity, the sooner your account will disappear, just through the costs of doing business.

True, there are some who have made spectacular profits, even when they have had to pay commissions, but it was only their outstanding ability to call the market, and to manipulate options on a day to day basis that allowed them to survive. Most of the traders who are able to make a living at trading options on a day to day basis generally are on the floor of the Options Exchange, because they do not incur the high commission costs. Day trading is a very costly art, and we have not covered it in depth because the author feels the discussion would be academic for the average investor, due to the commission costs incurred.

WHAT ABOUT THE DISCOUNT COMMISSION BROKERS?

You have all heard of them — they are a welcome sight; the discount broker, or what is termed the bargain broker, is one who gives you a discount on your commission costs —— in some cases, as much as 50% off. This sounds very attractive, and to many, it is a feasible alternative. But the major problem for the option player is the fact that the discount broker does not provide services; he only provides a trading facility.

In the options market, unlike the case in the stock market, the option player needs a great deal of backup from his brokerage house, in the form of a competent options specialist, a competent trading staff, and sophisticated option trading facilities. This support includes lines to the floor of the Exchanges, publications, and anything else that will aid him in making investment decisions. Remember, option trading requires far more activity than stock trading, far more surveillance, far more planning, and far more expertise. You may think you are an expert, but you should use all the help you can get, and with a discount broker, you receive relatively little, because you are not paying for that assistance.

The only other circumstance in which the author recommends the use of a discount broker is when you are strictly dealing in buying or selling stocks in the market, since the amount of services you require may be very minimal.

Therefore, although there is some difference in cost, it is well worth the added expense to obtain the guidance and aid of a full service options house. We will be discussing this very extensively in Chapter 25.

Of course, if you are an expert, have an excellent line of information to the floor of the Exchange, have no problem in calculating the very complex margin rules of the Options Exchange, have plenty of time, have the "equipment" to follow, monitor and execute your strategies, then the discount broker may be a good alternative.

Now that you know what the best strategies to use in your cost reduction program are, it is time to look at a few steps which you can follow to greatly reduce commission costs. They are very simple, and should not alter your overall strategies to any great degree. They may not provide as much action as you would like, but then, remember, the more action, the more your commission costs will rise and the smaller your profits will be.

STEPS TO REDUCE COMMISSION COSTS

1. Avoid Excessive Trading in Your Account

Remember, option portfolios have a high propensity for trading activity. Even the most conservative options account has a high degree of trading activity. As you get into this game, you may become over-zealous and do far more trading in your account than you should, and this will be a costly habit. The more trading you do, the more your costs will increase. So, attempt at all times to avoid trading activity if you can. Avoid strategies which require a lot of activity. If you can, when you finish one strategy, attempt to use some of the same positions in the old strategy to create a new one. This will reduce some of the activity that is required.

It is hard to describe in theory how to avoid trading activity. You should probably learn this art through experience. As you become an experienced option player, you will discover ways of avoiding such activity.

2. Plan for Commissions

Before you even enter a strategy, build your commission costs into the profit and loss picture of that strategy. Do not assume that they will be a certain percentage of your profit. Make sure they are built-in. If you have two roundtrip commissions that could be incurred in a strategy, build them in before you ever enter it. Map out your costs, know what those costs will be before they are ever incurred. This will greatly aid you in your selection process, and it will direct you towards strategies which have much higher profits, because of much lower commission costs.

In this text, we have factored out the commission costs in displaying our examples, as we mentioned before, and for good reason: to simplify the explanation, and to avoid the confusion of introducing yet another variable. But, because we have not dealt with commission costs does not mean that they should not be figured into your strategy design activities. They must be incorporated into your strategies before you even consider which one you will select. And the special forms that we have used here have room set aside for these commission costs. Use them. Make them a part of your investment decision.

3. Beware of the Over-Zealous Broker

Brokers have a tendency to ignore, or factor out commission costs, especially when they are recommending strategies to the customers. Your broker may not be aware of commission costs, but you had better be aware of them. Even the most competent options specialist around must be controlled by this kind of thinking. So, when your options specialist makes a recommendation to move into a strategy, check on the commission costs first. Then you should make the decision, incorporating those commission costs into your profit-loss scenario.

4. Get a Quantity Discount

Just as in any other business, the more options you buy or sell, the lower the price that you will pay for each option. Using this principle, attempt to move into strategies where you are buying and selling a quantity of options. In this way, you will reduce the commission costs per option, in many cases, significantly. The option player who comes into this game with a very small amount of capital, and only buys one option, or sells one option, is taking on huge commissions. The commission cost per option on a one-to-one basis is significant. In order to reduce that cost, buy and sell in quantity.

We strongly suggest that you always work with at least five options when you move in and out of positions. By doing this, you will reduce your commission costs down to $10 to $15 per option, and that can be a significant reduction in your overall profit-loss scenario.

The more options you buy, the more you sell, the lower your cost per option. The ideal number, of course, is *ten;* if you can get to a working level of ten options for each strategy, then you will have attained a minimal commission cost level. However, you might note that using more than ten options, although it may reduce your commission costs a slight bit more, may also create some trading problems. Many classes of options don't have the liquidity to take on large positions. And it is far more difficult to get the right price with a large position than with a smaller one.

5. Select a Brokerage House Carefully

We are in an era of competitive commission rates; every brokerage house charges different commissions, and you may want to look at the full range of brokerage houses to find those that will charge the lowest commissions for the number of services that you receive. A warning here: do not forsake a competent options specialist for a 5% or 10% difference in commissions. In the long run, you will pay for that difference, many times over.

6. Select the Cheapest Strategies

We have mentioned the priorities of the strategies based on commission costs per dollar of investment. Use that priority list. Naked options may have some inherent risks, but one thing is very true about them — they have low commission costs per dollar of investment, and that should be an important consideration when you are comparing investment alternatives.

7. Avoid Exercise

This is one of our Ten Commandments of option trading, and it is important, because exercise costs money. It costs commissions, and when you have an exercise, you will be shocked at the commission costs involved. By avoiding exercise, you avoid commission costs.

8. Let Options Expire

When you are an option writer, the name of the game is to write an option, and let it die. Let it pass on, thereby incurring only one commission, the commission to move into that position. One caution here: in many cases, an option will become almost worthless long before it will expire. In these situations, it is best to cover your positions and use your money wisely in other areas. Whenever you write naked options, there are margin requirements (collateral requirements) that must be put up, and if you are letting that money sit there because you are holding a naked option which is worthless, you are wasting the use of that money. So, although it is wise to let your options expire, should they become almost worthless before their life comes to an end, go ahead and take your profits, cover those positions, and put your money to use in some other option strategy.

Following some of these simple steps should greatly reduce your commission costs. Again, one of the key points of this chapter is to stress the importance of commission costs to the survival of the option player. When we get into the heat of the battle, when we are involved in playing the game, we have a tendency to rationalize commission costs; to flip them under a stone, to hide them from our sight. That practice can be a dangerous game.

On the other hand, don't let commissions interfere with your tactical and strategic actions once strategies are put into play. When there are profits to be made, take them. When you are required to get out of a strategy, *get out.* Do not consider commissions *at these points* in time, although you can consider tactics to reduce the commissions in taking

WATCH YOUR COMMISSION COSTS LIKE A PARANOID ACCOUNTANT

these actions. Once in the game, do not let commissions interfere with the critical, tactical maneuvers that you must make during the life of your strategies.

To conclude, remember, commission costs will probably eat up 15% to 30% of your portfolio every year. Plan for them, take defensive positions to reduce them, be cost conscious — put on your "accountant's hat" and control those costs.

Chapter 24

WINNING THE MARGIN GAME

To be a COMPLEAT OPTION PLAYER, you must know how to play the margin game, and in the new options market, this is probably the most confusing and complex subject that you will ever encounter. Even the experts, the back office people who handle the measuring of margin requirements and maintenance requirements, have trouble determining what the margin requirement is for each type of strategy. Even the best options specialists at times have questions; so, if you become confused and lost in the maze of requirements, you are not alone.

WHAT IS MARGIN?
WHAT ARE MARGIN REQUIREMENTS?

Many players in the options market never really have a clear understanding of what it's all about. They let their options specialist handle that problem, and they are amazed both at the figures he comes up with, and by the margin calls that they receive throughout the lives of their strategies.

Margin in the options market is *not* the same as in the stock market, where margin relates to the borrowing of money to take and maintain a stock position. In the options market, margin is *not* the borrowing of money from a brokerage house. Margin in options is a totally different concept, and because it is different, it has caused many problems.

So, clean the slates regarding your knowledge of margin requirements and margin calls, and let's talk about a new breed of cat — the margin requirements in the new options market.

A margin requirement is a deposit — of cash, or collateral — that you, the investor, put up *to guarantee that you will deliver on options that you have written.*

Therefore, the only option players who should be concerned with margins are those who are *writing* options. If you are writing covered options, you have already put up your margin requirements, this requirement being the 100 shares of stock underlying that option (covering the short position that you have written). So, when you are writing covered options, we do not have too heady a problem in calculating your margin requirement.

Instead, the problem arises when we are writing naked options, or are involved in spreads, ratio hedges, or ratio spreads. In this case we are required to put up cash, or collateral, to guarantee that we will deliver if the options we have written are ever exercised; (that is, you guarantee that you will make good on the option contracts you have written). This good faith deposit, if you would like to call it that, differs depending on which strategy we enter.

This deposit is required, and it is an important consideration in your strategy selection process, because it will determine your return on investment. Therefore, you want to select profitable strategies that require *very little margin.*

In determining the margin requirement for each strategy, a little knowledge and a few basic rules will do the job. If figures confuse you, you might want to leave this problem for your options specialist.

The only two entities that you can put up for this deposit are CASH or TREASURY BILLS. Treasury bills, as we have stated before, are an excellent way for the investor to put up collateral, but there are some brokerage houses that will not accept them. This is because they are making money from your margin account, and they would rather take that 5% to 10% return than give it to you. Stay away from such houses. One of the first questions that you should ask when determining whether to go with a firm is whether they will allow you to use Treasury bills as margin for your options account.

You probably have heard that you can put up stocks or bonds and use that as collateral against your naked options as part of your margin requirement. You can do this, but you will pay for it — you are putting up collateral which you will borrow against. The brokerage house is lending you money against these stocks or bonds, and you are *paying interest* on that money that you have borrowed.

Margin requirements are a major obstacle in the options game; make sure that you always know what your margin will be, and if you can't calculate your margin requirements, make sure somebody on your team calculates them for you before you ever enter a strategy. Too many option players are confused by this issue — they attempt to factor it out, just as they attempt to ignore commissions, and this habit is dangerous. You can't afford to ignore margins — they will get you one way or the other if you do.

TYPES OF MARGIN REQUIREMENTS

Now let's discuss the different kinds of margin requirements. There are two basic types of margin requirements, and you must understand the difference thoroughly. There are:

1. The INITIAL margin requirement
2. The MAINTENANCE margin requirement

The initial margin requirement is the amount of deposit that you must put down when you *first* enter your strategy. But the second type of margin, namely the maintenance margin requirement, will probably cause you more headaches than anything else. You need to pay maintenance margin in the following situation: you have taken a position, and suddenly the underlying stock price moves against your naked option positions; now you must pay additional good faith deposits, or maintenance margin.

You must pay because the potential value of the option has increased and now you must guarantee the good faith of that position. To do that, you must deposit additional margin (cash, or Treasury bills). You can easily calculate what the margin will be by yourself. But if you don't, your brokerage house will, and they will notify you when additional margin is required. At that time, you must immediately put up more margin to maintain that position.

At this point, let's go back first and discuss the initial margin requirement in depth. Then we will come back and look at maintenance margin requirements and discuss how to handle them.

INITIAL MARGIN REQUIREMENTS

We can best analyze the initial margin requirements by looking at all the different strategies that require these good faith deposits.

1. Covered Writing

As we mentioned at the beginning of this chapter, covered writing strategies have *no* special margin requirement, because you are writing options against their underlying stock. In addition, there is an advantage to this transaction — the option proceeds (the price of the option you have written) is directly credited to your account, and you can withdraw that money as soon as you write that option, even if you have purchased the stock on margin.

For example:

XRX = Xerox
Buy 100 XRX Common Stock at 50   Cost $2500
    with 50% margin

($5,000 x 50% = $2500)

Sell 1 XRX Oct 50 at 3   Less Proceeds $300
                                  Total Cost $2200

If you purchase XRX on 50% margin the total cost of this option writing position is only $2200.

2. Naked Writing

Next, when you write naked puts or calls, you must know about the special minimum margin requirements that have been established by the Chicago Board Options Exchange (CBOE). Note that many brokerage houses have higher margin requirements than the minimums. You should avoid these types of brokerage houses, if possible, for the more margin you have to put up, the lower your profit return will be. Therefore, as you select a brokerage house, make sure you find one that uses the CBOE minimum margin requirements.

The minimum margin requirement for writing one naked put or naked call is 30% of the value of the 100 shares of the underlying stock. This means that you must put up enough cash or Treasury bills to constitute a value equal to 30% of the underlying stock in order to establish that naked position — less the option proceeds. In addition, another segment to this margin rule exists. If the option exercise price is different from the stock price, an adjustment must be made to the initial margin requirement. If the option is in-the-money, (has intrinsic value), your margin requirement will increase above that 30% level. Thus each point that your option is out-of-the-money will reduce your margin requirement by $100, and each point that it is in-the-money will increase it by $100.

For examples of these cases, please refer to the next page . . .

EXAMPLE I

AN ON-THE-MONEY NAKED OPTION

Sell 1 XRX Jul 60 Put at 3
XRX Stock Price at 60
100 Shares x 60 = $6000

$6000 x 30% = $1800
Less Option Price . . . . ($300)
Initial Margin Requirement . . . $1500

EXAMPLE II

AN IN-THE-MONEY NAKED OPTION

Sell 1 XRX Jul 60 Put at 3
XRX Stock Price at 57

$5700 x 30% = $1710
Less Option Price . . . . ($300)
Margin Before Adjustment $1410

Exercise Price   60
XRX Stock Price   57
    Plus   3   = $300
Initial Margin Requirement. $1710

EXAMPLE III

AN OUT-OF-THE-MONEY NAKED OPTION

Sell XRX Jul 60 Call at 3
XRX Stock Price at 57

$5700 x 30% = $1710
Less Option Price   ($300)
Margin Before Adjustment $1410

Exercise Price   60
XRX Stock Price   57
    Less   3   = ($300)
Initial Margin Requirement $1110

3. The Naked Spread

The naked spread has still different margin rules from the writing of straight naked options. As you remember, when you write a naked spread, you are writing a put and a call with the same underlying stock. But the put and the call, although they have the same expiration dates, will have different exercise prices. Again, in determining the margin requirements for this strategy, we use the rule that we used for naked writing, which was: put up 30% of the value of the underlying stock.

However, in this case, there are some additional factors. In this instance, we have two naked options, not just one. The beauty of the naked spread comes out here, because the margin requirement is far more attractive. We only have to put up 30% of the value of the underlying stock, and for that good faith deposit, we get TWO naked options.

Again, there is an adjustment if the underlying stock price is not at the exercise price of one of the options. For each point that the stock price is out-of-the-money, the margin requirement is reduced by $100. For each point that the stock price is in-the-money of either option, the margin requirement will be increased by $100. Also, the margin is reduced by the proceeds you are credited from writing both options. Possibly an example will help to clarify these complex requirements.

EXAMPLE IV

A NAKED SPREAD

Sell 1 Sears Oct 60 Put at 3
Sell 1 Sears Oct 70 Call at 2½
Sears Stock Price of 65
100 Shares x 65 = $6500

$6500 x 30% =	$1950
Less proceeds from writing both options	(550)
	$1400

Less stock price distance from closest option exercise price (5 points)	(500)
Initial Margin Requirement	$900

Sears Stock Price	Total Margin Requirement	Maintenance Margin Requirement
72	1810	910
71	1680	780
70	1550	650
69	1420	520
68	1290	390
67	1160	260
66	1030	130
65 **Initial Price**	900	**Initial Margin** 0
64	970	70
63	1040	140
62	1110	210
61	1180	280
60	1250	350
59	1320	420
58	1390	490

4. The Naked Straddle

Now let's look at the straddle. Margin requirements for this strategy are very similar to those in the naked spread — we only have to put up one margin — 30% of the underlying stock. Thus again we get two naked options for the price of one, less the proceeds from writing both options.

If the underlying stock price is not at the exercise price of the options, it has to be in-the-money of either the put or the call. For every point that it is in-the-money, you must pay an additional $100 of initial margin. The following example shows the initial margin for an on-the-money straddle.

EXAMPLE V

A NAKED STRADDLE

Sell 1 Sears Oct 60 Put at 4
Sell 1 Sears Oct 60 Call at 3½
Sears Stock Price at 60
100 Shares x 60 = $6000

$6,000 x 30% = $1800

Less Option Proceeds   ($750)

Initial Margin Requirement $1050

Sears Stock Price		Total Margin Requirement	Maintenance Margin Requirement
68		2090	1040
67		1960	910
66		1830	780
65		1700	650
64		1570	520
63		1440	390
62		1310	260
61		1180	130
60	Initial Price	1050	0
59		1120	70
58		1190	140
57		1260	210
56		1330	280
55		1400	350
54		1470	420
53		1540	490
52		1610	560

5. The Ratio Hedge

The margin requirements for the ratio hedge can be quite fierce. In a ratio hedge, first of all, we have a covered writing position, 100 shares of stock, and in this instance, three written option positions. One of these options is covered, so that the value of that option is credited to our account, and can be used to meet the additional margin requirements for the strategy. Along with this one covered option, we also have two naked options. If you remember your naked option rules, you'll know that you must put up 30% of the value (less option proceeds) of the stock for each naked option, plus or minus $100 for each point that the stock is either above or below the exercise price.

Ratio hedges usually involve out-of-the-money options, so that the adjustment would be reduced, and we would normally require less than 30% of the value of the stock for each naked option. This requirement, of course, can add up if we have many naked positions. As a result, the investment in a ratio hedge can be quite high. We have to buy the stock, and it's true that we will get back the premium from all of the options, but we will also have to put up a very hefty good faith deposit for the two naked options. Should we write only two options against the stock, rather than three, we would only have one *naked* option, and therefore only have to put up 30% of the value of the stock for that one naked option. For example:

EXAMPLE VI

FNC = First National City

Buy 100 shares of FNC at 44   Cost $4400
Sell 3 FNC Apr 50 Calls at 4

30% of $4400 =	$1320.00
Multiply by no. of naked options	x 2
	$2640.00

Less proceeds from sale of
3 FNC Apr 50's   1200.00

Add margin required for options $1440

Total initial requirement $5840*

FNC Stock Price	Total Margin (plus Common stock) Requirement	Maintenance Margin Requirement	
58 Bail-out point	9480	3640	
56	8960	3120	
54	8440	2600	
52	7920	2080	
50	7400	1560	
48	6880	1040	Additional Margin Required
47	6620	780	
46	6360	520	
45	6100	260	
44 Initial Stock price	5840 Initial Margin Requirement	0	
43	5840	0	
42	5840	0	
41	5840	0	
40	5840	0	
38	5840	0	
36	5840	0	
34	5840	0	
32 Bail-out point	5840	0	

* An additional adjustment should be made to the initial and total margin requirements above. FNC is at 44, six points away from the exercise price of 50. Therefore, the margin requirement for each naked option should be reduced by $600; a total of $1200 for the strategy.

The same type of an adjustment must be made for the naked options in Example VII.

6. The Spread

Unlike the previous example, the one-on-one spread has no naked option writing positions. Therefore, the margin is much less than with the ratio hedge or the ratio spread. Spread margin requirements are very complicated and differ depending on whether you have a vertical, back or calendar spread.

We will only look at the requirements for (a) a vertical spread, where the long position is deeper in-the-money than the short position, and (b) at a calendar spread, where the long position has a longer life than the short position.

In each case, the margin requirement is the difference between the long side and the short side. You purchase one option and you reduce your purchase price by the amount of the premium (or price) of the written option.

For example: UPJ = Upjohn
I. Vertical Spread
Buy 1 UPJ Jan 85 Call at 10 3/4
Sell 1 UPJ Jan 100 Call at 4 3/4

Cost of UPJ Jan 85 Call. $1075
Less Proceeds from UPJ Jan 100 Call . . . ($475)

    Total Margin Required $600

II. Calendar Spread   **INA = INA Corp.**
Buy 1 INA Apr 30 Put at 3
Sell 1 INA Jan 30 Put at 2

Cost of INA Apr 30 Put $300
Less Proceeds from INA Jan 30 Put . . . . ($200)

    Total Margin Required $100

7. The Ratio Spread

The ratio (variable) spread, like the ratio hedge, has a complicated margin requirement. First we must look at the one-on-one spread, or the covered option, which is part of the ratio spread. Note that this is the one option writing position which is covered by the long option position. The margin requirement for that one-on-one spread is the difference between the long side and the short side. In other words, you purchase the long side and then you reduce your purchase price by the amount of premium which you receive from the short side.

In addition to that part of your strategy, you will also have one or two naked options that you have written against that long option position. These require the naked option writing margin requirement. For example:

EXAMPLE VII

(An actual ratio spread strategy recommended by the author on September 21, 1973. A strategy which has a profit range for the Upjohn stock price from 0 to 109.)

Buy 1 UPJ Jan 85 Call at 10 3/4
Sell 3 UPJ Jan 100 Calls at 4 3/4
UPJ Stock Price at 88

100 shares x 88 = $8800
30% of $8800 = $2640

Multiply by number of naked options   x 2
                                                        $5280

Less proceeds from 2 naked UPJ Jan 100's ($950)
Margin required for 2 naked options $4330

UPJ Jan 85 = $1075
Less proceeds from covered UPJ Jan 100   (475)
Margin required for 1-on-1 spread   600

      Initial Margin Requirement $4930*

UPJ Stock Price	Gross Profit	Gross Loss	Total Margin Requirement	Maintenance Margin Requirement
110		(150)	10,650	5,720
109 Bail-out Point	50		10,390	5.460
106	650		9,610	4,680
104	1050		9,090	4,160
102	1450		8,570	3,640
100	1850		8,050	3,120
98	1650		7,530	2,600
96	1450		7,010	2,080
94	1250		6,490	1,560
92	1050		5,970	1,040
90	850		5,450	520
88 Initial Price	650		4,930 Initial Margin	0
85 or lower	350		4,930 Requirement	0

MAINTENANCE MARGIN REQUIREMENTS

Now that we have covered the initial margin requirements for each type of strategy discussed in this text, it is time to look at the second type of good faith deposit that is required, and that is the *maintenance* requirement. If your strategies move in the right direction, you will never be bothered with a maintenance requirement. However, as soon as one of your strategies goes astray and moves in the wrong direction, and even though you may not be taking any realized or unrealized losses, (in fact, your strategy may still be in great shape based on your profit parameters), you may receive margin maintenance calls. This means you must put up additional deposits. Why? Because the stock price is approaching the exercise prices of your naked options.

Let's look again at each of the different types of strategies and determine when we would receive a margin call, requiring additional cash or Treasury bill deposits to be placed in your account.

1. Covered Writing

In the case of covered writing, you will never receive an option's maintenance call for additional margin as you have your 100 shares of stock covering the option position.

2. Naked Writing

With naked writing, you will always have a margin call if the underlying stock price moves one point towards the exercise price of the options you have written, whether they be puts or calls, unless you have reserve cash in the account.

For each point the stock price moves towards the exercise price of your call, you must put up an additional $130. For each point the stock price moves toward the exercise price of your put, you must put up an additional $70. If you have five naked call options, and the stock price moves two points towards the exercise price of those naked options, you will have to put up an additional $1,300. If they are puts, you will have to put up an additional $700. Naked options, then, may entail many maintenance calls, especially when the stock is moving in the wrong direction. So, prepare for these types of calls by building them into your initial strategy.

For example, using the out-of-the-money naked XRX Jul 60 call in Example III, we have displayed in Example VIII the maintenance margin requirement as the XRX stock price changes from its initial price of 57.

EXAMPLE VIII

XRX Stock Price	Total Margin Requirement	Maintenance Margin Requirement
65	2150	1040
64	2020	910
63	1890	780
62	1760	650
61	1630	520
60	1500	390
59	1370	260
58	1240	130
57 Initial Price	1110 Initial Requirement	0
56	1110	0
55	1110	0
54	1110	0
53	1110	0

3. The Naked Spread and the Straddle

The naked spread, like any other type of naked option writing strategy, receives maintenance calls if the stock price approaches either one or the other of the two naked options. Therefore, it is wise to throw in a little extra cash into your account to avoid this aggravation.

With a naked straddle, the same rule applies. Again, you are working with naked options, and for each point that the stock moves into the exercise price of the naked call option, $130 more is required. For each point that the stock moves into the exercise price of the naked put option, $70 more is required.

Example IV maps out the total margin required and the maintenance margin requirement (as part of the total requirement) at each price level of the Sears common stock for a naked spread.

Example V does the same for a Sears naked straddle.

4. The Ratio Hedge

The ratio hedge has naked options built into it, and because of this, you will again receive margin calls if the stock moves toward the exercise price of the naked options.

Example VI maps out the total margin requirement and the maintenance margin requirement for the First National City ratio hedge that is presented within the range of its profit parameters.

5. Spreads

The one-on-one spread has no maintenance margin requirements, because there are no naked option writing positions.

6. Ratio Spreads

The same problems that are incurred with ratio hedges are also encountered with ratio spreads. You have naked options, and therefore, you will have margin calls. You will be required to put up additional good faith deposits, even though the underlying stock price may be moving within the parameters of your strategy.

In Example VII we map out a ratio spread, showing the profit parameters, the total margin requirement, and an accumulated look at the margin maintenance calls. Again you have two naked options to contend with.

KEYS TO WINNING THE MARGIN GAME

Now that we have discovered the rules of the margin game, let's look at the keys to winning this game. Margins are important to the option player, because they will dictate his return on investment and may dictate the actions he will take in the midst of an option strategy.

Your maintenance margin requirement is an important determination of the freedom you will have to operate your options portfolio. You must always consider, not only the initial margin requirement, but the maximum maintenance requirement possible within the life of a strategy or an option position.

Find out the maximum amount of margin that may be required in the strategy before it reaches its bail-out points. Then you will know ahead of time exactly how much money you will have to set aside in your account to meet a potential maintenance requirement. If you don't have enough money in your account, and you cannot acquire that money, you will have to bail-out before you want to, and that can be a very costly process. Further, if you are forced out of strategy positions because of margin, your commission costs will really mount up. You will not be taking advantage of all the time that you spent in developing that strategy; you will be at the mercy of the moods and whims of the market, and that is one position the option player cannot afford to be in.

You CANNOT let margin calls dictate the actions you will take in the options market. Therefore, an important rule to follow is to MAKE SURE YOU HAVE ENOUGH MARGIN TO MEET ALL MAINTENANCE REQUIREMENTS. This is the key principle to winning the margin game. If you don't follow this principle, margin calls will dictate your option life, and as soon as that occurs, you will have a very short life as an options player, because you will be eaten alive by commissions. You will be forced to take action long before you should, and you will be covering positions in many cases when the premiums in your naked positions are much too fat. Margin management is a skill you will need to develop to be a COMPLEAT OPTION PLAYER.

Closing Comments

If you are confused by this margin game, you are not alone. One suggestion — use your options specialist to guide you in determining margins — that is what he gets paid to do. He will give you the initial margin requirement, and determine the maximum deposit that may be needed to maintain the profit parameters that you have designed into the strategy.

A key principle you have discovered in the material in this chapter is that the most ideal strategies which can be used to maximize your profit returns are the naked spread and the naked straddle. Why? Because your margin requirement in these is almost half that of the other naked writing strategies that have been presented, although they all have their advantages.

Therefore, in order to minimize your margin requirement, always look closely at the naked straddles and naked spreads. Opportunities in these areas will create the greatest return on each dollar invested.

Chapter 25

SELECTING
YOUR OPTIONS TEAM

Now we come to the important task of selecting the options team which will help determine whether you win or lose the options game.

The most important member of your team is the options specialist who will handle your account. The selection of the option specialist is one of the most important decisions in options trading.

WHY AN OPTIONS SPECIALIST?

You must have an options specialist; he is an indispensable member of your investment team. Unlike the case with the stock market, and with stock investment portfolios, an options portfolio demands a tremendous amount of attention, as there is far more activity and surveillance involved. Consequently, your broker is a far more important member of your team than if you were merely investing in stocks or bonds. Add to this the intricacies involved in the use of the new listed options, the confusion over margin requirements, and the complexity and number of strategies that can be designed through the use of listed options, and you will understand why you need a specialist. A specialist can answer many of

your questions, guide you, and carry out a lot of the legwork that is needed to design and implement profitable strategies in the new options market.

Even though you may be your own man or woman, a person who wishes to make his own decisions, and does not want the advice and help of a broker, the options specialist still can be a very indispensable aid to your success. He can clarify margin rules for you, help monitor your portfolio, and be a "devil's advocate" for the strategies and ideas that you develop. Many of you may have had "bad vibes" regarding brokers in the past. In the options game, however, it is very difficult to survive without an options broker to handle your account.

There is another alternative — you can have someone else manage you money, and maybe by watching what he does, you can learn something without an expensive trial and error education, possibly paying more than a little "tuition" in the process. There are investment managers around, and they do not work on commissions — they simply charge a small percentage fee based on the size of your portfolio.

However, one of the problems with using an investment manager or investment counselor is that they require large chunks of money to begin a management program, and you may not qualify. Another disadvantage is that, as a rule, investment managers specialize only in covered option writing programs, if they manage money in the options market. Although a covered option writing program should generate a good return, you may be looking for more action, and more potential return, and therefore may wish to use some of the more inherently profitable strategies available.

Investment managers who work for fees rather than commissions cannot afford to spend a tremendous amount of time handling a portfolio, and therefore will avoid managing complicated option portfolios. Their problem is that the regulatory agencies will not allow them to charge enough money to make it worthwhile to spend the time needed to manage an aggressive options portfolio. Therefore, they either stick with covered writing, or they avoid getting into the options market entirely.

Your only choice, then, is to go with a commissioned options specialist, who earns his bread through your commissions. This is unfortunate, because you and your options specialist may have conflicting interests. *You* wish to keep the commissions low, and in order for him to earn his living, *he* wishes to keep the commissions high. This is one tendency you will have to keep in line. You must control your commissions as we mentioned in Chapter 22, but you also must have a competent options specialist.

We've given you a large task to complete — to find a person who can be your partner — your team member in this options game. He will take a lot of weight off of your shoulders, and will definitely help your profit margins. He will answer all the questions that are outside the scope of this book. He will provide all the experience you do not have, and he will be a gold mine of new information, new ideas and new strategies.

BROKERS TO AVOID

Many an investor will say: "Well, I have a broker, I have had the same one for ten years, and he is a good broker." But this is analogous to going to your family General Practitioner for a skin ailment, instead of going to a Dermatologist.

You don't need an *all purpose* stock broker, you need a *specialist* in the options field, one who spends all his time in the options market. And, unlike calling in a medical specialist, consulting an options specialist will cost you no more than working with a general broker, as the commissions are the same — there is no additional cost for the options broker that you affiliate with.

Most stock brokers will claim that they know options pretty well. They will say that they have been dabbling in the options market since the new listed options were created. Be very wary of this type of statement; it takes a tremendous amount of time and effort to become a skilled option specialist. An all purpose stock broker will not have the depth, the knowledge and the information needed to do an effective job. He has just spread himself too thin.

In the process of seeking out a true options specialist, you are going to have difficulties, because the brokerage business tends to breed *salesmen* rather than stock technicians, or options technicians. In other words, usually the salesman is far more successful in obtaining new accounts than is the truly brilliant market specialist or options specialist. The salesman has "personality," he is often able to "con" the customer into believing that he knows it all.

In many cases, the salesman sells a package presented to him by his brokerage house, especially in the larger chain brokerage firms. Therefore, you are going to have to weed out the truly competent options specialist from the salesman who merely touts the ideas put out by his brokerage house. The salesman will not do the job for you — you need expertise — you need a specialist who knows what he is doing and knows his business; a good trader, a good strategist, a good technician. And you will probably have to shuffle through a few salesmen to get to that man. So, what we're looking for here is not "personality plus," but "intelligence plus."

Another type of specialist to avoid is one who works for one of the *large brokerage houses,* and has been totally trained and indoctrinated by that brokerage house. Normally, such brokers are sales oriented — they are trained to sell a package provided by management, and normally management highly discourages any kind of creativity on the part of their account executives. Such an option specialist would be little help to you because, in many cases, he would be representing management, and trying to push their bill of goods, rather than aiding you in designing and implementing strategies to your best advantage.

Also avoid the broker who has jumped on the bandwagon and suddenly calls himself an OPTIONS PRINCIPAL. Generally, he is in there to grab some of the commissions that have been highly touted in the brokerage industry, or he is a dropout from the stock market who is looking for a new method of grinding out commissions.

Again, learn to be leary of "active trading" option specialists. Remember, it is hard to survive in the market as a trader, and although the options specialist who does a lot of trading might be quite competent, following his habits can be dangerous.

The selection of an options specialist is as tough a job as selecting a spouse, or bringing a partner into your business, but we hope there is a lot less emotion involved in this process! You must find someone whom you feel comfortable with, and who is comfortable with you —— someone with whom you can communicate. Remember, he or she is human too, and likely to make mistakes at times. You have to be willing to forgive and forget in some cases. Attempt to avoid using your options specialist as a scapegoat because this game is tough enough as it is, and we want cooperation, not hostility in the process of getting these strategies off the ground, and building profits into your portfolio.

The options specialist is a broker who spends all his time in the options market, who has been in the options market at least since the advent of the new Options Exchange. Therefore, he has gained every minute of experience that has been available in this new options field. This kind of depth will provide you with a tremendous bank of knowledge when you need it, and you *will* need it.

HOW TO SELECT AN OPTIONS SPECIALIST

One way to avoid selecting a salesman in place of an options specialist is to look at his resume. You're right! Brokers usually don't have a resume, or if they did, they would be insulted if you asked them for one. However, a few good, well directed questions, as follows, may disclose some of the important aspects of their education and background.

1. Experience

How much experience does this so called options specialist

have — not stock experience, but options experience?

How long has he been an options specialist?

What track record does he have?

The ideal specialists started when the new listed options were born; they are the ones who foresaw the opportunities of this market, and were willing to stick their necks out, and commit themselves to this industry. Of course, the knowledge that you have gained through reading this text should help you to decipher the true blue, experienced specialist from the phony one, and it should not take long for you to determine whether or not he knows what he is talking about.

2. Originality and Creativity

Some big houses discourage this, but some of the smaller regional firms who still have New York Stock Exchange membership encourage this kind of attitude. Originality and creativity are two of the key attributes needed in the options market. There are so many strategies that can be designed in the options market, and so many ways of doing the same thing that the options market is a cornucopia of opportunities to the creative person. The creative and original go wild in the options market because there are so many new and imaginative strategies that can be designed — new and inventive ways of using margin and reducing commissions and improving profits. What you need on your options team is at least one creative person to trade ideas with you, to look for pitfalls in potential strategies, and to help you work out the complexities of the margin rules and the trading schemes that confront you as you play the game.

3. Mathematics Orientation

Mathematics and statistics are excellent prerequisites for entrance into the Options Exchange. You might want to look for an options specialist who has a math orientation, if this is not your forte.

SELECTING THE OPTION BROKERAGE HOUSE

Once you have selected what you feel are the prime candidates to represent your options portfolio, it is then time to look at the second criterion, the selection of the brokerage house.

There are several things to consider when attempting to select the brokerage house you are going to work with —— trading facilities, bookkeeping facilities, and an avenue to the floor of the Exchange. Normally, an extremely competent options specialist will be affiliated with a brokerage house which meets many of the needs of the option player. It will be a brokerage house that caters to options, one that has extremely good margin requirements, and that provides a tremendous amount of option supports. So, possibly your primary guide to identifying which brokerage house to work with is your options specialist.

If you haven't settled that question, then let's look more deeply at some of the other factors that you will want to investigate before you decide which brokerage house will service your account.

The most important consideration that you should review is the margin requirements. To generate a sufficient profit in this game, you must have the best margin requirements available in the market today. Consequently, you should only select brokerage houses which maintain the Chicago Board Options Exchange minimum margin requirements. Most firms today have moved in this direction, and are using these minimums, but there are a few that do not, and these are the firms that you should avoid..

The following are aspects to investigate in choosing a firm:

1. Trading Facilities

Does the firm have a direct telephone line to the floor of the Exchange?

How long does it take to get off an execution?

What types of orders will this firm accept?
(In many cases, some contingency orders will not be accepted by certain firms.)

2. Commissions

What kind of commissions does this firm charge?

Are the commissions above or below comparative commissions charged by other brokerage houses?

3. Services

How much research and development do they generate for you, not in the area of stocks, but in the area of optionable stock?

Will they provide you with charts, or with an accessibility to technical charts?

How well do they handle your bookkeeping problems?

4. Computers

What kind of computer services do they provide for the option trader?

Do they provide any kind of computer augmented information on a daily basis for their customers?

For the investor to maintain a competitive edge in the options market, the computer is becoming a more and more important part of that market. Eventually the option player will have to have a hand calculator at his side, which will continually calculate normal value prices for options, and generate different strategies that can be used at that moment in time.

When looking at different computer systems that each brokerage house provides, determine whether or not the strategy systems that are built into the computer systems are in-house or nationwide. Many of the large brokerage houses use a nationwide computer service which generates the same strategies to all their brokerage firms throughout the country. Unfortunately, such a widespread distribution of data nullifies the information that is provided before you can ever get to the floor of the Exchange, rendering such information almost worthless. On the other hand, a small brokerage house, which has in-house computer software, generates unique strategies which are distributed only to that house, and these can be a real advantage to the option player.

Again, even though you may not find all the advantages we have mentioned in an options house, if you can find a competent specialist, take him. Some of the small disadvantages you may encounter in the options house will be far offset by the aid and help you will receive from your man on the street.

To conclude — As we mentioned in the chapter on commissions, support from your brokerage house and from your options specialist is far more important in this new options game than it ever was in the stock market. You must have a competent options specialist to do a decent job, unless you are a well-seasoned expert in the options field. With a competent options specialist, you will get through this complex and confusing jungle and will reap the many profits that are available in this new options game.

Chapter 26

TOOLS NEEDED
FOR PROFESSIONAL PLAY

Now that you have a good feel for the tactics necessary for effective option trading, let's look at some of the aids that are in the toolbox of the professional option player.

1. Your Daily Newspaper

Most major daily newspapers now provide the daily prices for most of the Options Exchanges. The *Wall Street Journal* also furnishes a listing of the daily option prices for the Chicago Board Options Exchange, the Pacific Coast Options Exchange, the Baltimore-Washington Exchange, and the American Exchange, making it the best paper to have on hand to keep track of prices.

How do you make use of the newspaper? It keeps you in touch with the options market, is an indispensable aid for monitoring your positions, and it is your resource document for developing a strategy. From the data in the newspaper's options listings, you will derive your strategies.

Make sure that you collect the daily prices from this newspaper and keep them in a looseleaf notebook, in a file, or some place where you can have easy access to the prices for the past three months. This gives you a feel for the way the option prices have been behaving over the last few weeks and months so that you can more nearly estimate whether or not option prices for specific stocks are overpriced, under-priced, or normally priced at any point in time. This will greatly aid you in comparing strategies and anticipating what option prices will be in the next three to six months. These prices will give you a good feel for the options market, and are a very important intuitive aid as you play the game.

To recapitulate —— Your first major tools are your daily newspaper, and a three month collection of option prices; these will be indispensable in helping you to design, imple-ment and monitor option strategies.

2. Option Normal Value Tables

The second aid is one that you must also have to be com-petitive in this options market, namely your option normal value tables (The Appendix). These tables tell you what the price of an option should be at any one point in time, on any day in the life of that option. We have provided you with what we feel is a reasonable guide, a set of normal value tables for stocks which have average volatility. These tables in the Appendix of this text will be indispensable in the operation of your options portfolio, in the design of your strategies, in monitoring your strategies, and in telling you what will happen in the future if certain changes occur in the underlying stock prices of your strategies.

These tables are so important that the market makers on the Options Exchanges all receive a printout every morning which provides the normal value for all options on the Ex-change. So, in order to be competitive, you need to have the same information they have. You must know whether or not an option is over or underpriced, in order for you to main-tain a competitive edge with the market makers and profes-sional players on the floor of the Exchange.

If you would like to be even more accurate in determining the normal value of options, you might want to know that Hewlett-Packard makes a special handheld calculator, one of the marvels of our time, which will automatically calculate

THE NORMAL VALUE OPTION TABLES FORETELL OPTION PRICES IN THE FUTURE

for you the normal value for an option. At this writing, the retail price for this calculator is approximately $300. However, we believe you can also do a good job by yourself with the tables provided in this book.

In the future, you may need a more sophisticated means of determining normal value prices –– you may even need the aid of an on-line computer system. But for now, the normal value tables that we have presented should give you an important edge in this options market.

3. Stock Volatility Tables

Another indispensable tool of the option player is the all-important stock volatility table. You should know the volatility of your stocks backwards, forwards, and upside down, and also have an extremely good feel for the action and the movement of the prices that you are monitoring. The formula for identifying the volatility of a stock has been provided in Chapter 8. Determine the volatility for the past few years for all stock prices that you are monitoring. We strongly suggest that you then continue to update these volatility tables as time passes.

Remember the importance of volatility in determining which option strategies you will select. Use these tables in your selection process.

4. Stock Price Charts

Another aid to understanding the past price behavior of a stock are the stock charts – graphs that plot out the price action of stocks on a daily, weekly and monthly basis. These charts will be invaluable in helping you to better understand the underlying stock that you will be working with as you design option strategies.

There are many stock chart services available; some are quite expensive, so you may wish to use the services provided by your own brokerage house, or by your options specialist.

There are also excellent references in the library and you

can easily update your charts each week by a short visit to the library, using their Xerox machine to copy the reference material.

When deciding which type of charts to order, or to use, we strongly suggest that you work with daily stock price charts, not weekly or monthly ones. Remember, the life of an option is very short. We are not working with months and years; we are working with hours and days.

5. Strategy Forms

Now that you have some of the basics for designing strategies, you need some format to map out these strategies, and we strongly suggest a uniform, formalized *strategy sheet* where you can put all your strategies down on paper —— a worksheet of some type where you can map out your strategies, and easily compare the different types of strategies that you are considering.

We have used several forms in this text and include these forms in this chapter for your use. There are many types that you can design, and possibly the design of your strategy sheet will depend on what approach you will take in this options market. But a strategy sheet will force you to put your strategies down in black and white. It will also provide you with a record of which strategies were available, which ones you selected, and how they performed. It makes an excellent reference to review in or to find out where you made your errors, and what the actual outcomes were, as compared to the outcomes that you had projected in your preliminary work sheet.

You will also want to keep a *position record* to keep track of what positions you have at any one time.

6. Commission Charts

In Chapter 22, we talked about the importance of commissions, stressing the fact that you must be very cost conscious and watch your commissions like a paranoid accountant. To aid you in planning exactly what you are going to be

THE NAKED SPREAD (STRADDLE)
WORKSHEET

Date _____

WRITE _____ CALL(S) at _____ PROCEEDS = $ _____
(Sell)

WRITE _____ PUT(S) at _____ PROCEEDS = $ _____
(Sell)

STOCK PRICE _____

INITIAL MARGIN REQUIREMENT $ _____

MAXIMUM MARGIN REQUIREMENT $ _____

TOTAL PROCEEDS
RECEIVED $ _____

PROJECTED
COMMISSION COSTS $ _____

PRICE EXPIRATION DATE IN _____	PROCEEDS FROM CALL(S) (1)	VALUE OF CALL(S) (2)	= PROFIT OR (LOSS) FROM CALL(S) (3)	PROCEEDS FROM PUT(S) (4)	VALUE OF PUT(S) (5)	= PROFIT or (LOSS) FROM PUT(S) (6)	GROSS PROFIT OR (LOSS) (3) + (6) = (7)

THE RATIO SPREAD
WORKSHEET

BUY _____ at _____

WRITE _____ at _____
(Sell)

INITIAL MARGIN REQUIREMENT $ _____

MAXIMUM MARGIN REQUIREMENT $ _____

Date _____

COST = $ _____

PROCEEDS = $ _____

PROJECTED
COMMISSION
COSTS $

PRICE IN EXPIRATION DATE	(1) VALUE OF PURCHASED OPTION(S)	(2) COST OF OPTION(S)	(3) PROFIT OR (LOSS) FROM OPTIONS	(4) PROCEEDS FROM WRITTEN OPTIONS	(5) VALUE OF WRITTEN OPTIONS	(6) PROFIT OR (LOSS) FROM WRITTEN OPTIONS	(7) TOTAL GROSS PROFIT OR (LOSS) (3) + (6) = (7)
	—		=		—		=

THE SPREAD
WORKSHEET

Date _____

BUY _____ at _____

WRITE _____ at _____

MARGIN REQUIREMENT $ _____

(1) COST = $ _____

(2) PROCEEDS = $ _____

(3) TOTAL
RISK = _____   (1) - (2) = (3)

PROJECTED
COMMISSION
COSTS $ _____

PRICE EXPIRATION DATE IN	(4) VALUE OF PURCHASED OPTION(S)	(5) COST OF OPTION(S)	(6) PROFIT OR (LOSS) FROM OPTIONS	(7) PROCEEDS FROM WRITTEN OPTIONS	(8) VALUE OF WRITTEN OPTIONS	(9) PROFIT OR (LOSS) FROM WRITTEN OPTIONS	(10) TOTAL GROSS PROFIT OR (LOSS) (6) + (9) = (12)
		−	=		−	=	

paying, and when you are going to pay it, we have provided two commission charts in this chapter. One chart breaks down commissions by cost per commission, and the other rates commissions on a quantity basis.

The commissions listed are what we feel are the typical ones charged by the major firms today. But each firm differs, so these commissions may deviate one way or another from what you will actually pay for playing in the options market. However, you will find these charts to be an invaluable aid in deciding whether or not to enter a strategy. What is remarkable about these charts is the ease in which you can determine whether or not a trade is profitable, and what the costs to move in and out of an option position will be.

7. A Bookkeeping System

Another required piece of information that all option players and investors must have is some kind of a bookkeeping system, possibly of the type that you are now using for your stock portfolio. You need a system that will record the trades and provide a record for your own surveillance system, in effect, charting your own track record, and also — you guessed it — providing a record for the IRS to determine taxes you must pay.

You might also consider using a set of index cards and placing each active strategy on a card. When the strategy is terminated or expires, you may wish to record how much profit or loss you made on each card. In this way, you can gauge what kind of strategies are generating what kind of profits, and also, you can keep a more meaningful record for your portfolio (and for your own edification).

So, some sort of simple bookkeeping system is necessary, both as a matter of good management, and as a matter of meeting the requirements of the IRS. Possibly your accountant may be able to help you in designing the system if you are at a loss to determine how to set it up.

8. A Calendar

Another tool which is simple, but is something that all

COMMISSION SCHEDULE
PER OPTION ORDER

NUMBER OF OPTIONS IN ORDER

Price of Options	1	2	3	4	5	6	7	8	9	10	15	20	25	30	35	40	45	50
$1	25.00	26.60	33.90	41.20	48.50	55.80	63.10	70.40	77.70	85.00	111.50	138.00	164.50	189.00	213.50	238.00	262.50	287.00
2	25.00	29.20	37.80	46.40	55.00	63.60	72.20	80.80	89.40	98.00	129.00	158.00	182.00	216.00	245.00	274.00	303.00	332.00
3	25.00	31.80	41.70	51.60	61.50	71.40	81.30	91.20	100.30	109.00	142.50	176.00	209.50	243.00	276.50	310.00	343.50	377.00
4	25.00	34.40	45.60	56.80	68.00	79.20	89.20	98.80	108.40	118.00	156.00	194.00	232.00	270.00	308.00	346.00	394.00	422.00
5	25.00	37.00	49.50	62.00	74.50	85.00	95.50	106.00	116.50	127.00	169.50	212.00	254.50	297.00	339.50	392.00	417.00	452.00
6	25.00	39.60	52.40	67.20	79.00	90.40	101.80	113.20	124.60	136.00	183.00	230.00	277.00	324.00	368.00	406.00	444.00	482.00
7	25.00	42.20	57.30	71.20	83.50	95.80	108.10	120.40	133.70	145.00	196.50	248.00	299.50	348.00	389.00	430.00	468.00	502.00
8	25.00	44.80	61.20	74.80	88.00	101.20	114.40	127.60	140.80	154.00	210.00	266.00	322.00	366.00	410.00	450.00	486.00	522.00
9	25.00	47.40	64.30	78.40	92.50	106.60	120.70	134.80	148.90	163.00	223.50	284.00	337.00	384.00	428.00	466.00	504.00	542.00
10	25.00	50.00	67.00	82.00	97.00	112.00	127.00	142.00	157.00	172.00	237.00	302.00	352.00	402.00	442.00	482.00	522.00	562.00
11	26.30	52.60	69.70	85.60	101.00	117.40	133.30	149.20	165.10	181.00	250.50	314.00	367.00	414.00	456.00	498.00	540.00	582.00
12	27.60	55.20	72.40	89.20	106.00	122.80	139.60	156.40	173.20	190.00	264.00	326.00	382.00	426.00	470.00	514.00	558.00	602.00
13	28.90	57.40	75.10	92.80	110.50	128.20	145.90	163.60	181.30	199.00	277.50	338.00	392.00	438.00	484.00	530.00	576.00	622.00
14	30.20	59.20	77.80	96.40	115.00	133.60	152.20	170.80	189.40	208.00	288.00	350.00	402.00	450.00	498.00	546.00	594.00	642.00
15	31.50	61.00	80.50	100.00	119.50	139.00	158.50	178.60	197.50	217.00	297.00	362.00	412.00	462.00	512.00	562.00	612.00	662.00
20	38.00	70.00	94.00	118.00	142.00	166.00	190.00	214.00	238.00	262.00	342.00	402.00	462.00	522.00	582.00	642.00	702.00	762.00
25	44.50	79.00	107.50	130.00	164.50	193.00	221.50	250.00	271.00	292.00	372.00	442.00	512.00	582.00	652.00	722.00	792.00	862.00
30	49.00	88.00	121.00	154.00	187.00	220.00	250.00	274.00	298.00	322.00	402.00	482.00	562.00	642.00	722.00	802.00	882.00	962.00
35	53.50	97.00	134.50	172.00	209.50	244.00	271.00	298.00	322.00	342.00	432.00	522.00	612.00	702.00	792.00	882.00	972.00	1062.00
40	58.00	106.00	148.00	190.00	232.00	262.00	292.00	318.00	340.00	362.00	462.00	562.00	662.00	762.00	862.00	962.00	1062.00	1162.00
45	62.50	115.00	161.50	208.00	247.00	280.00	310.00	334.00	358.00	382.00	492.00	602.00	712.00	822.00	932.00	1042.00	1052.00	1262.00
50	65.00	124.00	175.00	226.00	262.00	298.00	324.00	350.00	376.00	402.00	522.00	642.00	762.00	882.00	1002.00	1122.00	1242.00	1362.00

Based on minimum CBOE commissions charged before May 1, 1975.

BASE COMMISSION COST PER OPTION

OPTION PRICE

Number of Options in Order	1	2	3	4	5	6	7	8	9	10	15	20	25	30	40	50
1	25.00	25.00	25.00	25.00	25.00	25.00	25.00	25.00	25.00	25.00	31.50	38.00	44.50	49.00	58.00	65.00
2	13.30	14.80	15.90	17.20	18.50	19.80	21.10	22.40	23.70	25.00	30.50	35.00	39.00	44.00	53.00	62.00
3	11.30	12.60	13.90	15.20	16.50	17.80	19.10	20.40	21.43	22.33	26.83	31.33	35.83	40.33	49.33	58.33
4	10.30	11.60	12.90	14.20	15.50	16.80	17.80	18.70	19.60	20.50	25.00	29.50	34.00	38.50	47.90	56.50
5	9.70	11.00	12.30	13.60	14.90	15.80	16.70	17.60	18.50	19.40	23.90	28.40	32.90	37.40	46.40	52.40
6	9.30	10.60	11.90	13.20	14.16	15.06	15.96	16.86	17.76	18.60	23.16	27.66	32.16	36.60	43.66	49.66
7	9.00	10.31	11.61	12.74	13.64	14.54	15.44	16.34	17.24	18.14	22.64	27.22	31.64	35.71	41.71	46.28
8	8.80	10.10	11.40	12.35	13.25	14.15	15.05	15.95	16.85	17.75	22.32	26.75	31.25	34.25	39.75	43.75
9	8.63	9.93	11.14	12.04	12.94	13.84	14.74	15.64	16.54	17.44	21.94	26.44	30.11	33.11	37.84	44.77
10	8.50	9.20	10.90	11.80	12.70	13.60	14.50	15.40	16.30	17.20	21.70	26.20	29.20	32.20	36.20	40.00
15	7.43	8.60	9.50	10.40	11.30	12.20	13.10	14.00	14.90	15.80	19.80	22.80	24.80	26.20	30.80	34.80
20	6.90	7.90	8.80	9.70	10.60	11.50	12.40	13.30	14.20	15.10	18.10	20.10	22.10	24.10	28.10	32.10
25	6.58	7.48	8.38	9.28	10.18	11.09	11.98	12.88	13.42	14.08	16.48	18.48	20.48	22.48	26.48	30.40
30	6.30	7.20	8.10	9.00	9.90	10.80	11.60	12.20	12.80	13.40	16.06	17.40	19.40	21.40	25.40	29.40
35	6.10	7.00	7.90	8.80	9.70	10.51	11.11	11.71	12.12	12.62	14.62	16.62	18.62	20.62	24.62	28.62
40	5.95	6.85	7.75	8.65	9.55	10.15	10.75	11.25	11.65	12.05	14.05	16.05	18.05	20.05	24.05	28.05
50	5.74	6.64	7.54	8.44	9.04	9.64	10.04	10.43	10.84	11.24	13.24	15.24	17.24	19.24	23.24	27.24

Listed options priced under $1 normally receive the following commission charges:

(a) $5 per option for options priced between 7/16 and 15/16.

(b) $2.50 per option for options priced between 1/16 and 6/16.

(c) Minimum commission charge per order will run from $20 to $25.

option players must have is a calendar —— one that spells out in red letters when options will expire. Believe it or not, investors forget about the fact that their options are sitting there wasting away; some investors even lose sight of the options' expiration date!

9. An Options Diary

A final tool which we recommend is an options diary. All you need is a notebook, which lists your successful strategies, tells why they were successful, and records what kind of return on investment you received. Then don't forget to put down a list of your errors; where did you go wrong —— did you get too greedy, did you ask for too much, did you take off one leg and hang on to the other? In other words, when did you stray from the beaten path? Remember, the player who makes the fewest errors will have the highest profits. Normally he is the player who is not afraid to pull the trigger every time, and although he will make errors, he makes fewer than most. The only way to eliminate errors is to study your past performance to find out where you are making mistakes.

Okay, you've now been given all the necessary tools that are needed for professional play. Actually, this list is not very long. Make sure that you *use* all these aids and your probability of success will be very high. If you just place them in your toolkit and never use them, well, we hope you are lucky, because you'll be substituting luck for method and training.

Chapter 27

THE TAX GAME

In this age of rising taxes, you cannot afford to ignore the tax aspects of the options game. Congress is continually in the mood for tax reform, and as a result of the 1976 Tax Reform Act, options are now treated like common stock profits and losses. This action has greatly encouraged the institutions to enter the options game. Unfortunately, at this time, listed options only have a maximum life of nine months, and therefore, profits taken from options can only result in a short-term capital gain or loss. However, in the future, we may see listed options with much longer lives, and this change may influence the way the I.R.S. treats some options.

How does this affect you? The tax consequences of options strategies may become important if you are exercised, and hold a long-term capital loss or gain in the underlying common stock. The *exercise price* is the price used to determine long-term capital gain or loss when a covered option is exercised. Exercise then, can have costly tax consequences.

One caution here —— options are far too volatile to allow any tax consideration to interfere with your option tactics once strategies are in play. The time to worry about tax considerations is earlier, when you are planning options strategies. In the initial stages of planning, a competent options specialist should be able to handle your particular tax problems.

Let's just stress this point again: taxes *are* important in the options game, just as taxes are a significant influence in all areas of our lives. Your tax position will determine whether or not options should be a part of your investment picture. We have not investigated taxes in depth, because the author feels that they are a separate consideration which may or may not encourage you to enter into the options game, just as the problem of taxes may preclude your investing in any of the equity markets.

Chapter 28

A LOOK INTO THE FUTURE

You are now prepared to enter the wonderful world of the listed option. You have been given the basics, the resources necessary for successful strategy design and the winning tools and tactics. Now, before you jump into this unusual game, let's take a peep into the future.

THINGS TO COME

Listed options are the hottest thing to hit Wall Street in over a decade. Almost every stock exchange in the United States has entered this game, and from now on listed options will also take on an international flavor. Europe, Australia and Canada are mapping out plans to initiate their own listed options exchanges.

On the home front, plans are in the works to begin trading listed options on the over-the-counter stocks; the American Stock Exchange is planning to trade listed options on gold and silver; and finally, there are plans in the works to trade listed options on all of the commodities. Several exchanges also plan to establish and trade listed options on Government fixed income securities.

All of these developments demonstrate the explosive

popularity of the new options game. The COMPLEAT OPTION PLAYER will be prepared for the multitude of opportunities that will develop as the options game enters new markets. As the listed option spreads to diverse markets and media, we may see other changes developing. The skilled player must be aware of these changes and be able to adapt to them.

At the present time, only 2% of the American population has some exposure to the new listed options. However, in the next few years, with the explosion of new listed option games, far more players will enter the options arena. The most significant force to enter the game will be institutional investors, and their influence in the options market cannot be ignored. As we mentioned in a previous chapter, institutions will be option writers, and normally, only call writers. They will provide excellent liquidity for the options market, but will depress call option premiums. Therefore, the option *buyer* will gain a strategic advantage.

THE COMING OF THE SPREAD

Floor brokers and market makers on the floor of the Exchange will increasingly gain more option sophistication and experience. Consequently, they will provide more liquidity and better executions for public orders.

For example: spreads can be very attractive, but until this time, they have been very difficult to execute. Now market makers feel far more comfortable with spreads —— most of the positions in their own accounts are spreads. As a result, the spread is becoming a trading vehicle in and of itself, and the traders on the floor of the Exchange are buying and selling spreads, just as they buy and sell puts and calls.

In the near future, "Spread Quotes" will probably be provided to the public on brokerage house quote machines, in a manner similar to the quotes now provided for common stock prices or listed put and call options.

Moreover, spreads will have a market of their own. For example:

THE XEROX SPREAD

Buy 1 XRX Jul 50 call
Sell 1 XRX Jul 60 call

may be quoted as: Bid 2   Asked 2½

In other words, you can buy the whole spread for $250, and sell it for $200.

As mentioned previously, along with spread quotes we will be seeing "Spread Commissions," one commission for the whole spread. Such developments will enable the small investor to participate in the spreading game without being eaten alive by commissions, or being endangered by poor executions.

Thus, spreads will become important investment and speculative vehicles, easy to enter and exit at low cost. The COMPLEAT OPTION PLAYER will use spreads generously, both as a defensive and offensive tactic.

CAUTION: BEWARE OF THE MARKET MAKERS

With the market makers' growing sophistication on the floor of the options exchanges, the game player will have fewer outstanding opportunities available to him. Market makers already are grabbing opportunities the moment they develop on the floor of the Exchange. In the future, their sophistication will grow, and really good opportunities may be harder and harder to find. Market makers will be continually watching for option prices to get out of line, or for spreads which are too wide or too narrow. Already they have at their finger tips the normal value of all options. However, as you know, we have also provided you with these prices in order for you to be competitive with the pros on the floor of the Exchange.

What do these future developments mean to the option player? Really good spots will be harder to find. Again, patience will be the key to success. You will have to wait for winning strategies to develop. The options player has two key advantages in his corner:

1. The advent of puts and other new option games will provide a multitude of opportunities. Winning strategies will continually be developing.

2. Public orders in the board broker's book have PRIORITY over market maker orders.

The options player who is flexible, who is willing to change strategies when opportunities dry up, and who is able to wait for strategies to develop with orders in the public book, will prosper in the future.

THE AGE OF THE COMPUTER

The fantastic growth of computer technology will have a strong influence in the options market. The increasing sophistication of market makers on the floor of the options exchanges is partially the result of this computer technology, as computers are used to identify strategies on an hour by hour basis. With a multitude of strategies available to the game player, the computer will become an aid in tracking and identifying potential and attractive option strategies.

Traders on the floor of the Exchange already have fancy computer models to identify option strategies. In the next few years, a computer that once was priced at over a million dollars will cost less than a hunderd dollars, and be the size of a hand calculator. You know the pros will use this technology — one which will key in on potential strategies very quickly. Therefore, opportunities will disappear rapidly. In the future, computers may not decide the survival of the option player, but they will surely aid him in winning the game.

PUTS: A MIRROR IMAGE OF CALLS

In the old OTC options market, puts were priced from 30% to 50% below the price of calls. But with the advent of the *listed* put, you may be surprised at their current prices. Believe it or not, a put may eventually be priced pretty closely to its corresponding call. Why? Because with listed options, market makers on the floor of the Exchange can *convert* listed puts into listed calls at a low cost.

You may be wondering what "conversion" is all about. How do you change a put into a call? The process is quite complicated, but if you pay no commission, you can develop an attractive arbitrage.

To carry out a conversion, we buy the put we wish to convert to a call, and then sell the corresponding call and buy 100 shares of the underlying common stock, or a deep-in-the-money call with little time value.

A detailed discussion of conversion is beyond the scope of this text, but the result is not. Market makers searching for attractive arbitrages will buy puts for conversion, pushing the put price very close to its corresponding call price.

An outstanding ploy if this scenario develops will be to write naked puts during rallies when calls are highly inflated. Highly inflated calls will result in highly inflated puts, even in a wild bull market. Why? Because of *conversion.* Think about it, and watch those put prices carefully.

BEWARE OF REGULATORS

Regulation in the United States is becoming a major problem, and is probably one of the major causes of inflation. It interferes more with business than it helps to protect the citizens of our nation. Regulation has grown out of all proportion, and it is surprising that with its massive influence in the securities industry, a listed Options Exchange was ever born and has been able to survive.

First of all, listed puts were not available for over three years because of the regulators. Option margin requirements and the whole future of options will continue to be highly influenced by regulation.

Further, the regulators are supposedly here to protect the small investor, but it seems they have done more to keep him out of the options game.

So, the regulators will have a strong influence; how strong this influence is will depend on how well we are able to control them.

THE DRYING OF THE WELL

Will the explosion in outstanding option opportunities ever end? Will this well of opportunities ever run dry? Once a game becomes extremely popular and the masses enter that game, the game is usually over.

But wait a minute — the options game is not such a simple game. Because of the very complex nature of the options game, because of a multitude of vehicles that can be used to participate in this game, the well may never run dry. If covered writing dries up because of heavy institutional participation, then option buying will become attractive. If the calendar put spread is overplayed, then maybe the calendar call spread will become attractive.

In other words, because there is such a huge number of vastly different strategies, when one strategy becomes over-played, another will pop up for the astute player. The option market is now and will probably continue to be in a state of continual adjustment. It will over-adjust to one strategy and then under-adjust to that strategy. The COMPLEAT OPTION PLAYER will take advantage of this over and under adjustment.

One thing you should remember — if the masses enter the options game, they will enter the simplest strategies, those that are easy to understand. Therefore, the COMPLEAT OPTION PLAYER will select strategies which are complex and difficult to follow, ones which are not popular. These are the strategies where outstanding opportunities will be gained.

But, before we assume that our options well will remain full of opportunities, there are some other factors to consider. The heavy influence in the securities industry of the regulators could some day destroy the options game. And, don't forget the influence of our illustrious Congress, which may some day tax reform us out of the game.

Finally, the well could also run dry if listed options become so widespread as to generate insufficient liquidity in each market. Liquidity is the key to success of the listed option, and without it, the game will die.

PREPARING FOR THE FUTURE

Now that you have had a look ahead, how can you prepare for the future? The author suggests that you follow these three steps:
1. Take a graduate course in spreading
2. Use all the aids you can get
3. Be flexible and patient

1. Take a graduate course in spreading

With the advent of spread quotes and spread commissions, spreads will become an outstanding investment media in the options market. We have only touched on spreading in this text, because it is such a complex art and science.

Once you have gotten your feet wet in the options market, your next step will be to begin to play around with spreads. Read everything you can about spreads and play a lot of different ones on paper. Remember, spreads take a lot of trading skill, and trading skill takes a lot of time to develop, so be patient and prepare yourself before you enter the spreading game.

Once in this unique game, you will find the opportunities limitless. Spreads are very complex, but because they are, they keep the masses out and the COMPLEAT OPTION PLAYER in the money.

2. Use all the aids you can get

To maintain that competitive edge over the increased sophistication by the market makers, the institutions and the public, the COMPLEAT OPTION PLAYER will utilize all the aids available to him. He will use the best computer technology available, the best options specialist available, and the best software (publications, charts, and other resource aids — see Chapter 26) that is available.

3. Be flexible and patient

You've heard this before, but in the future it will be even more important to be flexible and patient. Don't get stuck on a special strategy; move on to new option vehicles when old ones run out of gas. Then be patient and wait for really good opportunities to develop. You, the public investor, have the advantage in the options game only if you are willing to sit and wait for your key strategies to develop.

The time has come to wish you the best of luck in this super game. You have all the resources you need to win the options game. If you are still uncomfortable with the listed option, a re-reading or review of this book will help. Options are a very complicated subject even for the super-intelligent person.

If you use the tools and strategies we have given you and apply them according to the guidelines we have set, you will join the ranks of the COMPLEAT OPTION PLAYERS.

APPENDIX

NORMAL VALUE OPTION TABLES

HOW TO USE THE NORMAL VALUE OPTION TABLES

The Normal Value Option Tables are one of the most indispensable aids to the option player. They will tell him when to buy, when to sell, and project accurately what a specific option price will be in the future.

Normal Value Option Tables are the crystal ball of the option player. They are critical to his success, they will identify bargain priced options, and options which are ripe for naked or covered writing. The Normal Value Option Tables give the *true* option price, given the underlying common stock price, and the number of weeks left in the life of the option.

Options with exercise prices as high as $150 are provided in the tables. Very few optionable common stocks are priced above $150, and those that do reach these heights normally are split in order to make their shares more attractive to covered option writers. So, if you are evaluating a listed option with an exercise price at 150 or lower, you should be able to easily determine the true value of that option today, or at any time in the option's life.

The normal option prices presented in these tables are to be used as GUIDELINES — not as an absolute measure of value. The prices given are based on an underlying common stock with average volatility. Volatility is a key you will have to input in evaluating these normal prices. Common stocks with a higher than average volatility should have a higher price than the prices listed in the Normal Value Option Tables. Underlying common stocks with low volatility should have a lower price than the listed option prices in the tables.

Therefore, volatility should be carefully considered when you view the normal values we have given to each option. Use the volatility formula we have presented, or look at the underlying common stock's Beta Factor (provided by most chart services).

When the volatility is much greater than 20% or the Beta Factor is much greater than 1.00, the corresponding option price should be adjusted accordingly. The same adjustment should be made for underlying common stocks which have a volatility which is significantly below 20%, or maintain a Beta Factor well below 1.00.

Remember, the normal value prices are to be used as a guideline — a beacon to guide you in this fast moving and confusing game. You will find these tables invaluable, both in strategy design and in making tactical maneuvers. These tables will clearly tell you when option prices are out of line. So, keep these tables at your side when you play the options game.

INTERPOLATION

Under certain conditions, you will encounter an option *exercise price* not listed in our Normal Value Option Tables, such as 55 or 48 1/8, etc. In order to measure the normal price of options with abnormal exercise prices requires interpolation.

For example, you are evaluating an EXXON Oct 55 put with 6 weeks until expiration, with the stock price at 55.

This option is not presented in the tables. Therefore, identify the two option prices with the closest exercise prices and the same number of weeks to expiration. Add these two prices together and, in this case, divide by 2. This will give you the normal value of the Oct 55 option with 6 weeks remaining until expiration.

(a) Normal value of the Oct 50 put is when the underlying stock is 50.   1.7

(b) Add the normal value of the Oct 60 put when the underlying stock is 60.   + 2.1

NORMAL VALUE = $\dfrac{3.8}{2}$ = 1.9

Sum of (a) and (b) divided by 2 equals the normal value of the Oct 55 put option which is 1.9 ($190).

You can also use interpolation to measure the normal value of an option for a specific number of days rather than a specific number of weeks before expiration; although the author feels that the normal value prices given for each week will provide quite adequate guidelines, and such interpolation is probably unnecessary.

HOW TO FIND THE NORMAL VALUE OF AN OPTION

Using our Normal Value Option Tables is an easy task. For example, to find the real value of a Sears July 40 call with 10 weeks remaining, with Sears priced at $40 a share — turn to the Call tables and the page with the exercise price of 40. Look down the table to the point where the common stock price is 40. Move across to the column which states that 10 weeks are remaining, and you will find the normal value of the Sears July 40 call, which is 2.3 ($230).

Practice with a few more options and you will get the hang of using these tables quite rapidly. Then make sure that you continue to use these tables — they will give you a big edge in the options game.

THE NORMAL

VALUE LISTED

CALL OPTION

TABLES

LISTED CALL OPTION PRICE WHEN EXERCISE PRICE IS 10

NUMBER OF WEEKS BEFORE THE OPTION EXPIRES

Common Stock Price	1	2	3	4	5	6	7	8	9	10	11	12	13	14	15	16	17	18	19	20	21	22	23	24	25	26	27	28	29	30	31	32	33	34	35	36	37	38	39
14	4.0	4.0	4.0	4.0	4.0	4.0	4.0	4.1	4.1	4.1	4.1	4.1	4.1	4.1	4.1	4.1	4.1	4.1	4.1	4.1	4.1	4.1	4.2	4.2	4.2	4.2	4.2	4.2	4.2	4.2	4.2	4.2	4.2	4.2	4.2	4.2	4.2	4.2	4.3
13.5	3.5	3.5	3.5	3.5	3.5	3.6	3.6	3.6	3.6	3.6	3.6	3.6	3.6	3.6	3.6	3.6	3.7	3.7	3.7	3.7	3.7	3.7	3.7	3.7	3.7	3.7	3.7	3.8	3.8	3.8	3.8	3.8	3.8	3.8	3.8	3.8	3.8	3.8	3.9
13	3.0	3.0	3.0	3.0	3.1	3.1	3.1	3.1	3.1	3.1	3.1	3.1	3.2	3.2	3.2	3.2	3.2	3.2	3.2	3.2	3.2	3.3	3.3	3.3	3.3	3.3	3.3	3.3	3.3	3.4	3.4	3.4	3.4	3.4	3.4	3.4	3.4	3.4	3.5
12.5	2.5	2.5	2.5	2.6	2.6	2.6	2.6	2.6	2.6	2.6	2.7	2.7	2.7	2.7	2.7	2.7	2.7	2.8	2.8	2.8	2.8	2.8	2.8	2.8	2.9	2.9	2.9	2.9	2.9	2.9	2.9	3.0	3.0	3.0	3.0	3.0	3.0	3.0	3.1
12	2.0	2.0	2.1	2.1	2.1	2.1	2.1	2.1	2.2	2.2	2.2	2.2	2.2	2.2	2.3	2.3	2.3	2.3	2.3	2.3	2.4	2.4	2.4	2.4	2.4	2.4	2.5	2.5	2.5	2.5	2.5	2.5	2.6	2.6	2.6	2.6	2.6	2.6	2.7
11.5	1.5	1.5	1.6	1.6	1.6	1.6	1.6	1.7	1.7	1.7	1.7	1.7	1.8	1.8	1.8	1.8	1.8	1.8	1.9	1.9	1.9	1.9	1.9	2.0	2.0	2.0	2.0	2.0	2.1	2.1	2.1	2.1	2.1	2.2	2.2	2.2	2.2	2.2	2.3
11	1.0	1.1	1.1	1.2	1.2	1.2	1.2	1.2	1.3	1.3	1.3	1.3	1.3	1.4	1.4	1.4	1.4	1.4	1.5	1.5	1.5	1.5	1.6	1.6	1.6	1.6	1.6	1.6	1.7	1.7	1.7	1.7	1.7	1.8	1.8	1.8	1.8	1.9	1.9
10.5	0.6	0.7	0.7	0.7	0.8	0.8	0.8	0.8	0.9	0.9	0.9	0.9	0.9	1.0	1.0	1.0	1.0	1.0	1.1	1.1	1.1	1.1	1.2	1.2	1.2	1.2	1.2	1.3	1.3	1.3	1.3	1.3	1.3	1.4	1.4	1.4	1.4	1.4	1.5
10	0.2	0.3	0.3	0.4	0.4	0.4	0.5	0.5	0.5	0.6	0.6	0.6	0.6	0.7	0.7	0.7	0.7	0.8	0.8	0.8	0.8	0.8	0.9	0.9	0.9	0.9	0.9	0.9	1.0	1.0	1.0	1.0	1.0	1.0	1.1	1.1	1.1	1.1	1.1
9.5	0.0	0.1	0.1	0.2	0.2	0.2	0.3	0.3	0.3	0.4	0.4	0.4	0.4	0.5	0.5	0.5	0.5	0.6	0.6	0.6	0.6	0.6	0.7	0.7	0.7	0.7	0.7	0.7	0.8	0.8	0.8	0.8	0.8	0.8	0.9	0.9	0.9	0.9	0.9
9	0.0	0.0	0.0	0.0	0.0	0.0	0.1	0.1	0.1	0.2	0.2	0.2	0.2	0.2	0.3	0.3	0.3	0.4	0.4	0.4	0.4	0.4	0.5	0.5	0.5	0.5	0.5	0.5	0.6	0.6	0.6	0.6	0.6	0.6	0.7	0.7	0.7	0.7	0.7
8.5	0.0	0.0	0.0	0.0	0.0	0.0	0.1	0.1	0.1	0.1	0.1	0.2	0.2	0.2	0.2	0.2	0.3	0.3	0.3	0.3	0.3	0.3	0.3	0.3	0.3	0.3	0.3	0.3	0.4	0.4	0.4	0.4	0.4	0.4	0.5	0.5	0.5	0.5	0.5
8	0.0	0.0	0.0	0.0	0.0	0.0	0.0	0.0	0.0	0.0	0.0	0.0	0.0	0.1	0.1	0.1	0.1	0.1	0.1	0.1	0.2	0.2	0.2	0.2	0.2	0.2	0.2	0.2	0.2	0.2	0.2	0.3	0.3	0.3	0.3	0.3	0.3	0.3	0.3
7.5	0.0	0.0	0.0	0.0	0.0	0.0	0.0	0.0	0.0	0.0	0.0	0.0	0.0	0.0	0.0	0.0	0.0	0.0	0.0	0.0	0.0	0.0	0.0	0.0	0.0	0.0	0.0	0.0	0.0	0.0	0.1	0.1	0.1	0.1	0.1	0.1	0.1	0.1	0.1
7	0.0	0.0	0.0	0.0	0.0	0.0	0.0	0.0	0.0	0.0	0.0	0.0	0.0	0.0	0.0	0.0	0.0	0.0	0.0	0.0	0.0	0.0	0.0	0.0	0.0	0.0	0.0	0.0	0.0	0.0	0.0	0.0	0.0	0.0	0.0	0.0	0.0	0.0	0.0
6.5	0.0	0.0	0.0	0.0	0.0	0.0	0.0	0.0	0.0	0.0	0.0	0.0	0.0	0.0	0.0	0.0	0.0	0.0	0.0	0.0	0.0	0.0	0.0	0.0	0.0	0.0	0.0	0.0	0.0	0.0	0.0	0.0	0.0	0.0	0.0	0.0	0.0	0.0	0.0
6	0.0	0.0	0.0	0.0	0.0	0.0	0.0	0.0	0.0	0.0	0.0	0.0	0.0	0.0	0.0	0.0	0.0	0.0	0.0	0.0	0.0	0.0	0.0	0.0	0.0	0.0	0.0	0.0	0.0	0.0	0.0	0.0	0.0	0.0	0.0	0.0	0.0	0.0	0.0

LISTED CALL OPTION PRICE WHEN EXERCISE PRICE IS 15

NUMBER OF WEEKS BEFORE THE OPTION EXPIRES

Common Stock Price	1	2	3	4	5	6	7	8	9	10	11	12	13	14	15	16	17	18	19	20	21	22	23	24	25	26	27	28	29	30	31	32	33	34	35	36	37	38	39
21	6.0	6.0	6.0	6.0	6.0	6.1	6.1	6.1	6.1	6.1	6.1	6.1	6.1	6.1	6.1	6.2	6.2	6.2	6.2	6.2	6.2	6.2	6.2	6.2	6.2	6.3	6.3	6.3	6.3	6.3	6.3	6.3	6.3	6.3	6.3	6.4	6.4	6.4	6.4
20	5.0	5.0	5.0	5.1	5.1	5.1	5.1	5.1	5.1	5.1	5.2	5.2	5.2	5.2	5.2	5.2	5.3	5.3	5.3	5.3	5.3	5.3	5.3	5.4	5.4	5.4	5.4	5.4	5.4	5.4	5.5	5.5	5.5	5.5	5.5	5.5	5.6	5.6	5.6
19	4.0	4.0	4.1	4.1	4.1	4.1	4.1	4.2	4.2	4.2	4.2	4.2	4.3	4.3	4.3	4.3	4.3	4.4	4.4	4.4	4.4	4.4	4.5	4.5	4.5	4.5	4.5	4.6	4.6	4.6	4.6	4.6	4.7	4.7	4.7	4.7	4.7	4.8	4.8
18	3.0	3.1	3.1	3.1	3.1	3.2	3.2	3.2	3.2	3.3	3.3	3.3	3.3	3.4	3.4	3.4	3.4	3.5	3.5	3.5	3.5	3.6	3.6	3.6	3.6	3.6	3.7	3.7	3.7	3.8	3.8	3.8	3.8	3.9	3.9	3.9	3.9	4.0	4.0
17	2.0	2.1	2.1	2.1	2.2	2.2	2.2	2.2	2.3	2.3	2.3	2.4	2.4	2.4	2.4	2.5	2.5	2.5	2.6	2.6	2.6	2.7	2.7	2.7	2.8	2.8	2.8	2.8	2.9	2.9	2.9	3.0	3.0	3.0	3.1	3.1	3.1	3.2	3.2
16	1.1	1.2	1.2	1.3	1.3	1.4	1.4	1.5	1.5	1.5	1.6	1.6	1.6	1.7	1.7	1.8	1.8	1.8	1.9	1.9	1.9	1.9	2.0	2.0	2.0	2.0	2.0	2.1	2.1	2.1	2.1	2.2	2.2	2.3	2.3	2.4	2.4	2.5	2.5
15	0.3	0.4	0.5	0.5	0.6	0.7	0.7	0.8	0.8	0.8	0.9	0.9	1.0	1.0	1.0	1.1	1.1	1.1	1.2	1.2	1.2	1.3	1.3	1.3	1.3	1.4	1.4	1.4	1.4	1.5	1.5	1.5	1.5	1.6	1.6	1.6	1.6	1.6	1.7
14.5	0.1	0.2	0.3	0.3	0.4	0.5	0.5	0.6	0.6	0.6	0.7	0.7	0.8	0.8	0.8	0.9	0.9	0.9	1.0	1.0	1.0	1.1	1.1	1.1	1.1	1.2	1.2	1.2	1.2	1.3	1.3	1.3	1.3	1.4	1.4	1.4	1.4	1.4	1.5
14	0.0	0.0	0.1	0.1	0.2	0.3	0.3	0.4	0.4	0.4	0.5	0.5	0.6	0.6	0.6	0.7	0.7	0.7	0.8	0.8	0.8	0.9	0.9	0.9	0.9	1.0	1.0	1.0	1.0	1.1	1.1	1.1	1.1	1.2	1.2	1.2	1.2	1.2	1.3
13.5	0.0	0.0	0.0	0.0	0.0	0.1	0.1	0.2	0.2	0.2	0.3	0.3	0.4	0.4	0.4	0.5	0.5	0.5	0.6	0.6	0.6	0.7	0.7	0.7	0.7	0.8	0.8	0.8	0.8	0.9	0.9	0.9	0.9	1.0	1.0	1.0	1.0	1.0	1.1
13	0.0	0.0	0.0	0.0	0.0	0.0	0.0	0.0	0.0	0.0	0.1	0.1	0.2	0.2	0.2	0.3	0.3	0.3	0.4	0.4	0.4	0.5	0.5	0.5	0.5	0.6	0.6	0.6	0.6	0.7	0.7	0.7	0.7	0.8	0.8	0.8	0.8	0.8	0.9
12.5	0.0	0.0	0.0	0.0	0.0	0.0	0.0	0.0	0.0	0.0	0.0	0.0	0.0	0.0	0.0	0.1	0.1	0.1	0.2	0.2	0.2	0.3	0.3	0.3	0.3	0.4	0.4	0.4	0.4	0.5	0.5	0.5	0.5	0.6	0.6	0.6	0.6	0.6	0.7
12	0.0	0.0	0.0	0.0	0.0	0.0	0.0	0.0	0.0	0.0	0.0	0.0	0.0	0.0	0.0	0.0	0.0	0.0	0.0	0.0	0.0	0.1	0.1	0.1	0.1	0.2	0.2	0.2	0.2	0.3	0.3	0.3	0.3	0.4	0.4	0.4	0.4	0.4	0.5
11.5	0.0	0.0	0.0	0.0	0.0	0.0	0.0	0.0	0.0	0.0	0.0	0.0	0.0	0.0	0.0	0.0	0.0	0.0	0.0	0.0	0.0	0.0	0.0	0.0	0.0	0.0	0.0	0.0	0.0	0.1	0.1	0.1	0.1	0.2	0.2	0.2	0.2	0.2	0.3
11	0.0	0.0	0.0	0.0	0.0	0.0	0.0	0.0	0.0	0.0	0.0	0.0	0.0	0.0	0.0	0.0	0.0	0.0	0.0	0.0	0.0	0.0	0.0	0.0	0.0	0.0	0.0	0.0	0.0	0.0	0.0	0.0	0.0	0.0	0.0	0.0	0.0	0.0	0.1
10.5	0.0	0.0	0.0	0.0	0.0	0.0	0.0	0.0	0.0	0.0	0.0	0.0	0.0	0.0	0.0	0.0	0.0	0.0	0.0	0.0	0.0	0.0	0.0	0.0	0.0	0.0	0.0	0.0	0.0	0.0	0.0	0.0	0.0	0.0	0.0	0.0	0.0	0.0	0.0
10	0.0	0.0	0.0	0.0	0.0	0.0	0.0	0.0	0.0	0.0	0.0	0.0	0.0	0.0	0.0	0.0	0.0	0.0	0.0	0.0	0.0	0.0	0.0	0.0	0.0	0.0	0.0	0.0	0.0	0.0	0.0	0.0	0.0	0.0	0.0	0.0	0.0	0.0	0.0
9.5	0.0	0.0	0.0	0.0	0.0	0.0	0.0	0.0	0.0	0.0	0.0	0.0	0.0	0.0	0.0	0.0	0.0	0.0	0.0	0.0	0.0	0.0	0.0	0.0	0.0	0.0	0.0	0.0	0.0	0.0	0.0	0.0	0.0	0.0	0.0	0.0	0.0	0.0	0.0
9	0.0	0.0	0.0	0.0	0.0	0.0	0.0	0.0	0.0	0.0	0.0	0.0	0.0	0.0	0.0	0.0	0.0	0.0	0.0	0.0	0.0	0.0	0.0	0.0	0.0	0.0	0.0	0.0	0.0	0.0	0.0	0.0	0.0	0.0	0.0	0.0	0.0	0.0	0.0

LISTED CALL OPTION PRICE WHEN EXERCISE PRICE IS 20

NUMBER OF WEEKS BEFORE THE OPTION EXPIRES

Common Stock Price	1	2	3	4	5	6	7	8	9	10	11	12	13	14	15	16	17	18	19	20	21	22	23	24	25	26	27	28	29	30	31	32	33	34	35	36	37	38	39
28	8.0	8.0	8.0	8.1	8.1	8.1	8.1	8.1	8.1	8.1	8.1	8.2	8.2	8.2	8.2	8.2	8.2	8.2	8.2	8.3	8.3	8.3	8.3	8.3	8.3	8.3	8.4	8.4	8.4	8.4	8.4	8.4	8.4	8.4	8.5	8.5	8.5	8.5	8.5
27	7.0	7.0	7.1	7.1	7.1	7.1	7.1	7.1	7.2	7.2	7.2	7.2	7.2	7.3	7.3	7.3	7.3	7.3	7.3	7.4	7.4	7.4	7.4	7.4	7.5	7.5	7.5	7.5	7.5	7.5	7.6	7.6	7.6	7.6	7.6	7.7	7.7	7.7	7.7
26	6.0	6.0	6.1	6.1	6.1	6.1	6.1	6.2	6.2	6.2	6.2	6.3	6.3	6.3	6.4	6.4	6.4	6.4	6.4	6.5	6.5	6.5	6.5	6.6	6.6	6.6	6.6	6.7	6.7	6.7	6.7	6.7	6.8	6.8	6.8	6.8	6.9	6.9	6.9
25	5.0	5.1	5.1	5.1	5.1	5.2	5.2	5.2	5.3	5.3	5.3	5.3	5.4	5.4	5.4	5.5	5.5	5.5	5.5	5.6	5.6	5.6	5.7	5.7	5.7	5.7	5.8	5.8	5.8	5.9	5.9	5.9	5.9	6.0	6.0	6.0	6.1	6.1	6.1
24	4.0	4.1	4.1	4.1	4.2	4.2	4.2	4.3	4.3	4.3	4.4	4.4	4.4	4.5	4.5	4.5	4.6	4.6	4.6	4.7	4.7	4.7	4.8	4.8	4.8	4.9	4.9	4.9	5.0	5.0	5.0	5.1	5.1	5.1	5.2	5.2	5.2	5.3	5.3
23	3.0	3.1	3.1	3.2	3.2	3.2	3.3	3.3	3.3	3.4	3.4	3.5	3.5	3.5	3.6	3.6	3.7	3.7	3.7	3.8	3.8	3.9	3.9	3.9	4.0	4.0	4.0	4.1	4.1	4.2	4.2	4.2	4.3	4.3	4.4	4.4	4.4	4.5	4.5
22	2.1	2.1	2.2	2.2	2.3	2.3	2.4	2.5	2.5	2.6	2.7	2.7	2.7	2.8	2.9	2.9	3.0	3.0	3.0	3.0	3.1	3.1	3.1	3.1	3.2	3.2	3.3	3.3	3.3	3.4	3.4	3.4	3.5	3.5	3.6	3.6	3.6	3.7	3.7
21	1.1	1.2	1.2	1.3	1.4	1.5	1.6	1.7	1.8	1.8	1.9	1.9	1.9	2.0	2.0	2.1	2.2	2.2	2.2	2.3	2.3	2.3	2.4	2.4	2.5	2.5	2.5	2.5	2.6	2.6	2.7	2.7	2.8	2.8	2.8	2.8	2.9	2.9	2.9
20	0.4	0.5	0.6	0.7	0.8	0.9	1.0	1.0	1.1	1.1	1.2	1.2	1.3	1.3	1.4	1.4	1.5	1.5	1.6	1.6	1.6	1.7	1.7	1.7	1.8	1.8	1.8	1.9	1.9	1.9	2.0	2.0	2.0	2.1	2.1	2.1	2.2	2.2	2.2
19	0.0	0.1	0.2	0.3	0.4	0.5	0.6	0.6	0.7	0.7	0.8	0.8	0.9	0.9	1.0	1.0	1.1	1.1	1.2	1.2	1.2	1.3	1.3	1.3	1.4	1.4	1.4	1.5	1.5	1.5	1.6	1.6	1.6	1.7	1.7	1.7	1.8	1.8	1.8
18	0.0	0.0	0.0	0.0	0.0	0.1	0.2	0.2	0.3	0.3	0.4	0.4	0.5	0.5	0.6	0.6	0.7	0.7	0.8	0.8	0.8	0.9	0.9	0.9	1.0	1.0	1.0	1.1	1.1	1.1	1.2	1.2	1.2	1.3	1.3	1.3	1.4	1.4	1.4
17	0.0	0.0	0.0	0.0	0.0	0.0	0.0	0.0	0.0	0.0	0.0	0.0	0.1	0.1	0.2	0.2	0.3	0.3	0.4	0.4	0.4	0.5	0.5	0.5	0.6	0.6	0.6	0.7	0.7	0.7	0.8	0.8	0.8	0.9	0.9	0.9	1.0	1.0	1.0
16	0.0	0.0	0.0	0.0	0.0	0.0	0.0	0.0	0.0	0.0	0.0	0.0	0.0	0.0	0.0	0.0	0.0	0.0	0.0	0.0	0.0	0.1	0.1	0.1	0.2	0.2	0.2	0.3	0.3	0.3	0.4	0.4	0.4	0.5	0.5	0.5	0.6	0.6	0.6
15	0.0	0.0	0.0	0.0	0.0	0.0	0.0	0.0	0.0	0.0	0.0	0.0	0.0	0.0	0.0	0.0	0.0	0.0	0.0	0.0	0.0	0.0	0.0	0.0	0.0	0.0	0.0	0.0	0.0	0.0	0.1	0.1	0.1	0.1	0.1	0.1	0.2	0.2	0.2
14.5	0.0	0.0	0.0	0.0	0.0	0.0	0.0	0.0	0.0	0.0	0.0	0.0	0.0	0.0	0.0	0.0	0.0	0.0	0.0	0.0	0.0	0.0	0.0	0.0	0.0	0.0	0.0	0.0	0.0	0.0	0.0	0.0	0.0	0.0	0.0	0.0	0.0	0.0	0.0
14	0.0	0.0	0.0	0.0	0.0	0.0	0.0	0.0	0.0	0.0	0.0	0.0	0.0	0.0	0.0	0.0	0.0	0.0	0.0	0.0	0.0	0.0	0.0	0.0	0.0	0.0	0.0	0.0	0.0	0.0	0.0	0.0	0.0	0.0	0.0	0.0	0.0	0.0	0.0
13.5	0.0	0.0	0.0	0.0	0.0	0.0	0.0	0.0	0.0	0.0	0.0	0.0	0.0	0.0	0.0	0.0	0.0	0.0	0.0	0.0	0.0	0.0	0.0	0.0	0.0	0.0	0.0	0.0	0.0	0.0	0.0	0.0	0.0	0.0	0.0	0.0	0.0	0.0	0.0
13	0.0	0.0	0.0	0.0	0.0	0.0	0.0	0.0	0.0	0.0	0.0	0.0	0.0	0.0	0.0	0.0	0.0	0.0	0.0	0.0	0.0	0.0	0.0	0.0	0.0	0.0	0.0	0.0	0.0	0.0	0.0	0.0	0.0	0.0	0.0	0.0	0.0	0.0	0.0
12.5	0.0	0.0	0.0	0.0	0.0	0.0	0.0	0.0	0.0	0.0	0.0	0.0	0.0	0.0	0.0	0.0	0.0	0.0	0.0	0.0	0.0	0.0	0.0	0.0	0.0	0.0	0.0	0.0	0.0	0.0	0.0	0.0	0.0	0.0	0.0	0.0	0.0	0.0	0.0
12	0.0	0.0	0.0	0.0	0.0	0.0	0.0	0.0	0.0	0.0	0.0	0.0	0.0	0.0	0.0	0.0	0.0	0.0	0.0	0.0	0.0	0.0	0.0	0.0	0.0	0.0	0.0	0.0	0.0	0.0	0.0	0.0	0.0	0.0	0.0	0.0	0.0	0.0	0.0

LISTED CALL OPTION PRICE WHEN EXERCISE PRICE IS 25

NUMBER OF WEEKS BEFORE THE OPTION EXPIRES

Common Stock Price	1	2	3	4	5	6	7	8	9	10	11	12	13	14	15	16	17	18	19	20	21	22	23	24	25	26	27	28	29	30	31	32	33	34	35	36	37	38	39
35	10.0	10.0	10.0	10.1	10.1	10.1	10.1	10.1	10.1	10.2	10.2	10.2	10.2	10.2	10.2	10.3	10.3	10.3	10.3	10.3	10.3	10.4	10.4	10.4	10.4	10.4	10.4	10.5	10.5	10.5	10.5	10.5	10.5	10.6	10.6	10.6	10.6	10.6	10.6
34	9.0	9.0	9.1	9.1	9.1	9.1	9.2	9.2	9.2	9.2	9.2	9.3	9.3	9.3	9.3	9.3	9.4	9.4	9.4	9.4	9.5	9.5	9.5	9.5	9.5	9.6	9.6	9.6	9.6	9.6	9.7	9.7	9.7	9.7	9.8	9.8	9.8	9.8	9.8
33	8.0	8.1	8.1	8.1	8.1	8.2	8.2	8.2	8.2	8.3	8.3	8.3	8.3	8.4	8.4	8.4	8.5	8.5	8.5	8.5	8.6	8.6	8.6	8.6	8.7	8.7	8.7	8.7	8.8	8.8	8.8	8.9	8.9	8.9	8.9	9.0	9.0	9.0	9.0
32	7.0	7.1	7.1	7.1	7.2	7.2	7.2	7.3	7.3	7.3	7.3	7.4	7.4	7.4	7.5	7.5	7.5	7.6	7.6	7.6	7.7	7.7	7.7	7.8	7.8	7.8	7.9	7.9	7.9	8.0	8.0	8.0	8.0	8.1	8.1	8.1	8.2	8.2	8.2
31	6.0	6.1	6.1	6.1	6.2	6.2	6.3	6.3	6.4	6.4	6.4	6.4	6.5	6.5	6.6	6.6	6.6	6.7	6.7	6.7	6.8	6.8	6.8	6.9	6.9	7.0	7.0	7.0	7.1	7.1	7.1	7.2	7.2	7.3	7.3	7.3	7.4	7.4	7.4
30	5.0	5.1	5.1	5.2	5.2	5.3	5.3	5.3	5.4	5.4	5.5	5.5	5.5	5.6	5.6	5.7	5.7	5.8	5.8	5.8	5.9	5.9	6.0	6.0	6.0	6.1	6.1	6.2	6.2	6.3	6.3	6.3	6.4	6.4	6.5	6.5	6.6	6.6	6.6
29	4.0	4.1	4.1	4.2	4.2	4.3	4.3	4.4	4.4	4.4	4.5	4.5	4.6	4.6	4.7	4.8	4.8	4.8	4.9	4.9	5.0	5.0	5.1	5.1	5.2	5.2	5.3	5.3	5.4	5.4	5.5	5.5	5.6	5.6	5.6	5.7	5.7	5.8	5.8
28	3.1	3.1	3.2	3.2	3.3	3.3	3.4	3.4	3.5	3.5	3.6	3.6	3.7	3.7	3.8	3.8	3.9	3.9	4.0	4.0	4.1	4.1	4.2	4.3	4.3	4.4	4.4	4.5	4.5	4.6	4.6	4.7	4.7	4.8	4.8	4.9	4.9	5.0	5.0
27	2.2	2.3	2.4	2.4	2.5	2.6	2.6	2.7	2.7	2.8	2.9	2.9	3.0	3.0	3.1	3.1	3.2	3.2	3.3	3.3	3.4	3.4	3.5	3.5	3.6	3.6	3.6	3.7	3.7	3.8	3.8	3.9	3.9	4.0	4.1	4.1	4.1	4.2	4.2
26	1.3	1.4	1.6	1.7	1.8	1.9	1.9	1.9	2.0	2.0	2.1	2.1	2.2	2.3	2.4	2.5	2.5	2.5	2.6	2.6	2.7	2.7	2.7	2.8	2.8	2.9	2.9	3.0	3.0	3.0	3.1	3.1	3.2	3.2	3.3	3.3	3.3	3.3	3.4
25	0.4	0.6	0.8	0.9	1.0	1.1	1.2	1.3	1.4	1.4	1.5	1.5	1.6	1.7	1.7	1.8	1.8	1.9	1.9	2.0	2.0	2.1	2.1	2.2	2.2	2.3	2.3	2.4	2.4	2.4	2.5	2.5	2.6	2.6	2.6	2.7	2.7	2.7	2.8
24	0.0	0.2	0.4	0.5	0.6	0.7	0.8	0.9	1.0	1.0	1.1	1.1	1.2	1.3	1.3	1.4	1.4	1.5	1.5	1.6	1.6	1.7	1.7	1.8	1.8	1.9	1.9	2.0	2.0	2.0	2.1	2.1	2.2	2.2	2.3	2.3	2.3	2.3	2.4
23	0.0	0.0	0.0	0.1	0.2	0.3	0.4	0.5	0.5	0.6	0.7	0.7	0.8	0.9	0.9	1.0	1.0	1.1	1.1	1.2	1.2	1.3	1.3	1.4	1.4	1.5	1.5	1.6	1.6	1.6	1.7	1.7	1.8	1.8	1.9	1.9	1.9	1.9	2.0
22	0.0	0.0	0.0	0.0	0.0	0.0	0.1	0.2	0.2	0.3	0.3	0.4	0.4	0.5	0.5	0.6	0.6	0.7	0.7	0.8	0.9	0.9	1.0	1.0	1.0	1.1	1.1	1.2	1.2	1.2	1.3	1.3	1.4	1.4	1.4	1.5	1.5	1.5	1.6
21	0.0	0.0	0.0	0.0	0.0	0.0	0.0	0.0	0.1	0.1	0.2	0.2	0.3	0.3	0.4	0.4	0.5	0.5	0.6	0.6	0.6	0.7	0.7	0.8	0.8	0.8	0.9	0.9	0.9	1.0	1.0	1.0	1.1	1.1	1.1	1.1	1.2	1.2	1.2
20	0.0	0.0	0.0	0.0	0.0	0.0	0.0	0.0	0.0	0.0	0.0	0.0	0.0	0.1	0.1	0.1	0.2	0.2	0.2	0.3	0.3	0.3	0.4	0.4	0.4	0.4	0.5	0.5	0.5	0.5	0.6	0.6	0.6	0.6	0.7	0.7	0.7	0.7	0.8
19	0.0	0.0	0.0	0.0	0.0	0.0	0.0	0.0	0.0	0.0	0.0	0.0	0.0	0.0	0.0	0.0	0.0	0.0	0.1	0.1	0.1	0.1	0.2	0.2	0.2	0.2	0.2	0.3	0.3	0.3	0.3	0.3	0.3	0.4	0.4	0.4	0.4	0.4	0.4
18	0.0	0.0	0.0	0.0	0.0	0.0	0.0	0.0	0.0	0.0	0.0	0.0	0.0	0.0	0.0	0.0	0.0	0.0	0.0	0.0	0.0	0.0	0.0	0.0	0.0	0.0	0.0	0.0	0.0	0.0	0.0	0.0	0.0	0.0	0.0	0.0	0.0	0.0	0.0
17	0.0	0.0	0.0	0.0	0.0	0.0	0.0	0.0	0.0	0.0	0.0	0.0	0.0	0.0	0.0	0.0	0.0	0.0	0.0	0.0	0.0	0.0	0.0	0.0	0.0	0.0	0.0	0.0	0.0	0.0	0.0	0.0	0.0	0.0	0.0	0.0	0.0	0.0	0.0
16	0.0	0.0	0.0	0.0	0.0	0.0	0.0	0.0	0.0	0.0	0.0	0.0	0.0	0.0	0.0	0.0	0.0	0.0	0.0	0.0	0.0	0.0	0.0	0.0	0.0	0.0	0.0	0.0	0.0	0.0	0.0	0.0	0.0	0.0	0.0	0.0	0.0	0.0	0.0
15	0.0	0.0	0.0	0.0	0.0	0.0	0.0	0.0	0.0	0.0	0.0	0.0	0.0	0.0	0.0	0.0	0.0	0.0	0.0	0.0	0.0	0.0	0.0	0.0	0.0	0.0	0.0	0.0	0.0	0.0	0.0	0.0	0.0	0.0	0.0	0.0	0.0	0.0	0.0

LISTED CALL OPTION PRICE WHEN EXERCISE PRICE IS 30

NUMBER OF WEEKS BEFORE THE OPTION EXPIRES

Common Stock Price	1	2	3	4	5	6	7	8	9	10	11	12	13	14	15	16	17	18	19	20	21	22	23	24	25	26	27	28	29	30	31	32	33	34	35	36	37	38	39
42	12.0	12.0	12.1	12.1	12.1	12.1	12.1	12.2	12.2	12.2	12.2	12.2	12.3	12.3	12.3	12.3	12.3	12.4	12.4	12.4	12.4	12.4	12.5	12.5	12.5	12.5	12.5	12.5	12.6	12.6	12.6	12.6	12.6	12.7	12.7	12.7	12.7	12.7	12.8
41	11.0	11.0	11.1	11.1	11.1	11.1	11.2	11.2	11.2	11.2	11.3	11.3	11.3	11.3	11.4	11.4	11.4	11.4	11.5	11.5	11.5	11.5	11.6	11.6	11.6	11.6	11.7	11.7	11.7	11.7	11.8	11.8	11.8	11.8	11.9	11.9	11.9	11.9	12.0
40	10.0	10.1	10.1	10.1	10.1	10.2	10.2	10.2	10.3	10.3	10.3	10.4	10.4	10.4	10.4	10.5	10.5	10.5	10.6	10.6	10.6	10.7	10.7	10.7	10.7	10.8	10.8	10.8	10.9	10.9	10.9	11.0	11.0	11.0	11.0	11.1	11.1	11.1	11.2
39	9.0	9.1	9.1	9.1	9.2	9.2	9.2	9.3	9.3	9.3	9.4	9.4	9.5	9.5	9.5	9.6	9.6	9.6	9.7	9.7	9.7	9.8	9.8	9.8	9.8	9.9	9.9	9.9	9.9	10.0	10.0	10.1	10.1	10.2	10.2	10.3	10.3	10.3	10.4
38	8.0	8.1	8.1	8.2	8.2	8.2	8.3	8.3	8.4	8.4	8.4	8.5	8.5	8.6	8.6	8.6	8.7	8.7	8.8	8.8	8.8	8.9	8.9	9.0	9.0	9.0	9.1	9.1	9.2	9.2	9.3	9.3	9.3	9.4	9.4	9.5	9.5	9.5	9.6
37	7.0	7.1	7.1	7.2	7.2	7.3	7.3	7.4	7.4	7.5	7.5	7.5	7.6	7.6	7.7	7.7	7.8	7.8	7.9	7.9	8.0	8.0	8.0	8.1	8.1	8.2	8.2	8.3	8.3	8.4	8.4	8.4	8.5	8.5	8.6	8.6	8.7	8.7	8.8
36	6.1	6.1	6.2	6.2	6.3	6.3	6.4	6.4	6.5	6.5	6.6	6.6	6.7	6.7	6.8	6.8	6.9	6.9	7.0	7.0	7.1	7.1	7.2	7.2	7.3	7.3	7.4	7.4	7.5	7.5	7.6	7.6	7.7	7.7	7.8	7.8	7.9	7.9	8.0
35	5.1	5.1	5.2	5.2	5.3	5.3	5.4	5.4	5.5	5.5	5.6	5.6	5.7	5.7	5.8	5.9	5.9	6.0	6.0	6.1	6.2	6.2	6.3	6.3	6.4	6.4	6.5	6.6	6.6	6.7	6.7	6.8	6.8	6.9	6.9	7.0	7.1	7.1	7.2
34	4.1	4.1	4.2	4.2	4.3	4.4	4.4	4.5	4.5	4.6	4.6	4.7	4.8	4.8	4.9	5.0	5.0	5.1	5.2	5.2	5.3	5.3	5.4	5.5	5.5	5.6	5.6	5.7	5.8	5.8	5.9	5.9	6.0	6.1	6.1	6.2	6.2	6.3	6.4
33	3.2	3.2	3.2	3.3	3.4	3.5	3.6	3.6	3.7	3.8	3.8	3.9	4.0	4.0	4.1	4.2	4.2	4.3	4.4	4.4	4.5	4.5	4.6	4.6	4.7	4.8	4.8	4.9	4.9	5.0	5.0	5.1	5.2	5.3	5.3	5.4	5.4	5.5	5.6
32	2.2	2.3	2.4	2.5	2.6	2.7	2.8	2.9	2.9	3.0	3.1	3.1	3.2	3.3	3.4	3.4	3.5	3.6	3.6	3.7	3.7	3.8	3.9	3.9	4.0	4.0	4.1	4.1	4.2	4.2	4.3	4.3	4.4	4.4	4.5	4.5	4.6	4.7	4.8
31	1.3	1.5	1.6	1.8	1.9	2.0	2.1	2.2	2.2	2.3	2.3	2.4	2.5	2.6	2.6	2.7	2.8	2.9	2.9	3.0	3.0	3.1	3.2	3.3	3.3	3.3	3.4	3.4	3.5	3.5	3.6	3.6	3.7	3.8	3.8	3.9	3.9	4.0	4.0
30	0.5	0.8	0.9	1.1	1.2	1.3	1.4	1.5	1.6	1.7	1.8	1.8	1.9	2.0	2.1	2.1	2.2	2.3	2.4	2.4	2.4	2.5	2.6	2.6	2.7	2.7	2.8	2.9	2.9	2.9	3.0	3.0	3.1	3.1	3.2	3.2	3.3	3.3	3.3
29	0.1	0.4	0.5	0.7	0.8	1.0	1.1	1.2	1.2	1.3	1.4	1.4	1.5	1.6	1.7	1.7	1.8	1.9	1.9	2.0	2.0	2.1	2.2	2.2	2.3	2.3	2.4	2.4	2.5	2.5	2.6	2.6	2.7	2.7	2.8	2.8	2.8	2.9	2.9
28	0.0	0.0	0.1	0.3	0.4	0.5	0.7	0.8	0.9	1.0	1.0	1.0	1.1	1.2	1.3	1.3	1.4	1.5	1.5	1.6	1.6	1.7	1.8	1.8	1.9	1.9	2.0	2.0	2.1	2.1	2.2	2.2	2.3	2.3	2.4	2.4	2.4	2.5	2.5
27	0.0	0.0	0.0	0.1	0.2	0.2	0.3	0.3	0.4	0.5	0.6	0.6	0.7	0.8	0.8	0.9	1.0	1.1	1.1	1.2	1.3	1.3	1.4	1.4	1.5	1.5	1.6	1.6	1.7	1.7	1.8	1.8	1.9	1.9	2.0	2.0	2.0	2.1	2.1
26	0.0	0.0	0.0	0.0	0.0	0.1	0.1	0.2	0.2	0.3	0.4	0.4	0.5	0.6	0.6	0.7	0.8	0.9	0.9	1.0	1.0	1.1	1.2	1.2	1.3	1.3	1.4	1.4	1.5	1.5	1.6	1.6	1.7	1.7	1.8	1.8	1.9	1.9	2.0
25	0.0	0.0	0.0	0.0	0.0	0.0	0.0	0.0	0.0	0.1	0.2	0.2	0.3	0.4	0.5	0.5	0.6	0.7	0.7	0.8	0.8	0.9	1.0	1.0	1.1	1.1	1.2	1.2	1.3	1.3	1.4	1.4	1.5	1.5	1.6	1.6	1.6	1.7	1.7
24	0.0	0.0	0.0	0.0	0.0	0.0	0.0	0.0	0.0	0.0	0.0	0.0	0.1	0.2	0.2	0.3	0.3	0.4	0.5	0.5	0.6	0.6	0.7	0.8	0.8	0.9	0.9	1.0	1.1	1.1	1.2	1.2	1.3	1.3	1.4	1.4	1.5	1.5	1.6
23	0.0	0.0	0.0	0.0	0.0	0.0	0.0	0.0	0.0	0.0	0.0	0.0	0.0	0.0	0.0	0.0	0.0	0.0	0.0	0.1	0.2	0.2	0.3	0.3	0.4	0.4	0.5	0.5	0.6	0.6	0.7	0.7	0.7	0.8	0.8	0.8	0.9	0.9	0.9
22	0.0	0.0	0.0	0.0	0.0	0.0	0.0	0.0	0.0	0.0	0.0	0.0	0.0	0.0	0.0	0.0	0.0	0.0	0.0	0.0	0.0	0.0	0.0	0.0	0.0	0.0	0.0	0.0	0.1	0.1	0.2	0.2	0.3	0.3	0.4	0.4	0.4	0.5	0.5
21	0.0	0.0	0.0	0.0	0.0	0.0	0.0	0.0	0.0	0.0	0.0	0.0	0.0	0.0	0.0	0.0	0.0	0.0	0.0	0.0	0.0	0.0	0.0	0.0	0.0	0.0	0.0	0.0	0.0	0.0	0.0	0.0	0.0	0.0	0.0	0.0	0.0	0.1	0.1
20	0.0	0.0	0.0	0.0	0.0	0.0	0.0	0.0	0.0	0.0	0.0	0.0	0.0	0.0	0.0	0.0	0.0	0.0	0.0	0.0	0.0	0.0	0.0	0.0	0.0	0.0	0.0	0.0	0.0	0.0	0.0	0.0	0.0	0.0	0.0	0.0	0.0	0.0	0.0
19	0.0	0.0	0.0	0.0	0.0	0.0	0.0	0.0	0.0	0.0	0.0	0.0	0.0	0.0	0.0	0.0	0.0	0.0	0.0	0.0	0.0	0.0	0.0	0.0	0.0	0.0	0.0	0.0	0.0	0.0	0.0	0.0	0.0	0.0	0.0	0.0	0.0	0.0	0.0
18	0.0	0.0	0.0	0.0	0.0	0.0	0.0	0.0	0.0	0.0	0.0	0.0	0.0	0.0	0.0	0.0	0.0	0.0	0.0	0.0	0.0	0.0	0.0	0.0	0.0	0.0	0.0	0.0	0.0	0.0	0.0	0.0	0.0	0.0	0.0	0.0	0.0	0.0	0.0

LISTED CALL OPTION PRICE WHEN EXERCISE PRICE IS 35

NUMBER OF WEEKS BEFORE THE OPTION EXPIRES

Common Stock Price	1	2	3	4	5	6	7	8	9	10	11	12	13	14	15	16	17	18	19	20	21	22	23	24	25	26	27	28	29	30	31	32	33	34	35	36	37	38	39
49	14.0	14.0	14.1	14.1	14.1	14.1	14.2	14.2	14.2	14.2	14.3	14.3	14.3	14.3	14.3	14.4	14.4	14.4	14.4	14.5	14.5	14.5	14.5	14.5	14.6	14.6	14.6	14.6	14.7	14.7	14.7	14.7	14.8	14.8	14.8	14.8	14.8	14.9	14.9
48	13.0	13.1	13.1	13.1	13.1	13.2	13.2	13.2	13.3	13.3	13.3	13.3	13.4	13.4	13.4	13.4	13.5	13.5	13.5	13.6	13.6	13.6	13.6	13.7	13.7	13.7	13.8	13.8	13.8	13.8	13.9	13.9	13.9	14.0	14.0	14.0	14.0	14.1	14.1
47	12.0	12.1	12.1	12.1	12.1	12.2	12.2	12.3	12.3	12.3	12.4	12.4	12.4	12.5	12.5	12.5	12.5	12.6	12.6	12.7	12.7	12.7	12.7	12.8	12.8	12.9	12.9	12.9	13.0	13.0	13.0	13.1	13.1	13.1	13.2	13.2	13.2	13.3	13.3
46	11.0	11.1	11.1	11.2	11.2	11.2	11.3	11.3	11.3	11.4	11.4	11.5	11.5	11.5	11.6	11.6	11.7	11.7	11.7	11.8	11.8	11.8	11.9	11.9	12.0	12.0	12.0	12.1	12.1	12.1	12.2	12.2	12.3	12.3	12.3	12.4	12.4	12.5	12.5
45	10.0	10.1	10.1	10.2	10.2	10.3	10.3	10.3	10.4	10.4	10.5	10.5	10.6	10.6	10.7	10.7	10.7	10.8	10.8	10.9	10.9	11.0	11.0	11.0	11.1	11.1	11.2	11.2	11.2	11.3	11.3	11.4	11.4	11.5	11.5	11.6	11.6	11.6	11.7
44	9.0	9.1	9.1	9.2	9.2	9.3	9.3	9.4	9.4	9.4	9.5	9.6	9.6	9.7	9.7	9.8	9.8	9.9	9.9	9.9	10.0	10.1	10.1	10.2	10.2	10.3	10.3	10.4	10.4	10.5	10.5	10.6	10.6	10.6	10.7	10.7	10.8	10.8	10.9
43	8.1	8.1	8.2	8.2	8.3	8.3	8.4	8.4	8.5	8.5	8.6	8.6	8.7	8.7	8.8	8.9	8.9	9.0	9.0	9.1	9.1	9.2	9.2	9.3	9.3	9.4	9.4	9.5	9.5	9.6	9.6	9.7	9.7	9.8	9.8	9.9	9.9	10.0	10.1
42	7.1	7.1	7.2	7.2	7.3	7.3	7.4	7.5	7.5	7.6	7.6	7.7	7.8	7.8	7.9	7.9	8.0	8.0	8.1	8.2	8.2	8.3	8.3	8.4	8.4	8.5	8.5	8.6	8.7	8.7	8.8	8.8	8.9	8.9	9.0	9.1	9.1	9.2	9.3
41	6.1	6.1	6.2	6.3	6.3	6.4	6.4	6.5	6.6	6.6	6.7	6.8	6.8	6.9	7.0	7.0	7.1	7.2	7.2	7.3	7.3	7.4	7.5	7.5	7.6	7.7	7.7	7.8	7.9	7.9	8.0	8.0	8.1	8.2	8.2	8.3	8.4	8.4	8.5
40	5.1	5.2	5.2	5.3	5.3	5.4	5.5	5.5	5.6	5.7	5.7	5.8	5.9	6.0	6.0	6.1	6.2	6.2	6.3	6.4	6.4	6.5	6.6	6.6	6.7	6.8	6.9	6.9	7.0	7.1	7.1	7.2	7.3	7.3	7.4	7.5	7.6	7.6	7.7
39	4.1	4.1	4.2	4.3	4.3	4.4	4.5	4.5	4.6	4.7	4.7	4.8	4.9	5.0	5.0	5.1	5.2	5.3	5.3	5.4	5.5	5.6	5.6	5.7	5.8	5.9	5.9	6.0	6.1	6.2	6.2	6.3	6.4	6.5	6.6	6.6	6.7	6.8	6.9
38	3.2	3.2	3.3	3.4	3.4	3.5	3.6	3.7	3.8	3.9	3.9	4.0	4.1	4.2	4.3	4.4	4.4	4.5	4.6	4.7	4.8	4.8	4.9	5.0	5.1	5.1	5.2	5.3	5.4	5.4	5.5	5.6	5.6	5.7	5.8	5.9	5.9	6.0	6.1
37	2.2	2.3	2.4	2.5	2.5	2.6	2.7	2.8	2.9	3.0	3.1	3.2	3.3	3.4	3.5	3.6	3.7	3.7	3.8	3.9	4.0	4.1	4.1	4.2	4.3	4.4	4.4	4.5	4.6	4.6	4.7	4.8	4.8	4.9	5.0	5.0	5.1	5.2	5.3
36	1.4	1.6	1.8	1.9	2.0	2.1	2.2	2.4	2.5	2.6	2.7	2.8	2.8	2.9	3.0	3.1	3.2	3.2	3.3	3.4	3.5	3.6	3.6	3.7	3.7	3.8	3.9	3.9	4.0	4.1	4.1	4.2	4.2	4.3	4.4	4.4	4.5	4.5	4.6
35	0.6	0.9	1.1	1.2	1.4	1.5	1.6	1.8	1.9	2.0	2.1	2.2	2.3	2.4	2.5	2.6	2.6	2.7	2.8	2.9	2.9	3.0	3.0	3.1	3.2	3.2	3.3	3.3	3.4	3.5	3.5	3.6	3.6	3.7	3.7	3.8	3.8	3.9	3.9
34	0.2	0.5	0.7	0.8	1.0	1.1	1.2	1.4	1.5	1.6	1.7	1.8	1.8	1.9	2.0	2.1	2.2	2.2	2.3	2.4	2.5	2.5	2.6	2.6	2.7	2.7	2.8	2.9	2.9	3.0	3.0	3.1	3.1	3.2	3.3	3.3	3.4	3.4	3.5
33	0.0	0.1	0.3	0.4	0.6	0.7	0.8	1.0	1.1	1.2	1.3	1.4	1.4	1.5	1.6	1.7	1.8	1.8	1.9	2.0	2.0	2.1	2.2	2.2	2.3	2.3	2.4	2.4	2.5	2.6	2.6	2.7	2.7	2.8	2.9	2.9	3.0	3.0	3.1
32	0.0	0.0	0.1	0.2	0.3	0.4	0.5	0.6	0.7	0.8	0.9	1.0	1.0	1.1	1.2	1.3	1.4	1.4	1.5	1.6	1.7	1.7	1.8	1.8	1.9	2.0	2.0	2.1	2.2	2.2	2.3	2.3	2.4	2.4	2.5	2.5	2.6	2.6	2.7
31	0.0	0.0	0.0	0.1	0.2	0.3	0.3	0.4	0.5	0.6	0.7	0.7	0.8	0.9	1.0	1.0	1.1	1.2	1.2	1.3	1.3	1.4	1.5	1.5	1.6	1.6	1.7	1.7	1.8	1.9	1.9	2.0	2.0	2.1	2.1	2.2	2.2	2.3	2.3
30	0.0	0.0	0.0	0.0	0.1	0.1	0.2	0.3	0.4	0.4	0.5	0.6	0.6	0.7	0.8	0.8	0.9	1.0	1.0	1.1	1.1	1.2	1.2	1.3	1.3	1.4	1.4	1.5	1.5	1.6	1.6	1.7	1.7	1.7	1.8	1.8	1.9	1.9	1.9
29	0.0	0.0	0.0	0.0	0.0	0.1	0.1	0.2	0.2	0.3	0.4	0.4	0.5	0.5	0.6	0.7	0.7	0.8	0.8	0.9	0.9	1.0	1.0	1.1	1.1	1.1	1.2	1.2	1.3	1.3	1.3	1.4	1.4	1.4	1.4	1.5	1.5	1.5	1.5
28	0.0	0.0	0.0	0.0	0.0	0.0	0.1	0.1	0.2	0.2	0.3	0.3	0.4	0.4	0.5	0.5	0.6	0.6	0.6	0.7	0.7	0.8	0.8	0.8	0.9	0.9	0.9	1.0	1.0	1.0	1.0	1.1	1.1	1.1	1.1	1.1	1.1	1.1	1.1
27	0.0	0.0	0.0	0.0	0.0	0.0	0.0	0.0	0.1	0.1	0.2	0.2	0.3	0.3	0.4	0.4	0.4	0.5	0.5	0.5	0.6	0.6	0.6	0.6	0.7	0.7	0.7	0.7	0.7	0.7	0.7	0.7	0.7	0.7	0.7	0.7	0.7	0.7	0.7
26	0.0	0.0	0.0	0.0	0.0	0.0	0.0	0.0	0.0	0.0	0.0	0.1	0.1	0.1	0.1	0.2	0.2	0.2	0.2	0.2	0.3	0.3	0.3	0.3	0.3	0.3	0.3	0.3	0.3	0.3	0.3	0.3	0.3	0.3	0.3	0.3	0.3	0.3	0.3
25	0.0	0.0	0.0	0.0	0.0	0.0	0.0	0.0	0.0	0.0	0.0	0.0	0.0	0.0	0.0	0.0	0.0	0.0	0.0	0.0	0.0	0.0	0.0	0.0	0.0	0.0	0.0	0.0	0.0	0.0	0.0	0.0	0.0	0.0	0.0	0.0	0.0	0.0	0.0
24	0.0	0.0	0.0	0.0	0.0	0.0	0.0	0.0	0.0	0.0	0.0	0.0	0.0	0.0	0.0	0.0	0.0	0.0	0.0	0.0	0.0	0.0	0.0	0.0	0.0	0.0	0.0	0.0	0.0	0.0	0.0	0.0	0.0	0.0	0.0	0.0	0.0	0.0	0.0
23	0.0	0.0	0.0	0.0	0.0	0.0	0.0	0.0	0.0	0.0	0.0	0.0	0.0	0.0	0.0	0.0	0.0	0.0	0.0	0.0	0.0	0.0	0.0	0.0	0.0	0.0	0.0	0.0	0.0	0.0	0.0	0.0	0.0	0.0	0.0	0.0	0.0	0.0	0.0
22	0.0	0.0	0.0	0.0	0.0	0.0	0.0	0.0	0.0	0.0	0.0	0.0	0.0	0.0	0.0	0.0	0.0	0.0	0.0	0.0	0.0	0.0	0.0	0.0	0.0	0.0	0.0	0.0	0.0	0.0	0.0	0.0	0.0	0.0	0.0	0.0	0.0	0.0	0.0
21	0.0	0.0	0.0	0.0	0.0	0.0	0.0	0.0	0.0	0.0	0.0	0.0	0.0	0.0	0.0	0.0	0.0	0.0	0.0	0.0	0.0	0.0	0.0	0.0	0.0	0.0	0.0	0.0	0.0	0.0	0.0	0.0	0.0	0.0	0.0	0.0	0.0	0.0	0.0

LISTED CALL OPTION PRICE WHEN EXERCISE PRICE IS 40

NUMBER OF WEEKS BEFORE THE OPTION EXPIRES

Common Stock Price	2	3	4	5	6	7	8	9	10	11	12	13	14	15	16	17	18	19	20	21	22	23	24	25	26	27	28	29	30	31	32	33	34	35	36	37	38	39
56	16.0	16.1	16.1	16.1	16.2	16.2	16.2	16.2	16.3	16.3	16.3	16.3	16.4	16.4	16.4	16.4	16.5	16.5	16.5	16.5	16.6	16.6	16.6	16.7	16.7	16.7	16.7	16.8	16.8	16.8	16.8	16.9	16.9	16.9	16.9	17.0	17.0	17.0
55	15.0	15.1	15.1	15.1	15.2	15.2	15.2	15.3	15.3	15.3	15.3	15.4	15.4	15.4	15.5	15.5	15.5	15.6	15.6	15.6	15.7	15.7	15.7	15.8	15.8	15.8	15.9	15.9	15.9	16.0	16.0	16.0	16.1	16.1	16.1	16.1	16.2	16.2
54	14.0	14.1	14.1	14.1	14.2	14.2	14.3	14.3	14.4	14.4	14.4	14.5	14.5	14.5	14.6	14.6	14.6	14.7	14.7	14.7	14.8	14.8	14.9	14.9	14.9	15.0	15.0	15.1	15.1	15.1	15.2	15.2	15.2	15.3	15.3	15.3	15.4	15.4
53	13.0	13.1	13.1	13.2	13.2	13.3	13.3	13.4	13.4	13.5	13.5	13.5	13.6	13.6	13.7	13.7	13.7	13.8	13.8	13.8	13.9	13.9	14.0	14.0	14.1	14.1	14.1	14.2	14.2	14.3	14.3	14.4	14.4	14.5	14.5	14.5	14.6	14.6
52	12.0	12.1	12.1	12.2	12.2	12.3	12.4	12.4	12.5	12.5	12.6	12.6	12.7	12.7	12.7	12.8	12.8	12.9	12.9	13.0	13.0	13.0	13.1	13.2	13.2	13.3	13.3	13.4	13.4	13.5	13.5	13.6	13.6	13.6	13.7	13.7	13.8	13.8
51	11.1	11.1	11.2	11.2	11.3	11.3	11.4	11.4	11.5	11.5	11.6	11.6	11.7	11.7	11.8	11.8	11.9	11.9	12.0	12.0	12.1	12.1	12.2	12.2	12.3	12.3	12.4	12.5	12.5	12.6	12.6	12.7	12.7	12.8	12.8	12.9	12.9	13.0
50	10.1	10.1	10.2	10.2	10.3	10.4	10.4	10.5	10.5	10.6	10.6	10.7	10.7	10.8	10.9	10.9	11.0	11.0	11.1	11.1	11.2	11.3	11.3	11.4	11.5	11.5	11.6	11.7	11.7	11.8	11.8	11.9	11.9	12.0	12.0	12.1	12.2	12.2
49	9.1	9.1	9.2	9.2	9.3	9.4	9.4	9.5	9.6	9.6	9.7	9.8	9.8	9.9	9.9	10.0	10.1	10.1	10.2	10.2	10.3	10.4	10.4	10.5	10.6	10.6	10.7	10.8	10.8	10.9	11.0	11.0	11.1	11.2	11.2	11.3	11.4	11.4
48	8.1	8.1	8.2	8.3	8.3	8.4	8.5	8.5	8.6	8.7	8.7	8.8	8.9	8.9	9.0	9.1	9.1	9.2	9.3	9.3	9.4	9.5	9.6	9.6	9.7	9.8	9.9	9.9	10.0	10.1	10.1	10.2	10.3	10.4	10.4	10.5	10.6	10.6
47	7.1	7.1	7.2	7.3	7.4	7.4	7.5	7.6	7.6	7.7	7.8	7.9	7.9	8.0	8.1	8.2	8.3	8.3	8.4	8.5	8.6	8.7	8.7	8.8	8.9	9.0	9.0	9.1	9.2	9.2	9.3	9.4	9.5	9.5	9.6	9.7	9.7	9.8
46	6.1	6.2	6.2	6.3	6.3	6.5	6.5	6.6	6.7	6.8	6.9	6.9	7.0	7.1	7.2	7.3	7.3	7.4	7.5	7.6	7.7	7.7	7.8	7.8	7.9	8.0	8.1	8.2	8.3	8.4	8.4	8.5	8.6	8.7	8.8	8.9	8.9	9.0
45	5.1	5.2	5.2	5.3	5.4	5.4	5.5	5.7	5.7	5.8	5.8	5.9	6.0	6.1	6.2	6.2	6.3	6.4	6.4	6.5	6.6	6.7	6.7	6.8	6.9	7.0	7.1	7.2	7.3	7.4	7.5	7.6	7.6	7.7	7.8	7.9	8.0	8.2
44	4.1	4.2	4.3	4.3	4.4	4.6	4.7	4.8	4.9	5.0	5.0	5.1	5.2	5.3	5.3	5.4	5.5	5.5	5.6	5.6	5.7	5.7	5.8	5.9	5.9	6.0	6.0	6.2	6.2	6.2	6.3	6.3	6.4	6.4	6.5	6.5	6.7	7.4
43	3.2	3.3	3.5	3.6	3.7	3.8	4.0	4.1	4.2	4.3	4.4	4.5	4.6	4.8	4.9	5.0	5.0	5.1	5.2	5.3	5.3	5.5	5.5	5.6	5.7	5.8	5.8	5.9	6.0	6.2	6.2	6.2	6.3	6.3	6.4	6.5	6.7	6.8
42	2.3	2.5	2.7	2.9	3.1	3.2	3.4	3.5	3.6	3.7	3.9	4.0	4.2	4.3	4.4	4.5	4.5	4.6	4.7	4.7	4.9	4.9	5.1	5.1	5.2	5.2	5.3	5.4	5.5	5.5	5.6	5.7	5.7	5.8	5.8	5.9	6.0	6.1
41	1.5	1.7	1.9	2.1	2.3	2.4	2.6	2.7	2.9	3.0	3.2	3.3	3.5	3.6	3.7	3.8	3.8	3.9	4.0	4.1	4.1	4.3	4.3	4.4	4.5	4.6	4.6	4.6	4.7	4.7	4.7	4.8	4.8	4.9	5.0	5.1	5.2	5.2
40	0.7	1.0	1.2	1.4	1.6	1.9	2.0	2.1	2.3	2.4	2.5	2.6	2.7	2.8	2.9	3.0	3.0	3.1	3.2	3.2	3.3	3.4	3.5	3.6	3.6	3.7	3.8	3.8	3.9	4.0	4.0	4.1	4.1	4.2	4.3	4.3	4.4	4.4
39	0.3	0.6	0.8	1.0	1.2	1.3	1.5	1.6	1.7	1.9	2.0	2.1	2.2	2.3	2.4	2.5	2.6	2.7	2.7	2.9	2.9	3.0	3.0	3.1	3.2	3.2	3.3	3.4	3.5	3.6	3.6	3.7	3.7	3.8	3.9	3.9	4.0	4.0
38	0.0	0.2	0.4	0.6	0.8	0.9	1.1	1.2	1.3	1.5	1.6	1.7	1.8	1.9	2.0	2.1	2.2	2.2	2.3	2.4	2.5	2.6	2.7	2.7	2.8	2.8	2.9	3.0	3.0	3.1	3.2	3.2	3.3	3.3	3.4	3.5	3.6	3.6
37	0.0	0.0	0.2	0.4	0.5	0.7	0.8	0.9	1.1	1.2	1.3	1.4	1.5	1.6	1.7	1.7	1.8	1.9	2.0	2.0	2.1	2.2	2.3	2.3	2.4	2.4	2.5	2.6	2.6	2.7	2.8	2.8	2.9	2.9	3.0	3.1	3.1	3.2
36	0.0	0.0	0.0	0.2	0.3	0.4	0.5	0.6	0.7	0.8	0.9	1.0	1.1	1.2	1.2	1.3	1.4	1.5	1.6	1.6	1.7	1.8	1.9	1.9	2.0	2.0	2.1	2.2	2.2	2.3	2.4	2.4	2.5	2.6	2.7	2.7	2.8	2.8
35	0.0	0.0	0.0	0.0	0.0	0.1	0.2	0.3	0.4	0.5	0.6	0.7	0.8	0.9	1.0	1.1	1.2	1.3	1.4	1.5	1.5	1.6	1.6	1.7	1.8	1.8	1.9	2.0	2.0	2.1	2.2	2.2	2.3	2.3	2.4	2.4	2.4	2.4
34	0.0	0.0	0.0	0.0	0.0	0.0	0.1	0.1	0.2	0.3	0.4	0.5	0.6	0.7	0.8	0.8	0.9	1.0	1.1	1.2	1.3	1.3	1.4	1.5	1.6	1.6	1.7	1.8	1.8	1.9	2.0	2.0	2.1	2.1	2.2	2.3	2.4	2.0
33	0.0	0.0	0.0	0.0	0.0	0.0	0.0	0.0	0.2	0.2	0.4	0.5	0.6	0.7	0.8	0.9	0.9	1.0	1.1	1.2	1.3	1.3	1.4	1.5	1.5	1.5	1.6	1.6	1.6	1.6	1.6	1.6	1.6	1.6	1.6	1.6	1.6	1.6
32	0.0	0.0	0.0	0.0	0.0	0.0	0.0	0.0	0.0	0.0	0.0	0.1	0.2	0.4	0.4	0.5	0.6	0.8	0.8	0.9	1.0	1.0	1.1	1.2	1.2	1.2	1.2	1.2	1.2	1.2	1.2	1.2	1.2	1.2	1.2	1.2	1.2	1.2
31	0.0	0.0	0.0	0.0	0.0	0.0	0.0	0.0	0.0	0.0	0.0	0.0	0.0	0.0	0.0	0.1	0.2	0.3	0.4	0.5	0.5	0.6	0.6	0.7	0.7	0.8	0.8	0.8	0.8	0.8	0.8	0.8	0.8	0.8	0.8	0.8	0.8	0.8
30	0.0	0.0	0.0	0.0	0.0	0.0	0.0	0.0	0.0	0.0	0.0	0.0	0.0	0.0	0.0	0.0	0.0	0.0	0.0	0.1	0.1	0.2	0.2	0.2	0.3	0.3	0.4	0.4	0.4	0.4	0.4	0.4	0.4	0.4	0.4	0.4	0.4	0.4
29	0.0	0.0	0.0	0.0	0.0	0.0	0.0	0.0	0.0	0.0	0.0	0.0	0.0	0.0	0.0	0.0	0.0	0.0	0.0	0.0	0.0	0.0	0.0	0.0	0.0	0.0	0.0	0.0	0.0	0.0	0.0	0.0	0.0	0.0	0.0	0.0	0.0	0.0

LISTED CALL OPTION PRICE WHEN EXERCISE PRICE IS 45

NUMBER OF WEEKS BEFORE THE OPTION EXPIRES

Common Stock Price	1	2	3	4	5	6	7	8	9	10	11	12	13	14	15	16	17	18	19	20	21	22	23	24	25	26	27	28	29	30	31	32	33	34	35	36	37	38	39
63	18.0	18.1	18.1	18.1	18.1	18.2	18.2	18.2	18.3	18.3	18.3	18.4	18.4	18.4	18.4	18.5	18.5	18.5	18.6	18.6	18.6	18.6	18.7	18.7	18.7	18.8	18.8	18.8	18.9	18.9	18.9	18.9	19.0	19.0	19.0	19.1	19.1	19.1	19.1
62	17.0	17.1	17.1	17.1	17.2	17.2	17.2	17.3	17.3	17.3	17.4	17.4	17.4	17.5	17.5	17.6	17.6	17.6	17.7	17.7	17.7	17.8	17.8	17.8	17.9	17.9	18.0	18.0	18.0	18.0	18.1	18.1	18.1	18.2	18.2	18.2	18.3	18.3	18.3
61	16.0	16.1	16.1	16.2	16.2	16.2	16.3	16.3	16.4	16.4	16.4	16.5	16.5	16.6	16.6	16.6	16.6	16.7	16.8	16.8	16.8	16.9	16.9	16.9	17.0	17.0	17.0	17.1	17.1	17.1	17.2	17.3	17.3	17.3	17.4	17.4	17.4	17.5	17.5
60	15.0	15.1	15.1	15.2	15.2	15.3	15.3	15.4	15.4	15.4	15.5	15.5	15.6	15.6	15.7	15.7	15.7	15.8	15.9	15.9	15.9	16.0	16.0	16.1	16.1	16.2	16.2	16.3	16.3	16.3	16.4	16.4	16.5	16.5	16.6	16.6	16.6	16.7	16.7
59	14.0	14.1	14.1	14.2	14.2	14.3	14.3	14.4	14.4	14.5	14.5	14.6	14.6	14.7	14.7	14.8	14.8	14.9	14.9	15.0	15.0	15.1	15.1	15.2	15.2	15.3	15.3	15.4	15.4	15.5	15.5	15.6	15.6	15.7	15.7	15.8	15.8	15.9	15.9
58	13.1	13.1	13.2	13.2	13.3	13.3	13.4	13.4	13.5	13.6	13.6	13.7	13.7	13.8	13.8	13.9	13.9	14.0	14.0	14.1	14.2	14.2	14.3	14.3	14.4	14.4	14.5	14.5	14.6	14.7	14.7	14.8	14.8	14.9	14.9	15.0	15.0	15.1	15.1
57	12.1	12.1	12.2	12.2	12.3	12.4	12.4	12.5	12.5	12.6	12.7	12.7	12.8	12.8	12.9	13.0	13.0	13.1	13.1	13.2	13.3	13.3	13.4	13.4	13.5	13.6	13.6	13.7	13.7	13.8	13.9	13.9	14.0	14.0	14.1	14.2	14.2	14.3	14.3
56	11.1	11.1	11.2	11.2	11.3	11.4	11.4	11.5	11.6	11.6	11.7	11.8	11.8	11.9	12.0	12.0	12.1	12.1	12.2	12.3	12.4	12.4	12.5	12.6	12.6	12.7	12.8	12.8	12.9	13.0	13.0	13.1	13.2	13.2	13.3	13.4	13.4	13.5	13.5
55	10.1	10.1	10.2	10.3	10.4	10.4	10.5	10.6	10.6	10.7	10.8	10.8	10.9	11.0	11.1	11.1	11.2	11.3	11.3	11.4	11.5	11.5	11.6	11.6	11.8	11.8	11.9	12.0	12.0	12.1	12.2	12.3	12.3	12.4	12.5	12.5	12.6	12.6	12.7
54	9.1	9.2	9.2	9.3	9.4	9.5	9.5	9.6	9.7	9.8	9.8	9.9	9.9	10.1	10.1	10.2	10.3	10.4	10.5	10.5	10.6	10.7	10.7	10.8	10.9	11.0	11.0	11.1	11.2	11.3	11.3	11.4	11.5	11.6	11.6	11.7	11.8	11.9	11.9
53	8.1	8.2	8.2	8.3	8.4	8.5	8.6	8.6	8.7	8.8	8.9	9.0	9.0	9.1	9.2	9.3	9.4	9.4	9.5	9.6	9.7	9.8	9.9	9.9	10.0	10.1	10.2	10.3	10.3	10.4	10.5	10.6	10.6	10.7	10.8	10.9	11.0	11.1	11.1
52	7.1	7.2	7.3	7.3	7.4	7.5	7.6	7.7	7.8	7.9	7.9	8.0	8.1	8.2	8.3	8.4	8.5	8.5	8.7	8.7	8.8	8.9	9.0	9.0	9.1	9.3	9.3	9.4	9.5	9.6	9.7	9.7	9.8	9.9	10.0	10.1	10.2	10.3	10.3
51	6.1	6.2	6.3	6.4	6.5	6.5	6.6	6.7	6.8	6.9	7.0	7.1	7.2	7.3	7.4	7.5	7.6	7.6	7.8	7.8	7.9	8.0	8.1	8.2	8.3	8.4	8.5	8.5	8.6	8.7	8.8	8.9	9.0	9.1	9.1	9.3	9.4	9.5	9.5
50	5.1	5.2	5.3	5.4	5.5	5.6	5.7	5.8	5.9	6.0	6.1	6.2	6.2	6.3	6.5	6.6	6.7	6.7	6.9	6.9	7.0	7.1	7.2	7.3	7.4	7.5	7.6	7.7	7.8	7.9	8.0	8.1	8.1	8.3	8.4	8.5	8.6	8.7	8.7
49	4.2	4.3	4.3	4.5	4.6	4.7	4.8	4.9	5.0	5.1	5.2	5.3	5.4	5.5	5.5	5.6	5.8	5.8	6.0	6.0	6.1	6.2	6.3	6.4	6.5	6.6	6.7	6.9	7.0	7.0	7.1	7.2	7.3	7.4	7.5	7.6	7.8	7.9	8.0
48	3.3	3.4	3.4	3.6	3.7	3.8	3.9	4.1	4.2	4.3	4.4	4.5	4.6	4.6	4.7	4.8	4.9	5.0	5.1	5.2	5.3	5.4	5.5	5.6	5.7	5.8	5.9	6.0	6.1	6.2	6.3	6.4	6.5	6.6	6.7	6.8	7.0	7.1	7.2
47	2.4	2.6	2.6	2.8	3.1	3.3	3.3	3.4	3.5	3.7	3.8	4.0	4.0	4.1	4.2	4.3	4.4	4.5	4.6	4.7	4.8	4.9	4.9	5.1	5.2	5.3	5.4	5.5	5.6	5.7	5.8	5.9	6.0	6.1	6.2	6.3	6.3	6.4	6.4
46	1.6	1.8	1.9	2.2	2.4	2.6	2.7	2.9	3.0	3.1	3.3	3.4	3.5	3.6	3.7	3.8	3.8	3.9	4.1	4.2	4.2	4.4	4.4	4.5	4.6	4.7	4.8	4.9	5.0	5.1	5.2	5.2	5.3	5.3	5.5	5.4	5.5	5.6	5.6
45	0.8	1.0	1.1	1.2	1.4	1.6	1.7	1.9	2.0	2.1	2.3	2.4	2.5	2.6	2.7	2.8	2.9	3.0	3.1	3.2	3.3	3.4	3.5	3.6	3.7	3.8	3.9	4.0	4.1	4.1	4.2	4.3	4.4	4.4	4.5	4.6	4.7	4.9	5.0
44	0.4	0.6	0.8	1.0	1.2	1.4	1.5	1.6	1.8	1.9	2.0	2.1	2.2	2.3	2.4	2.5	2.6	2.7	2.8	2.9	3.0	3.0	3.1	3.2	3.3	3.4	3.4	3.5	3.6	3.7	3.7	3.8	3.9	3.9	4.0	4.1	4.1	4.2	4.2
43	0.1	0.3	0.6	0.8	1.0	1.1	1.3	1.4	1.5	1.6	1.7	1.9	2.0	2.1	2.2	2.3	2.4	2.4	2.5	2.6	2.7	2.8	2.8	2.9	3.0	3.1	3.1	3.2	3.3	3.4	3.4	3.5	3.6	3.6	3.7	3.7	3.8	3.8	3.8
42	0.0	0.0	0.0	0.4	0.6	0.8	1.0	1.1	1.2	1.3	1.5	1.6	1.7	1.8	1.9	2.0	2.0	2.1	2.2	2.3	2.4	2.5	2.5	2.6	2.7	2.8	2.8	2.9	3.0	3.0	3.1	3.2	3.2	3.3	3.3	3.4	3.4	3.4	3.4
41	0.0	0.0	0.0	0.0	0.2	0.4	0.5	0.7	0.8	0.9	1.1	1.2	1.3	1.4	1.5	1.6	1.7	1.8	1.9	2.0	2.0	2.1	2.2	2.3	2.4	2.4	2.5	2.6	2.6	2.7	2.8	2.8	2.9	2.9	3.0	3.0	3.0	3.0	3.0
40	0.0	0.0	0.0	0.0	0.0	0.2	0.2	0.3	0.4	0.5	0.7	0.8	0.9	1.0	1.1	1.2	1.3	1.4	1.5	1.6	1.6	1.7	1.8	1.9	2.0	2.0	2.1	2.2	2.2	2.3	2.4	2.4	2.5	2.5	2.6	2.6	2.6	2.6	2.6
39	0.0	0.0	0.0	0.0	0.0	0.0	0.0	0.1	0.2	0.3	0.3	0.4	0.5	0.6	0.7	0.8	0.9	1.0	1.1	1.2	1.2	1.3	1.4	1.5	1.5	1.6	1.7	1.7	1.8	1.9	1.9	2.0	2.0	2.1	2.1	2.2	2.2	2.2	2.2
38	0.0	0.0	0.0	0.0	0.0	0.0	0.0	0.0	0.0	0.0	0.1	0.3	0.4	0.5	0.6	0.7	0.8	0.9	1.0	1.0	1.1	1.2	1.2	1.3	1.4	1.4	1.5	1.5	1.6	1.6	1.7	1.7	1.7	1.8	1.8	1.8	1.8	1.8	1.8
37	0.0	0.0	0.0	0.0	0.0	0.0	0.0	0.0	0.0	0.0	0.0	0.1	0.1	0.4	0.5	0.6	0.7	0.8	0.9	1.0	1.0	1.1	1.2	1.3	1.3	1.4	1.5	1.6	1.6	1.7	1.7	1.8	1.8	1.9	1.9	2.0	2.1	2.1	1.4
36	0.0	0.0	0.0	0.0	0.0	0.0	0.0	0.0	0.0	0.0	0.0	0.0	0.0	0.1	0.1	0.4	0.5	0.6	0.7	0.8	0.9	1.0	1.0	1.1	1.2	1.2	1.2	1.3	1.3	1.4	1.5	1.5	1.6	1.6	1.7	1.7	1.2	1.1	1.0
35	0.0	0.0	0.0	0.0	0.0	0.0	0.0	0.0	0.0	0.0	0.0	0.0	0.0	0.0	0.0	0.1	0.2	0.3	0.4	0.5	0.6	0.7	0.7	0.8	0.9	1.0	1.1	1.1	1.1	1.2	1.3	1.3	1.4	0.7	0.3	0.4	0.3	0.3	0.6
34	0.0	0.0	0.0	0.0	0.0	0.0	0.0	0.0	0.0	0.0	0.0	0.0	0.0	0.0	0.0	0.0	0.0	0.1	0.1	0.3	0.4	0.5	0.6	0.7	0.7	0.8	0.9	1.0	1.0	1.1	1.1	0.1	0.2	0.7	0.3	0.0	0.0	0.0	0.2
33	0.0	0.0	0.0	0.0	0.0	0.0	0.0	0.0	0.0	0.0	0.0	0.0	0.0	0.0	0.0	0.0	0.0	0.0	0.0	0.1	0.1	0.1	0.2	0.0	0.1	0.1	0.2	0.2	0.3	0.0	0.0	0.1	0.1	0.2	0.2	0.0	0.0	0.0	0.0
32	0.0	0.0	0.0	0.0	0.0	0.0	0.0	0.0	0.0	0.0	0.0	0.0	0.0	0.0	0.0	0.0	0.0	0.0	0.0	0.0	0.0	0.0	0.0	0.0	0.0	0.0	0.0	0.0	0.0	0.0	0.0	0.0	0.0	0.0	0.0	0.0	0.0	0.0	0.0
31	0.0	0.0	0.0	0.0	0.0	0.0	0.0	0.0	0.0	0.0	0.0	0.0	0.0	0.0	0.0	0.0	0.0	0.0	0.0	0.0	0.0	0.0	0.0	0.0	0.0	0.0	0.0	0.0	0.0	0.0	0.0	0.0	0.0	0.0	0.0	0.0	0.0	0.0	0.0
30	0.0	0.0	0.0	0.0	0.0	0.0	0.0	0.0	0.0	0.0	0.0	0.0	0.0	0.0	0.0	0.0	0.0	0.0	0.0	0.0	0.0	0.0	0.0	0.0	0.0	0.0	0.0	0.0	0.0	0.0	0.0	0.0	0.0	0.0	0.0	0.0	0.0	0.0	0.0
29	0.0	0.0	0.0	0.0	0.0	0.0	0.0	0.0	0.0	0.0	0.0	0.0	0.0	0.0	0.0	0.0	0.0	0.0	0.0	0.0	0.0	0.0	0.0	0.0	0.0	0.0	0.0	0.0	0.0	0.0	0.0	0.0	0.0	0.0	0.0	0.0	0.0	0.0	0.0
28	0.0	0.0	0.0	0.0	0.0	0.0	0.0	0.0	0.0	0.0	0.0	0.0	0.0	0.0	0.0	0.0	0.0	0.0	0.0	0.0	0.0	0.0	0.0	0.0	0.0	0.0	0.0	0.0	0.0	0.0	0.0	0.0	0.0	0.0	0.0	0.0	0.0	0.0	0.0
27	0.0	0.0	0.0	0.0	0.0	0.0	0.0	0.0	0.0	0.0	0.0	0.0	0.0	0.0	0.0	0.0	0.0	0.0	0.0	0.0	0.0	0.0	0.0	0.0	0.0	0.0	0.0	0.0	0.0	0.0	0.0	0.0	0.0	0.0	0.0	0.0	0.0	0.0	0.0

LISTED CALL OPTION PRICE WHEN EXERCISE PRICE IS 50

NUMBER OF WEEKS BEFORE THE OPTION EXPIRES

Common Stock Price	1	2	3	4	5	6	7	8	9	10	11	12	13	14	15	16	17	18	19	20	21	22	23	24	25	26	27	28	29	30	31	32	33	34	35	36	37	38	39
65	15.1	15.1	15.2	15.2	15.3	15.3	15.4	15.5	15.5	15.6	15.6	15.7	15.8	15.8	15.9	15.9	16.0	16.0	16.1	16.2	16.2	16.3	16.3	16.4	16.5	16.5	16.6	16.6	16.7	16.8	16.8	16.9	16.9	17.0	17.0	17.1	17.2	17.2	17.3
64	14.1	14.1	14.2	14.3	14.3	14.4	14.4	14.5	14.6	14.6	14.7	14.8	14.8	14.9	15.0	15.0	15.1	15.1	15.2	15.3	15.3	15.4	15.5	15.5	15.6	15.6	15.7	15.8	15.8	15.9	16.0	16.0	16.1	16.2	16.2	16.3	16.3	16.4	16.5
63	13.1	13.1	13.2	13.3	13.3	13.4	13.5	13.5	13.6	13.7	13.8	13.8	13.9	14.0	14.0	14.1	14.2	14.2	14.3	14.4	14.4	14.5	14.5	14.6	14.7	14.8	14.9	14.9	15.0	15.1	15.1	15.2	15.3	15.3	15.4	15.5	15.5	15.6	15.7
62	12.1	12.1	12.2	12.3	12.4	12.4	12.5	12.6	12.7	12.7	12.8	12.9	13.0	13.0	13.1	13.2	13.3	13.3	13.4	13.5	13.5	13.6	13.7	13.8	13.8	13.9	14.0	14.1	14.1	14.2	14.2	14.3	14.4	14.5	14.6	14.7	14.7	14.8	14.9
61	11.1	11.2	11.2	11.3	11.4	11.5	11.6	11.6	11.7	11.8	11.9	11.9	12.0	12.1	12.1	12.2	12.3	12.3	12.4	12.6	12.6	12.7	12.7	12.8	12.9	13.0	13.0	13.1	13.2	13.3	13.4	13.4	13.5	13.6	13.7	13.8	13.9	13.9	14.1
60	10.1	10.2	10.3	10.3	10.4	10.5	10.6	10.7	10.8	10.8	10.9	11.0	11.1	11.2	11.3	11.3	11.4	11.5	11.5	11.7	11.7	11.8	11.9	11.9	12.0	12.1	12.2	12.3	12.4	12.5	12.5	12.6	12.7	12.8	12.9	13.0	13.1	13.2	13.3
59	9.1	9.2	9.3	9.4	9.4	9.5	9.6	9.7	9.8	9.9	9.9	10.1	10.1	10.2	10.3	10.4	10.5	10.6	10.7	10.8	10.9	11.0	11.0	11.1	11.2	11.3	11.4	11.5	11.6	11.7	11.7	11.8	11.9	12.0	12.1	12.2	12.3	12.4	12.5
58	8.1	8.2	8.3	8.4	8.5	8.6	8.7	8.7	8.8	8.9	9.0	9.1	9.2	9.3	9.4	9.5	9.6	9.7	9.8	9.9	9.9	10.0	10.1	10.2	10.3	10.4	10.5	10.5	10.6	10.7	10.8	10.9	11.0	11.1	11.2	11.3	11.5	11.6	11.7
57	7.1	7.2	7.3	7.4	7.4	7.6	7.7	7.8	7.9	8.0	8.1	8.2	8.3	8.4	8.5	8.6	8.7	8.8	8.9	9.0	9.1	9.2	9.3	9.4	9.5	9.6	9.7	9.8	9.9	9.9	10.1	10.2	10.3	10.4	10.5	10.6	10.7	10.8	10.9
56	6.1	6.2	6.3	6.4	6.5	6.6	6.7	6.8	6.9	7.0	7.1	7.3	7.3	7.4	7.6	7.7	7.8	7.9	8.0	8.1	8.2	8.3	8.4	8.5	8.6	8.7	8.8	8.9	9.0	9.1	9.2	9.3	9.4	9.6	9.7	9.8	9.9	9.9	10.1
55	5.2	5.2	5.3	5.4	5.5	5.6	5.8	5.9	6.0	6.1	6.3	6.4	6.5	6.6	6.7	6.8	6.9	7.0	7.1	7.2	7.3	7.4	7.5	7.6	7.7	7.8	7.9	8.0	8.1	8.2	8.3	8.4	8.5	8.6	8.8	8.9	9.0	9.1	9.2
54	4.2	4.3	4.4	4.5	4.6	4.7	4.8	5.0	5.1	5.3	5.4	5.5	5.6	5.7	5.9	6.0	6.1	6.2	6.3	6.4	6.5	6.6	6.7	6.8	6.8	7.0	7.1	7.2	7.3	7.4	7.5	7.6	7.7	7.9	8.0	8.1	8.2	8.3	8.4
53	3.3	3.4	3.5	3.6	3.8	3.9	4.1	4.2	4.4	4.5	4.7	4.8	4.9	5.0	5.1	5.2	5.3	5.5	5.6	5.7	5.8	5.9	6.0	6.1	6.2	6.3	6.4	6.5	6.6	6.7	6.8	7.0	7.0	7.2	7.3	7.4	7.5	7.6	7.7
52	2.3	2.5	2.7	2.9	3.2	3.3	3.5	3.7	3.9	4.0	4.2	4.3	4.5	4.6	4.7	4.9	5.0	5.1	5.2	5.3	5.4	5.5	5.6	5.7	5.8	5.9	6.0	6.1	6.2	6.3	6.4	6.5	6.6	6.7	6.7	6.8	6.9	7.0	7.0
51	1.4	1.7	2.0	2.2	2.4	2.6	2.8	2.9	3.1	3.2	3.4	3.5	3.6	3.7	3.8	4.0	4.1	4.2	4.3	4.4	4.5	4.6	4.7	4.8	4.9	5.0	5.1	5.2	5.3	5.4	5.5	5.6	5.7	5.8	5.9	6.0	6.1	6.1	6.2
50	0.9	1.3	1.6	1.8	2.0	2.2	2.4	2.5	2.7	2.8	3.0	3.1	3.2	3.3	3.4	3.6	3.7	3.8	3.9	4.0	4.1	4.2	4.3	4.4	4.4	4.5	4.6	4.7	4.8	4.9	5.0	5.1	5.2	5.3	5.3	5.4	5.5	5.5	5.6
49	0.5	0.9	1.1	1.4	1.6	1.8	2.0	2.1	2.3	2.4	2.6	2.7	2.8	2.9	3.0	3.2	3.3	3.4	3.5	3.6	3.7	3.8	3.9	4.0	4.0	4.1	4.2	4.3	4.4	4.5	4.5	4.6	4.7	4.8	4.9	4.9	5.0	5.1	5.2
48	0.1	0.5	0.8	1.0	1.2	1.4	1.6	1.7	1.9	2.0	2.2	2.3	2.4	2.5	2.6	2.7	2.8	2.9	3.0	3.1	3.2	3.3	3.4	3.5	3.5	3.6	3.7	3.8	3.9	4.0	4.0	4.1	4.2	4.3	4.4	4.5	4.6	4.7	4.8
47	0.0	0.1	0.3	0.6	0.8	1.0	1.3	1.4	1.6	1.7	1.9	2.0	2.1	2.2	2.3	2.4	2.5	2.6	2.7	2.8	2.9	3.0	3.1	3.2	3.3	3.4	3.4	3.5	3.6	3.7	3.8	3.9	4.0	4.0	4.1	4.2	4.3	4.3	4.4
46	0.0	0.0	0.1	0.3	0.4	0.6	0.8	1.0	1.2	1.4	1.5	1.7	1.8	1.9	2.0	2.1	2.2	2.3	2.4	2.5	2.6	2.7	2.8	2.9	2.9	3.0	3.1	3.2	3.3	3.3	3.4	3.5	3.6	3.6	3.7	3.8	3.9	3.9	4.0
45	0.0	0.0	0.0	0.1	0.2	0.4	0.5	0.7	0.8	1.1	1.2	1.4	1.5	1.6	1.7	1.9	2.0	2.1	2.2	2.3	2.4	2.5	2.5	2.6	2.7	2.8	2.9	2.9	3.0	3.1	3.1	3.2	3.3	3.3	3.4	3.5	3.5	3.6	3.6
44	0.0	0.0	0.0	0.0	0.1	0.2	0.4	0.5	0.6	0.8	1.0	1.1	1.2	1.4	1.5	1.6	1.7	1.8	1.9	2.0	2.1	2.2	2.3	2.3	2.4	2.5	2.6	2.7	2.7	2.8	2.9	3.0	3.0	3.1	3.2	3.3	3.4	3.5	3.6
43	0.0	0.0	0.0	0.0	0.0	0.1	0.2	0.3	0.5	0.6	0.8	1.0	1.1	1.2	1.3	1.5	1.6	1.7	1.8	1.9	2.0	2.1	2.1	2.2	2.3	2.4	2.4	2.5	2.6	2.7	2.7	2.8	2.9	2.9	3.0	3.0	3.1	3.1	3.2
42	0.0	0.0	0.0	0.0	0.0	0.0	0.1	0.2	0.3	0.4	0.6	0.7	0.8	1.0	1.1	1.2	1.3	1.4	1.5	1.6	1.7	1.8	1.8	1.9	2.0	2.1	2.1	2.2	2.3	2.4	2.4	2.5	2.5	2.6	2.6	2.7	2.7	2.8	2.8
41	0.0	0.0	0.0	0.0	0.0	0.0	0.0	0.1	0.2	0.4	0.5	0.6	0.7	0.8	1.0	1.1	1.2	1.3	1.3	1.5	1.6	1.6	1.7	1.8	1.8	1.9	2.0	2.0	2.1	2.1	2.2	2.2	2.3	2.3	2.4	2.4	2.4	2.4	2.4
40	0.0	0.0	0.0	0.0	0.0	0.0	0.0	0.0	0.1	0.3	0.4	0.5	0.6	0.7	0.8	1.0	1.1	1.2	1.2	1.4	1.4	1.5	1.6	1.6	1.7	1.8	1.8	1.9	1.9	2.0	2.0	2.0	2.0	2.0	2.0	2.0	2.0	2.0	2.0
39	0.0	0.0	0.0	0.0	0.0	0.0	0.0	0.0	0.0	0.1	0.2	0.3	0.4	0.4	0.6	0.7	0.8	0.9	1.0	1.0	1.1	1.2	1.2	1.3	1.4	1.4	1.5	1.5	1.5	1.6	1.6	1.6	1.6	1.6	1.6	1.6	1.6	1.6	1.6
38	0.0	0.0	0.0	0.0	0.0	0.0	0.0	0.0	0.0	0.0	0.1	0.2	0.3	0.4	0.5	0.6	0.6	0.7	0.8	0.8	0.9	1.0	1.0	1.0	1.1	1.1	1.1	1.2	1.2	1.2	1.2	1.2	1.2	1.2	1.2	1.2	1.2	1.2	1.2
37	0.0	0.0	0.0	0.0	0.0	0.0	0.0	0.0	0.0	0.0	0.0	0.1	0.2	0.3	0.3	0.4	0.5	0.5	0.6	0.6	0.7	0.7	0.7	0.8	0.8	0.8	0.8	0.8	0.8	0.8	0.8	0.8	0.8	0.8	0.8	0.8	0.8	0.8	0.8
36	0.0	0.0	0.0	0.0	0.0	0.0	0.0	0.0	0.0	0.0	0.0	0.0	0.0	0.1	0.1	0.2	0.2	0.3	0.3	0.3	0.4	0.4	0.4	0.4	0.4	0.4	0.4	0.4	0.4	0.4	0.4	0.4	0.4	0.4	0.4	0.4	0.4	0.4	0.4
35	0.0	0.0	0.0	0.0	0.0	0.0	0.0	0.0	0.0	0.0	0.0	0.0	0.0	0.0	0.0	0.0	0.0	0.0	0.0	0.0	0.0	0.0	0.0	0.0	0.0	0.0	0.0	0.0	0.0	0.0	0.0	0.0	0.0	0.0	0.0	0.0	0.0	0.0	0.0

LISTED CALL OPTION PRICE WHEN EXERCISE PRICE IS 60

NUMBER OF WEEKS BEFORE THE OPTION EXPIRES

Common Stock Price	1	2	3	4	5	6	7	8	9	10	11	12	13	14	15	16	17	18	19	20	21	22	23	24	25	26	27	28	29	30	31	32	33	34	35	36	37	38	39
78	18.1	18.1	18.2	18.3	18.3	18.4	18.5	18.6	18.6	18.7	18.8	18.8	18.9	19.0	19.1	19.1	19.2	19.3	19.3	19.4	19.5	19.5	19.6	19.7	19.7	19.8	19.8	19.9	20.0	20.1	20.2	20.2	20.3	20.4	20.4	20.5	20.6	20.7	20.7
77	17.1	17.2	17.2	17.3	17.4	17.4	17.5	17.5	17.6	17.7	17.8	17.9	18.0	18.1	18.1	18.2	18.3	18.4	18.4	18.5	18.6	18.7	18.7	18.8	18.8	19.0	19.0	19.1	19.2	19.3	19.3	19.4	19.5	19.6	19.6	19.7	19.8	19.9	19.9
76	16.1	16.2	16.2	16.3	16.3	16.4	16.5	16.6	16.6	16.7	16.8	16.9	17.0	17.1	17.2	17.2	17.3	17.4	17.4	17.5	17.6	17.7	17.8	17.8	17.9	18.0	18.1	18.2	18.2	18.3	18.4	18.5	18.5	18.6	18.7	18.8	18.9	19.0	19.1
75	15.1	15.2	15.3	15.3	15.4	15.4	15.6	15.7	15.8	15.9	15.9	16.0	16.1	16.2	16.2	16.4	16.4	16.5	16.6	16.7	16.8	16.9	17.0	17.0	17.1	17.2	17.3	17.5	17.5	17.6	17.6	17.7	17.8	17.9	18.0	18.1	18.2	18.2	18.3
74	14.1	14.2	14.3	14.3	14.4	14.5	14.6	14.7	14.7	14.8	14.9	15.0	15.1	15.2	15.2	15.3	15.4	15.5	15.6	15.7	15.8	15.8	15.9	16.0	16.1	16.1	16.2	16.3	16.4	16.4	16.5	16.6	16.7	16.9	17.0	17.1	17.2	17.3	17.5
73	13.1	13.2	13.2	13.3	13.4	13.4	13.5	13.6	13.7	13.8	13.8	13.9	14.0	14.1	14.2	14.2	14.3	14.4	14.5	14.6	14.6	14.7	14.8	14.9	15.0	15.0	15.1	15.2	15.3	15.4	15.5	15.5	15.6	15.7	15.8	15.9	16.0	16.6	16.7
72	12.1	12.2	12.3	12.3	12.4	12.5	12.5	12.6	12.7	12.8	12.9	13.0	13.0	13.1	13.2	13.3	13.4	13.4	13.5	13.6	13.7	13.8	13.8	13.9	14.0	14.1	14.2	14.3	14.4	14.4	14.5	14.6	14.7	14.8	14.9	15.0	15.1	15.8	15.9
71	11.1	11.2	11.3	11.3	11.4	11.5	11.5	11.6	11.7	11.8	11.9	12.0	12.0	12.1	12.2	12.3	12.4	12.4	12.5	12.6	12.7	12.8	12.9	13.0	13.0	13.1	13.2	13.3	13.4	13.5	13.6	13.6	13.7	13.8	13.9	14.0	14.1	15.0	15.1
70	10.1	10.2	10.3	10.4	10.4	10.5	10.6	10.6	10.7	10.8	10.9	11.0	11.1	11.1	11.2	11.3	11.4	11.5	11.6	11.6	11.7	11.8	11.9	12.0	12.1	12.2	12.3	12.3	12.4	12.5	12.6	12.7	12.8	12.9	13.0	13.1	13.2	14.2	14.3
69	9.1	9.2	9.3	9.4	9.5	9.5	9.6	9.7	9.8	9.9	10.0	10.1	10.2	10.2	10.4	10.5	10.5	10.6	10.7	10.8	10.9	11.0	11.1	11.2	11.3	11.4	11.5	11.6	11.6	11.7	11.8	11.9	12.0	12.1	12.2	12.3	12.4	13.4	13.5
68	8.1	8.2	8.4	8.5	8.6	8.6	8.7	8.8	8.9	9.0	9.1	9.2	9.3	9.3	9.5	9.6	9.7	9.8	9.9	10.0	10.1	10.2	10.3	10.4	10.5	10.6	10.7	10.8	10.9	11.0	11.1	11.2	11.3	11.4	11.6	11.7	11.8	12.6	12.7
67	7.1	7.3	7.4	7.5	7.6	7.8	7.9	8.0	8.1	8.3	8.4	8.5	8.6	8.8	8.9	8.9	9.0	9.1	9.3	9.4	9.5	9.7	9.8	9.9	10.0	10.2	10.3	10.5	10.5	10.7	10.8	10.9	11.0	11.1	11.3	11.4	11.6	11.7	11.9
66	6.2	6.3	6.4	6.6	6.7	6.8	7.0	7.1	7.2	7.4	7.5	7.6	7.7	8.0	8.1	8.1	8.2	8.4	8.5	8.6	8.8	8.9	9.0	9.1	9.3	9.4	9.5	9.6	9.8	9.9	10.0	10.1	10.2	10.3	10.5	10.7	10.7	10.8	11.0
65	5.2	5.3	5.4	5.5	5.8	5.8	6.0	6.1	6.3	6.5	6.6	6.7	6.8	7.1	7.2	7.3	7.4	7.6	7.7	7.8	8.0	8.1	8.2	8.3	8.5	8.6	8.7	8.8	8.9	9.1	9.2	9.3	9.4	9.5	9.6	9.7	9.8	10.0	10.1
64	4.2	4.4	4.5	4.9	5.0	5.0	5.1	5.2	5.4	5.6	5.8	5.8	6.0	6.2	6.3	6.5	6.6	6.8	7.0	7.1	7.2	7.4	7.4	7.6	7.6	7.7	7.8	8.0	8.1	8.2	8.3	8.4	8.5	8.6	8.8	9.0	9.1	9.2	9.3
63	3.3	3.4	3.7	3.8	4.1	4.3	4.3	4.6	4.8	4.8	5.0	5.2	5.3	5.5	5.6	5.7	5.8	5.9	6.1	6.2	6.3	6.4	6.6	6.7	6.8	7.0	7.1	7.2	7.3	7.5	7.6	7.7	7.9	8.0	8.1	8.2	8.3	8.4	8.5
62	2.3	2.5	2.8	3.1	3.1	3.3	3.6	3.6	3.8	4.0	4.1	4.3	4.5	4.6	4.7	4.9	5.0	5.3	5.3	5.4	5.6	5.7	5.9	6.0	6.1	6.2	6.3	6.4	6.5	6.7	6.8	6.9	7.0	7.1	7.3	7.4	7.6	7.7	7.8
61	1.5	1.9	2.2	2.4	2.5	2.8	2.8	3.0	3.2	3.4	3.5	3.7	3.8	4.0	4.1	4.3	4.5	4.5	4.6	4.8	4.9	5.0	5.1	5.3	5.4	5.5	5.6	5.7	5.8	5.9	6.1	6.2	6.3	6.4	6.6	6.7	6.8	7.0	7.1
60	1.1	1.5	1.8	2.0	2.2	2.4	2.6	2.8	3.0	3.2	3.4	3.6	3.7	3.9	4.0	4.2	4.3	4.4	4.5	4.7	4.8	4.9	5.0	5.1	5.3	5.4	5.5	5.6	5.7	5.8	5.9	6.0	6.1	6.2	6.3	6.4	6.5	6.6	6.7
59	0.7	1.1	1.4	1.7	1.8	2.0	2.2	2.4	2.6	2.8	3.0	3.2	3.3	3.5	3.6	3.8	4.0	4.0	4.1	4.3	4.4	4.6	4.7	4.8	4.9	5.0	5.1	5.2	5.4	5.5	5.6	5.7	5.7	5.8	5.9	6.0	6.1	6.2	6.3
58	0.3	0.7	1.0	1.2	1.4	1.6	1.8	2.0	2.2	2.4	2.6	2.7	2.9	3.0	3.2	3.3	3.5	3.6	3.7	3.9	4.0	4.1	4.2	4.4	4.5	4.6	4.7	4.8	4.9	5.0	5.1	5.2	5.3	5.4	5.5	5.6	5.7	5.8	5.9
57	0.0	0.3	0.6	0.8	1.0	1.2	1.4	1.6	1.8	2.0	2.1	2.3	2.4	2.5	2.7	2.9	3.0	3.2	3.3	3.4	3.5	3.7	3.8	3.9	4.0	4.1	4.2	4.3	4.4	4.6	4.7	4.8	4.9	5.0	5.1	5.2	5.3	5.4	5.5
56	0.0	0.0	0.3	0.4	0.6	0.8	1.0	1.2	1.4	1.6	1.7	1.9	2.0	2.1	2.3	2.4	2.5	2.7	2.8	2.9	3.0	3.2	3.3	3.4	3.5	3.6	3.7	3.8	3.9	4.0	4.1	4.2	4.3	4.4	4.6	4.7	4.8	4.9	5.1
55	0.0	0.0	0.0	0.2	0.4	0.6	0.8	1.0	1.1	1.3	1.4	1.5	1.7	1.8	1.9	2.1	2.2	2.3	2.5	2.6	2.7	2.8	2.9	3.0	3.1	3.2	3.3	3.5	3.6	3.6	3.7	3.8	3.9	4.0	4.1	4.3	4.4	4.5	4.7
54	0.0	0.0	0.0	0.0	0.2	0.4	0.6	0.8	0.9	1.1	1.2	1.4	1.5	1.6	1.8	1.9	2.0	2.1	2.3	2.4	2.5	2.6	2.7	2.8	2.9	3.0	3.1	3.2	3.3	3.4	3.5	3.6	3.7	3.8	3.9	4.0	4.1	4.2	4.3
53	0.0	0.0	0.0	0.0	0.0	0.2	0.4	0.6	0.7	0.9	1.0	1.1	1.3	1.4	1.5	1.7	1.8	1.9	2.0	2.1	2.3	2.4	2.5	2.5	2.6	2.7	2.8	2.9	3.0	3.1	3.2	3.3	3.3	3.4	3.5	3.6	3.7	3.8	3.9
52	0.0	0.0	0.0	0.0	0.0	0.0	0.2	0.4	0.5	0.7	0.8	1.0	1.1	1.2	1.3	1.5	1.6	1.7	1.8	1.9	2.0	2.1	2.2	2.3	2.4	2.5	2.6	2.6	2.7	2.8	2.9	3.0	3.1	3.1	3.2	3.3	3.4	3.5	3.5
51	0.0	0.0	0.0	0.0	0.0	0.0	0.0	0.2	0.4	0.5	0.6	0.8	0.9	1.0	1.1	1.2	1.3	1.5	1.6	1.7	1.7	1.8	1.9	2.0	2.1	2.2	2.3	2.4	2.5	2.5	2.6	2.7	2.8	2.8	2.9	3.0	3.0	3.1	3.1
50	0.0	0.0	0.0	0.0	0.0	0.0	0.0	0.0	0.2	0.4	0.5	0.6	0.7	0.8	1.0	1.1	1.2	1.3	1.4	1.5	1.6	1.6	1.7	1.8	1.9	2.0	2.0	2.1	2.2	2.3	2.3	2.4	2.5	2.5	2.6	2.6	2.7	2.7	2.7
49	0.0	0.0	0.0	0.0	0.0	0.0	0.0	0.0	0.0	0.2	0.3	0.5	0.6	0.7	0.8	0.9	1.0	1.1	1.1	1.2	1.3	1.4	1.5	1.6	1.6	1.7	1.8	1.8	1.9	2.0	2.0	2.1	2.1	2.2	2.2	2.3	2.3	2.3	2.3
48	0.0	0.0	0.0	0.0	0.0	0.0	0.0	0.0	0.0	0.0	0.2	0.3	0.4	0.5	0.6	0.7	0.8	0.9	1.0	1.0	1.1	1.2	1.2	1.3	1.4	1.4	1.5	1.5	1.6	1.6	1.7	1.7	1.8	1.8	1.8	1.9	1.9	1.9	1.9
47	0.0	0.0	0.0	0.0	0.0	0.0	0.0	0.0	0.0	0.0	0.0	0.2	0.3	0.4	0.5	0.6	0.6	0.7	0.8	0.8	0.9	0.9	1.0	1.1	1.1	1.2	1.2	1.3	1.3	1.3	1.4	1.4	1.5	1.5	1.5	1.5	1.5	1.5	1.5
46	0.0	0.0	0.0	0.0	0.0	0.0	0.0	0.0	0.0	0.0	0.0	0.0	0.2	0.3	0.3	0.4	0.5	0.5	0.6	0.6	0.7	0.7	0.8	0.8	0.9	0.9	0.9	1.0	1.0	1.0	1.1	1.1	1.1	1.1	1.2	1.2	1.1	1.1	1.1
45	0.0	0.0	0.0	0.0	0.0	0.0	0.0	0.0	0.0	0.0	0.0	0.0	0.0	0.2	0.2	0.3	0.3	0.4	0.4	0.5	0.5	0.5	0.6	0.6	0.6	0.7	0.7	0.7	0.7	0.8	0.8	0.8	0.8	0.8	0.7	0.7	0.7	0.7	0.7
44	0.0	0.0	0.0	0.0	0.0	0.0	0.0	0.0	0.0	0.0	0.0	0.0	0.0	0.0	0.1	0.1	0.2	0.2	0.2	0.3	0.3	0.3	0.3	0.4	0.4	0.4	0.4	0.4	0.4	0.5	0.5	0.4	0.4	0.4	0.4	0.4	0.3	0.3	0.3
43	0.0	0.0	0.0	0.0	0.0	0.0	0.0	0.0	0.0	0.0	0.0	0.0	0.0	0.0	0.0	0.0	0.0	0.0	0.0	0.0	0.0	0.0	0.0	0.1	0.1	0.1	0.1	0.1	0.1	0.2	0.2	0.1	0.1	0.1	0.1	0.0	0.0	0.0	0.0
42	0.0	0.0	0.0	0.0	0.0	0.0	0.0	0.0	0.0	0.0	0.0	0.0	0.0	0.0	0.0	0.0	0.0	0.0	0.0	0.0	0.0	0.0	0.0	0.0	0.0	0.0	0.0	0.0	0.0	0.0	0.0	0.0	0.0	0.0	0.0	0.0	0.0	0.0	0.0

LISTED CALL OPTION PRICE WHEN EXERCISE PRICE IS 70

NUMBER OF WEEKS BEFORE THE OPTION EXPIRES

Common Stock Price	1	2	3	4	5	6	7	8	9	10	11	12	13	14	15	16	17	18	19	20	21	22	23	24	25	26	27	28	29	30	31	32	33	34	35	36	37	38	39
91	21.1	21.2	21.2	21.3	21.4	21.5	21.6	21.7	21.7	21.8	21.9	22.0	22.0	22.1	22.2	22.3	22.4	22.5	22.6	22.6	22.7	22.8	22.9	23.0	23.0	23.1	23.2	23.3	23.4	23.4	23.5	23.6	23.7	23.8	23.9	23.9	24.0	24.1	24.2
90	20.1	20.2	20.3	20.3	20.4	20.5	20.6	20.6	20.7	20.9	20.9	21.0	21.1	21.1	21.3	21.3	21.4	21.6	21.6	21.7	21.8	21.9	22.0	22.1	22.2	22.2	22.3	22.4	22.5	22.6	22.6	22.8	22.9	22.9	23.0	23.1	23.2	23.3	23.4
89	19.1	19.2	19.3	19.4	19.5	19.6	19.6	19.7	19.8	19.9	20.0	20.1	20.2	20.3	20.4	20.5	20.6	20.7	20.7	20.8	20.9	21.0	21.1	21.2	21.3	21.4	21.5	21.6	21.7	21.8	21.8	21.9	22.0	22.1	22.2	22.3	22.4	22.5	22.6
88	18.1	18.2	18.3	18.4	18.5	18.6	18.7	18.7	18.8	18.9	19.0	19.2	19.2	19.3	19.4	19.5	19.6	19.7	19.7	19.9	19.9	20.1	20.2	20.3	20.4	20.5	20.6	20.7	20.8	20.9	20.9	21.1	21.2	21.3	21.4	21.5	21.6	21.7	21.8
87	17.1	17.2	17.3	17.4	17.5	17.6	17.7	17.8	17.9	18.0	18.1	18.2	18.3	18.4	18.5	18.6	18.7	18.8	18.9	18.9	19.0	19.1	19.3	19.3	19.5	19.7	19.8	19.9	19.9	20.1	20.2	20.3	20.4	20.5	20.6	20.7	20.8	20.9	21.0
86	16.1	16.2	16.3	16.4	16.5	16.6	16.8	16.8	16.9	17.1	17.2	17.3	17.4	17.5	17.6	17.7	17.8	17.9	18.1	18.1	18.3	18.4	18.5	18.6	18.7	18.8	18.9	19.0	19.1	19.2	19.3	19.4	19.5	19.6	19.8	19.9	20.0	20.1	20.2
85	15.1	15.2	15.3	15.4	15.6	15.7	15.8	15.9	16.0	16.1	16.2	16.3	16.5	16.6	16.7	16.8	16.9	17.0	17.2	17.2	17.4	17.5	17.6	17.7	17.8	18.0	18.1	18.2	18.3	18.4	18.5	18.6	18.7	18.8	18.9	19.0	19.2	19.3	19.4
84	14.1	14.2	14.4	14.5	14.6	14.7	14.8	14.9	15.1	15.2	15.3	15.4	15.5	15.6	15.8	15.9	16.0	16.1	16.2	16.4	16.5	16.6	16.7	16.8	16.9	17.1	17.2	17.3	17.4	17.5	17.6	17.8	17.9	18.0	18.1	18.2	18.3	18.5	18.6
83	13.1	13.2	13.4	13.5	13.6	13.7	13.9	14.0	14.1	14.2	14.3	14.5	14.6	14.7	14.8	15.0	15.1	15.2	15.4	15.5	15.6	15.7	15.8	16.0	16.1	16.2	16.3	16.4	16.6	16.7	16.8	16.9	17.0	17.2	17.3	17.4	17.5	17.7	17.8
82	12.1	12.3	12.4	12.5	12.6	12.8	12.9	13.0	13.2	13.3	13.4	13.5	13.7	13.8	13.9	14.0	14.2	14.3	14.4	14.6	14.7	14.8	14.9	15.1	15.2	15.3	15.5	15.6	15.6	15.8	15.8	16.0	16.2	16.3	16.5	16.6	16.7	16.9	17.0
81	11.1	11.3	11.4	11.5	11.7	11.8	11.9	12.1	12.2	12.3	12.5	12.6	12.7	12.9	13.0	13.1	13.3	13.4	13.5	13.7	13.8	13.9	14.1	14.2	14.3	14.5	14.6	14.7	14.9	15.0	15.1	15.3	15.4	15.5	15.7	15.8	15.9	16.1	16.2
80	10.1	10.4	10.5	10.6	10.7	10.8	11.0	11.1	11.2	11.4	11.5	11.7	11.8	11.9	12.1	12.2	12.3	12.5	12.6	12.8	12.9	13.0	13.2	13.3	13.5	13.6	13.7	13.9	14.0	14.1	14.3	14.4	14.6	14.7	14.8	15.0	15.1	15.2	15.4
79	9.1	9.3	9.4	9.6	9.7	9.9	10.0	10.1	10.3	10.4	10.6	10.7	10.9	11.0	11.1	11.3	11.4	11.6	11.7	11.9	12.0	12.2	12.3	12.4	12.6	12.7	12.9	13.0	13.2	13.3	13.4	13.6	13.7	13.9	14.0	14.2	14.3	14.4	14.6
78	8.1	8.3	8.4	8.6	8.7	8.9	9.0	9.2	9.3	9.5	9.6	9.8	10.0	10.1	10.2	10.4	10.5	10.7	10.8	11.0	11.1	11.3	11.4	11.6	11.7	11.9	12.0	12.2	12.3	12.5	12.6	12.7	12.9	13.0	13.2	13.3	13.5	13.6	13.8
77	7.1	7.3	7.5	7.6	7.8	8.0	8.1	8.3	8.4	8.6	8.7	8.9	9.0	9.2	9.3	9.5	9.6	9.8	9.9	10.1	10.2	10.4	10.5	10.7	10.8	11.0	11.1	11.3	11.4	11.6	11.7	11.8	12.0	12.1	12.3	12.4	12.6	12.6	12.8
76	6.2	6.4	6.7	6.7	6.9	7.0	7.2	7.4	7.5	7.7	7.9	8.0	8.2	8.3	8.4	8.6	8.8	8.9	9.0	9.2	9.3	9.5	9.6	9.8	9.9	10.1	10.2	10.4	10.5	10.7	10.8	10.9	11.1	11.2	11.4	11.5	11.6	11.7	11.8
75	5.2	5.4	5.5	5.8	6.0	6.1	6.3	6.5	6.6	6.8	7.0	7.1	7.4	7.5	7.7	7.8	8.0	8.2	8.3	8.4	8.6	8.7	8.9	9.0	9.2	9.3	9.5	9.6	9.7	9.9	10.0	10.1	10.3	10.4	10.5	10.6	10.8	10.6	10.8
74	4.3	4.6	4.9	5.1	5.3	5.5	5.7	5.8	6.0	6.1	6.3	6.4	6.6	6.8	6.9	7.1	7.3	7.4	7.6	7.7	7.9	8.1	8.2	8.4	8.5	8.7	8.8	9.0	9.1	9.3	9.4	9.6	9.7	9.9	10.0	10.2	10.3	10.4	10.5
73	3.4	3.8	4.0	4.3	4.5	4.7	4.9	5.1	5.3	5.5	5.6	5.8	6.0	6.1	6.3	6.5	6.6	6.8	7.0	7.1	7.3	7.4	7.6	7.7	7.9	8.0	8.2	8.3	8.5	8.6	8.8	8.9	9.1	9.2	9.4	9.5	9.6	9.7	9.9
72	2.4	3.0	3.3	3.6	3.9	4.1	4.3	4.5	4.7	4.9	5.1	5.3	5.5	5.6	5.8	5.9	6.1	6.3	6.5	6.6	6.8	6.9	7.1	7.2	7.4	7.5	7.7	7.8	7.9	8.1	8.2	8.4	8.4	8.5	8.6	8.7	8.8	8.9	9.0
71	1.8	2.2	2.6	2.9	3.2	3.4	3.6	3.8	4.0	4.2	4.4	4.5	4.7	4.9	5.1	5.2	5.4	5.5	5.7	5.8	6.0	6.2	6.3	6.5	6.6	6.7	6.9	7.0	7.1	7.3	7.4	7.4	7.6	7.7	7.8	7.9	8.0	8.1	8.2
70	1.2	1.8	2.2	2.5	2.8	3.0	3.3	3.5	3.7	3.9	4.1	4.3	4.3	4.7	4.8	5.0	5.1	5.3	5.4	5.6	5.8	5.8	6.0	6.1	6.2	6.4	6.5	6.6	6.7	6.8	6.8	7.0	7.2	7.3	7.4	7.5	7.6	7.7	7.8
69	0.8	1.4	1.8	2.1	2.4	2.7	2.9	3.1	3.3	3.5	3.7	3.9	3.9	4.3	4.4	4.6	4.7	4.9	5.0	5.2	5.3	5.4	5.6	5.7	5.9	6.0	6.1	6.2	6.3	6.4	6.5	6.6	6.8	6.9	7.0	7.1	7.2	7.3	7.4
68	0.4	1.0	1.4	1.7	2.0	2.3	2.5	2.7	2.9	3.1	3.3	3.5	3.5	3.7	4.0	4.1	4.3	4.5	4.6	4.8	4.9	5.0	5.2	5.3	5.4	5.5	5.7	5.8	5.9	6.0	6.1	6.2	6.4	6.5	6.6	6.7	6.8	6.9	7.0
67	0.2	0.6	1.0	1.3	1.6	1.9	2.1	2.3	2.5	2.7	2.9	3.1	3.1	3.3	3.6	3.8	3.9	4.1	4.2	4.4	4.5	4.7	4.8	4.9	5.1	5.2	5.3	5.4	5.5	5.6	5.7	5.8	6.0	6.1	6.2	6.3	6.4	6.5	6.6
66	0.0	0.4	0.7	1.1	1.2	1.6	1.7	1.9	2.1	2.3	2.5	2.7	2.7	2.9	3.2	3.4	3.5	3.7	3.8	4.0	4.1	4.3	4.4	4.5	4.7	4.8	4.9	5.0	5.1	5.2	5.3	5.4	5.6	5.7	5.8	5.9	6.0	6.1	6.2
65	0.0	0.2	0.4	0.9	1.0	1.2	1.4	1.6	1.8	2.0	2.1	2.3	2.5	2.7	2.8	3.0	3.1	3.3	3.4	3.6	3.7	3.8	4.0	4.1	4.3	4.4	4.5	4.6	4.7	4.8	4.9	5.0	5.2	5.3	5.4	5.5	5.6	5.7	5.8
64	0.0	0.1	0.3	0.5	0.7	1.0	1.1	1.3	1.5	1.7	1.9	2.0	2.3	2.4	2.6	2.6	2.8	3.0	3.2	3.3	3.5	3.6	3.7	3.8	4.0	4.1	4.2	4.3	4.4	4.4	4.5	4.7	4.8	4.9	5.0	5.1	5.2	5.3	5.4
63	0.0	0.0	0.2	0.4	0.4	0.6	0.9	1.1	1.2	1.4	1.5	1.7	1.9	2.1	2.2	2.4	2.6	2.7	2.8	3.0	3.2	3.3	3.4	3.5	3.7	3.8	3.9	4.0	4.1	4.1	4.2	4.4	4.4	4.5	4.6	4.7	4.8	4.9	5.0
62	0.0	0.0	0.1	0.2	0.4	0.5	0.7	0.9	1.1	1.2	1.3	1.5	1.7	1.9	2.0	2.1	2.3	2.5	2.5	2.8	2.8	3.0	3.2	3.3	3.4	3.5	3.6	3.8	3.8	3.9	4.0	4.1	4.0	4.2	4.2	4.4	4.5	4.5	4.6
61	0.0	0.0	0.0	0.1	0.2	0.3	0.5	0.7	0.8	1.0	1.1	1.3	1.5	1.5	1.8	1.8	2.0	2.1	2.2	2.4	2.5	2.6	2.8	2.9	3.0	3.1	3.3	3.4	3.5	3.6	3.7	3.8	3.9	4.0	4.1	4.2	4.3	4.4	4.6
60	0.0	0.0	0.0	0.0	0.1	0.2	0.3	0.5	0.6	0.7	0.9	1.1	1.3	1.4	1.6	1.6	1.8	2.0	2.1	2.2	2.3	2.4	2.6	2.7	2.8	2.9	3.1	3.0	3.1	3.3	3.3	3.4	3.6	3.7	3.8	3.9	4.0	4.1	4.2
59	0.0	0.0	0.0	0.0	0.0	0.1	0.2	0.3	0.5	0.6	0.7	0.9	1.1	1.2	1.2	1.4	1.6	1.7	1.8	1.9	2.0	2.2	2.3	2.4	2.5	2.6	2.7	2.8	2.9	3.0	3.1	3.2	3.3	3.4	3.5	3.6	3.7	3.8	3.9
58	0.0	0.0	0.0	0.0	0.0	0.0	0.1	0.2	0.3	0.5	0.6	0.7	0.9	1.0	1.1	1.2	1.3	1.5	1.5	1.7	1.8	1.9	2.0	2.2	2.2	2.4	2.5	2.6	2.7	2.8	2.9	2.9	3.1	3.2	3.3	3.4	3.5	3.6	3.7
57	0.0	0.0	0.0	0.0	0.0	0.0	0.0	0.1	0.2	0.3	0.5	0.6	0.7	0.8	1.0	1.1	1.2	1.3	1.4	1.6	1.6	1.8	1.9	2.0	2.1	2.3	2.3	2.5	2.6	2.7	2.8	2.9	3.0	3.1	3.2	3.3	3.4	3.5	3.6
56	0.0	0.0	0.0	0.0	0.0	0.0	0.0	0.0	0.1	0.2	0.3	0.5	0.6	0.7	0.8	0.9	1.1	1.2	1.3	1.4	1.5	1.6	1.8	1.9	2.0	2.1	2.2	2.3	2.4	2.5	2.6	2.6	2.9	3.0	3.0	3.1	3.2	3.3	3.4
55	0.0	0.0	0.0	0.0	0.0	0.0	0.0	0.0	0.0	0.1	0.2	0.3	0.5	0.6	0.7	0.8	0.9	1.0	1.2	1.3	1.3	1.4	1.6	1.7	1.8	1.9	2.0	2.1	2.2	2.3	2.4	2.5	2.6	2.7	2.8	2.9	3.0	3.1	3.2
54	0.0	0.0	0.0	0.0	0.0	0.0	0.0	0.0	0.0	0.0	0.1	0.2	0.3	0.5	0.5	0.7	0.8	0.9	1.0	1.1	1.2	1.3	1.4	1.5	1.6	1.7	1.8	1.9	2.0	2.1	2.2	2.3	2.4	2.5	2.6	2.7	2.8	2.9	3.0
53	0.0	0.0	0.0	0.0	0.0	0.0	0.0	0.0	0.0	0.0	0.0	0.1	0.2	0.3	0.4	0.6	0.7	0.8	0.9	1.0	1.1	1.2	1.3	1.4	1.5	1.6	1.7	1.8	1.9	2.0	2.1	2.2	2.3	2.4	2.5	2.6	2.7	2.8	3.0
52	0.0	0.0	0.0	0.0	0.0	0.0	0.0	0.0	0.0	0.0	0.0	0.0	0.1	0.2	0.3	0.4	0.5	0.6	0.7	0.8	0.9	1.0	1.1	1.2	1.3	1.4	1.5	1.6	1.7	1.8	1.9	2.0	2.1	2.2	2.3	2.4	2.5	2.5	2.6
51	0.0	0.0	0.0	0.0	0.0	0.0	0.0	0.0	0.0	0.0	0.0	0.0	0.0	0.1	0.2	0.3	0.4	0.5	0.6	0.7	0.8	0.9	1.0	1.1	1.2	1.3	1.3	1.5	1.5	1.7	1.7	1.8	1.9	2.0	2.1	2.1	2.2	2.3	2.2
50	0.0	0.0	0.0	0.0	0.0	0.0	0.0	0.0	0.0	0.0	0.0	0.0	0.0	0.0	0.0	0.2	0.3	0.4	0.5	0.6	0.6	0.8	0.9	1.0	1.0	1.1	1.3	1.3	1.4	1.5	1.6	1.7	1.8	1.9	1.9	1.5	1.5	1.3	1.4
49	0.0	0.0	0.0	0.0	0.0	0.0	0.0	0.0	0.0	0.0	0.0	0.0	0.0	0.0	0.0	0.0	0.0	0.1	0.2	0.3	0.4	0.5	0.6	0.7	0.8	0.9	1.0	1.0	1.1	1.2	1.3	1.3	1.4	1.5	1.4	1.1	1.0	0.8	0.6

LISTED CALL OPTION PRICE WHEN EXERCISE PRICE IS 80

Common Stock Price	NUMBER OF WEEKS BEFORE THE OPTION EXPIRES																																					
	1	2	3	4	5	6	7	8	9	10	11	12	13	14	15	16	17	18	19	20	21	22	23	24	25	26	27	28	29	30	31	32	33	34	35	36	37	38	39
104	24.1	24.2	24.3	24.4	24.5	24.6	24.7	24.7	24.8	24.9	25.0	25.1	25.2	25.3	25.4	25.5	25.6	25.7	25.8	25.9	26.0	26.1	26.1	26.2	26.3	26.4	26.5	26.6	26.7	26.8	26.9	27.0	27.1	27.2	27.3	27.4	27.5	27.5	27.6
102	22.1	22.2	22.3	22.4	22.5	22.6	22.7	22.8	22.9	23.0	23.1	23.2	23.3	23.5	23.6	23.7	23.8	23.9	24.0	24.1	24.2	24.3	24.4	24.5	24.6	24.7	24.8	24.9	25.0	25.1	25.2	25.3	25.4	25.5	25.6	25.7	25.8	25.9	26.0
100	20.1	20.2	20.3	20.5	20.6	20.7	20.8	20.9	21.0	21.1	21.3	21.4	21.5	21.6	21.7	21.8	21.9	22.0	22.2	22.3	22.4	22.5	22.6	22.7	22.8	23.0	23.1	23.2	23.3	23.4	23.5	23.6	23.8	23.9	24.0	24.1	24.2	24.3	24.4
99	19.1	19.2	19.4	19.5	19.6	19.7	19.8	19.9	20.1	20.2	20.3	20.4	20.5	20.7	20.8	20.9	21.0	21.1	21.3	21.4	21.5	21.6	21.7	21.9	22.0	22.1	22.2	22.3	22.5	22.6	22.7	22.8	22.9	23.0	23.2	23.3	23.4	23.5	23.6
98	18.1	18.2	18.4	18.5	18.6	18.7	18.9	19.0	19.1	19.2	19.4	19.5	19.6	19.7	19.9	19.9	20.1	20.2	20.4	20.5	20.6	20.7	20.9	21.0	21.1	21.2	21.4	21.5	21.6	21.7	21.8	22.0	22.1	22.2	22.3	22.5	22.6	22.7	22.8
97	17.1	17.3	17.4	17.5	17.6	17.8	17.9	18.0	18.2	18.3	18.4	18.6	18.7	18.8	18.9	19.1	19.2	19.3	19.5	19.6	19.7	19.8	19.9	20.1	20.2	20.4	20.5	20.6	20.7	20.9	21.0	21.1	21.3	21.4	21.5	21.7	21.8	21.9	22.0
96	16.1	16.3	16.4	16.5	16.7	16.8	16.9	17.1	17.2	17.3	17.5	17.6	17.7	17.9	18.0	18.1	18.3	18.4	18.6	18.7	18.8	19.0	19.1	19.2	19.4	19.5	19.6	19.8	19.9	20.0	20.2	20.3	20.4	20.6	20.7	20.8	21.0	21.1	21.2
95	15.1	15.3	15.4	15.6	15.7	15.8	16.0	16.1	16.3	16.4	16.5	16.7	16.8	17.0	17.1	17.2	17.4	17.5	17.7	17.8	17.9	18.1	18.2	18.3	18.5	18.6	18.8	18.9	19.0	19.2	19.3	19.5	19.6	19.7	19.9	20.0	20.2	20.3	20.4
94	14.1	14.3	14.4	14.6	14.7	14.9	15.0	15.2	15.3	15.4	15.6	15.7	15.9	16.0	16.2	16.3	16.5	16.6	16.7	16.9	17.0	17.2	17.3	17.5	17.6	17.8	17.9	18.0	18.2	18.3	18.5	18.6	18.8	18.9	19.1	19.2	19.4	19.5	19.6
93	13.1	13.3	13.4	13.6	13.7	13.9	14.0	14.2	14.3	14.5	14.6	14.8	14.9	15.1	15.2	15.4	15.5	15.7	15.8	16.0	16.1	16.3	16.4	16.6	16.7	16.9	17.0	17.2	17.3	17.5	17.6	17.8	17.9	18.1	18.2	18.4	18.5	18.7	18.8
92	12.2	12.3	12.5	12.6	12.8	12.9	13.1	13.2	13.4	13.5	13.7	13.9	14.0	14.2	14.3	14.5	14.6	14.8	14.9	15.1	15.3	15.4	15.6	15.7	15.9	16.0	16.2	16.3	16.5	16.6	16.8	17.0	17.1	17.3	17.4	17.6	17.7	17.9	18.0
91	11.2	11.3	11.5	11.6	11.8	12.0	12.1	12.3	12.4	12.6	12.8	12.9	13.1	13.2	13.4	13.6	13.7	13.9	14.0	14.2	14.4	14.5	14.7	14.8	15.0	15.2	15.3	15.5	15.6	15.8	16.0	16.1	16.3	16.4	16.6	16.8	16.9	17.1	17.2
90	10.2	10.3	10.5	10.7	10.8	11.0	11.2	11.3	11.5	11.7	11.8	12.0	12.1	12.3	12.5	12.6	12.8	13.0	13.1	13.3	13.5	13.6	13.8	14.0	14.1	14.3	14.5	14.6	14.8	15.0	15.1	15.3	15.4	15.6	15.8	15.9	16.1	16.3	16.4
89	9.2	9.3	9.5	9.7	9.9	10.0	10.2	10.4	10.5	10.7	10.9	11.0	11.2	11.4	11.6	11.7	11.9	12.1	12.2	12.4	12.6	12.7	12.9	13.1	13.3	13.4	13.6	13.8	13.9	14.1	14.3	14.4	14.6	14.8	15.0	15.1	15.3	15.5	15.6
88	8.2	8.3	8.5	8.7	8.9	9.1	9.3	9.5	9.6	9.8	9.9	10.1	10.2	10.4	10.6	10.7	11.0	11.2	11.3	11.4	11.6	11.7	11.9	12.1	12.3	12.4	12.6	12.8	13.0	13.2	13.4	13.5	13.7	13.9	14.1	14.2	14.4	14.6	14.7
87	7.2	7.4	7.5	7.8	7.9	8.2	8.4	8.6	8.6	8.8	9.0	9.1	9.3	9.5	9.7	9.8	10.1	10.3	10.4	10.5	10.7	10.8	11.0	11.2	11.4	11.5	11.7	11.9	12.1	12.3	12.5	12.6	12.8	13.0	13.2	13.4	13.5	13.7	13.8
86	6.2	6.4	6.6	6.8	7.0	7.3	7.5	7.7	7.7	7.9	8.0	8.2	8.4	8.6	8.8	8.9	9.2	9.4	9.5	9.6	9.8	9.9	10.1	10.3	10.5	10.6	10.8	11.0	11.2	11.4	11.7	11.7	11.9	12.1	12.3	12.5	12.6	12.8	12.9
85	5.3	5.4	5.6	5.9	6.1	6.4	6.6	6.8	6.8	6.9	7.1	7.3	7.5	7.7	7.9	8.0	8.3	8.5	8.6	8.7	8.9	9.0	9.2	9.4	9.6	9.7	9.9	10.1	10.3	10.5	10.9	10.9	11.1	11.2	11.4	11.6	11.7	11.9	12.0
84	4.3	4.4	4.6	4.9	5.2	5.5	5.7	5.9	6.1	6.2	6.3	6.5	6.7	6.9	7.1	7.3	7.5	7.6	7.8	8.0	8.1	8.3	8.4	8.6	8.7	8.9	9.0	9.3	9.4	9.6	10.0	10.1	10.2	10.3	10.5	10.7	10.8	11.0	11.1
83	2.4	3.4	3.7	4.1	4.4	4.7	5.0	5.2	5.5	5.7	5.9	6.1	6.3	6.5	6.7	6.9	7.1	7.2	7.4	7.6	7.7	7.9	8.0	8.2	8.3	8.5	8.6	8.7	8.9	9.0	9.1	9.3	9.4	9.5	9.6	9.9	10.0	10.2	10.2
82	2.4	2.8	3.3	3.6	4.0	4.3	4.6	4.8	5.1	5.3	5.5	5.7	5.9	6.1	6.3	6.6	6.7	6.8	7.0	7.2	7.3	7.5	7.6	7.8	7.9	8.1	8.2	8.3	8.5	8.6	8.7	8.9	9.0	9.1	9.2	9.3	9.5	9.6	9.7
81	1.8	2.4	2.9	3.2	3.6	3.9	4.2	4.4	4.7	4.9	5.1	5.3	5.5	5.7	5.9	6.1	6.3	6.4	6.6	6.8	6.9	7.1	7.2	7.4	7.5	7.7	7.8	7.9	8.1	8.2	8.3	8.5	8.6	8.7	8.8	8.9	9.1	9.2	9.3
80	1.4	2.0	2.5	2.8	3.2	3.5	3.8	4.0	4.3	4.5	4.7	4.9	5.1	5.3	5.5	5.7	5.9	6.0	6.2	6.4	6.5	6.7	6.8	7.0	7.1	7.3	7.4	7.5	7.7	7.8	7.9	8.1	8.2	8.3	8.4	8.5	8.7	8.8	8.9
79	1.0	1.6	2.1	2.4	2.8	3.1	3.4	3.6	3.9	4.1	4.3	4.5	4.7	4.9	5.1	5.3	5.5	5.6	5.8	6.0	6.1	6.3	6.4	6.6	6.7	6.9	7.0	7.1	7.3	7.4	7.5	7.7	7.8	7.9	8.0	8.1	8.3	8.4	8.5
78	0.6	1.2	1.7	2.0	2.4	2.7	3.0	3.2	3.5	3.7	3.9	4.1	4.3	4.5	4.7	4.9	5.1	5.2	5.4	5.6	5.7	5.9	6.0	6.2	6.3	6.5	6.6	6.7	6.9	7.0	7.1	7.3	7.4	7.5	7.6	7.7	7.9	8.0	8.1
77	0.2	0.8	1.3	1.6	2.0	2.3	2.6	2.8	3.1	3.3	3.5	3.7	3.9	4.1	4.3	4.5	4.7	4.8	5.0	5.2	5.3	5.5	5.6	5.8	5.9	6.1	6.2	6.3	6.5	6.6	6.7	6.9	7.0	7.1	7.2	7.3	7.5	7.6	7.7
76	0.0	0.4	0.9	1.2	1.6	1.9	2.2	2.4	2.7	2.9	3.1	3.3	3.5	3.7	3.9	4.1	4.3	4.4	4.6	4.8	4.9	5.1	5.2	5.4	5.5	5.7	5.8	5.9	6.1	6.2	6.3	6.5	6.6	6.7	6.8	6.9	7.1	7.2	7.3
75	0.0	0.0	0.5	0.8	1.2	1.5	1.8	2.0	2.3	2.5	2.7	2.9	3.1	3.3	3.5	3.7	3.9	4.0	4.2	4.4	4.5	4.7	4.8	5.0	5.1	5.3	5.4	5.5	5.7	5.8	5.9	6.1	6.2	6.3	6.4	6.5	6.7	6.8	6.9
74	0.0	0.0	0.1	0.4	0.8	1.1	1.4	1.6	1.9	2.1	2.3	2.5	2.7	2.9	3.1	3.3	3.5	3.6	3.8	4.0	4.1	4.3	4.4	4.6	4.7	4.9	5.0	5.1	5.3	5.4	5.5	5.7	5.8	5.9	6.0	6.1	6.3	6.4	6.5
73	0.0	0.0	0.0	0.0	0.4	0.7	1.0	1.2	1.5	1.7	1.9	2.1	2.3	2.5	2.7	2.9	3.1	3.2	3.4	3.6	3.7	3.9	4.0	4.2	4.3	4.5	4.6	4.7	4.9	5.0	5.1	5.3	5.4	5.5	5.6	5.7	5.9	6.0	6.1
72	0.0	0.0	0.0	0.0	0.0	0.3	0.6	0.8	1.1	1.3	1.5	1.7	1.9	2.1	2.3	2.5	2.7	2.8	3.0	3.2	3.3	3.5	3.6	3.8	3.9	4.1	4.2	4.3	4.5	4.6	4.7	4.9	5.0	5.1	5.2	5.3	5.5	5.6	5.7
71	0.0	0.0	0.0	0.0	0.0	0.0	0.2	0.4	0.7	0.9	1.1	1.3	1.5	1.7	1.9	2.1	2.3	2.4	2.6	2.8	2.9	3.1	3.2	3.4	3.5	3.7	3.8	3.9	4.1	4.2	4.3	4.5	4.6	4.7	4.8	4.9	5.1	5.2	5.3
70	0.0	0.0	0.0	0.0	0.0	0.0	0.0	0.0	0.3	0.5	0.7	0.9	1.1	1.3	1.5	1.7	1.9	2.0	2.2	2.4	2.5	2.7	2.8	3.0	3.1	3.3	3.4	3.5	3.7	3.8	3.9	4.1	4.2	4.3	4.4	4.5	4.7	4.8	4.9
69	0.0	0.0	0.0	0.0	0.0	0.0	0.0	0.0	0.0	0.1	0.3	0.5	0.7	0.9	1.1	1.3	1.5	1.6	1.8	2.0	2.1	2.3	2.4	2.6	2.7	2.9	3.0	3.1	3.3	3.4	3.5	3.7	3.8	3.9	4.0	4.1	4.3	4.4	4.5
68	0.0	0.0	0.0	0.0	0.0	0.0	0.0	0.0	0.0	0.0	0.0	0.1	0.3	0.5	0.7	0.9	1.1	1.2	1.4	1.6	1.7	1.9	2.0	2.2	2.3	2.5	2.6	2.7	2.9	3.0	3.1	3.3	3.4	3.5	3.6	3.7	3.9	4.0	4.1
67	0.0	0.0	0.0	0.0	0.0	0.0	0.0	0.0	0.0	0.0	0.0	0.0	0.0	0.1	0.3	0.5	0.7	0.8	1.0	1.2	1.3	1.5	1.6	1.8	1.9	2.1	2.2	2.3	2.5	2.6	2.7	2.9	3.0	3.1	3.2	3.3	3.5	3.6	3.7
66	0.0	0.0	0.0	0.0	0.0	0.0	0.0	0.0	0.0	0.0	0.0	0.0	0.0	0.0	0.0	0.1	0.3	0.4	0.6	0.8	0.9	1.1	1.2	1.4	1.5	1.7	1.8	1.9	2.1	2.2	2.3	2.5	2.6	2.7	2.8	2.9	3.1	3.2	3.3
65	0.0	0.0	0.0	0.0	0.0	0.0	0.0	0.0	0.0	0.0	0.0	0.0	0.0	0.0	0.0	0.0	0.0	0.0	0.2	0.4	0.5	0.7	0.8	1.0	1.1	1.3	1.4	1.5	1.7	1.8	1.9	2.1	2.2	2.3	2.4	2.5	2.7	2.8	2.9
64	0.0	0.0	0.0	0.0	0.0	0.0	0.0	0.0	0.0	0.0	0.0	0.0	0.0	0.0	0.0	0.0	0.0	0.0	0.0	0.0	0.1	0.3	0.4	0.6	0.7	0.9	1.0	1.1	1.3	1.4	1.5	1.7	1.8	1.9	2.0	2.1	2.3	2.4	2.5
63	0.0	0.0	0.0	0.0	0.0	0.0	0.0	0.0	0.0	0.0	0.0	0.0	0.0	0.0	0.0	0.0	0.0	0.0	0.0	0.0	0.0	0.0	0.0	0.2	0.3	0.5	0.6	0.7	0.9	1.0	1.1	1.3	1.4	1.5	1.7	1.8	1.9	2.0	2.1
62	0.0	0.0	0.0	0.0	0.0	0.0	0.0	0.0	0.0	0.0	0.0	0.0	0.0	0.0	0.0	0.0	0.0	0.0	0.0	0.0	0.0	0.0	0.0	0.0	0.0	0.1	0.2	0.3	0.5	0.6	0.7	0.9	1.0	1.1	1.2	1.3	1.5	1.6	1.7
61	0.0	0.0	0.0	0.0	0.0	0.0	0.0	0.0	0.0	0.0	0.0	0.0	0.0	0.0	0.0	0.0	0.0	0.0	0.0	0.0	0.0	0.0	0.0	0.0	0.0	0.0	0.0	0.0	0.1	0.2	0.3	0.5	0.6	0.7	0.8	0.9	1.1	1.2	1.3
60	0.0	0.0	0.0	0.0	0.0	0.0	0.0	0.0	0.0	0.0	0.0	0.0	0.0	0.0	0.0	0.0	0.0	0.0	0.0	0.0	0.0	0.0	0.0	0.0	0.0	0.0	0.0	0.0	0.0	0.0	0.0	0.1	0.2	0.3	0.4	0.5	0.7	0.8	0.9
59	0.0	0.0	0.0	0.0	0.0	0.0	0.0	0.0	0.0	0.0	0.0	0.0	0.0	0.0	0.0	0.0	0.0	0.0	0.0	0.0	0.0	0.0	0.0	0.0	0.0	0.0	0.0	0.0	0.0	0.0	0.0	0.0	0.0	0.0	0.0	0.1	0.3	0.4	0.5
58	0.0	0.0	0.0	0.0	0.0	0.0	0.0	0.0	0.0	0.0	0.0	0.0	0.0	0.0	0.0	0.0	0.0	0.0	0.0	0.0	0.0	0.0	0.0	0.0	0.0	0.0	0.0	0.0	0.0	0.0	0.0	0.0	0.0	0.0	0.0	0.0	0.0	0.0	0.1
57	0.0	0.0	0.0	0.0	0.0	0.0	0.0	0.0	0.0	0.0	0.0	0.0	0.0	0.0	0.0	0.0	0.0	0.0	0.0	0.0	0.0	0.0	0.0	0.0	0.0	0.0	0.0	0.0	0.0	0.0	0.0	0.0	0.0	0.0	0.0	0.0	0.0	0.0	0.0

LISTED CALL OPTION PRICE WHEN EXERCISE PRICE IS 90

Common Stock Price	NUMBER OF WEEKS BEFORE THE OPTION EXPIRES 1	2	3	4	5	6	7	8	9	10	11	12	13	14	15	16	17	18	19	20	21	22	23	24	25	26	27	28	29	30	31	32	33	34	35	36	37	38	39
118	28.1	28.2	28.3	28.4	28.5	28.6	28.7	28.8	28.9	29.0	29.1	29.2	29.3	29.4	29.5	29.6	29.7	29.8	29.9	29.9	30.1	30.2	30.3	30.4	30.5	30.6	30.7	30.8	30.9	31.0	31.1	31.2	31.3	31.4	31.5	31.6	31.7	31.8	31.9
116	26.1	26.2	26.3	26.4	26.6	26.7	26.8	26.9	27.0	27.1	27.2	27.3	27.4	27.5	27.7	27.8	27.9	28.0	28.1	28.2	28.3	28.4	28.5	28.6	28.8	28.9	29.0	29.1	29.2	29.3	29.4	29.5	29.6	29.7	29.8	29.9	30.1	30.2	30.3
114	24.1	24.2	24.4	24.5	24.6	24.7	24.8	25.0	25.1	25.2	25.3	25.4	25.6	25.7	25.8	25.9	26.0	26.2	26.3	26.4	26.5	26.6	26.8	26.9	27.0	27.1	27.3	27.4	27.5	27.6	27.7	27.9	28.0	28.1	28.2	28.3	28.5	28.6	28.7
112	22.1	22.3	22.4	22.5	22.7	22.8	22.9	23.0	23.2	23.3	23.4	23.6	23.7	23.8	24.0	24.1	24.2	24.4	24.5	24.6	24.7	24.9	25.0	25.1	25.3	25.4	25.5	25.7	25.8	25.9	26.0	26.2	26.3	26.4	26.6	26.7	26.8	27.0	27.1
110	20.1	20.3	20.4	20.6	20.7	20.8	21.0	21.1	21.3	21.4	21.5	21.7	21.8	22.0	22.1	22.3	22.4	22.5	22.7	22.8	23.0	23.1	23.2	23.4	23.5	23.7	23.8	23.9	24.1	24.2	24.4	24.5	24.6	24.8	24.9	25.1	25.2	25.4	25.5
108	18.2	18.3	18.5	18.6	18.8	18.9	19.1	19.2	19.4	19.5	19.7	19.8	19.9	20.1	20.3	20.4	20.6	20.7	20.9	21.0	21.2	21.3	21.5	21.6	21.8	21.9	22.1	22.2	22.4	22.5	22.7	22.8	23.0	23.1	23.3	23.4	23.6	23.7	23.9
106	16.2	16.3	16.5	16.6	16.8	17.0	17.1	17.3	17.5	17.6	17.8	17.9	18.1	18.3	18.4	18.6	18.7	18.9	19.1	19.2	19.4	19.6	19.7	19.9	20.0	20.2	20.4	20.5	20.7	20.8	21.0	21.2	21.3	21.5	21.6	21.8	22.0	22.1	22.3
104	14.2	14.3	14.5	14.7	14.9	15.0	15.2	15.4	15.5	15.7	15.9	16.1	16.2	16.4	16.6	16.7	16.9	17.1	17.3	17.4	17.6	17.8	17.9	18.1	18.3	18.5	18.6	18.8	19.0	19.1	19.3	19.5	19.7	19.8	20.0	20.2	20.4	20.5	20.7
102	12.2	12.4	12.5	12.7	12.9	13.1	13.3	13.5	13.6	13.8	14.0	14.2	14.4	14.5	14.7	14.9	15.1	15.3	15.5	15.6	15.8	16.0	16.2	16.4	16.5	16.7	16.9	17.1	17.3	17.5	17.6	17.8	18.0	18.2	18.4	18.5	18.7	18.9	19.1
100	10.2	10.4	10.6	10.8	11.0	11.2	11.3	11.5	11.7	11.9	12.1	12.3	12.5	12.7	12.9	13.1	13.3	13.5	13.7	13.8	14.0	14.2	14.4	14.6	14.8	15.0	15.2	15.4	15.6	15.8	16.0	16.1	16.3	16.5	16.7	16.9	17.1	17.3	17.5
99	9.2	9.4	9.6	9.8	10.0	10.2	10.4	10.6	10.7	10.9	11.1	11.4	11.6	11.8	12.0	12.2	12.4	12.6	12.8	12.9	13.1	13.3	13.5	13.7	13.9	14.1	14.3	14.5	14.7	14.9	15.1	15.2	15.4	15.6	15.8	16.0	16.2	16.4	16.6
98	8.2	8.4	8.6	8.8	9.1	9.3	9.4	9.6	9.8	10.0	10.2	10.5	10.7	10.9	11.1	11.3	11.5	11.7	11.9	12.0	12.2	12.4	12.6	12.8	13.0	13.2	13.4	13.6	13.8	14.0	14.2	14.3	14.5	14.7	14.9	15.1	15.3	15.4	15.7
97	7.2	7.4	7.6	7.9	8.1	8.3	8.5	8.7	8.8	9.0	9.3	9.6	9.8	10.0	10.2	10.4	10.6	10.8	11.0	11.1	11.3	11.5	11.7	11.9	12.1	12.3	12.5	12.7	12.9	13.1	13.3	13.4	13.6	13.8	14.0	14.2	14.4	14.6	14.8
96	6.3	6.5	6.7	6.9	7.2	7.4	7.5	7.7	7.9	8.1	8.4	8.7	8.9	9.1	9.3	9.5	9.7	9.9	10.1	10.2	10.4	10.6	10.8	11.0	11.2	11.4	11.6	11.8	12.0	12.2	12.4	12.5	12.7	12.9	13.1	13.3	13.5	13.7	13.9
95	5.3	5.5	5.7	6.0	6.3	6.5	6.6	6.8	7.0	7.2	7.5	7.8	8.0	8.2	8.4	8.6	8.8	9.0	9.2	9.3	9.5	9.7	9.9	10.1	10.3	10.5	10.7	10.9	11.1	11.3	11.5	11.6	11.8	12.0	12.2	12.4	12.6	12.8	13.0
94	4.4	4.5	4.8	5.1	5.4	5.6	5.8	6.1	6.4	6.7	6.9	7.1	7.4	7.6	7.8	8.0	8.2	8.4	8.6	8.8	8.9	9.1	9.3	9.4	9.6	9.8	9.9	10.1	10.2	10.4	10.6	10.7	10.9	11.1	11.3	11.5	11.7	11.9	12.1
93	3.4	3.5	4.0	4.4	4.8	5.1	5.4	5.7	6.0	6.3	6.5	6.7	7.0	7.2	7.4	7.6	7.8	8.0	8.2	8.4	8.5	8.7	8.9	9.0	9.2	9.4	9.5	9.7	9.8	9.9	10.1	10.3	10.4	10.5	10.7	10.8	10.9	11.1	11.2
92	2.5	3.1	3.6	4.0	4.4	4.7	5.0	5.3	5.6	5.9	6.1	6.3	6.6	6.8	7.0	7.2	7.4	7.6	7.8	8.0	8.1	8.3	8.5	8.6	8.8	9.0	9.1	9.3	9.4	9.6	9.7	9.9	9.9	10.1	10.3	10.4	10.5	10.7	10.8
91	2.0	2.7	3.2	3.6	4.0	4.3	4.6	4.9	5.2	5.5	5.7	5.9	6.2	6.4	6.6	6.8	7.0	7.2	7.4	7.6	7.7	7.9	8.1	8.2	8.4	8.6	8.7	8.9	9.0	9.2	9.3	9.5	9.6	9.7	9.9	10.0	10.1	10.3	10.4
90	1.6	2.3	2.8	3.2	3.6	3.9	4.2	4.5	4.8	5.1	5.3	5.5	5.8	6.0	6.2	6.4	6.6	6.8	7.0	7.2	7.3	7.5	7.7	7.8	8.0	8.2	8.3	8.5	8.6	8.8	8.9	9.1	9.2	9.3	9.5	9.6	9.7	9.9	10.0
89	1.2	1.9	2.4	2.8	3.2	3.5	3.8	4.1	4.4	4.7	4.9	5.1	5.4	5.6	5.8	6.0	6.2	6.4	6.6	6.8	6.9	7.1	7.3	7.4	7.6	7.8	7.9	8.1	8.2	8.4	8.5	8.7	8.8	8.9	9.1	9.2	9.3	9.5	9.6
88	0.8	1.5	2.0	2.4	2.8	3.1	3.4	3.7	4.0	4.3	4.5	4.7	5.0	5.2	5.4	5.6	5.8	6.0	6.2	6.4	6.5	6.7	6.9	7.0	7.2	7.4	7.5	7.7	7.8	8.0	8.1	8.3	8.4	8.5	8.7	8.8	8.9	9.1	9.2
87	0.4	1.1	1.6	2.0	2.4	2.7	3.0	3.3	3.6	3.9	4.1	4.3	4.6	4.8	5.0	5.2	5.4	5.6	5.8	6.0	6.1	6.3	6.5	6.6	6.8	7.0	7.1	7.3	7.4	7.6	7.7	7.9	8.0	8.1	8.3	8.4	8.5	8.7	8.8
86	0.0	0.7	1.2	1.6	2.0	2.3	2.6	2.9	3.2	3.5	3.7	3.9	4.2	4.4	4.6	4.8	5.0	5.2	5.4	5.6	5.7	5.9	6.1	6.2	6.4	6.6	6.7	6.9	7.0	7.2	7.3	7.5	7.6	7.7	7.9	8.0	8.1	8.3	8.4
85	0.0	0.3	0.8	1.2	1.6	1.9	2.2	2.5	2.8	3.1	3.3	3.5	3.8	4.0	4.2	4.4	4.6	4.8	5.0	5.2	5.3	5.5	5.7	5.8	6.0	6.2	6.3	6.5	6.6	6.8	6.9	7.1	7.2	7.3	7.5	7.6	7.7	7.9	8.0
84	0.0	0.0	0.4	0.8	1.2	1.5	1.8	2.1	2.4	2.7	2.9	3.1	3.4	3.6	3.8	4.0	4.2	4.4	4.6	4.8	4.9	5.1	5.3	5.4	5.6	5.8	5.9	6.1	6.2	6.4	6.5	6.7	6.8	6.9	7.1	7.2	7.3	7.5	7.6
83	0.0	0.0	0.0	0.4	0.8	1.1	1.4	1.7	2.0	2.3	2.5	2.7	3.0	3.2	3.4	3.6	3.8	4.0	4.2	4.4	4.5	4.7	4.9	5.0	5.2	5.4	5.5	5.7	5.8	6.0	6.1	6.3	6.4	6.5	6.7	6.8	6.9	7.1	7.2
82	0.0	0.0	0.0	0.0	0.4	0.7	1.0	1.3	1.6	1.9	2.1	2.3	2.6	2.8	3.0	3.2	3.4	3.6	3.8	4.0	4.1	4.3	4.5	4.6	4.8	5.0	5.1	5.3	5.4	5.6	5.7	5.9	6.0	6.1	6.3	6.4	6.5	6.7	6.8
81	0.0	0.0	0.0	0.0	0.0	0.3	0.6	0.9	1.2	1.5	1.7	1.9	2.2	2.4	2.6	2.8	3.0	3.2	3.4	3.6	3.7	3.9	4.1	4.2	4.4	4.6	4.7	4.9	5.0	5.2	5.3	5.5	5.6	5.7	5.9	6.0	6.1	6.3	6.4
80	0.0	0.0	0.0	0.0	0.0	0.0	0.2	0.5	0.8	1.1	1.3	1.5	1.8	2.0	2.2	2.4	2.6	2.8	3.0	3.2	3.3	3.5	3.7	3.8	4.0	4.2	4.3	4.5	4.6	4.8	4.9	5.1	5.2	5.3	5.5	5.6	5.7	5.9	6.0
79	0.0	0.0	0.0	0.0	0.0	0.0	0.0	0.1	0.4	0.7	0.9	1.1	1.4	1.6	1.8	2.0	2.2	2.4	2.6	2.8	2.9	3.1	3.3	3.4	3.6	3.8	3.9	4.1	4.2	4.4	4.5	4.7	4.8	4.9	5.1	5.2	5.3	5.5	5.6
78	0.0	0.0	0.0	0.0	0.0	0.0	0.0	0.0	0.0	0.3	0.5	0.7	1.0	1.2	1.4	1.6	1.8	2.0	2.2	2.4	2.5	2.7	2.9	3.0	3.2	3.4	3.5	3.7	3.8	4.0	4.1	4.3	4.4	4.5	4.7	4.8	4.9	5.1	5.2
77	0.0	0.0	0.0	0.0	0.0	0.0	0.0	0.0	0.0	0.0	0.1	0.3	0.6	0.8	1.0	1.2	1.4	1.6	1.8	2.0	2.1	2.3	2.5	2.6	2.8	3.0	3.1	3.3	3.4	3.6	3.7	3.8	4.0	4.1	4.3	4.4	4.5	4.7	4.8
76	0.0	0.0	0.0	0.0	0.0	0.0	0.0	0.0	0.0	0.0	0.0	0.0	0.2	0.4	0.6	0.8	1.0	1.2	1.4	1.6	1.7	1.9	2.1	2.2	2.4	2.6	2.7	2.9	3.0	3.2	3.3	3.5	3.6	3.7	3.9	4.0	4.1	4.3	4.4
75	0.0	0.0	0.0	0.0	0.0	0.0	0.0	0.0	0.0	0.0	0.0	0.0	0.0	0.0	0.2	0.4	0.6	0.8	1.0	1.2	1.3	1.5	1.7	1.8	2.0	2.2	2.3	2.5	2.6	2.8	2.9	3.1	3.2	3.3	3.5	3.6	3.7	3.9	4.0
74	0.0	0.0	0.0	0.0	0.0	0.0	0.0	0.0	0.0	0.0	0.0	0.0	0.0	0.0	0.0	0.0	0.2	0.4	0.6	0.8	0.9	1.1	1.3	1.4	1.6	1.8	1.9	2.1	2.2	2.4	2.5	2.7	2.8	2.9	3.1	3.2	3.3	3.5	3.6
73	0.0	0.0	0.0	0.0	0.0	0.0	0.0	0.0	0.0	0.0	0.0	0.0	0.0	0.0	0.0	0.0	0.0	0.0	0.2	0.4	0.5	0.7	0.9	1.0	1.2	1.4	1.5	1.7	1.8	2.0	2.1	2.3	2.4	2.5	2.7	2.8	2.9	3.1	3.2
72	0.0	0.0	0.0	0.0	0.0	0.0	0.0	0.0	0.0	0.0	0.0	0.0	0.0	0.0	0.0	0.0	0.0	0.0	0.0	0.0	0.1	0.3	0.5	0.6	0.8	1.0	1.1	1.3	1.4	1.6	1.7	1.9	2.0	2.1	2.3	2.4	2.5	2.7	2.8
71	0.0	0.0	0.0	0.0	0.0	0.0	0.0	0.0	0.0	0.0	0.0	0.0	0.0	0.0	0.0	0.0	0.0	0.0	0.0	0.0	0.0	0.0	0.1	0.2	0.4	0.6	0.7	0.9	1.0	1.2	1.3	1.5	1.6	1.7	1.9	2.0	2.1	2.3	2.4
70	0.0	0.0	0.0	0.0	0.0	0.0	0.0	0.0	0.0	0.0	0.0	0.0	0.0	0.0	0.0	0.0	0.0	0.0	0.0	0.0	0.0	0.0	0.0	0.0	0.0	0.2	0.3	0.5	0.6	0.8	0.9	1.1	1.2	1.3	1.5	1.6	1.7	1.9	2.0
69	0.0	0.0	0.0	0.0	0.0	0.0	0.0	0.0	0.0	0.0	0.0	0.0	0.0	0.0	0.0	0.0	0.0	0.0	0.0	0.0	0.0	0.0	0.0	0.0	0.0	0.0	0.0	0.1	0.2	0.4	0.5	0.7	0.8	0.9	1.1	1.2	1.3	1.5	1.6
68	0.0	0.0	0.0	0.0	0.0	0.0	0.0	0.0	0.0	0.0	0.0	0.0	0.0	0.0	0.0	0.0	0.0	0.0	0.0	0.0	0.0	0.0	0.0	0.0	0.0	0.0	0.0	0.0	0.0	0.0	0.1	0.3	0.4	0.5	0.7	0.8	0.9	1.1	1.2
67	0.0	0.0	0.0	0.0	0.0	0.0	0.0	0.0	0.0	0.0	0.0	0.0	0.0	0.0	0.0	0.0	0.0	0.0	0.0	0.0	0.0	0.0	0.0	0.0	0.0	0.0	0.0	0.0	0.0	0.0	0.0	0.0	0.0	0.1	0.3	0.4	0.5	0.7	0.8
66	0.0	0.0	0.0	0.0	0.0	0.0	0.0	0.0	0.0	0.0	0.0	0.0	0.0	0.0	0.0	0.0	0.0	0.0	0.0	0.0	0.0	0.0	0.0	0.0	0.0	0.0	0.0	0.0	0.0	0.0	0.0	0.0	0.0	0.0	0.0	0.0	0.1	0.3	0.4
65	0.0	0.0	0.0	0.0	0.0	0.0	0.0	0.0	0.0	0.0	0.0	0.0	0.0	0.0	0.0	0.0	0.0	0.0	0.0	0.0	0.0	0.0	0.0	0.0	0.0	0.0	0.0	0.0	0.0	0.0	0.0	0.0	0.0	0.0	0.0	0.0	0.0	0.0	0.0
64	0.0	0.0	0.0	0.0	0.0	0.0	0.0	0.0	0.0	0.0	0.0	0.0	0.0	0.0	0.0	0.0	0.0	0.0	0.0	0.0	0.0	0.0	0.0	0.0	0.0	0.0	0.0	0.0	0.0	0.0	0.0	0.0	0.0	0.0	0.0	0.0	0.0	0.0	0.0

LISTED CALL OPTION PRICE WHEN EXERCISE PRICE IS 100

NUMBER OF WEEKS BEFORE THE OPTION EXPIRES

Common Stock Price	1	2	3	4	5	6	7	8	9	10	11	12	13	14	15	16	17	18	19	20
130	30.1	30.2	30.3	30.5	30.6	30.7	30.8	30.9	31.0	31.2	31.3	31.4	31.5	31.6	31.8	31.9	32.0	32.1	32.2	32.3
128	28.1	28.3	28.4	28.5	28.6	28.8	28.9	29.0	29.1	29.3	29.4	29.5	29.7	29.8	29.9	30.0	30.2	30.3	30.4	30.5
126	26.1	26.3	26.4	26.5	26.7	26.8	27.0	27.1	27.2	27.4	27.5	27.6	27.8	27.9	28.1	28.2	28.3	28.5	28.6	28.7
124	24.1	24.3	24.4	24.6	24.7	24.9	25.0	25.2	25.3	25.5	25.6	25.8	25.9	26.1	26.2	26.4	26.5	26.7	26.8	26.9
122	22.2	22.3	22.5	22.6	22.8	22.9	23.1	23.3	23.4	23.6	23.7	23.9	24.1	24.2	24.4	24.5	24.7	24.8	25.0	25.2
120	20.2	20.3	20.5	20.7	20.8	21.0	21.2	21.3	21.5	21.7	21.8	22.0	22.2	22.4	22.5	22.7	22.9	23.0	23.2	23.4
118	18.2	18.4	18.5	18.7	18.9	19.1	19.2	19.4	19.6	19.8	19.9	20.1	20.3	20.5	20.7	20.9	21.0	21.2	21.4	21.6
116	16.2	16.4	16.6	16.8	16.9	17.1	17.3	17.5	17.7	17.9	18.1	18.3	18.5	18.6	18.8	19.0	19.2	19.4	19.6	19.8
114	14.2	14.4	14.6	14.8	15.0	15.2	15.4	15.6	15.8	16.0	16.2	16.4	16.6	16.8	17.0	17.2	17.4	17.6	17.8	18.0
112	12.2	12.4	12.6	12.8	13.0	13.3	13.5	13.7	13.9	14.1	14.3	14.5	14.7	14.9	15.1	15.3	15.6	15.8	16.0	16.2
110	10.2	10.4	10.6	10.8	11.0	11.3	11.5	11.7	12.0	12.2	12.4	12.6	12.8	13.0	13.4	13.6	13.9	14.1	14.2	14.4
108	8.2	8.4	8.7	8.9	9.2	9.4	9.6	9.8	10.1	10.3	10.6	10.8	11.0	11.2	11.7	11.9	12.2	12.4	12.6	12.8
106	6.3	6.5	6.8	7.0	7.3	7.5	7.7	7.9	8.2	8.6	8.8	9.0	9.3	9.6	10.0	10.2	10.5	10.7	10.9	11.1
104	4.4	4.6	4.8	5.2	5.6	6.0	6.3	6.6	6.9	7.2	7.5	7.8	8.0	8.3	8.5	8.7	8.9	9.1	9.4	9.6
102	2.6	3.3	4.0	4.4	4.8	5.2	5.5	5.8	6.1	6.4	6.7	7.0	7.2	7.5	7.7	7.9	8.1	8.3	8.6	8.8
100	1.8	2.5	3.1	3.6	4.0	4.4	4.7	5.0	5.3	5.6	5.9	6.2	6.4	6.7	6.9	7.1	7.3	7.5	7.8	8.0
99	1.4	2.1	2.7	3.2	3.6	4.0	4.3	4.6	4.9	5.2	5.5	5.8	6.0	6.3	6.5	6.7	6.9	7.1	7.4	7.6
98	1.0	1.7	2.3	2.8	3.2	3.6	3.9	4.2	4.5	4.8	5.1	5.4	5.6	5.9	6.1	6.3	6.5	6.7	7.0	7.2
97	0.6	1.3	1.9	2.4	2.8	3.2	3.5	3.8	4.1	4.4	4.7	5.0	5.2	5.5	5.7	5.9	6.1	6.3	6.6	6.8
96	0.2	0.9	1.5	2.0	2.4	2.8	3.1	3.4	3.7	4.0	4.3	4.6	4.8	5.1	5.3	5.5	5.7	5.9	6.2	6.4
95	0.0	0.5	1.1	1.6	2.0	2.4	2.7	3.0	3.3	3.6	3.9	4.2	4.4	4.7	4.9	5.1	5.3	5.5	5.8	6.0
94	0.0	0.1	0.7	1.2	1.6	2.0	2.3	2.6	2.9	3.2	3.5	3.8	4.0	4.3	4.5	4.7	4.9	5.1	5.4	5.6
93	0.0	0.0	0.3	0.8	1.2	1.6	1.9	2.2	2.5	2.8	3.1	3.4	3.6	3.9	4.1	4.3	4.5	4.7	5.0	5.2
92	0.0	0.0	0.0	0.4	0.8	1.2	1.5	1.8	2.1	2.4	2.7	3.0	3.2	3.5	3.7	3.9	4.1	4.3	4.6	4.8
91	0.0	0.0	0.0	0.0	0.4	0.8	1.1	1.4	1.7	2.0	2.3	2.6	2.8	3.1	3.3	3.5	3.7	3.9	4.2	4.4
90	0.0	0.0	0.0	0.0	0.0	0.4	0.7	1.0	1.3	1.6	1.9	2.2	2.4	2.7	2.9	3.1	3.3	3.5	3.8	4.0
89	0.0	0.0	0.0	0.0	0.0	0.0	0.3	0.6	0.9	1.2	1.5	1.8	2.0	2.3	2.5	2.7	2.9	3.1	3.4	3.6
88	0.0	0.0	0.0	0.0	0.0	0.0	0.0	0.2	0.5	0.8	1.1	1.4	1.6	1.9	2.1	2.3	2.5	2.7	3.0	3.2
87	0.0	0.0	0.0	0.0	0.0	0.0	0.0	0.0	0.1	0.4	0.7	1.0	1.2	1.5	1.7	1.9	2.1	2.3	2.6	2.8
86	0.0	0.0	0.0	0.0	0.0	0.0	0.0	0.0	0.0	0.0	0.3	0.6	0.8	1.1	1.3	1.5	1.7	1.9	2.2	2.4
85	0.0	0.0	0.0	0.0	0.0	0.0	0.0	0.0	0.0	0.0	0.0	0.2	0.4	0.7	0.9	1.1	1.3	1.5	1.8	2.0
84	0.0	0.0	0.0	0.0	0.0	0.0	0.0	0.0	0.0	0.0	0.0	0.0	0.0	0.3	0.5	0.7	0.9	1.1	1.4	1.6
83	0.0	0.0	0.0	0.0	0.0	0.0	0.0	0.0	0.0	0.0	0.0	0.0	0.0	0.0	0.1	0.3	0.5	0.7	1.0	1.2
82	0.0	0.0	0.0	0.0	0.0	0.0	0.0	0.0	0.0	0.0	0.0	0.0	0.0	0.0	0.0	0.0	0.1	0.3	0.6	0.8
81	0.0	0.0	0.0	0.0	0.0	0.0	0.0	0.0	0.0	0.0	0.0	0.0	0.0	0.0	0.0	0.0	0.0	0.0	0.2	0.4
80	0.0	0.0	0.0	0.0	0.0	0.0	0.0	0.0	0.0	0.0	0.0	0.0	0.0	0.0	0.0	0.0	0.0	0.0	0.0	0.0
79	0.0	0.0	0.0	0.0	0.0	0.0	0.0	0.0	0.0	0.0	0.0	0.0	0.0	0.0	0.0	0.0	0.0	0.0	0.0	0.0
78	0.0	0.0	0.0	0.0	0.0	0.0	0.0	0.0	0.0	0.0	0.0	0.0	0.0	0.0	0.0	0.0	0.0	0.0	0.0	0.0
77	0.0	0.0	0.0	0.0	0.0	0.0	0.0	0.0	0.0	0.0	0.0	0.0	0.0	0.0	0.0	0.0	0.0	0.0	0.0	0.0
76	0.0	0.0	0.0	0.0	0.0	0.0	0.0	0.0	0.0	0.0	0.0	0.0	0.0	0.0	0.0	0.0	0.0	0.0	0.0	0.0
75	0.0	0.0	0.0	0.0	0.0	0.0	0.0	0.0	0.0	0.0	0.0	0.0	0.0	0.0	0.0	0.0	0.0	0.0	0.0	0.0
74	0.0	0.0	0.0	0.0	0.0	0.0	0.0	0.0	0.0	0.0	0.0	0.0	0.0	0.0	0.0	0.0	0.0	0.0	0.0	0.0
73	0.0	0.0	0.0	0.0	0.0	0.0	0.0	0.0	0.0	0.0	0.0	0.0	0.0	0.0	0.0	0.0	0.0	0.0	0.0	0.0
72	0.0	0.0	0.0	0.0	0.0	0.0	0.0	0.0	0.0	0.0	0.0	0.0	0.0	0.0	0.0	0.0	0.0	0.0	0.0	0.0
71	0.0	0.0	0.0	0.0	0.0	0.0	0.0	0.0	0.0	0.0	0.0	0.0	0.0	0.0	0.0	0.0	0.0	0.0	0.0	0.0
70	0.0	0.0	0.0	0.0	0.0	0.0	0.0	0.0	0.0	0.0	0.0	0.0	0.0	0.0	0.0	0.0	0.0	0.0	0.0	0.0

Common Stock Price	21	22	23	24	25	26	27	28	29	30	31	32	33	34	35	36	37	38	39
130	32.4	32.6	32.7	32.8	32.9	33.0	33.2	33.3	33.4	33.5	33.6	33.7	33.8	34.0	34.1	34.2	34.3	34.4	34.6
128	30.7	30.8	30.9	31.0	31.2	31.3	31.4	41.6	31.7	31.8	31.9	32.1	32.2	32.3	32.4	32.6	32.7	32.8	33.0
126	28.9	29.0	29.2	29.3	29.4	29.6	29.7	29.8	29.9	30.1	30.3	30.4	30.5	30.7	30.8	30.9	31.1	31.2	31.3
124	27.1	27.2	27.4	27.5	27.7	27.8	28.0	28.1	28.3	28.4	28.6	28.7	28.9	29.0	29.2	29.3	29.5	29.6	29.8
122	25.3	25.5	25.6	25.8	25.9	26.1	26.3	26.4	26.6	26.7	26.9	27.0	27.2	27.4	27.5	27.7	27.8	28.0	28.2
120	23.5	23.7	23.9	24.0	24.2	24.4	24.5	24.7	24.9	25.0	25.2	25.4	25.5	25.7	25.9	26.0	26.2	26.4	26.6
118	21.7	21.9	22.1	22.3	22.5	22.6	22.8	23.0	23.2	23.3	23.5	23.7	23.9	24.1	24.2	24.4	24.6	24.8	25.0
116	19.9	20.1	20.3	20.5	20.7	20.9	21.1	21.3	21.5	21.7	21.8	22.0	22.2	22.4	22.6	22.8	23.0	23.2	23.4
114	18.2	18.4	18.6	18.8	19.0	19.2	19.4	19.6	19.8	19.9	20.2	20.4	20.6	20.8	21.0	21.2	21.4	21.6	21.8
112	16.4	16.6	16.8	17.0	17.2	17.4	17.6	17.9	18.1	18.3	18.5	18.7	18.9	19.1	19.3	19.5	19.7	19.9	20.1
110	14.6	14.9	15.1	15.3	15.5	15.7	15.9	16.2	16.4	16.6	16.7	16.9	17.1	17.3	17.4	17.6	17.8	18.0	18.2
108	13.0	13.2	13.4	13.6	13.8	14.0	14.2	14.5	14.7	14.9	15.0	15.2	15.4	15.6	15.7	15.7	15.9	16.1	16.3
106	11.3	11.5	11.7	11.9	12.1	12.3	12.5	12.8	13.0	13.2	13.3	13.5	13.7	13.9	14.0	14.0	14.1	14.3	14.5
104	9.8	9.9	10.1	10.3	10.5	10.7	10.8	11.0	11.2	11.3	11.5	11.7	11.8	12.0	12.1	12.3	12.4	12.6	12.7
102	9.0	9.1	9.3	9.5	9.7	9.9	10.0	10.2	10.4	10.5	10.7	10.9	11.0	11.2	11.3	11.5	11.6	11.8	11.9
100	8.2	8.3	8.5	8.7	8.9	9.1	9.2	9.4	9.6	9.7	9.9	10.1	10.2	10.4	10.5	10.7	10.8	11.0	11.1
99	7.8	7.9	8.1	8.3	8.5	8.7	8.8	9.0	9.2	9.3	9.5	9.7	9.8	9.9	10.1	10.3	10.4	10.6	10.7
98	7.4	7.5	7.7	7.9	8.1	8.3	8.4	8.6	8.8	8.9	9.1	9.3	9.4	9.6	9.7	9.9	10.0	10.2	10.3
97	7.0	7.1	7.3	7.5	7.7	7.9	8.0	8.2	8.4	8.5	8.7	8.9	9.0	9.2	9.3	9.5	9.6	9.8	9.9
96	6.6	6.7	6.9	7.1	7.3	7.5	7.6	7.8	8.0	8.1	8.3	8.5	8.6	8.8	8.9	9.1	9.2	9.4	9.5
95	6.2	6.3	6.5	6.7	6.9	7.1	7.2	7.4	7.6	7.7	7.9	8.1	8.2	8.4	8.5	8.7	8.8	9.0	9.1
94	5.8	5.9	6.1	6.3	6.5	6.7	6.8	7.0	7.2	7.3	7.5	7.7	7.8	8.0	8.1	8.3	8.4	8.6	8.7
93	5.4	5.5	5.7	5.9	6.1	6.3	6.4	6.6	6.8	6.9	7.1	7.3	7.4	7.6	7.7	7.9	8.0	8.2	8.3
92	5.0	5.1	5.3	5.5	5.7	5.9	6.0	6.2	6.4	6.5	6.7	6.9	7.0	7.2	7.3	7.5	7.6	7.8	7.9
91	4.6	4.7	4.9	5.1	5.3	5.5	5.6	5.8	6.0	6.1	6.3	6.5	6.6	6.8	6.9	7.1	7.2	7.4	7.5
90	4.2	4.3	4.5	4.7	4.9	5.1	5.2	5.4	5.6	5.7	5.9	6.1	6.2	6.4	6.5	6.7	6.8	7.0	7.1
89	3.8	3.9	4.1	4.3	4.5	4.7	4.8	5.0	5.2	5.3	5.5	5.7	5.8	6.0	6.1	6.3	6.4	6.6	6.7
88	3.4	3.5	3.7	3.9	4.1	4.3	4.4	4.6	4.8	4.9	5.1	5.3	5.4	5.6	5.7	5.9	6.0	6.2	6.3
87	3.0	3.1	3.3	3.5	3.7	3.9	4.0	4.2	4.4	4.5	4.7	4.9	5.0	5.2	5.3	5.5	5.6	5.8	5.9
86	2.6	2.7	2.9	3.1	3.3	3.5	3.6	3.8	4.0	4.1	4.3	4.5	4.6	4.8	4.9	5.1	5.2	5.4	5.5
85	2.2	2.3	2.5	2.7	2.9	3.1	3.2	3.4	3.6	3.7	3.9	4.1	4.2	4.4	4.5	4.7	4.8	5.0	5.1
84	1.8	1.9	2.1	2.3	2.5	2.7	2.8	3.0	3.2	3.3	3.5	3.7	3.8	4.0	4.1	4.3	4.4	4.6	4.7
83	1.4	1.5	1.7	1.9	2.1	2.3	2.4	2.6	2.8	2.9	3.1	3.3	3.4	3.6	3.7	3.9	4.0	4.2	4.3
82	1.0	1.1	1.3	1.5	1.7	1.9	2.0	2.2	2.4	2.5	2.7	2.9	3.0	3.2	3.3	3.5	3.6	3.8	3.9
81	0.6	0.7	0.9	1.1	1.3	1.5	1.6	1.8	2.0	2.1	2.3	2.5	2.6	2.8	2.9	3.1	3.2	3.4	3.5
80	0.2	0.3	0.5	0.7	0.9	1.1	1.2	1.4	1.6	1.7	1.9	2.1	2.2	2.4	2.5	2.7	2.8	3.0	3.1
79	0.0	0.0	0.1	0.3	0.5	0.7	0.8	1.0	1.2	1.3	1.5	1.7	1.8	2.0	2.1	2.3	2.4	2.6	2.7
78	0.0	0.0	0.0	0.0	0.1	0.3	0.4	0.6	0.8	0.9	1.1	1.3	1.4	1.6	1.7	1.9	2.0	2.2	2.3
77	0.0	0.0	0.0	0.0	0.0	0.0	0.0	0.2	0.4	0.5	0.7	0.9	1.0	1.2	1.3	1.5	1.6	1.8	1.9
76	0.0	0.0	0.0	0.0	0.0	0.0	0.0	0.0	0.0	0.1	0.3	0.5	0.6	0.8	0.9	1.1	1.2	1.4	1.5
75	0.0	0.0	0.0	0.0	0.0	0.0	0.0	0.0	0.0	0.0	0.0	0.1	0.2	0.4	0.5	0.7	0.8	1.0	1.1
74	0.0	0.0	0.0	0.0	0.0	0.0	0.0	0.0	0.0	0.0	0.0	0.0	0.0	0.0	0.1	0.3	0.4	0.6	0.7
73	0.0	0.0	0.0	0.0	0.0	0.0	0.0	0.0	0.0	0.0	0.0	0.0	0.0	0.0	0.0	0.0	0.0	0.2	0.3
72	0.0	0.0	0.0	0.0	0.0	0.0	0.0	0.0	0.0	0.0	0.0	0.0	0.0	0.0	0.0	0.0	0.0	0.0	0.0
71	0.0	0.0	0.0	0.0	0.0	0.0	0.0	0.0	0.0	0.0	0.0	0.0	0.0	0.0	0.0	0.0	0.0	0.0	0.0
70	0.0	0.0	0.0	0.0	0.0	0.0	0.0	0.0	0.0	0.0	0.0	0.0	0.0	0.0	0.0	0.0	0.0	0.0	0.0

LISTED CALL OPTION PRICE WHEN EXERCISE PRICE IS 110

NUMBER OF WEEKS BEFORE THE OPTION EXPIRES

Common Stock Price	1	2	3	4	5	6	7	8	9	10	11	12	13	14	15	16	17	18	19	20
144	34.1	34.2	34.4	34.5	34.6	34.7	34.9	35.0	35.1	35.2	35.4	35.5	35.6	35.7	35.8	36.0	36.1	36.2	36.3	36.5
142	32.1	32.3	32.4	32.5	32.7	32.8	32.9	33.1	33.2	33.3	33.5	33.6	33.7	33.9	34.0	34.1	34.3	34.4	34.5	34.7
140	30.1	30.3	30.4	30.6	30.7	30.9	31.0	31.1	31.3	31.4	31.6	31.7	31.9	32.0	32.2	32.3	32.4	32.6	32.7	32.9
138	28.2	28.3	28.5	28.6	28.8	28.9	29.1	29.2	29.4	29.5	29.7	29.8	30.0	30.2	30.3	30.5	30.6	30.8	30.9	31.1
136	26.2	26.3	26.4	26.7	26.8	27.0	27.1	27.3	27.5	27.6	27.8	28.0	28.1	28.3	28.5	28.6	28.8	29.0	29.1	29.3
134	24.2	24.3	24.5	24.7	24.9	25.0	25.2	25.4	25.6	25.7	25.9	26.1	26.3	26.4	26.6	26.8	27.0	27.1	27.3	27.5
132	22.2	22.4	22.6	22.7	22.9	23.1	23.3	23.5	23.7	23.8	24.0	24.2	24.4	24.6	24.8	25.0	25.1	25.3	25.5	25.7
130	20.2	20.4	20.6	20.8	21.0	21.2	21.4	21.6	21.8	22.0	22.1	22.3	22.5	22.7	22.9	23.1	23.3	23.5	23.7	23.9
128	18.2	18.4	18.6	18.8	19.0	19.2	19.4	19.6	19.8	20.1	20.3	20.5	20.7	20.9	21.1	21.3	21.5	21.7	21.9	22.1
126	16.2	16.4	16.6	16.9	17.1	17.3	17.5	17.7	17.9	18.2	18.4	18.6	18.8	19.0	19.2	19.4	19.7	19.9	20.1	20.3
124	14.2	14.5	14.7	14.9	15.1	15.4	15.6	15.8	16.0	16.3	16.5	16.7	16.9	17.2	17.4	17.6	17.8	18.1	18.3	18.5
122	12.2	12.5	12.7	12.9	13.2	13.4	13.7	13.9	14.1	14.4	14.6	14.8	15.1	15.3	15.5	15.8	16.0	16.2	16.5	16.7
120	10.2	10.5	10.7	11.0	11.3	11.5	11.8	12.0	12.3	12.6	12.8	13.0	13.2	13.5	13.7	14.0	14.2	14.5	14.8	15.0
118	8.3	8.5	8.8	9.1	9.4	9.6	9.9	10.2	10.5	10.8	11.0	11.2	11.5	11.8	12.0	12.3	12.5	12.8	13.0	13.2
116	6.3	6.6	6.8	7.2	7.5	7.7	8.1	8.4	8.7	9.0	9.3	9.6	9.9	10.3	10.5	10.8	11.0	11.3	11.5	11.7
114	4.5	4.7	5.0	5.5	6.0	6.4	6.8	7.1	7.5	7.8	8.1	8.4	8.7	8.9	9.2	9.4	9.7	9.9	10.1	10.4
112	2.8	3.6	4.2	4.7	5.2	5.6	6.0	6.3	6.7	7.0	7.3	7.6	7.9	8.1	8.4	8.6	8.9	9.1	9.3	9.6
110	2.0	2.8	3.4	3.9	4.4	4.8	5.2	5.5	5.9	6.2	6.5	6.8	7.1	7.3	7.6	7.8	8.1	8.3	8.5	8.8
108	1.2	2.0	2.6	3.1	3.6	4.0	4.4	4.7	5.1	5.4	5.7	6.0	6.3	6.5	6.8	7.0	7.3	7.5	7.7	8.0
106	0.4	1.2	1.8	2.3	2.8	3.2	3.6	3.9	4.3	4.6	4.9	5.2	5.5	5.7	6.0	6.2	6.5	6.7	6.9	7.2
104	0.0	0.4	1.0	1.5	2.0	2.4	2.8	3.1	3.5	3.8	4.1	4.4	4.7	4.9	5.2	5.4	5.7	5.9	6.1	6.4
102	0.0	0.0	0.2	0.7	1.2	1.6	2.0	2.3	2.7	3.0	3.3	3.6	3.9	4.1	4.4	4.6	4.9	5.1	5.3	5.6
100	0.0	0.0	0.0	0.0	0.4	0.8	1.2	1.5	1.9	2.2	2.5	2.8	3.1	3.3	3.6	3.8	4.1	4.3	4.5	4.8
99	0.0	0.0	0.0	0.0	0.0	0.4	0.8	1.1	1.5	1.8	2.1	2.4	2.7	2.9	3.2	3.4	3.7	3.9	4.1	4.4
98	0.0	0.0	0.0	0.0	0.0	0.0	0.4	0.7	1.1	1.4	1.7	2.0	2.3	2.5	2.8	3.0	3.3	3.5	3.7	4.0
97	0.0	0.0	0.0	0.0	0.0	0.0	0.0	0.3	0.7	1.0	1.3	1.6	1.9	2.1	2.4	2.6	2.9	3.1	3.3	3.6
96	0.0	0.0	0.0	0.0	0.0	0.0	0.0	0.0	0.3	0.6	0.9	1.2	1.5	1.7	2.0	2.2	2.5	2.7	2.9	3.2
95	0.0	0.0	0.0	0.0	0.0	0.0	0.0	0.0	0.0	0.2	0.5	0.8	1.1	1.3	1.6	1.8	2.1	2.3	2.5	2.8
94	0.0	0.0	0.0	0.0	0.0	0.0	0.0	0.0	0.0	0.0	0.1	0.4	0.7	0.9	1.2	1.4	1.7	1.9	2.1	2.4
93	0.0	0.0	0.0	0.0	0.0	0.0	0.0	0.0	0.0	0.0	0.0	0.0	0.3	0.5	0.8	1.0	1.3	1.5	1.7	2.0
92	0.0	0.0	0.0	0.0	0.0	0.0	0.0	0.0	0.0	0.0	0.0	0.0	0.0	0.1	0.4	0.6	0.9	1.1	1.3	1.6
91	0.0	0.0	0.0	0.0	0.0	0 0	0.0	0.0	0.0	0.0	0.0	0.0	0.0	0.0	0.0	0.2	0.5	0.7	0.9	1.2
90	0.0	0.0	0.0	0.0	0.0	0.0	0.0	0.0	0.0	0.0	0.0	0.0	0.0	0.0	0.0	0.0	0.1	0.3	0.5	0.8
89	0.0	0.0	0.0	0.0	0.0	0.0	0.0	0.0	0.0	0.0	0.0	0.0	0.0	0.0	0.0	0.0	0.0	0.0	0.1	0.4
88	0.0	0.0	0.0	0.0	0.0	0.0	0.0	0.0	0.0	0.0	0.0	0.0	0.0	0.0	0.0	0.0	0.0	0.0	0.0	0.0
87	0.0	0.0	0.0	0.0	0.0	0.0	0.0	0.0	0.0	0.0	0.0	0.0	0.0	0.0	0.0	0.0	0.0	0.0	0.0	0.0
86	0.0	0.0	0.0	0.0	0.0	0.0	0.0	0.0	0.0	0.0	0.0	0.0	0.0	0.0	0.0	0.0	0.0	0.0	0.0	0.0
85	0.0	0.0	0.0	0.0	0.0	0.0	0.0	0.0	0.0	0.0	0.0	0.0	0.0	0.0	0.0	0.0	0.0	0.0	0.0	0.0
84	0.0	0.0	0.0	0.0	0.0	0.0	0.0	0.0	0.0	0.0	0.0	0.0	0.0	0.0	0.0	0.0	0.0	0.0	0.0	0.0
83	0.0	0.0	0.0	0.0	0.0	0.0	0.0	0.0	0.0	0.0	0.0	0.0	0.0	0.0	0.0	0.0	0.0	0.0	0.0	0.0
82	0.0	0.0	0.0	0.0	0.0	0.0	0.0	0.0	0.0	0.0	0.0	0.0	0.0	0.0	0.0	0.0	0.0	0.0	0.0	0.0
81	0.0	0.0	0.0	0.0	0.0	0.0	0.0	0.0	0.0	0.0	0.0	0.0	0.0	0.0	0.0	0.0	0.0	0.0	0.0	0.0
80	0.0	0.0	0.0	0.0	0.0	0.0	0.0	0.0	0.0	0.0	0.0	0.0	0.0	0.0	0.0	0.0	0.0	0.0	0.0	0.0
79	0.0	0.0	0.0	0.0	0.0	0.0	0.0	0.0	0.0	0.0	0.0	0.0	0.0	0.0	0.0	0.0	0.0	0.0	0.0	0.0
78	0.0	0.0	0.0	0.0	0.0	0.0	0.0	0.0	0.0	0.0	0.0	0.0	0.0	0.0	0.0	0.0	0.0	0.0	0.0	0.0
77	0.0	0.0	0.0	0.0	0.0	0.0	0.0	0.0	0.0	0.0	0.0	0.0	0.0	0.0	0.0	0.0	0.0	0.0	0.0	0.0

Common Stock Price	21	22	23	24	25	26	27	28	29	30	31	32	33	34	35	36	37	38	39
144	36.6	36.7	36.8	37.0	37.1	37.2	37.3	37.4	37.6	37.7	37.8	37.9	38.1	38.2	38.3	38.4	38.6	38.7	38.8
142	34.8	34.9	35.1	35.2	35.3	35.5	35.6	35.7	35.9	36.0	36.1	36.3	36.4	36.5	36.7	36.8	36.9	37.1	37.2
140	33.0	33.2	33.3	33.4	33.6	33.7	33.9	34.0	34.2	34.3	34.5	34.6	34.7	34.9	35.0	35.2	35.3	35.5	35.6
138	31.2	31.4	31.5	31.7	31.8	32.0	32.2	32.3	32.5	32.6	32.8	32.9	33.1	33.2	33.4	33.5	33.7	33.9	34.0
136	29.4	29.6	29.8	29.9	30.1	30.3	30.4	30.6	30.8	30.9	31.1	31.3	31.4	31.6	31.7	31.9	32.1	32.2	32.4
134	27.7	27.8	28.0	28.2	28.4	28.5	28.7	28.9	29.1	29.2	29.4	29.6	29.8	29.9	30.1	30.3	30.5	30.6	30.8
132	25.9	26.1	26.2	26.4	26.6	26.8	27.0	27.2	27.4	27.5	27.7	27.9	28.1	28.3	28.5	28.7	28.8	29.0	29.2
130	24.1	24.3	24.5	24.7	24.9	25.1	25.3	25.5	25.7	25.9	26.0	26.2	26.4	26.6	26.8	27.0	27.2	27.4	27.6
128	22.3	22.5	22.7	22.9	23.1	23.3	23.5	23.7	24.0	24.2	24.4	24.6	24.8	25.0	25.2	25.4	25.6	25.8	26.0
126	20.5	20.7	21.0	21.2	21.4	21.6	21.8	22.0	22.2	22.5	22.7	22.9	23.1	23.3	23.5	23.8	24.0	24.2	24.4
124	18.7	19.0	19.2	19.4	19.6	19.9	20.1	20.3	20.5	20.8	21.0	21.2	21.5	21.7	21.9	22.1	22.4	22.6	22.8
122	17.0	17.2	17.4	17.7	17.9	18.1	18.4	18.6	18.8	19.1	19.3	19.6	19.8	20.0	20.3	20.5	20.7	21.0	21.2
120	15.3	15.5	15.7	16.0	16.1	16.3	16.6	16.8	17.0	17.3	17.5	17.8	18.0	18.2	18.5	18.7	18.9	19.2	19.4
118	13.5	13.7	13.9	14.2	14.4	14.6	14.9	15.1	15.2	15.5	15.7	16.0	16.2	16.4	16.7	16.9	17.1	17.4	17.6
116	12.0	12.2	12.4	12.7	12.9	13.1	13.3	13.5	13.7	14.0	14.2	14.5	14.7	14.8	14.9	15.1	15.3	15.6	15.8
114	10.6	10.8	11.0	11.2	11.4	11.6	11.8	12.0	12.1	12.3	12.5	12.7	12.8	13.0	13.2	13.3	13.5	13.7	13.8
112	9.8	9.9	10.2	10.4	10.6	10.8	11.0	11.2	11.3	11.5	11.7	11.9	12.0	12.2	12.4	12.5	12.7	12.9	13.0
110	9.0	9.2	9.4	9.6	9.8	9.9	10.2	10.4	10.5	10.7	10.9	11.1	11.2	11.4	11.6	11.7	11.9	12.1	12.2
108	8.2	8.4	8.6	8.8	9.0	9.2	9.4	9.6	9.7	9.9	10.1	10.3	10.4	10.6	10.8	10.9	11.1	11.3	11.4
106	7.4	7.6	7.8	8.0	8.2	8.4	8.6	8.8	8.9	9.1	9.3	9.5	9.6	9.8	9.9	10.1	10.3	10.5	10.6
104	6.6	6.8	7.0	7.2	7.4	7.6	7.8	8.0	8.1	8.3	8.5	8.7	8.8	9.0	9.2	9.3	9.5	9.7	9.8
102	5.8	6.0	6.2	6.4	6.6	6.8	7.0	7.2	7.3	7.5	7.7	7.9	8.0	8.2	8.4	8.5	8.7	8.9	9.0
100	5.0	5.2	5.4	5.6	5.8	6.0	6.2	6.4	6.5	6.7	6.9	7.1	7.2	7.4	7.6	7.7	7.9	8.1	8.2
99	4.6	4.8	5.0	5.2	5.4	5.6	5.8	6.0	6.1	6.3	6.5	6.7	6.8	7.0	7.2	7.3	7.5	7.7	7.8
98	4.2	4.4	4.6	4.8	5.0	5.2	5.4	5.6	5.7	5.9	6.1	6.3	6.4	6.6	6.8	6.9	7.1	7.3	7.4
97	3.8	4.0	4.2	4.4	4.6	4.8	5.0	5.2	5.3	5.5	5.7	5.9	6.0	6.2	6.4	6.5	6.7	6.9	7.0
96	3.4	3.6	3.8	4.0	4.2	4.4	4.6	4.8	4.9	5.1	5.3	5.5	5.6	5.8	6.0	6.1	6.3	6.5	6.6
95	3.0	3.2	3.4	3.6	3.8	4.0	4.2	4.4	4.5	4.7	4.9	5.1	5.2	5.4	5.6	5.7	5.9	6.1	6.2
94	2.6	2.8	3.0	3.2	3.4	3.6	3.8	4.0	4.1	4.3	4.5	4.7	4.8	5.0	5.2	5.3	5.5	5.7	5.8
93	2.2	2.4	2.6	2.8	3.0	3.2	3.4	3.6	3.7	3.9	4.1	4.3	4.4	4.6	4.8	4.9	5.1	5.3	5.4
92	1.8	2.0	2.2	2.4	2.6	2.8	3.0	3.2	3.3	3.5	3.7	3.9	4.0	4.2	4.4	4.5	4.7	4.9	5.0
91	1.4	1.6	1.8	2.0	2.2	2.4	2.6	2.8	2.9	3.1	3.3	3.5	3.6	3.8	4.0	4.1	4.3	4.5	4.6
90	1.0	1.2	1.4	1.6	1.8	2.0	2.2	2.4	2.5	2.7	2.9	3.1	3.2	3.4	3.6	3.7	3.9	4.1	4.2
89	0.6	0.8	1.0	1.2	1.4	1.6	1.8	2.0	2.1	2.3	2.5	2.7	2.8	3.0	3.2	3.3	3.5	3.7	3.8
88	0.2	0.4	0.6	0.8	1.0	1.2	1.4	1.6	1.7	1.9	2.1	2.3	2.4	2.6	2.8	2.9	3.1	3.3	3.4
87	0.0	0.0	0.2	0.4	0.6	0.8	1.0	1.2	1.3	1.5	1.7	1.9	2.0	2.2	2.4	2.5	2.7	2.9	3.0
86	0.0	0.0	0.0	0.0	0.2	0.4	0.6	0.8	0.9	1.1	1.3	1.5	1.6	1.8	2.0	2.1	2.3	2.5	2.6
85	0.0	0.0	0.0	0.0	0.0	0.0	0.2	0.4	0.5	0.7	0.9	1.1	1.2	1.4	1.6	1.7	1.9	2.1	2.2
84	0.0	0.0	0.0	0.0	0.0	0.0	0.0	0.0	0.1	0.3	0.5	0.7	0.8	1.0	1.2	1.3	1.5	1.7	1.8
83	0.0	0.0	0.0	0.0	0.0	0.0	0.0	0.0	0.0	0.0	0.1	0.3	0.4	0.6	0.8	0.9	1.1	1.3	1.4
82	0.0	0.0	0.0	0.0	0.0	0.0	0.0	0.0	0.0	0.0	0.0	0.0	0.0	0.2	0.4	0.5	0.7	0.9	1.0
81	0.0	0.0	0.0	0.0	0.0	0.0	0.0	0.0	0.0	0.0	0.0	0.0	0.0	0.0	0.0	0.1	0.3	0.5	0.6
80	0.0	0.0	0.0	0.0	0.0	0.0	0.0	0.0	0.0	0.0	0.0	0.0	0.0	0.0	0.0	0.0	0.0	0.1	0.2
79	0.0	0.0	0.0	0.0	0.0	0.0	0.0	0.0	0.0	0.0	0.0	0.0	0.0	0.0	0.0	0.0	0.0	0.0	0.0
78	0.0	0.0	0.0	0.0	0.0	0.0	0.0	0.0	0.0	0.0	0.0	0.0	0.0	0.0	0.0	0.0	0.0	0.0	0.0
77	0.0	0.0	0.0	0.0	0.0	0.0	0.0	0.0	0.0	0.0	0.0	0.0	0.0	0.0	0.0	0.0	[illegible]	0.0	0.0

LISTED CALL OPTION PRICE WHEN EXERCISE PRICE IS 120

NUMBER OF WEEKS BEFORE THE OPTION EXPIRES

Common Stock Price	1	2	3	4	5	6	7	8	9	10	11	12	13	14	15	16	17	18	19	20	21	22	23	24	25	26	27	28	29	30	31	32	33	34	35	36	37	38	39
156	36.1	36.3	36.4	36.6	36.7	36.8	37.0	37.1	37.3	37.4	37.5	37.7	37.8	38.0	38.1	38.2	38.4	38.5	38.7	38.8	38.9	39.1	39.2	39.4	39.5	39.6	39.8	39.9	40.1	40.2	40.3	40.5	40.6	40.8	40.9	41.0	41.2	41.3	41.5
154	34.2	34.3	34.5	34.6	34.8	34.9	35.1	35.2	35.4	35.5	35.7	35.8	36.0	36.1	36.3	36.4	36.6	36.7	36.9	37.0	37.2	37.3	37.5	37.6	37.8	37.9	38.1	38.2	38.4	38.5	38.7	38.8	39.0	39.1	39.3	39.4	39.6	39.7	39.9
152	32.2	32.3	32.5	32.6	32.8	33.0	33.1	33.3	33.4	33.6	33.8	33.9	34.1	34.2	34.4	34.6	34.7	34.9	35.0	35.2	35.4	35.5	35.7	35.9	36.0	36.2	36.3	36.5	36.7	36.8	37.0	37.1	37.3	37.5	37.6	37.8	37.9	38.1	38.3
150	30.2	30.3	30.5	30.7	30.9	31.0	31.2	31.4	31.5	31.7	31.9	32.0	32.2	32.4	32.6	32.7	32.9	33.1	33.2	33.4	33.6	33.8	33.9	34.1	34.3	34.4	34.6	34.8	35.0	35.1	35.3	35.5	35.6	35.8	36.0	36.1	36.3	36.5	36.7
148	28.2	28.4	28.5	28.7	28.9	29.1	29.3	29.4	29.6	29.8	29.9	30.2	30.4	30.5	30.7	30.9	31.1	31.3	31.4	31.6	31.8	32.0	32.2	32.3	32.5	32.7	32.9	33.1	33.3	33.4	33.6	33.8	34.0	34.2	34.3	34.5	34.7	34.9	35.1
146	26.2	26.4	26.6	26.8	27.0	27.1	27.3	27.5	27.7	27.9	28.1	28.3	28.5	28.7	28.9	29.1	29.2	29.4	29.6	29.8	30.0	30.2	30.4	30.6	30.8	31.0	31.2	31.4	31.5	31.7	31.9	32.1	32.3	32.5	32.7	32.9	33.1	33.3	33.5
144	24.2	24.4	24.6	24.8	25.0	25.2	25.4	25.6	25.8	26.0	26.2	26.4	26.6	26.8	27.0	27.2	27.4	27.6	27.8	28.0	28.2	28.4	28.6	28.8	29.0	29.2	29.4	29.6	29.8	30.0	30.2	30.4	30.7	30.9	31.1	31.3	31.5	31.7	31.9
142	22.2	22.4	22.6	22.8	23.1	23.3	23.5	23.7	23.9	24.1	24.3	24.5	24.8	25.0	25.2	25.4	25.6	25.8	26.0	26.2	26.4	26.7	26.9	27.1	27.3	27.5	27.7	27.9	28.1	28.4	28.6	28.8	29.0	29.2	29.4	29.6	29.8	30.0	30.3
140	20.2	20.4	20.7	20.9	21.1	21.3	21.6	21.8	22.0	22.2	22.4	22.7	22.9	23.1	23.3	23.6	23.8	24.0	24.2	24.4	24.7	24.9	25.1	25.3	25.6	25.8	26.0	26.2	26.4	26.7	26.9	27.1	27.3	27.5	27.8	28.0	28.2	28.4	28.7
138	18.2	18.5	18.7	18.9	19.2	19.4	19.6	19.9	20.1	20.3	20.6	20.8	21.0	21.3	21.5	21.7	21.9	22.2	22.4	22.6	22.9	23.1	23.3	23.6	23.8	24.0	24.3	24.5	24.7	25.0	25.2	25.4	25.7	25.9	26.1	26.4	26.6	26.8	27.1
136	16.2	16.5	16.7	17.0	17.2	17.5	17.7	17.9	18.2	18.4	18.7	18.9	19.2	19.4	19.6	19.9	20.1	20.4	20.6	20.9	21.1	21.3	21.6	21.8	22.1	22.3	22.5	22.8	23.0	23.3	23.5	23.8	24.0	24.2	24.5	24.7	25.0	25.2	25.5
134	14.3	14.5	14.8	15.0	15.3	15.6	15.8	16.0	16.3	16.5	16.8	17.0	17.3	17.5	17.8	18.0	18.3	18.6	18.8	19.1	19.3	19.6	19.8	20.1	20.3	20.6	20.8	21.1	21.3	21.6	21.8	22.1	22.3	22.6	22.8	23.1	23.4	23.6	23.9
132	12.3	12.5	12.8	13.0	13.3	13.5	13.9	14.1	14.4	14.6	15.0	15.3	15.6	15.8	16.1	16.3	16.6	16.9	17.1	17.4	17.6	17.9	18.1	18.4	18.7	18.9	19.2	19.4	19.7	19.9	20.2	20.4	20.7	21.0	21.2	21.5	21.7	22.0	22.2
130	10.3	10.5	10.8	11.1	11.4	11.6	12.1	12.3	12.6	12.8	13.2	13.5	13.9	14.1	14.4	14.6	14.9	15.2	15.4	15.7	15.9	16.2	16.4	16.7	16.9	17.2	17.4	17.7	17.9	18.2	18.4	18.7	18.9	19.2	19.3	19.4	19.6	19.8	20.1
128	8.4	8.6	8.9	9.2	9.5	9.8	10.3	10.5	10.8	11.1	11.5	11.8	12.2	12.4	12.7	12.9	13.2	13.5	13.7	14.0	14.2	14.5	14.7	15.0	15.2	15.5	15.7	16.0	16.2	16.5	16.7	17.0	17.2	17.5	17.6	17.8	17.9	18.0	18.2
126	6.5	6.7	7.0	7.3	7.6	8.0	8.3	8.6	8.9	9.3	9.6	9.8	10.1	10.3	10.5	10.8	11.0	11.3	11.5	11.8	12.1	12.3	12.6	12.8	13.1	13.3	13.6	13.8	14.1	14.3	14.6	14.8	15.1	15.3	15.6	15.8	16.0	16.2	16.4
124	4.6	4.9	5.3	5.9	6.4	6.8	7.2	7.6	8.0	8.4	8.7	9.0	9.3	9.6	9.9	10.1	10.4	10.7	10.9	11.2	11.4	11.7	11.9	12.1	12.3	12.5	12.7	12.9	13.1	13.3	13.5	13.7	13.9	14.2	14.4	14.6	14.8	15.0	15.2
122	2.9	3.8	4.5	5.1	5.6	6.0	6.4	6.8	7.2	7.6	7.9	8.2	8.5	8.8	9.1	9.3	9.6	9.9	10.1	10.4	10.6	10.9	11.1	11.3	11.5	11.7	11.9	12.1	12.3	12.5	12.7	12.9	13.1	13.3	13.6	13.8	14.0	14.3	14.5
120	0.5	1.3	2.1	2.7	3.2	3.6	4.0	4.4	4.8	5.2	5.5	5.8	6.1	6.4	6.7	7.0	7.2	7.5	7.7	8.0	8.2	8.4	8.6	8.9	9.1	9.3	9.5	9.7	9.9	10.1	10.3	10.5	10.7	10.8	11.0	11.2	11.4	11.6	11.7
118	0.0	0.6	1.3	1.8	2.2	2.7	3.1	3.5	3.9	4.3	4.6	4.9	5.2	5.5	5.8	6.1	6.4	6.7	6.9	7.2	7.4	7.6	7.8	8.1	8.3	8.5	8.7	9.0	9.2	9.4	9.6	9.8	10.0	10.2	10.4	10.6	10.8	11.0	11.2
116	0.0	0.3	0.8	1.3	1.7	2.1	2.5	2.9	3.3	3.7	4.0	4.3	4.6	4.9	5.2	5.5	5.8	6.1	6.3	6.6	6.8	7.1	7.3	7.5	7.7	8.0	8.2	8.4	8.6	8.8	9.0	9.2	9.4	9.6	9.8	10.0	10.2	10.4	10.6
114	0.0	0.1	0.5	0.9	1.3	1.6	2.0	2.4	2.8	3.2	3.5	3.8	4.1	4.4	4.7	5.0	5.3	5.6	5.9	6.1	6.4	6.6	6.8	7.0	7.3	7.5	7.7	7.9	8.1	8.3	8.5	8.7	8.9	9.1	9.4	9.6	9.8	10.0	10.2
112	0.0	0.0	0.3	0.6	0.9	1.3	1.6	2.0	2.4	2.8	3.1	3.4	3.7	4.0	4.3	4.5	4.8	5.1	5.4	5.7	5.9	6.1	6.4	6.6	6.8	7.0	7.3	7.5	7.7	7.9	8.0	8.2	8.4	8.7	8.9	9.1	9.3	9.5	9.7
110	0.0	0.0	0.1	0.3	0.6	0.9	1.2	1.5	1.9	2.3	2.6	2.9	3.2	3.5	3.7	4.0	4.3	4.5	4.8	5.0	5.3	5.5	5.7	6.0	6.2	6.5	6.7	6.9	7.1	7.3	7.5	7.7	7.9	8.0	8.3	8.5	8.7	8.9	9.1
108	0.0	0.0	0.0	0.2	0.4	0.7	0.9	1.2	1.5	1.8	2.1	2.4	2.7	2.9	3.2	3.5	3.7	3.9	4.2	4.4	4.7	4.9	5.2	5.4	5.7	5.9	6.1	6.3	6.5	6.7	6.9	7.1	7.3	7.5	7.8	8.0	8.2	8.4	8.5
106	0.0	0.0	0.0	0.0	0.2	0.4	0.6	0.9	1.1	1.4	1.7	1.8	2.1	2.4	2.7	2.9	3.2	3.5	3.7	3.9	4.2	4.4	4.6	4.9	5.1	5.3	5.5	5.7	5.9	6.1	6.3	6.5	6.7	6.8	7.0	7.2	7.4	7.6	7.7
104	0.0	0.0	0.0	0.0	0.0	0.2	0.4	0.6	0.8	1.2	1.5	1.8	2.0	2.2	2.4	2.6	2.9	3.2	3.4	3.6	3.9	4.1	4.3	4.5	4.7	4.9	5.1	5.3	5.5	5.7	5.9	6.1	6.3	6.5	6.7	6.9	7.1	7.3	7.5?
102	0.0	0.0	0.0	0.0	0.0	0.0	0.2	0.4	0.6	0.8	1.0	1.2	1.5	1.8	2.1	2.3	2.5	2.7	2.9	3.2	3.4	3.6	3.8	4.1	4.3	4.5	4.7	4.9	5.1	5.3	5.5	5.7	5.9	6.1	6.2	6.4	6.6	6.8	6.9
100	0.0	0.0	0.0	0.0	0.0	0.0	0.0	0.2	0.4	0.6	0.8	1.0	1.2	1.5	1.8	2.0	2.2	2.4	2.6	2.8	3.0	3.2	3.5	3.7	3.9	4.1	4.3	4.5	4.7	4.9	5.1	5.3	5.5	5.7	5.9	6.1	6.3	6.5	6.6
98	0.0	0.0	0.0	0.0	0.0	0.0	0.0	0.0	0.2	0.4	0.6	0.8	1.0	1.2	1.4	1.6	1.9	2.1	2.3	2.5	2.7	2.9	3.1	3.3	3.5	3.7	3.9	4.1	4.3	4.5	4.7	4.9	5.1	5.3	5.5	5.6	5.8	6.0	6.2
97	0.0	0.0	0.0	0.0	0.0	0.0	0.0	0.0	0.0	0.3	0.5	0.7	0.9	1.1	1.3	1.5	1.7	1.9	2.1	2.3	2.6	2.8	3.0	3.2	3.4	3.6	3.8	4.0	4.2	4.4	4.6	4.8	5.0	5.2	5.4	5.6	5.8	6.0	6.1
96	0.0	0.0	0.0	0.0	0.0	0.0	0.0	0.0	0.0	0.1	0.3	0.5	0.7	0.9	1.1	1.3	1.5	1.7	1.9	2.1	2.3	2.5	2.7	2.9	3.1	3.3	3.5	3.7	3.9	4.1	4.3	4.5	4.6	4.8	5.0	5.2	5.4	5.6	5.8
95	0.0	0.0	0.0	0.0	0.0	0.0	0.0	0.0	0.0	0.0	0.1	0.3	0.5	0.7	0.9	1.1	1.3	1.5	1.7	1.9	2.1	2.3	2.5	2.7	2.9	3.1	3.3	3.5	3.6	3.8	4.0	4.2	4.4	4.6	4.8	4.9	5.1	5.3	5.5
94	0.0	0.0	0.0	0.0	0.0	0.0	0.0	0.0	0.0	0.0	0.0	0.1	0.3	0.5	0.7	0.9	1.1	1.3	1.5	1.7	1.9	2.1	2.3	2.5	2.7	2.9	3.1	3.3	3.5	3.7	3.9	4.0	4.2	4.4	4.6	4.8	5.0	5.2	5.3
93	0.0	0.0	0.0	0.0	0.0	0.0	0.0	0.0	0.0	0.0	0.0	0.0	0.1	0.3	0.5	0.7	0.9	1.1	1.3	1.5	1.7	1.9	2.1	2.3	2.5	2.7	2.9	3.1	3.3	3.5	3.7	3.9	4.0	4.2	4.4	4.6	4.8	4.9	5.1
92	0.0	0.0	0.0	0.0	0.0	0.0	0.0	0.0	0.0	0.0	0.0	0.0	0.0	0.1	0.3	0.5	0.7	0.9	1.1	1.3	1.5	1.7	1.9	2.1	2.3	2.5	2.7	2.9	3.1	3.3	3.5	3.7	3.9	4.0	4.2	4.4	4.6	4.8	4.9
91	0.0	0.0	0.0	0.0	0.0	0.0	0.0	0.0	0.0	0.0	0.0	0.0	0.0	0.0	0.1	0.3	0.5	0.7	0.9	1.1	1.3	1.4	1.6	1.8	2.0	2.2	2.4	2.6	2.8	3.0	3.2	3.4	3.6	3.8	4.0	4.2	4.4	4.6	4.8
90	0.0	0.0	0.0	0.0	0.0	0.0	0.0	0.0	0.0	0.0	0.0	0.0	0.0	0.0	0.0	0.1	0.3	0.5	0.7	0.9	1.1	1.2	1.4	1.6	1.8	2.0	2.2	2.4	2.6	2.8	3.0	3.2	3.4	3.6	3.8	4.0	4.2	4.4	4.5
89	0.0	0.0	0.0	0.0	0.0	0.0	0.0	0.0	0.0	0.0	0.0	0.0	0.0	0.0	0.0	0.0	0.1	0.3	0.5	0.7	0.9	1.0	1.2	1.4	1.6	1.8	2.0	2.2	2.3	2.5	2.7	2.9	3.1	3.3	3.4	3.6	3.8	4.0	4.1
88	0.0	0.0	0.0	0.0	0.0	0.0	0.0	0.0	0.0	0.0	0.0	0.0	0.0	0.0	0.0	0.0	0.0	0.1	0.3	0.5	0.6	0.8	1.0	1.2	1.4	1.6	1.7	1.9	2.1	2.3	2.5	2.7	2.9	3.1	3.2	3.4	3.6	3.8	3.9
87	0.0	0.0	0.0	0.0	0.0	0.0	0.0	0.0	0.0	0.0	0.0	0.0	0.0	0.0	0.0	0.0	0.0	0.0	0.1	0.3	0.4	0.6	0.8	1.0	1.2	1.3	1.5	1.7	1.9	2.1	2.2	2.4	2.6	2.8	3.0	3.2	3.4	3.6	3.7
86	0.0	0.0	0.0	0.0	0.0	0.0	0.0	0.0	0.0	0.0	0.0	0.0	0.0	0.0	0.0	0.0	0.0	0.0	0.0	0.1	0.2	0.4	0.6	0.8	0.9	1.1	1.3	1.5	1.7	1.8	2.0	2.2	2.4	2.6	2.8	2.9	3.1	3.2	3.3
85	0.0	0.0	0.0	0.0	0.0	0.0	0.0	0.0	0.0	0.0	0.0	0.0	0.0	0.0	0.0	0.0	0.0	0.0	0.0	0.0	0.1	0.2	0.4	0.6	0.7	0.9	1.1	1.3	1.5	1.6	1.8	2.0	2.2	2.4	2.6	2.8	2.9	3.0	3.2
84	0.0	0.0	0.0	0.0	0.0	0.0	0.0	0.0	0.0	0.0	0.0	0.0	0.0	0.0	0.0	0.0	0.0	0.0	0.0	0.0	0.0	0.1	0.2	0.4	0.5	0.7	0.9	1.0	1.2	1.4	1.5	1.7	1.9	2.1	2.2	2.4	2.5	2.7	2.9

LISTED CALL OPTION PRICE WHEN EXERCISE PRICE IS 130

Common Stock Price	NUMBER OF WEEKS BEFORE THE OPTION EXPIRES 1	2	3	4	5	6	7	8	9	10	11	12	13	14	15	16	17	18	19	20	21	22	23	24	25	26	27	28	29	30	31	32	33	34	35	36	37	38	39
170	40.1	40.3	40.4	40.6	40.7	40.9	41.0	41.2	41.3	41.5	41.6	41.8	41.9	42.1	42.2	42.3	42.5	42.6	42.8	42.9	43.1	43.2	43.4	43.5	43.7	43.8	44.0	44.1	44.2	44.4	44.5	44.7	44.8	45.0	45.1	45.3	45.4	45.6	45.7
168	38.2	38.3	38.5	38.6	38.8	38.9	39.1	39.3	39.4	39.6	39.7	39.9	40.0	40.2	40.4	40.5	40.7	40.8	41.0	41.1	41.3	41.4	41.6	41.8	41.9	42.1	42.2	42.4	42.5	42.7	42.9	43.0	43.2	43.3	43.5	43.6	43.8	44.0	44.1
166	36.2	36.3	36.5	36.7	36.8	37.0	37.2	37.3	37.5	37.7	37.8	38.0	38.2	38.3	38.5	38.7	38.8	39.0	39.2	39.3	39.5	39.7	39.8	40.0	40.2	40.3	40.5	40.7	40.8	41.0	41.2	41.3	41.5	41.7	41.8	42.0	42.2	42.3	42.5
164	34.2	34.4	34.5	34.7	34.9	35.1	35.2	35.4	35.6	35.8	36.0	36.1	36.3	36.5	36.7	36.8	37.0	37.2	37.4	37.5	37.7	37.9	38.1	38.3	38.4	38.6	38.8	39.0	39.1	39.3	39.5	39.7	39.9	40.0	40.2	40.4	40.6	40.7	40.9
162	32.2	32.4	32.6	32.8	32.9	33.1	33.3	33.5	33.7	33.9	34.1	34.3	34.4	34.6	34.8	35.0	35.2	35.4	35.6	35.8	35.9	36.1	36.3	36.5	36.7	36.9	37.1	37.3	37.4	37.6	37.8	38.0	38.2	38.4	38.6	38.8	38.9	39.1	39.3
160	30.2	30.4	30.6	30.8	31.0	31.2	31.4	31.6	31.8	32.0	32.2	32.4	32.6	32.8	33.0	33.2	33.4	33.6	33.8	34.0	34.2	34.4	34.5	34.7	34.9	35.1	35.3	35.5	35.7	35.9	36.1	36.3	36.5	36.7	36.9	37.1	37.3	37.5	37.7
158	28.2	28.4	28.6	28.8	29.0	29.2	29.5	29.7	29.9	30.1	30.3	30.5	30.7	30.9	31.1	31.3	31.5	31.7	32.0	32.2	32.4	32.6	32.8	33.0	33.2	33.4	33.6	33.8	34.0	34.2	34.5	34.7	34.9	35.1	35.3	35.5	35.7	35.9	36.1
156	26.2	26.4	26.7	26.9	27.1	27.3	27.5	27.7	28.0	28.2	28.4	28.6	28.8	29.1	29.3	29.5	29.7	29.9	30.1	30.4	30.6	30.8	31.0	31.2	31.5	31.7	31.9	32.1	32.3	32.6	32.8	33.0	33.2	33.4	33.6	33.9	34.1	34.3	34.5
154	24.2	24.5	24.7	24.9	25.1	25.4	25.6	25.8	26.1	26.3	26.5	26.7	27.0	27.2	27.4	27.7	27.9	28.1	28.3	28.6	28.8	29.0	29.3	29.5	29.7	29.9	30.2	30.4	30.6	30.9	31.1	31.3	31.5	31.8	32.0	32.2	32.5	32.7	32.9
152	22.2	22.5	22.7	23.0	23.2	23.4	23.7	23.9	24.1	24.4	24.6	24.9	25.1	25.3	25.6	25.8	26.1	26.3	26.5	26.8	27.0	27.3	27.5	27.7	28.0	28.2	28.4	28.7	28.9	29.2	29.4	29.6	29.9	30.1	30.4	30.6	30.8	31.1	31.3
150	20.2	20.5	20.7	21.0	21.2	21.5	21.7	22.0	22.2	22.5	22.7	23.0	23.2	23.5	23.7	24.0	24.2	24.5	24.7	25.0	25.2	25.5	25.7	26.0	26.2	26.5	26.7	27.0	27.2	27.5	27.7	28.0	28.2	28.5	28.7	29.0	29.2	29.5	29.7
148	18.3	18.5	18.8	19.0	19.3	19.6	19.8	20.1	20.3	20.6	20.9	21.1	21.4	21.6	21.9	22.1	22.4	22.7	22.9	23.2	23.4	23.7	24.0	24.2	24.5	24.7	25.0	25.3	25.5	25.8	26.0	26.3	26.6	26.8	27.1	27.3	27.6	27.9	28.1
146	16.3	16.5	16.8	17.1	17.3	17.6	17.9	18.2	18.4	18.7	19.0	19.2	19.5	19.8	20.0	20.3	20.6	20.9	21.1	21.4	21.7	21.9	22.2	22.5	22.7	23.0	23.3	23.5	23.8	24.1	24.4	24.6	24.9	25.2	25.4	25.7	26.0	26.2	26.5
144	14.3	14.6	14.8	15.1	15.4	15.7	16.0	16.2	16.5	16.8	17.1	17.4	17.6	17.9	18.2	18.5	18.8	19.0	19.3	19.6	19.9	20.2	20.4	20.7	21.0	21.3	21.6	21.8	22.1	22.4	22.7	23.0	23.2	23.5	23.8	24.1	24.4	24.6	24.9
142	12.3	12.6	12.8	13.1	13.4	13.8	14.1	14.3	14.6	14.9	15.3	15.6	15.8	16.1	16.4	16.7	17.0	17.2	17.5	17.8	18.2	18.5	18.7	19.0	19.3	19.6	19.9	20.1	20.4	20.7	20.9	21.2	21.4	21.6	21.9	22.2	22.5	22.7	23.0
140	10.4	10.6	10.9	11.2	11.5	12.0	12.3	12.5	12.8	13.1	13.5	13.9	14.1	14.4	14.7	15.0	15.3	15.5	15.7	16.0	16.4	16.7	16.9	17.2	17.5	17.8	18.1	18.3	18.6	18.9	19.2	19.5	19.7	19.9	20.4	20.6	21.0	21.4	21.5
138	8.5	8.7	9.0	9.3	9.7	10.1	10.4	10.7	11.1	11.5	11.8	12.2	12.4	12.7	13.0	13.3	13.6	13.8	14.1	14.5	14.9	15.2	15.4	15.7	16.0	16.3	16.6	16.9	17.2	17.5	17.8	18.1	18.4	18.7	19.0	19.3	19.6	19.8	19.9
136	6.6	6.8	7.1	7.4	8.0	8.6	9.0	9.4	9.8	10.2	10.6	10.9	11.1	11.5	11.8	12.1	12.4	12.6	12.9	13.2	13.6	13.9	14.1	14.4	14.7	15.0	15.3	15.5	15.8	16.1	16.4	16.5	16.7	16.9	17.1	17.4	17.8	17.9	17.9
134	4.7	5.0	5.6	6.2	6.8	7.3	7.7	8.1	8.5	8.9	9.3	9.6	9.9	10.3	10.6	10.9	11.1	11.4	11.7	11.9	12.2	12.4	12.7	12.9	13.2	13.4	13.6	13.8	14.1	14.3	14.5	14.7	14.9	15.1	15.3	15.5	15.7	15.9	16.0
132	3.1	4.1	4.8	5.4	6.0	6.5	6.9	7.3	7.7	8.1	8.5	8.8	9.1	9.5	9.8	10.1	10.3	10.6	10.9	11.1	11.4	11.6	11.9	12.1	12.4	12.6	12.8	13.0	13.3	13.5	13.7	13.9	14.1	14.3	14.5	14.7	14.9	15.1	15.2
130	2.3	3.3	4.0	4.6	5.2	5.7	6.1	6.5	6.9	7.3	7.7	8.0	8.3	8.7	9.0	9.3	9.5	9.8	10.1	10.3	10.6	10.8	11.1	11.3	11.6	11.8	12.0	12.2	12.5	12.7	12.9	13.1	13.3	13.5	13.7	13.9	14.1	14.3	14.4
128	1.5	2.5	3.2	3.8	4.4	4.9	5.3	5.7	6.1	6.5	6.9	7.2	7.5	7.9	8.2	8.5	8.7	9.0	9.3	9.5	9.8	10.0	10.3	10.5	10.8	11.0	11.2	11.4	11.7	11.9	12.1	12.3	12.5	12.7	12.9	13.1	13.3	13.5	13.6
126	0.7	1.7	2.4	3.0	3.6	4.1	4.5	4.9	5.3	5.7	6.1	6.4	6.7	7.1	7.4	7.7	7.9	8.2	8.5	8.7	9.0	9.2	9.5	9.7	9.9	10.2	10.4	10.6	10.9	11.1	11.3	11.5	11.7	11.9	12.1	12.3	12.5	12.7	12.8
124	0.0	0.9	1.6	2.2	2.8	3.3	3.7	4.1	4.5	4.9	5.3	5.6	5.9	6.3	6.6	6.9	7.1	7.4	7.7	7.9	8.2	8.4	8.7	8.9	9.2	9.4	9.6	9.8	10.1	10.3	10.5	10.7	10.9	11.1	11.3	11.5	11.7	11.9	12.0
122	0.0	0.1	0.8	1.4	2.0	2.5	2.9	3.3	3.7	4.1	4.5	4.8	5.1	5.5	5.8	6.1	6.3	6.6	6.9	7.1	7.4	7.6	7.9	8.1	8.4	8.6	8.8	9.0	9.3	9.5	9.7	9.9	10.1	10.3	10.5	10.7	10.9	11.1	11.2
120	0.0	0.0	0.0	0.6	1.2	1.7	2.1	2.5	2.9	3.3	3.7	4.0	4.3	4.7	5.0	5.3	5.5	5.8	6.1	6.3	6.6	6.8	7.1	7.3	7.6	7.8	8.0	8.2	8.5	8.7	8.9	9.1	9.3	9.5	9.7	9.9	10.1	10.3	10.4
118	0.0	0.0	0.0	0.0	0.4	0.9	1.3	1.7	2.1	2.5	2.9	3.2	3.5	3.9	4.2	4.5	4.7	5.0	5.3	5.5	5.8	6.0	6.3	6.5	6.8	7.0	7.2	7.4	7.7	7.9	8.1	8.3	8.5	8.7	8.9	9.1	9.3	9.5	9.6
116	0.0	0.0	0.0	0.0	0.0	0.1	0.5	0.9	1.3	1.7	2.1	2.4	2.7	3.1	3.4	3.7	3.9	4.2	4.5	4.7	5.0	5.2	5.5	5.7	6.0	6.2	6.4	6.6	6.9	7.1	7.3	7.5	7.7	7.9	8.1	8.3	8.5	8.7	8.8
114	0.0	0.0	0.0	0.0	0.0	0.0	0.0	0.1	0.5	0.9	1.3	1.6	1.9	2.3	2.6	2.9	3.1	3.4	3.7	3.9	4.2	4.4	4.7	4.9	5.2	5.4	5.6	5.8	6.1	6.3	6.5	6.7	6.9	7.1	7.3	7.5	7.7	7.9	8.0
112	0.0	0.0	0.0	0.0	0.0	0.0	0.0	0.0	0.0	0.1	0.5	0.8	1.1	1.5	1.8	2.1	2.3	2.6	2.9	3.1	3.4	3.6	3.9	4.1	4.4	4.6	4.8	5.0	5.3	5.5	5.7	5.9	6.1	6.3	6.5	6.7	6.9	7.1	7.2
110	0.0	0.0	0.0	0.0	0.0	0.0	0.0	0.0	0.0	0.0	0.0	0.0	0.3	0.7	1.0	1.3	1.5	1.8	2.1	2.3	2.6	2.8	3.1	3.3	3.6	3.8	4.0	4.2	4.5	4.7	4.9	5.1	5.3	5.5	5.7	5.9	6.1	6.3	6.4
108	0.0	0.0	0.0	0.0	0.0	0.0	0.0	0.0	0.0	0.0	0.0	0.0	0.0	0.0	0.2	0.5	0.7	1.0	1.3	1.5	1.8	2.0	2.3	2.5	2.8	3.0	3.2	3.4	3.7	3.9	4.1	4.3	4.5	4.7	4.9	5.1	5.3	5.5	5.6
106	0.0	0.0	0.0	0.0	0.0	0.0	0.0	0.0	0.0	0.0	0.0	0.0	0.0	0.0	0.0	0.0	0.0	0.2	0.5	0.7	1.0	1.2	1.5	1.7	2.0	2.2	2.4	2.6	2.9	3.1	3.3	3.5	3.7	3.9	4.1	4.3	4.5	4.7	4.8
104	0.0	0.0	0.0	0.0	0.0	0.0	0.0	0.0	0.0	0.0	0.0	0.0	0.0	0.0	0.0	0.0	0.0	0.0	0.0	0.0	0.2	0.4	0.7	0.9	1.2	1.4	1.6	1.8	2.1	2.3	2.5	2.7	2.9	3.1	3.3	3.5	3.7	3.9	4.0
102	0.0	0.0	0.0	0.0	0.0	0.0	0.0	0.0	0.0	0.0	0.0	0.0	0.0	0.0	0.0	0.0	0.0	0.0	0.0	0.0	0.0	0.0	0.0	0.1	0.4	0.6	0.8	1.0	1.3	1.5	1.7	1.9	2.1	2.3	2.5	2.7	2.9	3.1	3.2
100	0.0	0.0	0.0	0.0	0.0	0.0	0.0	0.0	0.0	0.0	0.0	0.0	0.0	0.0	0.0	0.0	0.0	0.0	0.0	0.0	0.0	0.0	0.0	0.0	0.0	0.0	0.0	0.2	0.5	0.7	0.9	1.1	1.3	1.5	1.7	1.9	2.1	2.3	2.4
99	0.0	0.0	0.0	0.0	0.0	0.0	0.0	0.0	0.0	0.0	0.0	0.0	0.0	0.0	0.0	0.0	0.0	0.0	0.0	0.0	0.0	0.0	0.0	0.0	0.0	0.0	0.0	0.0	0.1	0.3	0.5	0.7	0.9	1.1	1.3	1.5	1.7	1.9	2.0
98	0.0	0.0	0.0	0.0	0.0	0.0	0.0	0.0	0.0	0.0	0.0	0.0	0.0	0.0	0.0	0.0	0.0	0.0	0.0	0.0	0.0	0.0	0.0	0.0	0.0	0.0	0.0	0.0	0.0	0.0	0.1	0.3	0.5	0.7	0.9	1.1	1.3	1.5	1.6
97	0.0	0.0	0.0	0.0	0.0	0.0	0.0	0.0	0.0	0.0	0.0	0.0	0.0	0.0	0.0	0.0	0.0	0.0	0.0	0.0	0.0	0.0	0.0	0.0	0.0	0.0	0.0	0.0	0.0	0.0	0.0	0.0	0.1	0.3	0.5	0.7	0.9	1.1	1.2
96	0.0	0.0	0.0	0.0	0.0	0.0	0.0	0.0	0.0	0.0	0.0	0.0	0.0	0.0	0.0	0.0	0.0	0.0	0.0	0.0	0.0	0.0	0.0	0.0	0.0	0.0	0.0	0.0	0.0	0.0	0.0	0.0	0.0	0.0	0.1	0.3	0.5	0.7	0.8
95	0.0	0.0	0.0	0.0	0.0	0.0	0.0	0.0	0.0	0.0	0.0	0.0	0.0	0.0	0.0	0.0	0.0	0.0	0.0	0.0	0.0	0.0	0.0	0.0	0.0	0.0	0.0	0.0	0.0	0.0	0.0	0.0	0.0	0.0	0.0	0.0	0.1	0.3	0.4
94	0.0	0.0	0.0	0.0	0.0	0.0	0.0	0.0	0.0	0.0	0.0	0.0	0.0	0.0	0.0	0.0	0.0	0.0	0.0	0.0	0.0	0.0	0.0	0.0	0.0	0.0	0.0	0.0	0.0	0.0	0.0	0.0	0.0	0.0	0.0	0.0	0.0	0.0	0.0
93	0.0	0.0	0.0	0.0	0.0	0.0	0.0	0.0	0.0	0.0	0.0	0.0	0.0	0.0	0.0	0.0	0.0	0.0	0.0	0.0	0.0	0.0	0.0	0.0	0.0	0.0	0.0	0.0	0.0	0.0	0.0	0.0	0.0	0.0	0.0	0.0	0.0	0.0	0.0
92	0.0	0.0	0.0	0.0	0.0	0.0	0.0	0.0	0.0	0.0	0.0	0.0	0.0	0.0	0.0	0.0	0.0	0.0	0.0	0.0	0.0	0.0	0.0	0.0	0.0	0.0	0.0	0.0	0.0	0.0	0.0	0.0	0.0	0.0	0.0	0.0	0.0	0.0	0.0
91	0.0	0.0	0.0	0.0	0.0	0.0	0.0	0.0	0.0	0.0	0.0	0.0	0.0	0.0	0.0	0.0	0.0	0.0	0.0	0.0	0.0	0.0	0.0	0.0	0.0	0.0	0.0	0.0	0.0	0.0	0.0	0.0	0.0	0.0	0.0	0.0	0.0	0.0	0.0

LISTED CALL OPTION PRICE WHEN EXERCISE PRICE IS 140

NUMBER OF WEEKS BEFORE THE OPTION EXPIRES

Common Stock Price	1	2	3	4	5	6	7	8	9	10	11	12	13	14	15	16	17	18	19	20	21	22	23	24	25	26	27	28	29	30	31	32	33	34	35	36	37	38	39
182	42.2	42.3	42.5	42.7	42.8	43.0	43.1	43.3	43.5	43.6	43.8	44.0	44.1	44.3	44.4	44.6	44.8	44.9	45.1	45.3	45.4	45.6	45.8	45.9	46.1	46.2	46.4	46.6	46.7	46.9	47.1	47.2	47.4	47.6	47.7	47.9	48.0	48.2	48.4
180	40.2	40.3	40.5	40.7	40.9	41.0	41.2	41.4	41.6	41.7	41.9	42.1	42.3	42.4	42.6	42.8	43.0	43.1	43.3	43.5	43.6	43.8	44.0	44.2	44.3	44.5	44.7	44.9	45.0	45.2	45.4	45.6	45.7	45.9	46.1	46.2	46.4	46.6	46.8
178	38.2	38.4	38.6	38.7	38.9	39.1	39.3	39.5	39.7	39.8	40.0	40.2	40.4	40.6	40.8	40.9	41.1	41.3	41.5	41.7	41.9	42.0	42.2	42.4	42.6	42.8	43.0	43.1	43.3	43.5	43.7	43.9	44.1	44.3	44.4	44.6	44.8	45.0	45.2
176	36.2	36.4	36.6	36.8	37.0	37.2	37.4	37.6	37.7	37.9	38.1	38.3	38.5	38.7	38.9	39.1	39.3	39.5	39.7	39.9	40.1	40.3	40.5	40.7	40.9	41.0	41.2	41.4	41.6	41.8	42.0	42.2	42.4	42.6	42.8	43.0	43.2	43.4	43.6
174	34.2	34.4	34.6	34.8	35.0	35.2	35.4	35.6	35.8	36.0	36.2	36.4	36.5	36.7	36.9	37.1	37.3	37.5	37.7	37.9	38.1	38.3	38.5	38.7	38.9	39.1	39.3	39.5	39.7	39.9	40.1	40.3	40.5	40.7	40.9	41.2	41.4	41.6	42.0
172	32.2	32.4	32.6	32.8	33.0	33.1	33.3	33.5	33.7	33.9	34.1	34.3	34.5	34.6	34.8	35.0	35.2	35.4	35.6	35.8	36.0	36.2	36.4	36.7	36.9	37.1	37.3	37.5	37.7	37.9	38.1	38.3	38.5	38.7	38.9	39.2	39.5	39.9	40.4
170	30.2	30.4	30.7	30.7	30.9	31.1	31.3	31.6	31.8	32.0	32.2	32.5	32.7	32.9	33.1	33.4	33.6	33.8	34.0	34.3	34.5	34.7	34.9	35.2	35.4	35.6	35.8	36.1	36.3	36.5	36.7	37.0	37.2	37.4	37.6	37.9	38.1	38.3	38.8
168	28.2	28.5	28.7	28.9	29.2	29.4	29.6	29.9	30.1	30.4	30.6	30.8	31.1	31.3	31.5	31.8	32.0	32.2	32.5	32.7	32.9	33.2	33.4	33.6	33.8	34.1	34.3	34.5	34.8	35.0	35.3	35.5	35.8	36.0	36.2	36.5	36.7	36.9	37.2
166	26.2	26.5	26.7	27.0	27.2	27.5	27.7	28.0	28.2	28.5	28.7	29.0	29.2	29.4	29.7	29.9	30.2	30.4	30.7	30.9	31.2	31.4	31.6	31.9	32.1	32.4	32.6	32.9	33.1	33.4	33.6	33.9	34.1	34.4	34.6	34.8	35.1	35.3	35.6
164	24.3	24.5	24.8	25.0	25.3	25.5	25.8	26.0	26.3	26.6	26.8	27.1	27.3	27.6	27.8	28.1	28.3	28.6	28.9	29.1	29.4	29.6	29.9	30.1	30.4	30.6	30.9	31.1	31.4	31.7	31.9	32.2	32.4	32.7	32.9	33.2	33.5	33.7	34.0
162	22.3	22.5	22.8	23.1	23.3	23.6	23.9	24.1	24.4	24.7	25.0	25.2	25.5	25.7	26.0	26.3	26.6	26.8	27.1	27.3	27.6	27.9	28.1	28.4	28.6	28.9	29.2	29.4	29.7	29.9	30.2	30.5	30.8	31.0	31.3	31.6	31.8	32.1	32.4
160	20.3	20.6	20.8	21.1	21.4	21.7	21.9	22.2	22.5	22.8	23.0	23.3	23.6	23.9	24.1	24.4	24.7	25.0	25.2	25.5	25.8	26.1	26.4	26.6	26.9	27.2	27.5	27.7	28.0	28.3	28.6	28.8	29.1	29.4	29.7	29.9	30.2	30.5	30.8
158	18.3	18.6	18.9	19.1	19.4	19.7	20.0	20.3	20.6	20.9	21.2	21.4	21.7	22.0	22.3	22.6	22.9	23.1	23.4	23.7	24.0	24.3	24.6	24.9	25.2	25.4	25.7	26.0	26.3	26.6	26.9	27.2	27.5	27.8	28.0	28.3	28.6	28.9	29.2
156	16.3	16.6	16.9	17.2	17.5	17.8	18.1	18.4	18.7	19.0	19.3	19.6	19.9	20.2	20.5	20.7	21.0	21.3	21.6	21.9	22.2	22.4	22.7	23.0	23.3	23.7	24.0	24.3	24.6	24.9	25.2	25.5	25.8	26.1	26.4	26.7	27.0	27.3	27.6
154	14.3	14.6	14.9	15.2	15.6	15.9	16.2	16.5	16.8	17.1	17.4	17.7	18.0	18.3	18.6	18.8	19.1	19.4	19.7	20.0	20.3	20.6	20.9	21.2	21.5	21.8	22.1	22.4	22.7	23.0	23.3	23.6	23.9	24.2	24.5	24.8	25.1	25.4	26.1
152	12.4	12.9	13.3	13.7	14.0	14.3	14.6	14.9	15.2	15.5	15.8	16.1	16.4	16.7	17.0	17.2	17.5	17.8	18.1	18.4	18.7	19.0	19.3	19.6	19.9	20.2	20.5	20.8	21.1	21.4	21.7	22.0	22.3	22.6	22.9	23.2	23.5	23.9	24.3
150	10.5	10.7	11.0	11.4	11.8	12.1	12.4	12.7	13.1	13.4	13.7	14.0	14.3	14.6	14.9	15.1	15.4	15.7	16.0	16.3	16.6	16.9	17.2	17.5	17.8	18.1	18.4	18.7	19.0	19.3	19.6	19.9	20.2	20.5	20.8	21.1	21.4	21.8	22.3
148	8.6	9.1	9.5	9.9	10.2	10.6	10.9	11.2	11.6	11.9	12.2	12.5	12.8	13.1	13.4	13.6	13.9	14.2	14.5	14.8	15.1	15.4	15.6	15.9	16.2	16.5	16.8	17.1	17.4	17.7	18.0	18.3	18.6	18.9	19.2	19.4	19.7	20.1	20.5
146	6.7	7.3	7.7	8.0	8.5	8.9	9.3	9.7	9.9	10.3	10.7	10.9	11.2	11.4	11.7	12.0	12.4	12.7	13.0	13.3	13.5	13.8	14.1	14.3	14.6	14.9	15.2	15.5	15.8	16.0	16.3	16.5	16.7	16.9	17.1	17.3	17.9	18.3	19.2
144	4.8	5.1	5.9	6.6	7.2	7.7	8.2	8.6	9.1	9.5	9.9	10.2	10.6	10.9	11.2	11.6	11.9	12.2	12.5	12.8	13.0	13.3	13.5	13.8	14.1	14.3	14.6	14.9	15.2	15.5	15.7	16.0	16.3	16.6	16.9	17.1	17.3	17.5	18.0
142	3.3	4.3	5.1	5.8	6.4	6.9	7.4	7.8	8.3	8.7	9.1	9.5	9.8	10.2	10.4	10.9	11.2	11.4	11.7	11.9	12.2	12.5	12.7	13.0	13.3	13.5	13.8	14.0	14.3	14.6	14.9	15.1	15.3	15.5	15.7	15.9	16.1	16.7	17.2
140	2.5	3.5	4.3	5.0	5.6	6.1	6.7	7.0	7.4	7.9	8.3	8.6	9.0	9.4	9.8	10.1	10.6	10.9	11.4	11.7	11.9	12.2	12.5	12.7	13.0	13.2	13.5	13.7	14.0	14.2	14.4	14.7	14.9	15.1	15.3	15.5	15.7	15.9	16.4
138	1.7	2.7	3.5	4.2	4.8	5.3	5.9	6.3	6.7	7.1	7.5	7.8	8.2	8.5	8.8	9.2	9.5	9.8	10.1	10.3	10.6	10.9	11.1	11.4	11.7	11.9	12.1	12.4	12.6	12.9	13.1	13.3	13.6	13.9	14.1	14.3	14.6	14.8	15.6
136	0.9	1.7	2.4	3.0	3.5	4.0	4.5	5.0	5.4	5.8	6.2	6.6	6.9	7.3	7.6	8.0	8.4	8.7	9.0	9.3	9.6	9.9	10.1	10.4	10.6	10.9	11.1	11.4	11.6	11.8	12.0	12.3	12.5	12.7	12.9	13.1	13.3	13.8	14.8
134	0.1	1.1	1.8	2.3	2.9	3.4	3.8	4.3	4.6	5.1	5.4	5.8	6.1	6.4	6.8	7.1	7.4	7.7	8.0	8.2	8.5	8.8	9.0	9.3	9.5	9.8	10.0	10.3	10.5	10.7	11.0	11.3	11.5	11.7	11.9	12.1	12.5	13.0	14.0
132	0.0	0.3	0.8	1.3	1.8	2.2	2.6	3.0	3.5	3.8	4.2	4.6	4.9	5.3	5.6	6.0	6.3	6.6	6.9	7.2	7.4	7.7	7.9	8.2	8.5	8.7	9.0	9.2	9.5	9.6	9.9	10.1	10.3	10.5	10.7	10.9	11.3	12.2	13.2
130	0.0	0.0	0.3	0.7	1.1	1.6	1.9	2.3	2.7	3.1	3.5	3.9	4.2	4.5	4.8	5.2	5.5	5.8	6.1	6.4	6.6	6.9	7.1	7.4	7.6	7.9	8.2	8.4	8.6	8.8	9.0	9.3	9.5	9.7	9.9	10.1	10.7	11.7	12.4
128	0.0	0.0	0.0	0.3	0.6	1.0	1.4	1.8	2.2	2.5	2.9	3.2	3.6	3.9	4.2	4.6	5.0	5.3	5.5	5.8	6.1	6.3	6.5	6.8	7.0	7.3	7.5	7.7	8.0	8.2	8.4	8.6	8.8	9.0	9.2	9.5	9.9	10.9	11.6
126	0.0	0.0	0.0	0.0	0.3	0.6	1.0	1.4	1.8	2.1	2.5	2.8	3.1	3.4	3.7	4.0	4.4	4.7	5.0	5.3	5.5	5.8	6.0	6.3	6.5	6.7	6.9	7.1	7.3	7.5	7.7	7.9	8.1	8.3	8.5	8.7	9.1	9.5	10.8
124	0.0	0.0	0.0	0.0	0.0	0.3	0.6	1.0	1.4	1.7	2.0	2.3	2.6	2.9	3.2	3.5	3.9	4.2	4.5	4.7	5.0	5.2	5.5	5.7	5.9	6.1	6.3	6.5	6.7	6.9	7.1	7.3	7.5	7.7	7.9	8.1	8.5	8.9	9.9
122	0.0	0.0	0.0	0.0	0.0	0.0	0.3	0.6	1.0	1.3	1.6	1.9	2.1	2.4	2.7	3.0	3.3	3.6	3.9	4.2	4.4	4.6	4.8	5.0	5.2	5.4	5.6	5.8	6.0	6.2	6.4	6.6	6.8	7.0	7.2	7.5	7.9	8.2	9.2
120	0.0	0.0	0.0	0.0	0.0	0.0	0.0	0.3	0.6	0.9	1.2	1.4	1.7	2.0	2.3	2.6	2.9	3.1	3.4	3.7	3.9	4.1	4.3	4.5	4.7	4.9	5.1	5.3	5.4	5.6	5.8	6.0	6.2	6.4	6.7	7.0	7.4	7.7	8.4
118	0.0	0.0	0.0	0.0	0.0	0.0	0.0	0.0	0.3	0.6	0.9	1.1	1.4	1.6	1.9	2.1	2.4	2.6	2.9	3.1	3.4	3.6	3.8	3.9	4.1	4.3	4.5	4.7	4.9	5.1	5.3	5.5	5.7	5.9	6.1	6.3	6.6	7.0	7.6
116	0.0	0.0	0.0	0.0	0.0	0.0	0.0	0.0	0.0	0.3	0.6	0.8	1.0	1.2	1.5	1.7	2.0	2.2	2.5	2.7	2.9	3.1	3.3	3.5	3.7	3.9	4.1	4.3	4.5	4.7	4.9	5.1	5.3	5.5	5.7	6.1	6.3	6.6	6.8
114	0.0	0.0	0.0	0.0	0.0	0.0	0.0	0.0	0.0	0.0	0.3	0.5	0.7	0.9	1.1	1.4	1.6	1.8	2.1	2.3	2.5	2.7	2.9	3.1	3.3	3.5	3.7	3.9	4.1	4.3	4.5	4.7	4.9	5.1	5.3	5.5	5.8	6.0	6.0
112	0.0	0.0	0.0	0.0	0.0	0.0	0.0	0.0	0.0	0.0	0.0	0.3	0.5	0.7	0.8	1.0	1.3	1.5	1.7	1.9	2.1	2.3	2.5	2.7	2.9	3.1	3.3	3.5	3.7	3.9	4.1	4.3	4.5	4.7	4.9	5.2	5.4	5.6	5.4
110	0.0	0.0	0.0	0.0	0.0	0.0	0.0	0.0	0.0	0.0	0.0	0.0	0.2	0.4	0.6	0.8	1.0	1.2	1.4	1.6	1.8	2.0	2.1	2.3	2.6	2.8	3.0	3.2	3.4	3.6	3.8	4.0	4.2	4.4	4.6	4.8	5.0	5.0	4.4
108	0.0	0.0	0.0	0.0	0.0	0.0	0.0	0.0	0.0	0.0	0.0	0.0	0.0	0.2	0.4	0.6	0.8	1.0	1.2	1.3	1.5	1.7	1.9	2.1	2.3	2.5	2.7	2.9	3.0	3.2	3.4	3.6	3.8	4.0	4.2	4.4	4.2	4.2	3.6
106	0.0	0.0	0.0	0.0	0.0	0.0	0.0	0.0	0.0	0.0	0.0	0.0	0.0	0.0	0.2	0.4	0.6	0.7	0.9	1.1	1.3	1.5	1.7	1.8	2.0	2.2	2.3	2.5	2.7	2.8	3.0	3.2	3.4	3.5	3.7	3.7	3.5	3.4	2.8
104	0.0	0.0	0.0	0.0	0.0	0.0	0.0	0.0	0.0	0.0	0.0	0.0	0.0	0.0	0.0	0.2	0.4	0.5	0.7	0.9	1.0	1.2	1.4	1.5	1.7	1.9	2.0	2.2	2.4	2.4	2.6	2.7	2.9	2.9	2.7	2.9	2.7	2.6	2.0
102	0.0	0.0	0.0	0.0	0.0	0.0	0.0	0.0	0.0	0.0	0.0	0.0	0.0	0.0	0.0	0.0	0.2	0.3	0.5	0.7	0.8	1.0	1.1	1.3	1.5	1.5	1.7	1.8	1.4	2.1	1.9	2.1	1.5	2.5	1.9	1.3	1.5	1.8	1.2
100	0.0	0.0	0.0	0.0	0.0	0.0	0.0	0.0	0.0	0.0	0.0	0.0	0.0	0.0	0.0	0.0	0.0	0.2	0.3	0.5	0.6	0.7	0.9	1.0	1.0	1.1	1.3	1.4	0.6	0.8	0.3	1.3	0.7	0.9	1.1	0.5	0.7	0.0	0.0
99	0.0	0.0	0.0	0.0	0.0	0.0	0.0	0.0	0.0	0.0	0.0	0.0	0.0	0.0	0.0	0.0	0.0	0.0	0.2	0.3	0.5	0.5	0.7	0.5	0.5	0.0	0.0	0.4	0.6	0.8	0.3	1.3	0.7	0.9	0.3	0.5	0.7	0.0	0.0
98	0.0	0.0	0.0	0.0	0.0	0.0	0.0	0.0	0.0	0.0	0.0	0.0	0.0	0.0	0.0	0.0	0.0	0.0	0.0	0.0	0.0	0.0	0.0	0.0	0.0	0.0	0.0	0.0	0.0	0.0	0.0	0.0	0.0	0.0	0.0	0.0	0.0	0.0	0.0

LISTED CALL OPTION PRICE WHEN EXERCISE PRICE IS 150

Common Stock Price	NUMBER OF WEEKS BEFORE THE OPTION EXPIRES																																					
	1	2	3	4	5	6	7	8	9	10	11	12	13	14	15	16	17	18	19	20	21	22	23	24	25	26	27	28	29	30	31	32	33	34	35	36	37	38	39
196	46.2	46.3	46.5	46.7	46.8	47.0	47.2	47.4	47.5	47.7	47.9	48.0	48.2	48.4	48.5	48.7	48.9	49.1	49.2	49.4	49.6	49.7	49.9	50.1	50.2	50.4	50.6	50.8	50.9	51.1	51.3	51.4	51.6	51.8	51.9	52.1	52.3	52.5	52.6
194	44.2	44.4	44.5	44.7	44.9	45.1	45.3	45.4	45.6	45.8	46.0	46.2	46.3	46.5	46.7	46.9	47.1	47.2	47.4	47.6	47.8	48.0	48.1	48.3	48.5	48.7	48.9	49.0	49.2	49.4	49.6	49.8	49.9	50.1	50.3	50.5	50.7	50.8	51.0
192	42.2	42.4	42.6	42.8	43.0	43.1	43.3	43.5	43.7	43.9	44.1	44.3	44.5	44.7	44.9	45.0	45.2	45.4	45.6	45.8	46.0	46.2	46.4	46.6	46.8	46.9	47.1	47.3	47.5	47.7	47.9	48.1	48.3	48.5	48.7	48.9	49.0	49.2	49.4
190	40.2	40.4	40.6	40.8	41.0	41.2	41.4	41.6	41.8	42.0	42.2	42.4	42.6	42.8	43.0	43.2	43.4	43.6	43.8	44.0	44.2	44.4	44.6	44.8	45.0	45.2	45.4	45.6	45.8	46.0	46.2	46.4	46.6	46.8	47.0	47.2	47.4	47.6	47.8
188	38.2	38.4	38.6	38.8	39.1	39.3	39.5	39.7	39.9	40.1	40.3	40.5	40.7	41.0	41.2	41.4	41.6	41.8	42.0	42.2	42.4	42.6	42.9	43.1	43.3	43.5	43.7	43.9	44.1	44.3	44.5	44.7	45.0	45.2	45.4	45.6	45.8	46.0	46.2
186	36.2	36.4	36.7	36.9	37.1	37.3	37.5	37.8	38.0	38.2	38.4	38.7	38.9	39.1	39.3	39.5	39.8	39.9	40.2	40.4	40.6	40.9	41.1	41.3	41.5	41.8	42.0	42.2	42.4	42.6	42.9	43.1	43.3	43.5	43.7	44.0	44.2	44.4	44.6
184	34.2	34.5	34.7	34.9	35.2	35.4	35.6	35.9	36.1	36.3	36.5	36.8	37.0	37.2	37.5	37.7	37.9	38.2	38.4	38.6	38.9	39.1	39.3	39.6	39.8	40.0	40.2	40.5	40.7	40.9	41.2	41.4	41.6	41.9	42.1	42.3	42.6	42.8	43.0
182	32.2	32.5	32.7	33.0	33.2	33.5	33.7	33.9	34.2	34.4	34.7	34.9	35.1	35.4	35.6	35.9	36.1	36.4	36.6	36.8	37.1	37.3	37.6	37.8	38.0	38.3	38.5	38.8	39.0	39.3	39.5	39.7	39.9	40.2	40.5	40.7	40.9	41.2	41.4
180	30.3	30.5	30.8	31.0	31.3	31.5	31.8	32.0	32.3	32.5	32.8	33.0	33.3	33.5	33.8	34.0	34.3	34.5	34.8	35.0	35.3	35.5	35.8	36.0	36.3	36.6	36.8	37.1	37.3	37.6	37.8	38.1	38.3	38.6	38.8	39.1	39.3	39.6	39.8
178	28.3	28.5	28.8	29.0	29.3	29.6	29.8	30.1	30.4	30.6	30.9	31.1	31.4	31.7	31.9	32.2	32.5	32.7	33.0	33.2	33.5	33.8	34.0	34.3	34.6	34.8	35.1	35.3	35.6	35.9	36.1	36.4	36.7	36.9	37.2	37.4	37.7	38.0	38.2
176	26.3	26.5	26.8	27.1	27.4	27.6	27.9	28.2	28.5	28.7	29.0	29.3	29.5	29.8	30.1	30.4	30.6	30.9	31.2	31.4	31.7	32.0	32.3	32.5	32.8	33.1	33.4	33.6	33.9	34.2	34.4	34.7	35.0	35.3	35.5	35.8	36.1	36.4	36.6
174	24.3	24.6	24.8	25.1	25.4	25.7	26.0	26.3	26.5	26.8	27.1	27.4	27.7	28.0	28.2	28.5	28.8	29.1	29.4	29.7	29.9	30.2	30.5	30.8	31.1	31.4	31.6	31.9	32.2	32.5	32.8	33.0	33.3	33.6	33.9	34.2	34.5	34.7	35.0
172	22.3	22.6	22.9	23.2	23.5	23.8	24.1	24.3	24.6	24.9	25.2	25.5	25.8	26.1	26.4	26.7	27.0	27.3	27.6	27.9	28.2	28.4	28.7	29.0	29.3	29.6	29.9	30.2	30.5	30.8	31.1	31.4	31.7	32.0	32.3	32.5	32.8	33.1	33.4
170	20.3	20.6	20.9	21.2	21.5	21.8	22.1	22.4	22.7	23.0	23.3	23.6	23.9	24.2	24.5	24.9	25.2	25.5	25.8	26.1	26.4	26.7	27.0	27.3	27.6	27.9	28.2	28.5	28.8	29.1	29.4	29.7	30.0	30.3	30.6	30.9	31.2	31.5	31.8
168	18.3	18.6	18.9	19.3	19.6	19.9	20.2	20.5	20.8	21.1	21.4	21.8	22.1	22.4	22.7	23.0	23.3	23.6	24.0	24.3	24.6	24.9	25.2	25.5	25.8	26.1	26.5	26.8	27.1	27.4	27.7	28.0	28.3	28.7	29.0	29.3	29.6	29.9	30.2
166	16.3	16.6	17.0	17.3	17.6	17.9	18.3	18.6	18.9	19.2	19.6	19.9	20.2	20.5	20.9	21.2	21.5	21.8	22.2	22.5	22.8	23.1	23.4	23.8	24.1	24.4	24.7	25.1	25.4	25.7	26.0	26.4	26.7	27.0	27.3	27.7	28.0	28.3	28.6
164	14.3	14.6	15.0	15.4	15.7	16.0	16.3	16.6	16.9	17.2	17.6	18.0	18.3	18.6	19.0	19.3	19.6	19.9	20.3	20.6	20.9	21.2	21.5	21.9	22.2	22.5	22.8	23.2	23.5	23.8	24.1	24.5	24.8	25.1	25.4	25.8	26.1	26.4	26.7
162	12.4	12.7	13.1	13.4	13.8	14.1	14.4	14.7	15.0	15.3	15.7	16.1	16.4	16.7	17.1	17.4	17.7	18.0	18.4	18.7	19.0	19.3	19.6	20.0	20.3	20.6	20.9	21.2	21.6	21.9	22.2	22.6	22.9	23.2	23.5	23.9	24.2	24.5	24.8
160	10.5	10.8	11.2	11.5	11.9	12.2	12.5	12.8	13.1	13.4	13.8	14.2	14.5	14.8	15.2	15.5	15.8	16.1	16.5	16.8	17.1	17.4	17.7	18.1	18.2	18.7	19.0	19.4	19.7	20.0	20.3	20.7	21.0	21.3	21.6	22.0	22.3	22.6	22.9
158	8.7	8.9	9.3	9.6	10.0	10.4	10.6	10.9	11.2	11.6	12.1	12.4	12.8	13.2	13.5	13.9	14.2	14.5	14.8	15.1	15.4	15.7	16.0	16.3	16.5	16.8	17.1	17.5	17.8	18.1	18.4	18.8	19.1	19.4	19.7	20.1	20.4	20.7	21.0
156	6.8	7.0	7.5	7.9	8.4	8.9	9.5	9.9	10.4	10.8	11.3	11.6	12.0	12.4	12.7	13.1	13.4	13.7	14.0	14.3	14.6	14.9	15.2	15.5	15.7	16.0	16.3	16.5	16.8	17.0	17.3	17.5	17.7	18.0	18.2	18.4	18.6	18.8	19.1
154	4.9	5.4	6.2	6.9	7.6	8.1	8.7	9.1	9.6	10.0	10.5	10.8	11.2	11.6	11.9	12.3	12.6	12.9	13.2	13.5	13.8	14.1	14.4	14.7	14.9	15.2	15.5	15.7	16.0	16.2	16.5	16.7	16.9	17.2	17.4	17.6	17.8	18.0	18.3
152	3.5	4.6	5.4	6.1	6.8	7.3	7.9	8.3	8.8	9.2	9.7	10.0	10.4	10.8	11.1	11.5	11.8	12.1	12.4	12.7	13.0	13.3	13.6	13.9	14.1	14.4	14.7	14.9	15.2	15.4	15.7	15.9	16.1	16.4	16.6	16.8	17.0	17.2	17.5
150	2.7	3.8	4.6	5.3	6.0	6.5	7.1	7.5	8.0	8.4	8.9	9.2	9.6	9.9	10.3	10.7	11.0	11.3	11.6	11.9	12.2	12.5	12.8	13.1	13.3	13.6	13.9	14.1	14.4	14.6	14.9	15.1	15.3	15.6	15.8	16.0	16.2	16.4	16.7
148	1.9	3.0	3.8	4.5	5.2	5.7	6.3	6.7	7.2	7.6	8.1	8.4	8.8	9.2	9.5	9.9	10.2	10.5	10.8	11.1	11.4	11.7	12.0	12.3	12.5	12.8	13.1	13.3	13.6	13.8	14.1	14.3	14.5	14.8	15.0	15.2	15.4	15.6	15.9
146	1.1	2.2	3.0	3.7	4.4	4.9	5.5	5.9	6.4	6.8	7.3	7.6	8.0	8.4	8.7	9.1	9.4	9.7	10.0	10.3	10.6	10.9	11.2	11.5	11.7	12.0	12.3	12.5	12.8	13.0	13.3	13.5	13.7	14.0	14.2	14.4	14.6	14.8	15.1
144	0.3	1.4	2.2	2.9	3.6	4.1	4.7	5.1	5.6	6.0	6.5	6.8	7.2	7.6	7.9	8.3	8.6	8.9	9.2	9.5	9.8	10.1	10.4	10.7	10.9	11.2	11.5	11.7	12.0	12.2	12.5	12.7	12.9	13.2	13.4	13.6	13.8	14.0	14.3
142	0.0	0.6	1.4	2.1	2.8	3.3	3.9	4.3	4.8	5.2	5.7	6.0	6.4	6.8	7.1	7.5	7.8	8.1	8.4	8.7	9.0	9.3	9.6	9.9	10.1	10.4	10.7	10.9	11.2	11.4	11.7	11.9	12.1	12.4	12.6	12.8	13.0	13.2	13.5
140	0.0	0.0	0.6	1.3	2.0	2.5	3.1	3.5	4.0	4.4	4.9	5.2	5.6	6.0	6.3	6.7	7.0	7.3	7.6	7.9	8.2	8.5	8.8	9.1	9.3	9.6	9.9	10.1	10.4	10.6	10.9	11.1	11.3	11.6	11.8	12.0	12.2	12.4	12.7
138	0.0	0.0	0.0	0.5	1.2	1.7	2.3	2.7	3.2	3.6	4.1	4.4	4.8	5.2	5.5	5.9	6.2	6.5	6.8	7.1	7.4	7.7	8.0	8.3	8.5	8.8	9.1	9.3	9.6	9.8	10.1	10.3	10.5	10.8	11.0	11.2	11.4	11.6	11.9
136	0.0	0.0	0.0	0.0	0.4	0.9	1.5	1.9	2.4	2.8	3.3	3.6	4.0	4.4	4.7	5.1	5.4	5.7	6.0	6.3	6.6	6.9	7.2	7.5	7.7	8.0	8.3	8.5	8.8	9.0	9.3	9.5	9.7	9.9	10.2	10.4	10.6	10.8	11.1
134	0.0	0.0	0.0	0.0	0.0	0.1	0.7	1.1	1.6	2.0	2.5	2.8	3.2	3.6	3.9	4.3	4.6	4.9	5.2	5.5	5.8	6.1	6.4	6.7	6.9	7.2	7.5	7.7	8.0	8.2	8.5	8.7	8.9	9.2	9.4	9.6	9.8	10.0	10.3
132	0.0	0.0	0.0	0.0	0.0	0.0	0.0	0.3	0.8	1.2	1.7	2.0	2.4	2.8	3.1	3.5	3.8	4.1	4.4	4.7	5.0	5.3	5.6	5.9	6.1	6.4	6.7	6.9	7.2	7.4	7.7	7.9	8.1	8.4	8.6	8.8	9.0	9.2	9.5
130	0.0	0.0	0.0	0.0	0.0	0.0	0.0	0.0	0.0	0.4	0.9	1.2	1.6	2.0	2.3	2.7	3.0	3.3	3.6	3.9	4.2	4.5	4.8	5.1	5.3	5.6	5.9	6.1	6.4	6.6	6.9	7.1	7.3	7.6	7.8	8.0	8.2	8.4	8.7
128	0.0	0.0	0.0	0.0	0.0	0.0	0.0	0.0	0.0	0.0	0.1	0.4	0.8	1.2	1.5	1.9	2.2	2.5	2.8	3.1	3.4	3.7	4.0	4.3	4.5	4.8	5.1	5.3	5.6	5.8	6.1	6.3	6.5	6.8	7.0	7.2	7.4	7.6	7.9
126	0.0	0.0	0.0	0.0	0.0	0.0	0.0	0.0	0.0	0.0	0.0	0.0	0.0	0.4	0.7	1.1	1.4	1.7	2.0	2.3	2.6	2.9	3.2	3.5	3.7	4.0	4.3	4.5	4.8	5.0	5.3	5.5	5.7	6.0	6.2	6.4	6.6	6.8	7.1
124	0.0	0.0	0.0	0.0	0.0	0.0	0.0	0.0	0.0	0.0	0.0	0.0	0.0	0.0	0.0	0.3	0.6	0.9	1.2	1.5	1.8	2.1	2.4	2.7	2.9	3.2	3.5	3.7	4.0	4.2	4.5	4.7	4.9	5.2	5.4	5.6	5.8	6.0	6.3
122	0.0	0.0	0.0	0.0	0.0	0.0	0.0	0.0	0.0	0.0	0.0	0.0	0.0	0.0	0.0	0.0	0.0	0.1	0.4	0.7	1.0	1.3	1.6	1.9	2.1	2.4	2.7	2.9	3.2	3.4	3.7	3.9	4.1	4.4	4.6	4.8	5.0	5.2	5.5
120	0.0	0.0	0.0	0.0	0.0	0.0	0.0	0.0	0.0	0.0	0.0	0.0	0.0	0.0	0.0	0.0	0.0	0.0	0.0	0.0	0.2	0.5	0.8	1.1	1.3	1.6	1.9	2.1	2.4	2.6	2.9	3.1	3.3	3.6	3.8	4.0	4.2	4.4	4.7
118	0.0	0.0	0.0	0.0	0.0	0.0	0.0	0.0	0.0	0.0	0.0	0.0	0.0	0.0	0.0	0.0	0.0	0.0	0.0	0.0	0.0	0.0	0.0	0.3	0.5	0.8	1.1	1.3	1.6	1.8	2.1	2.3	2.5	2.8	3.0	3.2	3.4	3.6	3.9
116	0.0	0.0	0.0	0.0	0.0	0.0	0.0	0.0	0.0	0.0	0.0	0.0	0.0	0.0	0.0	0.0	0.0	0.0	0.0	0.0	0.0	0.0	0.0	0.0	0.0	0.0	0.3	0.5	0.8	1.0	1.3	1.5	1.7	2.0	2.2	2.4	2.6	2.8	3.1
114	0.0	0.0	0.0	0.0	0.0	0.0	0.0	0.0	0.0	0.0	0.0	0.0	0.0	0.0	0.0	0.0	0.0	0.0	0.0	0.0	0.0	0.0	0.0	0.0	0.0	0.0	0.0	0.0	0.0	0.2	0.5	0.7	0.9	1.2	1.4	1.6	1.8	2.0	2.3
112	0.0	0.0	0.0	0.0	0.0	0.0	0.0	0.0	0.0	0.0	0.0	0.0	0.0	0.0	0.0	0.0	0.0	0.0	0.0	0.0	0.0	0.0	0.0	0.0	0.0	0.0	0.0	0.0	0.0	0.0	0.0	0.0	0.1	0.4	0.6	0.8	1.0	1.2	1.5
110	0.0	0.0	0.0	0.0	0.0	0.0	0.0	0.0	0.0	0.0	0.0	0.0	0.0	0.0	0.0	0.0	0.0	0.0	0.0	0.0	0.0	0.0	0.0	0.0	0.0	0.0	0.0	0.0	0.0	0.0	0.0	0.0	0.0	0.0	0.0	0.0	0.2	0.4	0.7
108	0.0	0.0	0.0	0.0	0.0	0.0	0.0	0.0	0.0	0.0	0.0	0.0	0.0	0.0	0.0	0.0	0.0	0.0	0.0	0.0	0.0	0.0	0.0	0.0	0.0	0.0	0.0	0.0	0.0	0.0	0.0	0.0	0.0	0.0	0.0	0.0	0.0	0.0	0.0
106	0.0	0.0	0.0	0.0	0.0	0.0	0.0	0.0	0.0	0.0	0.0	0.0	0.0	0.0	0.0	0.0	0.0	0.0	0.0	0.0	0.0	0.0	0.0	0.0	0.0	0.0	0.0	0.0	0.0	0.0	0.0	0.0	0.0	0.0	0.0	0.0	0.0	0.0	0.0

THE NORMAL

VALUE LISTED

PUT OPTION

TABLES

LISTED PUT OPTION PRICE WHEN EXERCISE PRICE IS 10

NUMBER OF WEEKS BEFORE THE OPTION EXPIRES

Common Stock Price	1	2	3	4	5	6	7	8	9	10	11	12	13	14	15	16	17	18	19	20	21	22	23	24	25	26	27	28	29	30	31	32	33	34	35	36	37	38	39
14	0.0	0.0	0.0	0.0	0.0	0.0	0.0	0.0	0.0	0.0	0.0	0.0	0.0	0.0	0.0	0.0	0.0	0.0	0.0	0.0	0.0	0.0	0.0	0.0	0.0	0.0	0.0	0.0	0.0	0.0	0.0	0.0	0.0	0.0	0.0	0.0	0.0	0.0	0.0
13.5	0.0	0.0	0.0	0.0	0.0	0.0	0.0	0.0	0.0	0.0	0.0	0.0	0.0	0.0	0.0	0.0	0.0	0.0	0.0	0.0	0.0	0.0	0.0	0.0	0.0	0.0	0.0	0.0	0.0	0.0	0.0	0.0	0.0	0.0	0.0	0.0	0.0	0.0	0.1
13	0.0	0.0	0.0	0.0	0.0	0.0	0.0	0.0	0.0	0.0	0.0	0.0	0.0	0.0	0.0	0.0	0.0	0.0	0.0	0.0	0.0	0.0	0.0	0.0	0.0	0.0	0.0	0.0	0.0	0.0	0.1	0.1	0.1	0.1	0.1	0.1	0.1	0.1	0.2
12.5	0.0	0.0	0.0	0.0	0.0	0.0	0.0	0.0	0.0	0.0	0.0	0.0	0.0	0.0	0.0	0.0	0.1	0.1	0.1	0.1	0.1	0.1	0.1	0.1	0.1	0.1	0.1	0.1	0.1	0.1	0.2	0.2	0.2	0.2	0.2	0.2	0.2	0.2	0.2
12	0.0	0.0	0.0	0.0	0.0	0.0	0.0	0.0	0.0	0.0	0.0	0.1	0.1	0.1	0.1	0.1	0.1	0.1	0.1	0.2	0.2	0.2	0.2	0.2	0.2	0.2	0.2	0.2	0.2	0.2	0.3	0.3	0.3	0.3	0.3	0.3	0.3	0.3	0.4
11.5	0.0	0.0	0.0	0.0	0.0	0.0	0.0	0.0	0.1	0.1	0.1	0.1	0.1	0.1	0.2	0.2	0.2	0.2	0.2	0.2	0.3	0.3	0.3	0.3	0.3	0.3	0.4	0.4	0.4	0.4	0.4	0.4	0.4	0.4	0.4	0.4	0.4	0.5	0.5
11	0.0	0.0	0.0	0.0	0.0	0.0	0.1	0.1	0.1	0.1	0.1	0.1	0.2	0.2	0.2	0.2	0.2	0.2	0.3	0.3	0.3	0.3	0.3	0.3	0.4	0.4	0.4	0.4	0.4	0.5	0.5	0.5	0.5	0.5	0.6	0.6	0.6	0.6	0.6
10.5	0.0	0.0	0.0	0.0	0.1	0.1	0.1	0.1	0.2	0.2	0.2	0.2	0.2	0.3	0.3	0.3	0.3	0.3	0.4	0.4	0.4	0.4	0.4	0.5	0.5	0.5	0.5	0.5	0.5	0.6	0.6	0.7	0.7	0.7	0.7	0.7	0.7	0.7	0.7
10	0.1	0.1	0.1	0.2	0.2	0.2	0.2	0.3	0.3	0.3	0.3	0.3	0.4	0.4	0.4	0.4	0.4	0.5	0.5	0.5	0.5	0.5	0.6	0.6	0.6	0.6	0.6	0.7	0.7	0.8	0.8	0.8	0.8	0.8	0.8	0.9	0.9	0.9	0.9
9.5	0.5	0.5	0.5	0.6	0.6	0.6	0.7	0.7	0.7	0.8	0.8	0.8	0.8	0.9	0.9	0.9	0.9	1.0	1.0	1.0	1.0	1.1	1.1	1.1	1.1	1.1	1.2	1.2	1.2	1.2	1.2	1.2	1.3	1.3	1.3	1.3	1.4	1.4	1.4
9	1.0	1.0	1.0	1.1	1.1	1.1	1.2	1.2	1.2	1.2	1.3	1.3	1.3	1.3	1.4	1.4	1.4	1.4	1.5	1.5	1.5	1.5	1.5	1.6	1.6	1.6	1.6	1.6	1.6	1.6	1.6	1.6	1.6	1.7	1.7	1.7	1.7	1.7	1.7
8.5	1.5	1.5	1.5	1.5	1.6	1.6	1.6	1.6	1.7	1.7	1.7	1.7	1.8	1.8	1.8	1.8	1.8	1.9	1.9	1.9	1.9	1.9	1.9	2.0	2.0	2.0	2.0	2.0	2.0	2.0	2.0	2.0	2.0	2.0	2.0	2.1	2.1	2.1	2.1
8	2.0	2.0	2.0	2.0	2.1	2.1	2.1	2.1	2.1	2.2	2.2	2.2	2.2	2.2	2.2	2.3	2.3	2.3	2.3	2.3	2.3	2.3	2.4	2.4	2.4	2.4	2.4	2.4	2.4	2.4	2.4	2.4	2.4	2.4	2.4	2.4	2.4	2.4	2.4
7.5	2.5	2.5	2.5	2.5	2.5	2.5	2.6	2.6	2.6	2.6	2.6	2.6	2.6	2.6	2.6	2.7	2.7	2.7	2.7	2.7	2.7	2.7	2.7	2.7	2.7	2.7	2.7	2.7	2.7	2.7	2.7	2.7	2.7	2.8	2.8	2.8	2.8	2.8	2.8
7	3.0	3.0	3.0	3.0	3.0	3.0	3.0	3.0	3.0	3.0	3.0	3.0	3.0	3.0	3.0	3.0	3.0	3.0	3.0	3.0	3.0	3.0	3.0	3.0	3.1	3.1	3.1	3.1	3.1	3.1	3.1	3.1	3.1	3.1	3.1	3.1	3.1	3.1	3.1
6.5	3.5	3.5	3.5	3.5	3.5	3.5	3.5	3.5	3.5	3.5	3.5	3.5	3.5	3.5	3.5	3.5	3.5	3.5	3.5	3.5	3.5	3.5	3.5	3.5	3.5	3.5	3.5	3.5	3.5	3.5	3.5	3.5	3.5	3.5	3.5	3.5	3.5	3.5	3.5
6	4.0	4.0	4.0	4.0	4.0	4.0	4.0	4.0	4.0	4.0	4.0	4.0	4.0	4.0	4.0	4.0	4.0	4.0	4.0	4.0	4.0	4.0	4.0	4.0	4.0	4.0	4.0	4.0	4.0	4.0	4.0	4.0	4.0	4.0	4.0	4.0	4.0	4.0	4.0

LISTED PUT OPTION PRICE WHEN EXERCISE PRICE IS 15

Common Stock Price	NUMBER OF WEEKS BEFORE THE OPTION EXPIRES																																						
	1	2	3	4	5	6	7	8	9	10	11	12	13	14	15	16	17	18	19	20	21	22	23	24	25	26	27	28	29	30	31	32	33	34	35	36	37	38	39
21	0.0	0.0	0.0	0.0	0.0	0.0	0.0	0.0	0.0	0.0	0.0	0.0	0.0	0.0	0.0	0.0	0.0	0.0	0.0	0.0	0.0	0.0	0.0	0.0	0.0	0.0	0.0	0.0	0.0	0.0	0.0	0.0	0.0	0.0	0.0	0.0	0.0	0.0	0.0
20	0.0	0.0	0.0	0.0	0.0	0.0	0.0	0.0	0.0	0.0	0.0	0.0	0.0	0.0	0.0	0.0	0.0	0.0	0.0	0.0	0.0	0.0	0.0	0.0	0.0	0.0	0.0	0.0	0.0	0.0	0.0	0.0	0.0	0.0	0.1	0.1	0.1	0.1	0.1
19	0.0	0.0	0.0	0.0	0.0	0.0	0.0	0.0	0.0	0.0	0.0	0.0	0.0	0.0	0.0	0.0	0.0	0.0	0.0	0.0	0.0	0.0	0.0	0.0	0.1	0.1	0.1	0.1	0.1	0.2	0.2	0.2	0.2	0.2	0.3	0.3	0.3	0.3	0.3
18	0.0	0.0	0.0	0.0	0.0	0.0	0.0	0.0	0.0	0.0	0.0	0.0	0.0	0.0	0.0	0.1	0.1	0.1	0.1	0.2	0.2	0.2	0.2	0.2	0.3	0.3	0.3	0.3	0.3	0.4	0.4	0.4	0.4	0.4	0.5	0.5	0.5	0.5	0.5
17	0.0	0.0	0.0	0.0	0.0	0.0	0.0	0.0	0.1	0.1	0.1	0.2	0.2	0.2	0.3	0.3	0.3	0.3	0.4	0.4	0.4	0.4	0.4	0.5	0.5	0.5	0.5	0.6	0.6	0.6	0.6	0.6	0.7	0.7	0.7	0.7	0.7	0.8	0.8
16	0.0	0.0	0.1	0.1	0.2	0.2	0.3	0.3	0.3	0.4	0.4	0.4	0.5	0.5	0.5	0.6	0.6	0.6	0.6	0.7	0.7	0.7	0.7	0.7	0.7	0.8	0.8	0.8	0.8	0.9	0.9	0.9	0.9	0.9	1.0	1.0	1.0	1.0	1.0
15	0.2	0.3	0.4	0.4	0.5	0.5	0.6	0.6	0.6	0.7	0.7	0.7	0.8	0.8	0.8	0.9	0.9	0.9	0.9	0.9	1.0	1.0	1.0	1.0	1.0	1.1	1.1	1.1	1.1	1.2	1.2	1.2	1.2	1.2	1.3	1.3	1.3	1.3	1.3
14.5	0.5	0.6	0.6	0.6	0.7	0.7	0.8	0.8	0.8	0.9	0.9	0.9	1.0	1.0	1.0	1.1	1.1	1.2	1.2	1.2	1.3	1.3	1.3	1.3	1.4	1.5	1.5	1.5	1.6	1.6	1.6	1.6	1.7	1.7	1.8	1.8	1.9	1.9	1.9
14	1.0	1.1	1.1	1.1	1.2	1.2	1.2	1.3	1.3	1.3	1.4	1.4	1.4	1.5	1.5	1.5	1.6	1.6	1.6	1.7	1.7	1.7	1.7	1.8	1.8	1.9	1.9	1.9	1.9	2.0	2.0	2.0	2.1	2.1	2.1	2.2	2.2	2.2	2.3
13.5	1.5	1.6	1.6	1.6	1.6	1.7	1.7	1.7	1.7	1.8	1.8	1.8	1.9	1.9	1.9	1.9	2.0	2.0	2.0	2.0	2.1	2.1	2.1	2.2	2.2	2.2	2.3	2.3	2.3	2.3	2.4	2.4	2.4	2.5	2.5	2.5	2.6	2.6	2.6
13	2.0	2.0	2.1	2.1	2.1	2.1	2.2	2.2	2.2	2.2	2.3	2.3	2.3	2.3	2.4	2.4	2.4	2.4	2.5	2.5	2.5	2.5	2.5	2.6	2.6	2.6	2.7	2.7	2.7	2.7	2.8	2.8	2.8	2.8	2.9	2.9	2.9	2.9	3.0
12.5	2.5	2.5	2.6	2.6	2.6	2.6	2.6	2.7	2.7	2.7	2.7	2.8	2.8	2.8	2.8	2.8	2.8	2.9	2.9	2.9	2.9	3.0	3.0	3.0	3.0	3.0	3.0	3.1	3.1	3.1	3.2	3.2	3.2	3.2	3.2	3.3	3.3	3.3	3.3
12	3.0	3.0	3.0	3.1	3.1	3.1	3.1	3.1	3.2	3.2	3.2	3.2	3.2	3.2	3.3	3.3	3.3	3.3	3.3	3.3	3.4	3.4	3.4	3.4	3.4	3.4	3.5	3.5	3.5	3.5	3.5	3.5	3.5	3.6	3.6	3.6	3.6	3.6	3.7
11.5	3.5	3.5	3.5	3.6	3.6	3.6	3.6	3.6	3.6	3.6	3.6	3.7	3.7	3.7	3.7	3.7	3.7	3.7	3.8	3.8	3.8	3.8	3.8	3.8	3.8	3.8	3.8	3.9	3.9	3.9	3.9	3.9	3.9	3.9	4.0	4.0	4.0	4.0	4.0
11	4.0	4.0	4.0	4.0	4.0	4.1	4.1	4.1	4.1	4.1	4.1	4.1	4.1	4.1	4.1	4.1	4.1	4.2	4.2	4.2	4.2	4.2	4.2	4.2	4.2	4.2	4.2	4.3	4.3	4.3	4.3	4.3	4.3	4.3	4.3	4.3	4.3	4.4	4.4
10.5	4.5	4.5	4.5	4.5	4.5	4.5	4.5	4.5	4.5	4.6	4.6	4.6	4.6	4.6	4.6	4.6	4.6	4.6	4.6	4.6	4.6	4.6	4.6	4.6	4.6	4.6	4.6	4.6	4.7	4.7	4.7	4.7	4.7	4.7	4.7	4.7	4.7	4.7	4.7
10	5.0	5.0	5.0	5.0	5.0	5.0	5.0	5.0	5.0	5.0	5.0	5.0	5.0	5.0	5.0	5.0	5.0	5.0	5.0	5.0	5.0	5.0	5.0	5.0	5.0	5.0	5.0	5.0	5.0	5.0	5.0	5.0	5.0	5.0	5.0	5.0	5.1	5.1	5.1
9.5	5.5	5.5	5.5	5.5	5.5	5.5	5.5	5.5	5.5	5.5	5.5	5.5	5.5	5.5	5.5	5.5	5.5	5.5	5.5	5.5	5.5	5.5	5.5	5.5	5.5	5.5	5.5	5.5	5.5	5.5	5.5	5.5	5.5	5.5	5.5	5.5	5.5	5.5	5.5
9	6.0	6.0	6.0	6.0	6.0	6.0	6.0	6.0	6.0	6.0	6.0	6.0	6.0	6.0	6.0	6.0	6.0	6.0	6.0	6.0	6.0	6.0	6.0	6.0	6.0	6.0	6.0	6.0	6.0	6.0	6.0	6.0	6.0	6.0	6.0	6.0	6.0	6.0	6.0

LISTED PUT OPTION PRICE WHEN EXERCISE PRICE IS 20

NUMBER OF WEEKS BEFORE THE OPTION EXPIRES

Common Stock Price	1	2	3	4	5	6	7	8	9	10	11	12	13	14	15	16	17	18	19	20	21	22	23	24	25	26	27	28	29	30	31	32	33	34	35	36	37	38	39
28	0.0	0.0	0.0	0.0	0.0	0.0	0.0	0.0	0.0	0.0	0.0	0.0	0.0	0.0	0.0	0.0	0.0	0.0	0.0	0.0	0.0	0.0	0.0	0.0	0.0	0.0	0.0	0.0	0.0	0.0	0.0	0.0	0.0	0.0	0.0	0.0	0.0	0.0	0.0
27	0.0	0.0	0.0	0.0	0.0	0.0	0.0	0.0	0.0	0.0	0.1	0.1	0.1	0.1	0.1	0.1	0.1	0.1	0.1	0.1	0.1	0.1	0.1	0.1	0.1	0.1	0.1	0.1	0.1	0.1	0.1	0.1	0.1	0.1	0.1	0.1	0.1	0.1	0.1
26	0.0	0.0	0.1	0.1	0.1	0.1	0.1	0.1	0.1	0.1	0.2	0.2	0.2	0.2	0.2	0.2	0.2	0.2	0.2	0.2	0.2	0.2	0.2	0.2	0.2	0.2	0.2	0.3	0.3	0.3	0.3	0.3	0.3	0.3	0.3	0.3	0.3	0.3	0.3
25	0.0	0.1	0.1	0.1	0.2	0.2	0.2	0.2	0.2	0.2	0.3	0.3	0.3	0.3	0.3	0.3	0.3	0.3	0.3	0.4	0.4	0.4	0.4	0.4	0.4	0.4	0.4	0.4	0.4	0.4	0.4	0.5	0.5	0.5	0.5	0.5	0.5	0.5	0.5
24	0.0	0.1	0.2	0.2	0.2	0.3	0.3	0.3	0.3	0.3	0.4	0.4	0.4	0.4	0.4	0.4	0.5	0.5	0.5	0.5	0.5	0.5	0.5	0.5	0.6	0.6	0.6	0.6	0.6	0.6	0.6	0.6	0.6	0.7	0.7	0.7	0.7	0.7	0.7
23	0.0	0.1	0.2	0.3	0.3	0.3	0.4	0.4	0.4	0.4	0.5	0.5	0.5	0.5	0.5	0.6	0.6	0.6	0.6	0.6	0.7	0.7	0.7	0.7	0.7	0.7	0.7	0.8	0.8	0.8	0.8	0.8	0.8	0.8	0.9	0.9	0.9	0.9	0.9
22	0.0	0.2	0.3	0.3	0.4	0.4	0.5	0.5	0.6	0.6	0.6	0.6	0.7	0.7	0.7	0.8	0.8	0.8	0.8	0.8	0.9	0.9	0.9	0.9	1.0	1.0	1.0	1.0	1.0	1.1	1.1	1.1	1.1	1.1	1.1	1.2	1.2	1.2	1.2
21	0.0	0.2	0.3	0.4	0.5	0.5	0.6	0.6	0.7	0.7	0.8	0.8	0.8	0.9	0.9	0.9	1.0	1.0	1.0	1.1	1.1	1.1	1.1	1.2	1.2	1.2	1.2	1.3	1.3	1.3	1.3	1.4	1.4	1.4	1.4	1.4	1.5	1.5	1.5
20	0.0	0.3	0.4	0.5	0.6	0.7	0.7	0.8	0.8	0.9	0.9	1.0	1.0	1.1	1.1	1.1	1.2	1.2	1.2	1.3	1.3	1.3	1.4	1.4	1.4	1.5	1.5	1.5	1.5	1.6	1.6	1.6	1.7	1.7	1.7	1.7	1.8	1.8	1.8
19	1.0	1.3	1.4	1.5	1.6	1.7	1.7	1.8	1.8	1.9	1.9	2.0	2.0	2.1	2.1	2.1	2.2	2.2	2.2	2.3	2.3	2.3	2.4	2.4	2.4	2.5	2.5	2.5	2.5	2.6	2.6	2.6	2.7	2.7	2.7	2.7	2.8	2.8	2.8
18	2.0	2.2	2.3	2.4	2.5	2.5	2.6	2.6	2.7	2.7	2.8	2.8	2.8	2.9	2.9	2.9	3.0	3.0	3.0	3.1	3.1	3.1	3.1	3.2	3.2	3.2	3.2	3.3	3.3	3.3	3.3	3.4	3.4	3.4	3.4	3.4	3.5	3.5	3.5
17	3.0	3.2	3.3	3.3	3.4	3.4	3.5	3.5	3.6	3.6	3.6	3.6	3.7	3.7	3.7	3.8	3.8	3.8	3.8	3.8	3.9	3.9	3.9	3.9	4.0	4.0	4.0	4.0	4.0	4.1	4.1	4.1	4.1	4.1	4.1	4.2	4.2	4.2	4.2
16	4.0	4.1	4.2	4.3	4.3	4.3	4.4	4.4	4.4	4.4	4.5	4.5	4.5	4.5	4.5	4.6	4.6	4.6	4.6	4.6	4.7	4.7	4.7	4.7	4.7	4.7	4.7	4.8	4.8	4.8	4.8	4.8	4.8	4.8	4.9	4.9	4.9	4.9	4.9
15	5.0	5.1	5.1	5.2	5.2	5.2	5.2	5.3	5.3	5.3	5.3	5.3	5.3	5.4	5.4	5.4	5.4	5.4	5.4	5.4	5.4	5.4	5.5	5.5	5.5	5.5	5.5	5.5	5.5	5.5	5.5	5.5	5.6	5.6	5.6	5.6	5.6	5.6	5.6
14.5	5.5	5.6	5.6	5.6	5.6	5.6	5.7	5.7	5.7	5.7	5.7	5.7	5.7	5.7	5.7	5.8	5.8	5.8	5.8	5.8	5.8	5.8	5.8	5.8	5.8	5.8	5.8	5.8	5.8	5.9	5.9	5.9	5.9	5.9	5.9	5.9	5.9	5.9	5.9
14	6.0	6.0	6.1	6.1	6.1	6.1	6.1	6.1	6.1	6.1	6.2	6.2	6.2	6.2	6.2	6.2	6.2	6.2	6.2	6.2	6.2	6.2	6.2	6.2	6.2	6.2	6.2	6.3	6.3	6.3	6.3	6.3	6.3	6.3	6.3	6.3	6.3	6.3	6.3
13.5	6.5	6.5	6.5	6.5	6.5	6.5	6.5	6.5	6.5	6.5	6.6	6.6	6.6	6.6	6.6	6.6	6.6	6.6	6.6	6.6	6.6	6.6	6.6	6.6	6.6	6.6	6.6	6.6	6.6	6.6	6.6	6.6	6.6	6.6	6.6	6.6	6.6	6.6	6.6
13	7.0	7.0	7.0	7.0	7.0	7.0	7.0	7.0	7.0	7.0	7.0	7.0	7.0	7.0	7.0	7.0	7.0	7.0	7.0	7.0	7.0	7.0	7.0	7.0	7.0	7.0	7.0	7.0	7.0	7.0	7.0	7.0	7.0	7.0	7.0	7.0	7.0	7.0	7.0
12.5	7.5	7.5	7.5	7.5	7.5	7.5	7.5	7.5	7.5	7.5	7.5	7.5	7.5	7.5	7.5	7.5	7.5	7.5	7.5	7.5	7.5	7.5	7.5	7.5	7.5	7.5	7.5	7.5	7.5	7.5	7.5	7.5	7.5	7.5	7.5	7.5	7.5	7.5	7.5
12	8.0	8.0	8.0	8.0	8.0	8.0	8.0	8.0	8.0	8.0	8.0	8.0	8.0	8.0	8.0	8.0	8.0	8.0	8.0	8.0	8.0	8.0	8.0	8.0	8.0	8.0	8.0	8.0	8.0	8.0	8.0	8.0	8.0	8.0	8.0	8.0	8.0	8.0	8.0

LISTED PUT OPTION PRICE WHEN EXERCISE PRICE IS 25

NUMBER OF WEEKS BEFORE THE OPTION EXPIRES

Common Stock Price	1	2	3	4	5	6	7	8	9	10	11	12	13	14	15	16	17	18	19	20	21	22	23	24	25	26	27	28	29	30	31	32	33	34	35	36	37	38	39
35	0.0	0.0	0.0	0.0	0.0	0.0	0.0	0.0	0.0	0.0	0.0	0.0	0.0	0.0	0.0	0.0	0.0	0.0	0.0	0.0	0.0	0.0	0.0	0.0	0.0	0.0	0.0	0.0	0.0	0.0	0.0	0.0	0.0	0.0	0.0	0.0	0.0	0.0	0.0
34	0.0	0.0	0.0	0.0	0.0	0.0	0.0	0.0	0.0	0.0	0.0	0.0	0.0	0.0	0.0	0.0	0.0	0.0	0.0	0.0	0.0	0.0	0.0	0.0	0.0	0.0	0.0	0.0	0.0	0.0	0.0	0.0	0.0	0.0	0.0	0.0	0.0	0.1	0.1
33	0.0	0.0	0.0	0.0	0.0	0.0	0.0	0.0	0.0	0.0	0.0	0.0	0.0	0.0	0.0	0.0	0.0	0.0	0.0	0.0	0.0	0.0	0.0	0.0	0.0	0.1	0.1	0.1	0.1	0.1	0.1	0.1	0.1	0.1	0.2	0.2	0.2	0.3	0.3
32	0.0	0.0	0.0	0.0	0.0	0.0	0.0	0.0	0.0	0.0	0.0	0.0	0.0	0.0	0.0	0.0	0.0	0.0	0.0	0.0	0.0	0.0	0.0	0.0	0.0	0.1	0.1	0.1	0.2	0.2	0.2	0.3	0.3	0.3	0.4	0.4	0.4	0.4	0.5
31	0.0	0.0	0.0	0.0	0.0	0.0	0.0	0.0	0.0	0.0	0.0	0.0	0.0	0.0	0.0	0.0	0.0	0.0	0.0	0.0	0.1	0.1	0.2	0.2	0.2	0.3	0.3	0.3	0.4	0.4	0.4	0.5	0.5	0.5	0.6	0.6	0.6	0.6	0.7
30	0.0	0.0	0.0	0.0	0.0	0.0	0.0	0.0	0.0	0.0	0.0	0.0	0.0	0.0	0.1	0.1	0.1	0.2	0.2	0.3	0.3	0.3	0.4	0.4	0.4	0.5	0.5	0.5	0.6	0.6	0.6	0.7	0.7	0.7	0.8	0.8	0.8	0.9	0.9
29	0.0	0.0	0.0	0.0	0.0	0.0	0.0	0.0	0.0	0.0	0.1	0.1	0.2	0.2	0.3	0.3	0.4	0.4	0.4	0.5	0.5	0.6	0.6	0.6	0.7	0.7	0.7	0.8	0.8	0.8	0.9	0.9	0.9	1.0	1.0	1.0	1.1	1.1	1.1
28	0.0	0.0	0.0	0.0	0.0	0.0	0.1	0.1	0.2	0.3	0.3	0.4	0.4	0.5	0.5	0.6	0.6	0.7	0.7	0.8	0.8	0.8	0.9	0.9	0.9	1.0	1.0	1.0	1.1	1.1	1.1	1.1	1.2	1.2	1.2	1.3	1.3	1.3	1.4
27	0.0	0.0	0.0	0.1	0.2	0.3	0.3	0.4	0.5	0.5	0.6	0.6	0.7	0.7	0.8	0.8	0.9	0.9	1.0	1.0	1.0	1.1	1.1	1.2	1.2	1.2	1.3	1.3	1.3	1.4	1.4	1.4	1.5	1.5	1.5	1.5	1.6	1.6	1.6
26	0.0	0.0	0.0	0.1	0.2	0.3	0.4	0.5	0.6	0.7	0.8	0.9	1.0	1.0	1.1	1.1	1.2	1.2	1.3	1.3	1.4	1.4	1.4	1.5	1.5	1.5	1.6	1.6	1.6	1.7	1.7	1.7	1.8	1.8	1.8	1.8	1.9	1.9	1.9
25	0.4	0.5	0.6	0.7	0.8	0.9	0.9	1.0	1.1	1.1	1.2	1.3	1.3	1.4	1.4	1.4	1.5	1.5	1.6	1.6	1.6	1.7	1.7	1.7	1.8	1.8	1.8	1.9	1.9	1.9	2.0	2.0	2.0	2.1	2.1	2.1	2.2	2.2	2.2
24	1.1	1.1	1.2	1.2	1.3	1.4	1.4	1.5	1.5	1.6	1.7	1.7	1.8	1.8	1.9	2.0	2.0	2.1	2.1	2.2	2.3	2.3	2.4	2.4	2.5	2.6	2.6	2.7	2.7	2.8	2.9	2.9	3.0	3.0	3.2	3.2	3.3	3.4	3.4
23	2.1	2.1	2.2	2.2	2.3	2.3	2.4	2.4	2.5	2.5	2.6	2.6	2.7	2.7	2.8	2.8	2.9	2.9	3.0	3.0	3.1	3.1	3.2	3.2	3.3	3.4	3.4	3.5	3.5	3.6	3.6	3.7	3.7	3.8	3.8	3.9	3.9	4.0	4.0
22	3.0	3.1	3.1	3.1	3.2	3.3	3.3	3.4	3.4	3.4	3.5	3.5	3.6	3.6	3.7	3.7	3.8	3.8	3.8	3.9	3.9	4.0	4.0	4.1	4.1	4.1	4.2	4.2	4.3	4.3	4.4	4.4	4.5	4.5	4.5	4.6	4.6	4.7	4.7
21	4.0	4.1	4.1	4.1	4.2	4.3	4.3	4.3	4.4	4.4	4.4	4.5	4.5	4.5	4.6	4.6	4.6	4.7	4.7	4.7	4.8	4.8	4.8	4.9	4.9	4.9	5.0	5.0	5.0	5.1	5.1	5.2	5.2	5.2	5.3	5.3	5.3	5.4	5.4
20	5.0	5.1	5.1	5.1	5.1	5.2	5.2	5.2	5.3	5.3	5.3	5.3	5.4	5.4	5.4	5.5	5.5	5.5	5.5	5.6	5.6	5.6	5.7	5.7	5.7	5.7	5.8	5.8	5.8	5.9	5.9	5.9	5.9	6.0	6.0	6.0	6.1	6.1	6.1
19	6.0	6.0	6.1	6.1	6.1	6.1	6.1	6.2	6.2	6.2	6.2	6.2	6.3	6.3	6.3	6.3	6.4	6.4	6.4	6.4	6.4	6.5	6.5	6.5	6.5	6.5	6.6	6.6	6.6	6.6	6.6	6.7	6.7	6.7	6.7	6.7	6.8	6.8	6.8
18	7.0	7.0	7.0	7.0	7.1	7.1	7.1	7.1	7.1	7.1	7.1	7.2	7.2	7.2	7.2	7.2	7.2	7.2	7.3	7.3	7.3	7.3	7.3	7.3	7.3	7.3	7.3	7.4	7.4	7.4	7.4	7.4	7.4	7.4	7.4	7.5	7.5	7.5	7.5
17	8.0	8.0	8.0	8.0	8.0	8.0	8.0	8.0	8.0	8.0	8.1	8.1	8.1	8.1	8.1	8.1	8.1	8.1	8.1	8.1	8.1	8.1	8.1	8.1	8.1	8.1	8.1	8.1	8.1	8.1	8.2	8.2	8.2	8.2	8.2	8.2	8.2	8.2	8.2
16	9.0	9.0	9.0	9.0	9.0	9.0	9.0	9.0	9.0	9.0	9.0	9.0	9.0	9.0	9.0	9.0	9.0	9.0	9.0	9.0	9.0	9.0	9.0	9.0	9.0	9.0	9.0	9.0	9.0	9.0	9.0	9.0	9.0	9.0	9.0	9.0	9.0	9.0	9.0
15	10.0	10.0	10.0	10.0	10.0	10.0	10.0	10.0	10.0	10.0	10.0	10.0	10.0	10.0	10.0	10.0	10.0	10.0	10.0	10.0	10.0	10.0	10.0	10.0	10.0	10.0	10.0	10.0	10.0	10.0	10.0	10.0	10.0	10.0	10.0	10.0	10.0	10.0	10.0

LISTED PUT OPTION PRICE WHEN EXERCISE PRICE IS 30

NUMBER OF WEEKS BEFORE THE OPTION EXPIRES

Common Stock Price	1	2	3	4	5	6	7	8	9	10	11	12	13	14	15	16	17	18	19	20	21	22	23	24	25	26	27	28	29	30	31	32	33	34	35	36	37	38	39
42	0.0	0.0	0.0	0.0	0.0	0.0	0.0	0.0	0.0	0.0	0.0	0.0	0.0	0.0	0.0	0.0	0.0	0.0	0.0	0.0	0.0	0.0	0.0	0.0	0.0	0.0	0.0	0.0	0.0	0.0	0.0	0.0	0.0	0.0	0.0	0.0	0.0	0.0	0.0
41	0.0	0.0	0.0	0.0	0.0	0.0	0.0	0.0	0.0	0.0	0.0	0.0	0.0	0.0	0.0	0.0	0.0	0.0	0.0	0.0	0.0	0.0	0.0	0.0	0.0	0.0	0.0	0.0	0.0	0.0	0.1	0.1	0.1	0.1	0.1	0.1	0.1	0.1	0.1
40	0.0	0.0	0.0	0.0	0.0	0.1	0.1	0.1	0.1	0.1	0.1	0.1	0.1	0.1	0.1	0.1	0.2	0.2	0.2	0.2	0.2	0.2	0.2	0.2	0.2	0.2	0.2	0.2	0.2	0.2	0.3	0.3	0.3	0.3	0.3	0.3	0.3	0.3	0.3
39	0.0	0.0	0.0	0.1	0.1	0.1	0.1	0.1	0.1	0.2	0.2	0.2	0.2	0.2	0.2	0.2	0.3	0.3	0.3	0.3	0.3	0.3	0.3	0.3	0.4	0.4	0.4	0.4	0.4	0.4	0.4	0.4	0.4	0.4	0.5	0.5	0.5	0.5	0.5
38	0.0	0.0	0.0	0.1	0.1	0.1	0.1	0.2	0.2	0.2	0.2	0.2	0.2	0.3	0.3	0.3	0.3	0.3	0.3	0.4	0.4	0.4	0.4	0.4	0.4	0.4	0.4	0.5	0.5	0.5	0.5	0.5	0.5	0.5	0.6	0.6	0.6	0.6	0.6
37	0.0	0.0	0.1	0.1	0.1	0.2	0.2	0.2	0.3	0.3	0.3	0.3	0.4	0.4	0.4	0.4	0.5	0.5	0.5	0.5	0.5	0.6	0.6	0.6	0.6	0.7	0.7	0.7	0.7	0.7	0.8	0.8	0.8	0.8	0.8	0.8	0.9	0.9	0.9
36	0.0	0.0	0.1	0.1	0.2	0.2	0.2	0.3	0.3	0.3	0.4	0.4	0.4	0.5	0.5	0.5	0.6	0.6	0.6	0.6	0.7	0.7	0.7	0.7	0.8	0.8	0.8	0.8	0.9	0.9	0.9	0.9	1.0	1.0	1.0	1.0	1.1	1.1	1.1
35	0.0	0.0	0.1	0.2	0.2	0.2	0.3	0.3	0.4	0.4	0.5	0.5	0.5	0.6	0.6	0.6	0.7	0.7	0.7	0.8	0.8	0.8	0.9	0.9	0.9	0.9	1.0	1.0	1.0	1.1	1.1	1.1	1.1	1.2	1.2	1.2	1.2	1.3	1.3
34	0.0	0.1	0.1	0.2	0.2	0.3	0.3	0.4	0.4	0.5	0.5	0.6	0.6	0.6	0.7	0.7	0.8	0.8	0.8	0.9	0.9	1.0	1.0	1.0	1.1	1.1	1.1	1.2	1.2	1.2	1.3	1.3	1.3	1.3	1.4	1.4	1.4	1.5	1.5
33	0.0	0.1	0.1	0.2	0.3	0.3	0.4	0.5	0.5	0.6	0.6	0.7	0.7	0.8	0.8	0.9	0.9	1.0	1.0	1.1	1.1	1.1	1.2	1.2	1.3	1.3	1.3	1.4	1.4	1.5	1.5	1.5	1.6	1.6	1.7	1.7	1.7	1.8	1.8
32	0.0	0.1	0.2	0.2	0.3	0.4	0.5	0.5	0.6	0.7	0.7	0.8	0.8	0.9	1.0	1.0	1.1	1.1	1.2	1.2	1.3	1.3	1.4	1.4	1.5	1.5	1.6	1.6	1.7	1.7	1.8	1.8	1.8	1.9	1.9	2.0	2.0	2.1	2.1
31	0.1	0.3	0.4	0.5	0.6	0.7	0.8	0.9	1.0	1.0	1.1	1.2	1.2	1.3	1.4	1.4	1.5	1.5	1.6	1.6	1.7	1.7	1.8	1.8	1.9	1.9	1.9	2.0	2.0	2.1	2.1	2.1	2.2	2.2	2.3	2.3	2.3	2.4	2.4
30	0.4	0.6	0.7	0.8	0.9	1.0	1.1	1.2	1.3	1.3	1.4	1.5	1.5	1.6	1.7	1.7	1.8	1.8	1.9	1.9	2.0	2.0	2.1	2.1	2.2	2.2	2.2	2.3	2.3	2.4	2.4	2.4	2.5	2.5	2.6	2.6	2.6	2.7	2.7
29	1.1	1.3	1.4	1.6	1.7	1.8	1.9	2.0	2.1	2.1	2.2	2.3	2.3	2.4	2.5	2.5	2.6	2.6	2.7	2.8	2.8	2.9	2.9	3.0	3.0	3.1	3.1	3.2	3.2	3.2	3.3	3.3	3.4	3.4	3.4	3.5	3.5	3.6	3.6
28	2.1	2.3	2.4	2.6	2.7	2.8	2.9	2.9	3.0	3.1	3.2	3.2	3.3	3.4	3.4	3.5	3.5	3.6	3.6	3.7	3.7	3.8	3.8	3.9	3.9	4.0	4.0	4.1	4.1	4.1	4.2	4.2	4.3	4.3	4.4	4.4	4.4	4.5	4.5
27	3.1	3.3	3.4	3.5	3.6	3.7	3.8	3.8	3.9	4.0	4.0	4.1	4.1	4.2	4.3	4.3	4.4	4.4	4.4	4.5	4.5	4.6	4.6	4.7	4.7	4.7	4.8	4.8	4.9	4.9	4.9	5.0	5.0	5.0	5.1	5.1	5.1	5.2	5.2
26	4.0	4.2	4.3	4.4	4.4	4.5	4.6	4.7	4.7	4.8	4.8	4.9	4.9	5.0	5.0	5.1	5.1	5.2	5.2	5.3	5.3	5.3	5.4	5.4	5.4	5.5	5.5	5.6	5.6	5.6	5.7	5.7	5.7	5.8	5.8	5.8	5.8	5.9	5.9
25	5.0	5.1	5.2	5.3	5.4	5.4	5.5	5.6	5.6	5.7	5.7	5.8	5.8	5.8	5.9	5.9	6.0	6.0	6.0	6.1	6.1	6.1	6.2	6.2	6.2	6.3	6.3	6.3	6.3	6.4	6.4	6.4	6.4	6.5	6.5	6.5	6.6	6.6	6.6
24	6.0	6.1	6.2	6.2	6.3	6.4	6.4	6.5	6.5	6.5	6.6	6.6	6.6	6.7	6.7	6.7	6.8	6.8	6.8	6.9	6.9	6.9	6.9	7.0	7.0	7.0	7.0	7.1	7.1	7.1	7.1	7.2	7.2	7.2	7.2	7.2	7.3	7.3	7.3
23	7.0	7.1	7.1	7.2	7.2	7.3	7.3	7.3	7.4	7.4	7.4	7.5	7.5	7.5	7.5	7.6	7.6	7.6	7.6	7.7	7.7	7.7	7.7	7.7	7.8	7.8	7.8	7.8	7.8	7.9	7.9	7.9	7.9	7.9	7.9	8.0	8.0	8.0	8.0
22	8.0	8.1	8.1	8.1	8.2	8.2	8.2	8.2	8.3	8.3	8.3	8.3	8.3	8.4	8.4	8.4	8.4	8.4	8.4	8.5	8.5	8.5	8.5	8.5	8.5	8.5	8.6	8.6	8.6	8.6	8.6	8.6	8.6	8.6	8.7	8.7	8.7	8.7	8.7
21	9.0	9.0	9.1	9.1	9.1	9.1	9.1	9.1	9.2	9.2	9.2	9.2	9.2	9.2	9.2	9.2	9.2	9.2	9.3	9.3	9.3	9.3	9.3	9.3	9.3	9.3	9.3	9.3	9.3	9.3	9.3	9.4	9.4	9.4	9.4	9.4	9.4	9.4	9.4
20	10.0	10.0	10.0	10.0	10.0	10.0	10.0	10.0	10.0	10.0	10.0	10.0	10.0	10.1	10.1	10.1	10.1	10.1	10.1	10.1	10.1	10.1	10.1	10.1	10.1	10.1	10.1	10.1	10.1	10.1	10.1	10.1	10.1	10.1	10.1	10.1	10.1	10.1	10.1
19	11.0	11.0	11.0	11.0	11.0	11.0	11.0	11.0	11.0	11.0	11.0	11.0	11.0	11.0	11.0	11.0	11.0	11.0	11.0	11.0	11.0	11.0	11.0	11.0	11.0	11.0	11.0	11.0	11.0	11.0	11.0	11.0	11.0	11.0	11.0	11.0	11.0	11.0	11.0
18	12.0	12.0	12.0	12.0	12.0	12.0	12.0	12.0	12.0	12.0	12.0	12.0	12.0	12.0	12.0	12.0	12.0	12.0	12.0	12.0	12.0	12.0	12.0	12.0	12.0	12.0	12.0	12.0	12.0	12.0	12.0	12.0	12.0	12.0	12.0	12.0	12.0	12.0	12.0

NUMBER OF WEEKS BEFORE THE OPTION EXPIRES

Common Stock Price	1	2	3	4	5	6	7	8	9	10	11	12	13	14	15	16	17	18	19	20	21	22	23	24	25	26	27	28	29	30	31	32	33	34	35	36	37	38	39
49	0.0	0.0	0.0	0.0	0.0	0.0	0.0	0.0	0.0	0.0	0.0	0.0	0.0	0.0	0.0	0.0	0.0	0.0	0.0	0.0	0.0	0.0	0.0	0.0	0.0	0.0	0.0	0.0	0.0	0.0	0.0	0.0	0.0	0.0	0.0	0.0	0.0	0.0	0.0
48	0.0	0.0	0.0	0.0	0.0	0.0	0.0	0.0	0.0	0.0	0.0	0.0	0.0	0.0	0.0	0.0	0.0	0.0	0.0	0.0	0.0	0.0	0.0	0.0	0.0	0.0	0.0	0.0	0.0	0.0	0.0	0.0	0.0	0.0	0.0	0.0	0.0	0.0	0.1
47	0.0	0.0	0.0	0.0	0.0	0.0	0.0	0.0	0.0	0.0	0.0	0.0	0.0	0.0	0.0	0.0	0.0	0.0	0.0	0.0	0.0	0.0	0.0	0.0	0.0	0.1	0.1	0.1	0.1	0.1	0.1	0.1	0.2	0.2	0.2	0.2	0.2	0.2	0.3
46	0.0	0.0	0.0	0.0	0.0	0.0	0.0	0.0	0.0	0.0	0.0	0.0	0.0	0.1	0.1	0.1	0.1	0.2	0.2	0.2	0.2	0.3	0.3	0.3	0.3	0.3	0.3	0.3	0.4	0.4	0.4	0.4	0.4	0.4	0.4	0.4	0.4	0.4	0.4
45	0.0	0.0	0.0	0.0	0.0	0.0	0.0	0.0	0.0	0.0	0.0	0.1	0.1	0.1	0.2	0.2	0.2	0.3	0.3	0.3	0.4	0.4	0.4	0.4	0.5	0.5	0.5	0.5	0.5	0.6	0.6	0.6	0.6	0.6	0.6	0.6	0.7	0.6	0.6
44	0.0	0.0	0.0	0.0	0.0	0.0	0.0	0.0	0.0	0.2	0.2	0.2	0.3	0.3	0.4	0.4	0.4	0.5	0.5	0.5	0.6	0.6	0.6	0.6	0.6	0.7	0.7	0.7	0.7	0.8	0.8	0.8	0.8	0.8	0.8	0.8	0.8	0.8	0.8
43	0.0	0.0	0.0	0.0	0.0	0.0	0.0	0.0	0.0	0.2	0.3	0.3	0.4	0.5	0.5	0.6	0.6	0.7	0.7	0.7	0.8	0.8	0.8	0.8	0.9	0.9	0.9	1.0	1.0	1.1	1.1	1.1	1.2	1.0	1.1	1.1	1.1	1.0	1.0
42	0.0	0.0	0.0	0.0	0.0	0.0	0.0	0.0	0.1	0.2	0.3	0.4	0.5	0.6	0.7	0.7	0.8	0.8	0.9	0.9	0.9	0.9	1.0	1.0	1.1	1.1	1.2	1.2	1.3	1.1	1.1	1.2	1.2	1.3	1.1	1.1	1.2	1.2	1.2
41	0.0	0.0	0.0	0.0	0.0	0.1	0.2	0.3	0.4	0.4	0.5	0.6	0.6	0.7	0.8	0.8	0.9	1.0	1.0	1.1	1.1	1.2	1.2	1.3	1.3	1.1	1.2	1.2	1.3	1.3	1.4	1.4	1.5	1.5	1.5	1.3	1.4	1.4	1.5
40	0.0	0.0	0.0	0.0	0.2	0.3	0.4	0.5	0.6	0.6	0.7	0.8	0.9	1.0	1.0	1.1	1.2	1.3	1.1	1.1	1.2	1.2	1.3	1.3	1.3	1.4	1.4	1.5	1.5	1.6	1.6	1.7	1.7	1.5	1.6	1.6	1.6	1.7	1.7
39	0.0	0.0	0.0	0.1	0.2	0.3	0.5	0.6	0.6	0.8	0.8	0.8	0.9	1.0	1.2	1.2	1.2	1.3	1.3	1.3	1.4	1.5	1.5	1.6	1.6	1.7	1.7	1.5	1.5	1.6	1.9	1.9	1.7	2.0	1.8	1.8	2.1	1.9	2.0
38	0.0	0.0	0.0	0.3	0.5	0.6	0.7	0.8	0.9	1.0	1.0	1.1	1.2	1.3	1.3	1.4	1.5	1.5	1.6	1.6	1.7	1.7	1.8	1.8	1.9	1.9	2.0	2.0	2.1	1.8	1.9	1.9	2.3	2.0	2.1	2.1	2.1	2.2	2.2
37	0.0	0.1	0.3	0.4	0.5	0.7	1.0	1.1	1.2	1.3	1.4	1.4	1.5	1.6	1.6	1.7	1.7	1.8	1.9	1.9	2.0	2.0	1.8	1.8	2.1	1.9	2.0	2.0	2.1	2.1	2.2	2.3	2.3	2.3	2.4	2.1	2.4	2.5	2.5
36	0.0	0.4	0.6	0.7	0.8	0.9	1.0	1.1	1.2	1.3	1.3	1.4	1.5	1.6	1.6	1.7	2.1	2.1	2.2	2.2	2.3	2.3	2.4	2.4	2.5	2.5	2.6	2.3	2.4	2.4	2.5	2.5	2.6	2.6	2.6	2.7	2.7	2.8	2.8
35	0.0	0.5	0.7	0.9	1.1	1.4	1.5	1.6	1.7	1.8	1.9	2.0	2.1	2.2	2.3	2.4	2.5	2.6	2.6	2.7	2.7	2.8	2.8	2.9	2.9	3.0	3.0	3.0	3.1	2.7	2.8	2.8	2.9	2.9	2.9	3.0	3.0	3.1	3.1
34	1.1	1.3	1.4	1.5	1.6	1.7	1.7	1.8	1.9	2.0	2.0	2.1	2.2	2.3	2.3	2.4	2.5	2.6	2.7	2.7	2.8	2.9	3.0	3.1	3.2	3.3	3.3	3.4	3.5	3.6	3.7	3.7	3.7	3.8	3.8	3.9	3.9	3.9	4.0
33	2.1	2.2	2.2	2.3	2.4	2.5	2.6	2.6	2.7	2.8	2.9	2.9	3.0	3.1	3.2	3.3	4.2	4.3	4.4	4.4	4.5	4.6	4.6	4.7	4.8	4.9	4.9	5.0	4.3	4.4	4.5	4.5	4.6	4.7	4.8	4.8	4.8	4.9	4.9
32	3.1	3.1	3.2	3.3	3.4	3.4	3.5	3.6	3.6	3.7	3.8	3.9	3.9	4.0	4.1	4.1	5.0	5.1	5.2	5.3	5.4	5.4	5.5	5.5	5.6	5.7	5.7	5.8	5.8	5.1	5.2	5.3	5.3	5.4	5.5	5.6	5.6	5.7	5.8
31	4.1	4.1	4.2	4.3	4.3	4.4	4.4	4.5	4.6	4.6	4.7	4.8	4.8	4.9	5.0	5.0	5.9	6.0	6.1	6.1	6.2	6.2	6.3	6.3	6.4	6.4	6.5	6.6	5.9	5.9	6.0	6.0	6.1	6.2	6.2	6.3	6.3	6.4	6.5
30	5.1	5.1	5.2	5.2	5.3	5.3	5.4	5.4	5.5	5.6	5.6	5.7	5.7	5.8	5.8	5.9	6.8	6.9	6.9	7.0	7.0	7.0	7.1	7.1	7.2	7.2	7.3	7.3	6.6	6.7	6.7	6.8	6.8	6.9	6.9	7.0	7.1	7.1	7.2
29	6.0	6.1	6.1	6.2	6.2	6.3	6.3	6.4	6.4	6.5	6.5	6.6	6.6	6.7	6.7	6.8	7.7	7.8	7.8	7.9	7.9	8.0	8.0	8.0	8.1	8.1	8.2	8.2	7.4	7.4	7.5	7.5	7.6	7.6	7.7	7.7	7.8	7.8	7.9
28	7.0	7.1	7.1	7.2	7.2	7.2	7.3	7.3	7.3	7.4	7.5	7.5	7.5	7.6	7.6	7.6	8.5	8.6	8.6	8.6	8.7	8.7	8.7	8.8	8.8	8.8	8.9	8.9	8.2	8.2	8.3	8.3	8.3	8.4	8.4	8.5	8.5	8.5	8.6
27	8.0	8.1	8.1	8.1	8.2	8.2	8.2	8.2	8.3	8.3	8.4	8.4	8.4	8.4	8.5	8.5	9.4	9.4	9.5	9.5	9.5	9.5	9.6	9.6	9.6	9.6	9.7	9.7	8.9	9.0	9.0	9.0	9.1	9.1	9.1	9.2	9.2	9.2	9.2
26	9.0	9.0	9.1	9.1	9.1	9.1	9.2	9.2	9.2	9.2	9.3	9.3	9.3	9.3	9.4	9.4	10.3	10.3	10.3	10.3	10.3	10.4	10.4	10.4	10.4	10.4	10.4	10.5	9.7	9.7	9.7	9.8	9.8	9.8	9.9	9.9	9.9	9.9	9.9
25	10.0	10.0	10.0	10.1	10.1	10.1	10.1	10.1	10.1	10.2	10.2	10.2	10.2	10.2	10.2	10.3	11.2	11.2	11.2	11.2	11.2	11.2	11.2	11.2	11.2	11.2	11.2	11.2	10.5	10.5	10.5	10.5	10.5	10.5	10.6	10.6	10.6	10.6	10.6
24	11.0	11.0	11.0	11.0	11.0	11.1	11.1	11.1	11.1	11.1	11.1	11.1	11.1	11.1	11.1	11.1	11.1	11.1	11.2	11.2	11.2	11.2	11.2	11.2	11.2	11.2	11.2	11.2	11.2	11.3	11.3	11.3	11.3	11.3	11.3	11.3	11.3	11.3	11.3

LISTED PUT OPTION PRICE WHEN EXERCISE PRICE IS 40

NUMBER OF WEEKS BEFORE THE OPTION EXPIRES

Common Stock Price	1	2	3	4	5	6	7	8	9	10	11	12	13	14	15	16	17	18	19	20	21	22	23	24	25	26	27	28	29	30	31	32	33	34	35	36	37	38	39
56	0.0	0.0	0.0	0.0	0.0	0.0	0.0	0.0	0.0	0.0	0.0	0.0	0.0	0.0	0.0	0.0	0.0	0.0	0.0	0.0	0.0	0.0	0.0	0.0	0.0	0.0	0.0	0.0	0.0	0.0	0.0	0.0	0.0	0.0	0.0	0.0	0.0	0.0	0.0
55	0.0	0.0	0.0	0.0	0.0	0.0	0.0	0.0	0.0	0.0	0.0	0.0	0.0	0.0	0.0	0.0	0.0	0.0	0.0	0.0	0.0	0.0	0.0	0.0	0.0	0.0	0.0	0.0	0.0	0.0	0.0	0.0	0.0	0.0	0.0	0.0	0.0	0.0	0.1
54	0.0	0.0	0.0	0.0	0.0	0.0	0.0	0.0	0.0	0.0	0.0	0.0	0.0	0.0	0.0	0.0	0.0	0.0	0.0	0.0	0.0	0.0	0.0	0.0	0.0	0.0	0.0	0.0	0.0	0.0	0.0	0.0	0.0	0.1	0.1	0.1	0.1	0.2	0.2
53	0.0	0.0	0.0	0.0	0.0	0.0	0.0	0.0	0.0	0.0	0.0	0.0	0.0	0.0	0.0	0.0	0.0	0.0	0.0	0.0	0.0	0.0	0.0	0.0	0.0	0.0	0.0	0.0	0.1	0.1	0.1	0.2	0.2	0.2	0.3	0.3	0.3	0.4	0.4
52	0.0	0.0	0.0	0.0	0.0	0.0	0.0	0.0	0.0	0.0	0.0	0.0	0.0	0.0	0.0	0.0	0.0	0.0	0.0	0.0	0.0	0.0	0.0	0.0	0.1	0.1	0.1	0.2	0.2	0.2	0.3	0.3	0.3	0.4	0.4	0.5	0.5	0.5	0.6
51	0.0	0.0	0.0	0.0	0.0	0.0	0.0	0.0	0.0	0.0	0.0	0.0	0.0	0.0	0.0	0.0	0.0	0.0	0.0	0.0	0.1	0.1	0.2	0.2	0.3	0.3	0.4	0.4	0.5	0.5	0.5	0.6	0.6	0.6	0.7	0.7	0.7	0.8	0.8
50	0.0	0.0	0.0	0.0	0.0	0.0	0.0	0.0	0.0	0.0	0.0	0.0	0.0	0.0	0.0	0.0	0.0	0.1	0.1	0.2	0.2	0.3	0.3	0.4	0.4	0.5	0.5	0.6	0.6	0.7	0.7	0.7	0.8	0.8	0.8	0.9	0.9	0.9	1.0
49	0.0	0.0	0.0	0.0	0.0	0.0	0.0	0.0	0.0	0.0	0.0	0.0	0.0	0.0	0.1	0.1	0.2	0.2	0.3	0.3	0.4	0.5	0.5	0.6	0.6	0.7	0.7	0.8	0.8	0.9	0.9	0.9	1.0	1.0	1.0	1.1	1.1	1.1	1.2
48	0.0	0.0	0.0	0.0	0.0	0.0	0.0	0.0	0.0	0.0	0.0	0.1	0.1	0.2	0.3	0.3	0.4	0.4	0.5	0.6	0.6	0.7	0.7	0.8	0.8	0.9	0.9	1.0	1.0	1.1	1.1	1.1	1.2	1.2	1.2	1.3	1.3	1.3	1.4
47	0.0	0.0	0.0	0.0	0.0	0.0	0.0	0.0	0.1	0.1	0.2	0.3	0.3	0.4	0.5	0.5	0.6	0.7	0.7	0.8	0.8	0.9	1.0	1.0	1.1	1.1	1.2	1.2	1.3	1.3	1.4	1.4	1.4	1.5	1.5	1.5	1.6	1.6	1.6
46	0.0	0.0	0.0	0.0	0.0	0.1	0.2	0.2	0.3	0.4	0.4	0.5	0.6	0.6	0.7	0.8	0.8	0.9	1.0	1.0	1.1	1.1	1.2	1.3	1.3	1.4	1.4	1.5	1.5	1.6	1.6	1.7	1.7	1.7	1.8	1.8	1.8	1.9	1.9
45	0.0	0.0	0.0	0.1	0.2	0.3	0.4	0.5	0.6	0.6	0.7	0.8	0.9	0.9	1.0	1.1	1.1	1.2	1.3	1.3	1.4	1.4	1.5	1.5	1.6	1.6	1.7	1.7	1.8	1.8	1.8	1.9	1.9	1.9	2.0	2.0	2.0	2.1	2.1
44	0.0	0.1	0.2	0.2	0.3	0.4	0.5	0.6	0.6	0.7	0.8	0.9	0.9	1.0	1.1	1.1	1.2	1.3	1.3	1.4	1.4	1.5	1.5	1.6	1.6	1.7	1.7	1.8	1.8	1.9	1.9	2.0	2.0	2.1	2.1	2.2	2.2	2.3	2.4
43	0.0	0.1	0.2	0.3	0.4	0.5	0.6	0.7	0.8	0.9	1.0	1.1	1.2	1.2	1.3	1.4	1.5	1.5	1.6	1.7	1.7	1.8	1.9	1.9	2.0	2.0	2.1	2.1	2.2	2.3	2.3	2.4	2.4	2.5	2.5	2.6	2.6	2.6	2.7
42	0.2	0.4	0.5	0.6	0.7	0.8	0.9	1.0	1.1	1.2	1.3	1.4	1.4	1.5	1.6	1.7	1.7	1.8	1.9	1.9	2.0	2.1	2.1	2.2	2.2	2.3	2.3	2.4	2.4	2.5	2.5	2.6	2.6	2.7	2.7	2.7	2.8	2.8	2.9
41	0.3	0.5	0.7	0.8	1.0	1.1	1.2	1.3	1.4	1.5	1.6	1.7	1.7	1.8	1.9	2.0	2.0	2.1	2.2	2.2	2.3	2.4	2.4	2.5	2.5	2.6	2.6	2.7	2.7	2.8	2.8	2.9	2.9	3.0	3.0	3.0	3.1	3.1	3.2
40	0.6	0.8	1.0	1.1	1.3	1.4	1.5	1.6	1.7	1.8	1.9	2.0	2.1	2.1	2.2	2.3	2.4	2.4	2.5	2.6	2.6	2.7	2.7	2.8	2.9	2.9	3.0	3.0	3.1	3.1	3.2	3.2	3.3	3.3	3.4	3.4	3.5	3.5	3.6
39	1.1	1.2	1.4	1.5	1.6	1.7	1.8	1.9	2.0	2.1	2.2	2.3	2.4	2.5	2.6	2.6	2.7	2.8	2.9	3.0	3.1	3.1	3.2	3.3	3.4	3.5	3.6	3.7	3.8	3.9	3.9	4.0	4.1	4.2	4.3	4.3	4.4	4.4	4.5
38	2.1	2.2	2.4	2.5	2.6	2.7	2.8	2.9	3.0	3.1	3.2	3.3	3.4	3.5	3.5	3.6	3.7	3.8	3.9	4.0	4.0	4.1	4.2	4.3	4.4	4.4	4.5	4.6	4.7	4.7	4.8	4.9	5.0	5.0	5.1	5.2	5.2	5.3	5.4
37	3.1	3.2	3.4	3.5	3.6	3.7	3.8	3.9	4.0	4.1	4.2	4.3	4.4	4.5	4.5	4.6	4.7	4.8	4.9	5.0	5.0	5.1	5.2	5.3	5.3	5.4	5.5	5.6	5.6	5.7	5.8	5.9	5.9	6.0	6.1	6.1	6.2	6.2	6.3
36	4.1	4.2	4.4	4.5	4.6	4.7	4.8	4.9	5.0	5.1	5.2	5.2	5.3	5.4	5.5	5.6	5.6	5.7	5.8	5.9	5.9	6.0	6.1	6.1	6.2	6.3	6.3	6.4	6.4	6.5	6.6	6.6	6.7	6.7	6.8	6.8	6.9	6.9	7.0
35	5.1	5.2	5.3	5.4	5.5	5.6	5.7	5.8	5.8	5.9	6.0	6.1	6.1	6.2	6.3	6.3	6.4	6.5	6.5	6.6	6.7	6.7	6.8	6.8	6.9	7.0	7.0	7.1	7.1	7.2	7.2	7.3	7.3	7.4	7.4	7.5	7.6	7.6	7.7
34	6.1	6.2	6.3	6.4	6.5	6.6	6.7	6.7	6.8	6.9	7.0	7.0	7.1	7.2	7.2	7.3	7.3	7.4	7.5	7.5	7.6	7.6	7.7	7.7	7.8	7.8	7.9	7.9	8.0	8.0	8.1	8.1	8.2	8.2	8.3	8.3	8.3	8.4	8.4
33	7.1	7.2	7.2	7.3	7.4	7.5	7.5	7.6	7.7	7.7	7.8	7.8	7.9	8.0	8.0	8.1	8.1	8.2	8.2	8.3	8.3	8.4	8.4	8.5	8.5	8.6	8.6	8.7	8.7	8.8	8.8	8.8	8.9	8.9	9.0	9.0	9.0	9.1	9.1
32	8.0	8.1	8.1	8.2	8.2	8.3	8.3	8.4	8.4	8.5	8.5	8.5	8.6	8.6	8.7	8.7	8.7	8.8	8.8	8.9	8.9	9.0	9.0	9.0	9.1	9.1	9.2	9.2	9.3	9.3	9.4	9.4	9.5	9.5	9.6	9.6	9.7	9.7	9.8
31	9.0	9.1	9.1	9.2	9.2	9.2	9.3	9.3	9.3	9.4	9.4	9.5	9.5	9.5	9.6	9.6	9.6	9.7	9.7	9.8	9.8	9.8	9.9	9.9	9.9	10.0	10.0	10.1	10.1	10.1	10.2	10.2	10.2	10.3	10.3	10.4	10.4	10.4	10.5
30	10.0	10.1	10.1	10.1	10.1	10.2	10.2	10.2	10.3	10.3	10.3	10.4	10.4	10.4	10.4	10.5	10.5	10.5	10.6	10.6	10.6	10.7	10.7	10.7	10.7	10.8	10.8	10.8	10.9	10.9	10.9	11.0	11.0	11.0	11.0	11.1	11.1	11.1	11.2
29	11.0	11.0	11.1	11.1	11.1	11.1	11.2	11.2	11.2	11.2	11.3	11.3	11.3	11.3	11.4	11.4	11.4	11.4	11.4	11.5	11.5	11.5	11.5	11.5	11.6	11.6	11.6	11.6	11.6	11.7	11.7	11.7	11.7	11.7	11.8	11.8	11.8	11.8	11.9
28	12.0	12.0	12.0	12.0	12.1	12.1	12.1	12.1	12.1	12.1	12.2	12.2	12.2	12.2	12.2	12.2	12.3	12.3	12.3	12.3	12.3	12.3	12.3	12.3	12.4	12.4	12.4	12.4	12.4	12.4	12.4	12.5	12.5	12.5	12.5	12.5	12.5	12.5	12.6
27	13.0	13.0	13.0	13.0	13.0	13.0	13.0	13.1	13.1	13.1	13.1	13.1	13.1	13.1	13.1	13.1	13.1	13.1	13.1	13.1	13.1	13.1	13.1	13.2	13.2	13.2	13.2	13.2	13.2	13.2	13.2	13.2	13.2	13.2	13.2	13.2	13.2	13.2	13.2

LISTED PUT OPTION PRICE WHEN EXERCISE PRICE IS 45

NUMBER OF WEEKS BEFORE THE OPTION EXPIRES

Common Stock Price	1	2	3	4	5	6	7	8	9	10	11	12	13	14	15	16	17	18	19	20	21	22	23	24	25	26	27	28	29	30	31	32	33	34	35	36	37	38	39
63	0.0	0.0	0.0	0.0	0.0	0.0	0.0	0.0	0.0	0.0	0.0	0.0	0.0	0.0	0.0	0.0	0.0	0.0	0.0	0.0	0.0	0.0	0.0	0.0	0.0	0.0	0.0	0.0	0.0	0.0	0.0	0.0	0.0	0.0	0.0	0.0	0.0	0.0	0.0
62	0.0	0.0	0.0	0.0	0.0	0.0	0.0	0.0	0.0	0.0	0.0	0.0	0.0	0.0	0.0	0.0	0.0	0.0	0.0	0.0	0.0	0.0	0.0	0.0	0.0	0.0	0.0	0.0	0.0	0.0	0.0	0.0	0.0	0.0	0.0	0.0	0.0	0.0	0.1
61	0.0	0.0	0.0	0.0	0.0	0.0	0.0	0.0	0.0	0.0	0.0	0.0	0.0	0.0	0.0	0.0	0.0	0.0	0.0	0.0	0.0	0.0	0.0	0.0	0.0	0.0	0.0	0.0	0.0	0.0	0.0	0.0	0.0	0.0	0.0	0.1	0.1	0.2	0.2
60	0.0	0.0	0.0	0.0	0.0	0.0	0.0	0.0	0.0	0.0	0.0	0.0	0.0	0.0	0.0	0.0	0.0	0.0	0.0	0.0	0.0	0.0	0.0	0.0	0.0	0.0	0.0	0.0	0.0	0.1	0.1	0.2	0.3	0.3	0.4	0.4	0.3	0.2	0.4
59	0.0	0.0	0.0	0.0	0.0	0.0	0.0	0.0	0.0	0.0	0.0	0.0	0.0	0.0	0.0	0.0	0.0	0.0	0.0	0.0	0.0	0.0	0.0	0.0	0.0	0.2	0.2	0.2	0.3	0.3	0.4	0.4	0.5	0.6	0.6	0.6	0.5	0.5	0.6
58	0.0	0.0	0.0	0.0	0.0	0.0	0.0	0.0	0.0	0.0	0.0	0.0	0.0	0.0	0.0	0.0	0.0	0.0	0.0	0.0	0.0	0.2	0.3	0.3	0.4	0.4	0.5	0.6	0.6	0.7	0.7	0.8	0.8	0.7	0.8	0.8	0.7	0.7	0.8
57	0.0	0.0	0.0	0.0	0.0	0.0	0.0	0.0	0.0	0.0	0.0	0.0	0.0	0.0	0.0	0.2	0.5	0.3	0.4	0.5	0.5	0.6	0.7	0.7	0.8	0.9	0.7	0.9	1.0	1.0	1.0	1.0	0.9	0.9	1.0	1.0	0.9	0.9	1.0
56	0.0	0.0	0.0	0.0	0.0	0.0	0.0	0.0	0.0	0.0	0.0	0.3	0.1	0.3	0.5	0.4	0.5	0.6	0.6	0.7	0.8	0.8	0.9	1.0	1.0	0.9	1.2	1.0	1.3	1.1	1.2	1.2	1.3	1.3	1.2	1.0	1.3	1.1	1.2
55	0.0	0.0	0.0	0.0	0.0	0.0	0.0	0.0	0.0	0.0	0.2	0.5	0.6	0.5	0.8	0.7	0.7	0.8	0.9	1.0	1.0	1.1	1.1	1.1	1.2	1.3	1.4	1.2	1.5	1.3	1.4	1.4	1.5	1.6	1.6	1.4	1.3	1.3	1.4
54	0.0	0.0	0.0	0.0	0.0	0.0	0.0	0.0	0.0	0.1	0.4	0.8	0.9	0.6	0.6	0.9	0.9	1.0	1.1	1.2	1.2	1.3	1.4	1.3	1.4	1.5	1.6	1.6	1.5	1.6	1.6	1.7	1.6	1.6	1.6	1.7	1.5	1.5	1.6
53	0.0	0.0	0.0	0.0	0.0	0.0	0.0	0.0	0.2	0.3	0.7	1.0	0.9	1.0	1.0	1.1	1.2	1.3	1.4	1.4	1.5	1.6	1.6	1.4	1.5	1.6	1.2	1.4	1.5	1.6	1.7	1.7	1.5	2.0	1.9	1.7	2.0	1.8	1.8
52	0.0	0.0	0.0	0.0	0.0	0.0	0.0	0.1	0.6	0.6	1.2	1.3	1.4	1.2	1.4	1.5	1.5	1.6	1.8	1.8	1.8	2.1	1.8	1.4	1.8	1.8	1.9	2.0	2.0	2.1	2.0	1.9	2.0	2.0	2.1	2.1	2.0	2.3	2.1
51	0.0	0.0	0.0	0.0	0.0	0.1	0.3	0.4	1.0	1.1	1.5	1.6	1.7	1.5	1.6	1.7	1.7	2.1	1.8	2.0	2.0	1.6	2.2	2.2	2.3	2.4	2.2	2.5	2.5	2.6	2.7	2.4	2.2	2.3	2.3	2.4	2.2	2.3	2.3
50	0.0	0.0	0.0	0.1	0.3	0.5	1.0	1.2	1.4	1.4	1.5	1.8	1.9	1.9	1.9	1.9	2.0	2.1	2.3	2.3	2.4	2.4	2.4	2.6	2.6	2.7	2.8	2.6	2.5	2.3	2.6	2.4	2.6	2.3	2.3	2.4	2.5	2.5	2.6
49	0.0	0.0	0.2	0.4	0.8	1.0	1.3	1.4	1.6	1.7	1.8	2.0	2.1	2.1	2.2	2.3	2.3	2.4	2.5	2.6	2.6	2.7	2.7	2.8	2.9	2.7	3.0	2.9	2.8	2.6	2.8	2.4	2.6	2.6	2.6	2.7	2.7	2.5	2.6
48	0.0	0.1	0.5	0.7	1.1	1.3	1.7	1.8	2.0	2.1	2.1	2.2	2.3	2.4	2.5	2.6	2.6	2.7	2.8	2.9	2.9	3.0	3.1	3.1	3.2	3.3	3.1	3.1	3.1	2.9	3.0	3.0	3.1	3.1	2.9	2.9	3.0	3.0	3.1
47	0.0	0.4	0.8	1.3	1.4	1.6	2.0	2.2	2.3	2.4	2.4	2.5	2.6	2.7	2.8	2.9	3.0	3.0	3.1	3.2	3.3	3.4	3.4	3.5	3.6	3.6	3.7	3.7	3.7	3.5	3.5	3.6	3.7	3.4	3.5	3.6	3.6	3.3	3.7
46	0.3	0.6	1.1	1.5	1.7	2.6	2.4	2.5	2.7	2.8	2.8	2.8	2.9	3.0	3.1	3.2	3.3	3.4	3.4	3.5	3.6	3.7	3.7	3.8	3.9	3.9	4.0	4.1	4.1	4.4	4.5	4.5	4.6	4.6	4.7	4.7	4.6	4.8	4.9
45	0.6	0.9	1.3	1.3	1.4	1.8	2.5	2.7	2.9	3.1	3.1	3.1	3.2	3.3	3.4	3.5	3.6	3.7	3.7	3.8	3.9	4.0	4.1	4.2	4.4	4.5	4.9	5.8	5.8	4.4	4.5	4.5	4.6	4.6	4.7	4.7	5.7	4.8	5.8
44	1.1	1.2	1.5	1.5	1.7	2.6	1.9	2.0	2.2	2.3	2.4	2.5	2.6	2.7	2.8	3.0	3.1	3.1	4.0	3.3	3.4	3.5	3.6	3.7	3.8	4.8	4.1	4.2	4.3	4.4	4.5	4.5	4.6	4.6	4.7	4.7	5.7	4.8	5.8
43	2.1	2.2	2.3	2.4	2.5	2.8	2.7	2.8	3.0	3.1	3.3	3.3	3.5	3.5	3.6	3.7	3.8	4.0	4.0	4.1	4.3	4.3	4.5	4.5	4.7	4.8	4.9	5.0	5.1	5.2	5.3	5.4	5.4	5.5	5.5	6.5	5.7	5.7	5.8
42	3.1	3.2	3.3	3.4	3.5	3.6	3.7	3.8	3.9	4.0	4.1	4.2	4.3	4.3	4.5	4.6	4.7	4.8	4.9	5.0	5.1	5.2	5.3	5.4	5.5	5.6	5.7	5.8	5.8	5.9	6.0	6.1	6.2	6.3	6.4	6.5	6.5	6.6	6.7
41	4.1	4.2	4.3	4.4	4.5	4.5	4.6	4.7	4.8	4.9	5.0	5.1	5.2	5.3	5.4	5.4	5.5	5.6	5.7	5.8	5.9	6.0	6.1	6.2	6.3	6.4	6.4	6.5	6.6	6.7	6.8	6.9	7.0	7.1	7.2	7.3	7.3	7.4	7.5
40	5.1	5.2	5.2	5.3	5.4	5.5	5.6	5.7	5.7	5.8	5.9	6.0	6.2	6.2	6.2	6.3	6.4	6.5	6.6	6.7	6.8	6.8	6.9	7.0	7.1	7.2	7.2	7.3	7.4	7.5	7.6	7.6	7.7	7.8	7.9	8.0	8.0	8.1	8.2
39	6.1	6.1	6.2	6.3	6.4	6.4	6.5	6.6	6.7	6.7	6.8	6.9	7.0	7.0	7.1	7.2	7.3	7.3	7.4	7.5	7.6	7.6	7.7	7.8	7.9	7.9	8.0	8.1	8.2	8.2	8.3	8.4	8.5	8.5	8.6	8.7	8.8	8.8	8.9
38	7.1	7.1	7.2	7.3	7.3	7.4	7.5	7.5	7.6	7.7	7.7	7.8	7.9	8.0	8.0	8.1	8.1	8.2	8.3	8.3	8.4	8.5	8.5	8.6	8.7	8.7	8.8	8.9	8.9	9.0	9.1	9.1	9.2	9.3	9.3	9.4	9.5	9.5	9.6
37	8.1	8.1	8.2	8.2	8.3	8.4	8.4	8.5	8.5	8.6	8.7	8.7	8.8	8.8	8.9	9.0	9.0	9.1	9.1	9.2	9.3	9.3	9.4	9.4	9.5	9.6	9.6	9.7	9.7	9.8	9.9	9.9	9.9	10.0	10.1	10.1	10.1	10.2	10.3
36	9.1	9.1	9.2	9.2	9.3	9.3	9.4	9.4	9.5	9.5	9.6	9.6	9.7	9.7	9.8	9.8	9.9	9.9	9.9	10.0	10.1	10.1	10.2	10.2	10.3	10.3	10.4	10.4	10.5	10.5	10.6	10.6	10.7	10.7	10.8	10.8	10.9	10.9	11.0
35	10.0	10.1	10.1	10.2	10.2	10.3	10.3	10.3	10.4	10.4	10.5	10.5	10.6	10.6	10.7	10.7	10.7	10.8	10.8	10.9	10.9	11.0	11.0	11.1	11.1	11.1	11.2	11.2	11.3	11.3	11.3	11.4	11.4	11.5	11.5	11.6	11.6	11.6	11.7
34	11.0	11.1	11.1	11.1	11.2	11.2	11.2	11.3	11.3	11.4	11.4	11.4	11.5	11.5	11.5	11.6	11.6	11.6	11.7	11.7	11.8	11.8	11.8	11.9	11.9	11.9	12.0	12.0	12.0	12.1	12.1	12.1	12.2	12.2	12.2	12.3	12.3	12.4	12.4
33	12.0	12.1	12.1	12.1	12.1	12.2	12.2	12.2	12.2	12.3	12.3	12.3	12.4	12.4	12.4	12.4	12.5	12.5	12.5	12.6	12.6	12.6	12.6	12.7	12.7	12.7	12.7	12.8	12.8	12.8	12.9	12.9	12.9	12.9	13.0	13.0	13.0	13.1	13.1
32	13.0	13.0	13.1	13.1	13.1	13.1	13.1	13.2	13.2	13.2	13.2	13.2	13.3	13.3	13.3	13.3	13.3	13.4	13.4	13.4	13.4	13.4	13.5	13.5	13.5	13.5	13.5	13.6	13.6	13.6	13.6	13.6	13.7	13.7	13.7	13.7	13.7	13.8	13.8
31	14.0	14.0	14.0	14.0	14.1	14.1	14.1	14.1	14.1	14.1	14.1	14.1	14.2	14.2	14.2	14.2	14.2	14.2	14.2	14.3	14.3	14.3	14.3	14.3	14.3	14.3	14.3	14.3	14.4	14.4	14.4	14.4	14.4	14.4	14.4	14.4	14.4	14.5	14.5
30	15.0	15.0	15.0	15.0	15.0	15.0	15.0	15.0	15.0	15.0	15.0	15.1	15.1	15.1	15.1	15.1	15.1	15.1	15.1	15.1	15.1	15.1	15.1	15.1	15.1	15.1	15.1	15.1	15.1	15.1	15.1	15.1	15.1	15.1	15.1	15.2	15.2	15.2	15.2

LISTED PUT OPTION PRICE WHEN EXERCISE PRICE IS 50

NUMBER OF WEEKS BEFORE THE OPTION EXPIRES

Common Stock Price	1	2	3	4	5	6	7	8	9	10	11	12	13	14	15	16	17	18	19	20	21	22	23	24	25	26	27	28	29	30	31	32	33	34	35	36	37	38	39
65	0.0	0.0	0.0	0.0	0.0	0.0	0.0	0.0	0.0	0.0	0.0	0.0	0.0	0.0	0.0	0.0	0.0	0.0	0.0	0.0	0.0	0.0	0.0	0.0	0.0	0.0	0.0	0.1	0.1	0.2	0.3	0.3	0.4	0.5	0.5	0.6	0.6	0.7	0.8
64	0.0	0.0	0.0	0.0	0.0	0.0	0.0	0.0	0.0	0.0	0.0	0.0	0.0	0.0	0.0	0.0	0.0	0.0	0.0	0.0	0.0	0.0	0.0	0.0	0.0	0.1	0.1	0.3	0.3	0.4	0.5	0.5	0.6	0.6	0.7	0.8	0.8	0.9	0.9
63	0.0	0.0	0.0	0.0	0.0	0.0	0.0	0.0	0.0	0.0	0.0	0.0	0.0	0.0	0.0	0.0	0.0	0.0	0.0	0.0	0.0	0.0	0.1	0.2	0.3	0.3	0.4	0.5	0.5	0.6	0.7	0.7	0.8	0.8	0.9	1.0	1.0	1.1	1.1
62	0.0	0.0	0.0	0.0	0.0	0.0	0.0	0.0	0.0	0.0	0.0	0.0	0.0	0.0	0.0	0.0	0.0	0.0	0.1	0.2	0.2	0.3	0.4	0.5	0.5	0.6	0.7	0.7	0.8	0.9	0.9	1.0	1.0	1.1	1.1	1.2	1.2	1.3	1.3
61	0.0	0.0	0.0	0.0	0.0	0.0	0.0	0.0	0.0	0.0	0.0	0.0	0.0	0.0	0.1	0.2	0.3	0.4	0.4	0.5	0.6	0.6	0.7	0.8	0.8	0.9	1.0	1.0	1.1	1.1	1.2	1.3	1.3	1.4	1.4	1.5	1.5	1.6	1.6
60	0.0	0.0	0.0	0.0	0.0	0.0	0.0	0.0	0.0	0.0	0.0	0.0	0.1	0.2	0.3	0.4	0.5	0.5	0.6	0.7	0.8	0.8	0.9	1.0	1.0	1.1	1.2	1.2	1.3	1.4	1.4	1.5	1.5	1.6	1.6	1.7	1.7	1.8	1.8
59	0.0	0.0	0.0	0.0	0.0	0.0	0.0	0.0	0.0	0.0	0.1	0.2	0.3	0.4	0.5	0.6	0.7	0.7	0.8	0.9	1.0	1.0	1.1	1.2	1.2	1.3	1.4	1.4	1.5	1.6	1.6	1.7	1.7	1.8	1.8	1.9	1.9	2.0	2.0
58	0.0	0.0	0.0	0.0	0.0	0.0	0.0	0.0	0.1	0.2	0.3	0.4	0.5	0.6	0.7	0.8	0.9	0.9	1.0	1.1	1.1	1.2	1.3	1.4	1.4	1.5	1.6	1.6	1.7	1.8	1.8	1.9	1.9	2.0	2.0	2.1	2.1	2.2	2.2
57	0.0	0.0	0.0	0.0	0.0	0.0	0.2	0.3	0.4	0.5	0.6	0.7	0.8	0.9	1.0	1.1	1.2	1.3	1.4	1.4	1.5	1.6	1.7	1.7	1.8	1.9	1.9	2.0	2.1	2.1	2.2	2.3	2.3	2.3	2.4	2.4	2.5	2.5	2.5
56	0.0	0.0	0.0	0.0	0.1	0.3	0.4	0.5	0.6	0.7	0.8	0.9	1.0	1.1	1.2	1.3	1.4	1.5	1.6	1.6	1.7	1.8	1.9	1.9	2.0	2.1	2.1	2.2	2.3	2.3	2.4	2.4	2.5	2.5	2.6	2.6	2.7	2.7	2.7
55	0.0	0.0	0.1	0.3	0.4	0.6	0.7	0.8	0.9	1.0	1.1	1.2	1.3	1.4	1.5	1.6	1.7	1.7	1.8	1.9	2.0	2.0	2.1	2.2	2.2	2.3	2.4	2.4	2.5	2.6	2.6	2.7	2.7	2.8	2.8	2.9	2.9	3.0	3.0
54	0.0	0.1	0.3	0.5	0.7	0.8	1.0	1.1	1.2	1.3	1.4	1.5	1.6	1.7	1.8	1.9	2.0	2.1	2.1	2.2	2.3	2.4	2.4	2.5	2.6	2.7	2.7	2.8	2.9	2.9	3.0	3.0	3.1	3.1	3.2	3.2	3.3	3.3	3.3
53	0.0	0.3	0.6	0.8	1.0	1.1	1.3	1.4	1.5	1.6	1.7	1.8	1.9	2.0	2.1	2.2	2.3	2.3	2.4	2.5	2.6	2.6	2.7	2.8	2.8	2.9	3.0	3.0	3.1	3.1	3.2	3.3	3.3	3.4	3.4	3.5	3.5	3.5	3.5
52	0.1	0.4	0.6	0.8	1.0	1.1	1.3	1.4	1.5	1.6	1.7	1.8	2.0	2.0	2.1	2.2	2.3	2.4	2.5	2.6	2.6	2.7	2.8	2.9	2.9	3.0	3.1	3.1	3.2	3.3	3.3	3.4	3.4	3.5	3.6	3.6	3.7	3.8	3.8
51	0.4	0.7	0.9	1.1	1.3	1.4	1.6	1.7	1.8	1.9	2.0	2.1	2.2	2.3	2.4	2.5	2.6	2.7	2.7	2.8	2.9	3.0	3.0	3.1	3.2	3.2	3.3	3.4	3.4	3.5	3.6	3.6	3.7	3.8	3.8	3.9	4.0	4.0	4.1
50	0.7	1.0	1.2	1.4	1.6	1.7	1.9	2.0	2.1	2.3	2.4	2.5	2.6	2.7	2.8	2.9	3.0	3.0	3.1	3.2	3.3	3.3	3.4	3.5	3.6	3.6	3.7	3.8	3.8	3.9	4.0	4.0	4.1	4.1	4.2	4.3	4.3	4.4	4.4
49	1.1	1.3	1.4	1.6	1.6	1.7	1.8	1.9	2.0	2.1	2.3	2.4	2.5	2.6	2.7	2.8	2.9	3.0	3.1	3.2	3.3	3.4	3.5	3.5	3.6	3.6	3.7	3.8	3.8	3.9	4.0	4.0	4.1	4.1	4.2	4.3	4.3	4.4	5.3
48	2.1	2.2	2.4	2.5	2.6	2.7	2.8	3.0	3.0	3.1	3.2	3.3	3.4	3.5	3.6	3.7	3.8	3.9	3.9	4.0	4.1	4.2	4.3	4.3	4.4	4.5	4.6	4.6	4.7	4.8	4.9	4.9	5.0	5.1	5.1	5.2	5.3	5.3	6.2
47	3.1	3.2	3.4	3.5	3.6	3.7	3.8	3.9	4.0	4.1	4.2	4.3	4.5	4.6	4.7	4.8	4.8	4.9	5.0	5.1	5.2	5.3	5.3	5.4	5.5	5.6	5.7	5.8	5.8	5.9	6.0	6.1	6.2	6.3	6.4	6.7	6.8	7.0	7.1
46	4.1	4.2	4.3	4.4	4.5	4.6	4.7	4.8	4.9	5.0	5.1	5.2	5.4	5.5	5.6	5.7	5.7	5.8	6.0	6.1	6.2	6.3	6.4	6.5	6.6	6.7	6.8	6.9	7.0	7.1	7.2	7.3	7.4	7.5	7.6	7.7	7.8	7.9	8.0
45	5.1	5.2	5.3	5.4	5.5	5.6	5.7	5.8	5.9	6.0	6.1	6.2	6.2	6.3	6.4	6.5	6.6	6.7	6.8	6.9	7.0	7.1	7.2	7.3	7.4	7.5	7.6	7.6	7.7	7.9	8.0	8.1	8.2	8.3	8.4	8.5	8.6	8.7	8.7
44	6.1	6.2	6.3	6.4	6.5	6.5	6.6	6.7	6.8	6.9	7.0	7.1	7.1	7.2	7.3	7.4	7.5	7.6	7.7	7.8	7.9	8.0	8.1	8.1	8.2	8.3	8.4	8.5	8.6	8.6	8.7	8.8	8.9	9.0	9.1	9.1	9.2	9.4	9.4
43	7.1	7.2	7.2	7.3	7.4	7.5	7.6	7.6	7.7	7.8	7.9	8.0	8.0	8.1	8.2	8.3	8.4	8.4	8.5	8.6	8.7	8.8	8.8	8.9	9.0	9.1	9.2	9.3	9.3	9.4	9.5	9.6	9.7	9.7	9.8	9.9	9.9	10.1	10.1
42	8.1	8.1	8.2	8.3	8.3	8.4	8.5	8.5	8.6	8.7	8.8	8.8	8.9	9.0	9.0	9.1	9.2	9.2	9.3	9.4	9.4	9.5	9.6	9.6	9.7	9.8	9.9	9.9	10.0	10.1	10.1	10.2	10.3	10.3	10.4	10.5	10.6	10.7	10.8
41	9.1	9.1	9.2	9.2	9.3	9.3	9.4	9.5	9.6	9.6	9.7	9.8	9.8	9.9	10.0	10.0	10.1	10.1	10.2	10.2	10.4	10.4	10.5	10.6	10.6	10.7	10.7	10.8	10.9	10.9	11.0	11.1	11.1	11.2	11.3	11.3	11.4	11.5	11.5
40	10.1	10.1	10.2	10.2	10.3	10.3	10.4	10.5	10.5	10.6	10.6	10.7	10.7	10.8	10.9	10.9	11.0	11.0	11.1	11.1	11.2	11.3	11.3	11.4	11.4	11.5	11.5	11.6	11.7	11.7	11.8	11.8	11.9	11.9	12.0	12.0	12.1	12.2	12.2
39	11.0	11.1	11.1	11.2	11.2	11.3	11.3	11.4	11.4	11.5	11.5	11.6	11.6	11.7	11.7	11.8	11.8	11.9	11.9	12.0	12.0	12.1	12.1	12.2	12.2	12.3	12.3	12.4	12.4	12.5	12.5	12.6	12.6	12.7	12.7	12.8	12.8	12.9	12.9
38	12.0	12.1	12.1	12.2	12.2	12.2	12.3	12.3	12.4	12.4	12.5	12.5	12.6	12.6	12.7	12.7	12.7	12.8	12.8	12.9	12.9	12.9	13.0	13.0	13.1	13.1	13.1	13.2	13.2	13.3	13.3	13.3	13.4	13.4	13.5	13.5	13.5	13.6	13.6
37	13.0	13.1	13.1	13.1	13.2	13.2	13.2	13.3	13.3	13.3	13.4	13.4	13.5	13.5	13.5	13.6	13.6	13.6	13.7	13.7	13.7	13.8	13.8	13.8	13.9	13.9	13.9	14.0	14.0	14.0	14.1	14.1	14.1	14.2	14.2	14.2	14.2	14.3	14.3
36	14.0	14.1	14.1	14.1	14.1	14.2	14.2	14.2	14.2	14.3	14.3	14.3	14.3	14.4	14.4	14.4	14.4	14.5	14.5	14.5	14.5	14.6	14.6	14.6	14.6	14.7	14.7	14.7	14.7	14.8	14.8	14.8	14.8	14.9	14.9	14.9	14.9	15.0	15.0
35	15.0	15.0	15.1	15.1	15.1	15.1	15.1	15.1	15.2	15.2	15.2	15.2	15.2	15.2	15.3	15.3	15.3	15.3	15.3	15.3	15.4	15.4	15.4	15.4	15.4	15.5	15.5	15.5	15.5	15.5	15.5	15.6	15.6	15.6	15.6	15.6	15.7	15.7	15.7

LISTED PUT OPTION PRICE WHEN EXERCISE PRICE IS 60

NUMBER OF WEEKS BEFORE THE OPTION EXPIRES

Common Stock Price	1	2	3	4	5	6	7	8	9	10	11	12	13	14	15	16	17	18	19	20	21	22	23	24	25	26	27	28	29	30	31	32	33	34	35	36	37	38	39
78	0.0	0.0	0.0	0.0	0.0	0.0	0.0	0.0	0.0	0.0	0.0	0.0	0.0	0.0	0.0	0.0	0.0	0.0	0.0	0.0	0.0	0.0	0.0	0.0	0.0	0.0	0.0	0.1	0.2	0.2	0.3	0.4	0.5	0.5	0.6	0.7	0.8	0.8	0.9
77	0.0	0.0	0.0	0.0	0.0	0.0	0.0	0.0	0.0	0.0	0.0	0.0	0.0	0.0	0.0	0.0	0.0	0.0	0.0	0.0	0.0	0.0	0.0	0.0	0.0	0.0	0.2	0.3	0.3	0.4	0.5	0.6	0.6	0.7	0.8	0.9	1.0	1.0	1.1
76	0.0	0.0	0.0	0.0	0.0	0.0	0.0	0.0	0.0	0.0	0.0	0.0	0.0	0.0	0.0	0.0	0.0	0.0	0.0	0.0	0.0	0.0	0.0	0.0	0.2	0.3	0.4	0.5	0.5	0.6	0.7	0.8	0.9	0.9	1.0	1.1	1.2	1.2	1.3
75	0.0	0.0	0.0	0.0	0.0	0.0	0.0	0.0	0.0	0.0	0.0	0.0	0.0	0.0	0.0	0.0	0.0	0.0	0.0	0.0	0.0	0.0	0.0	0.2	0.3	0.4	0.5	0.6	0.7	0.8	0.9	1.0	1.1	1.1	1.2	1.3	1.4	1.4	1.5
74	0.0	0.0	0.0	0.0	0.0	0.0	0.0	0.0	0.0	0.0	0.0	0.0	0.0	0.0	0.0	0.0	0.0	0.0	0.0	0.0	0.0	0.0	0.2	0.3	0.4	0.5	0.6	0.7	0.8	0.9	1.0	1.1	1.2	1.3	1.4	1.5	1.5	1.6	1.7
73	0.0	0.0	0.0	0.0	0.0	0.0	0.0	0.0	0.0	0.0	0.0	0.0	0.0	0.0	0.0	0.0	0.0	0.0	0.0	0.0	0.0	0.2	0.3	0.4	0.5	0.6	0.7	0.8	0.9	1.0	1.1	1.2	1.3	1.4	1.5	1.6	1.7	1.8	1.9
72	0.0	0.0	0.0	0.0	0.0	0.0	0.0	0.0	0.0	0.0	0.0	0.0	0.0	0.0	0.0	0.0	0.0	0.0	0.0	0.0	0.2	0.3	0.4	0.5	0.6	0.7	0.8	0.9	1.0	1.1	1.3	1.4	1.5	1.6	1.7	1.8	1.9	2.0	2.1
71	0.0	0.0	0.0	0.0	0.0	0.0	0.0	0.0	0.0	0.0	0.0	0.0	0.0	0.0	0.0	0.0	0.0	0.0	0.0	0.2	0.3	0.4	0.5	0.7	0.8	0.9	1.0	1.1	1.3	1.4	1.5	1.6	1.8	1.9	2.0	2.1	2.2	2.3	2.4
70	0.0	0.0	0.0	0.0	0.0	0.0	0.0	0.0	0.0	0.0	0.0	0.0	0.0	0.0	0.0	0.0	0.0	0.0	0.2	0.3	0.4	0.5	0.6	0.8	0.9	1.0	1.1	1.3	1.4	1.5	1.7	1.8	1.9	2.0	2.2	2.3	2.4	2.5	2.6
69	0.0	0.0	0.0	0.0	0.0	0.0	0.0	0.0	0.0	0.0	0.0	0.0	0.0	0.0	0.0	0.0	0.0	0.2	0.3	0.4	0.5	0.7	0.8	0.9	1.0	1.2	1.3	1.4	1.6	1.7	1.8	2.0	2.1	2.2	2.4	2.5	2.6	2.7	2.8
68	0.0	0.0	0.0	0.0	0.0	0.0	0.0	0.0	0.0	0.0	0.0	0.0	0.0	0.0	0.0	0.0	0.2	0.3	0.4	0.5	0.7	0.8	0.9	1.1	1.2	1.3	1.5	1.6	1.8	1.9	2.1	2.2	2.3	2.5	2.6	2.8	2.9	3.0	3.1
67	0.0	0.0	0.0	0.0	0.0	0.0	0.0	0.0	0.0	0.0	0.0	0.0	0.0	0.0	0.0	0.2	0.3	0.4	0.6	0.7	0.8	1.0	1.1	1.3	1.4	1.5	1.7	1.8	2.0	2.1	2.3	2.4	2.6	2.7	2.9	3.0	3.1	3.2	3.3
66	0.0	0.0	0.0	0.0	0.0	0.0	0.0	0.0	0.0	0.0	0.0	0.0	0.0	0.0	0.2	0.3	0.5	0.6	0.7	0.9	1.0	1.2	1.3	1.5	1.6	1.8	1.9	2.1	2.2	2.4	2.5	2.7	2.8	3.0	3.1	3.3	3.4	3.5	3.6
65	0.0	0.0	0.0	0.0	0.0	0.0	0.0	0.0	0.0	0.0	0.0	0.0	0.0	0.2	0.3	0.5	0.6	0.8	0.9	1.1	1.2	1.4	1.5	1.7	1.9	2.0	2.2	2.3	2.5	2.6	2.8	3.0	3.1	3.3	3.4	3.6	3.7	3.8	3.9
64	0.0	0.0	0.0	0.0	0.0	0.0	0.0	0.0	0.0	0.0	0.0	0.0	0.2	0.4	0.5	0.7	0.8	1.0	1.1	1.3	1.5	1.6	1.8	1.9	2.1	2.3	2.4	2.6	2.7	2.9	3.1	3.2	3.4	3.5	3.7	3.8	4.0	4.0	4.1
63	0.0	0.0	0.0	0.0	0.0	0.0	0.0	0.0	0.0	0.0	0.0	0.2	0.4	0.5	0.7	0.9	1.0	1.2	1.4	1.5	1.7	1.9	2.0	2.2	2.4	2.5	2.7	2.9	3.0	3.2	3.4	3.5	3.7	3.9	4.0	4.2	4.3	4.3	4.4
62	0.0	0.0	0.0	0.0	0.0	0.0	0.0	0.0	0.0	0.0	0.2	0.4	0.6	0.8	0.9	1.1	1.3	1.5	1.6	1.8	2.0	2.2	2.3	2.5	2.7	2.9	3.0	3.2	3.4	3.6	3.7	3.9	4.1	4.2	4.4	4.5	4.6	4.6	4.7
61	0.0	0.0	0.0	0.0	0.0	0.0	0.0	0.0	0.0	0.2	0.4	0.6	0.8	1.0	1.2	1.4	1.6	1.7	1.9	2.1	2.3	2.5	2.7	2.9	3.1	3.2	3.4	3.6	3.8	4.0	4.2	4.3	4.5	4.6	4.7	4.8	4.9	4.9	5.0
60	0.9	1.0	1.1	1.2	1.4	1.5	1.6	1.7	1.8	1.9	2.0	2.1	2.3	2.4	2.5	2.6	2.7	2.8	2.9	3.0	3.2	3.3	3.4	3.5	3.6	3.7	3.8	3.9	4.0	4.2	4.3	4.4	4.5	4.6	4.7	4.8	5.0	5.1	5.3
59	1.2	1.3	1.4	1.6	1.7	1.8	2.0	2.1	2.2	2.3	2.5	2.6	2.7	2.9	3.0	3.1	3.3	3.4	3.5	3.6	3.8	3.9	4.0	4.2	4.3	4.4	4.6	4.7	4.8	5.0	5.1	5.2	5.4	5.5	5.6	5.8	5.9	6.0	6.1
58	2.1	2.2	2.3	2.5	2.6	2.7	2.8	3.0	3.1	3.2	3.3	3.5	3.6	3.7	3.8	4.0	4.1	4.2	4.4	4.5	4.6	4.7	4.9	5.0	5.1	5.2	5.4	5.5	5.6	5.7	5.9	6.0	6.1	6.2	6.4	6.5	6.6	6.7	6.8
57	3.1	3.2	3.3	3.4	3.6	3.7	3.8	3.9	4.0	4.2	4.3	4.4	4.5	4.6	4.8	4.9	5.0	5.1	5.2	5.4	5.5	5.6	5.7	5.8	6.0	6.1	6.2	6.3	6.5	6.6	6.7	6.8	6.9	7.1	7.2	7.3	7.4	7.5	7.6
56	4.1	4.2	4.3	4.4	4.5	4.7	4.8	4.9	5.0	5.1	5.2	5.3	5.5	5.6	5.7	5.8	5.9	6.0	6.2	6.3	6.4	6.5	6.6	6.7	6.9	7.0	7.1	7.2	7.3	7.4	7.5	7.7	7.8	7.9	8.0	8.1	8.2	8.2	8.3
55	5.1	5.2	5.3	5.4	5.5	5.6	5.8	5.9	6.0	6.1	6.2	6.3	6.4	6.5	6.6	6.8	6.9	7.0	7.1	7.2	7.3	7.4	7.5	7.6	7.8	7.9	8.0	8.1	8.2	8.3	8.4	8.5	8.6	8.8	8.9	9.0	9.0	9.1	9.1
54	6.1	6.2	6.3	6.4	6.5	6.6	6.7	6.8	6.9	7.1	7.2	7.3	7.4	7.5	7.6	7.7	7.8	7.9	8.0	8.1	8.2	8.3	8.4	8.5	8.6	8.7	8.8	8.9	9.0	9.1	9.2	9.3	9.4	9.5	9.6	9.7	9.7	9.8	9.8
53	7.1	7.2	7.3	7.4	7.5	7.6	7.7	7.8	7.9	8.0	8.1	8.2	8.3	8.4	8.5	8.6	8.7	8.8	8.9	9.0	9.1	9.2	9.3	9.4	9.5	9.6	9.7	9.8	9.9	10.0	10.1	10.2	10.2	10.3	10.4	10.5	10.5	10.6	10.6
52	8.1	8.2	8.3	8.4	8.4	8.5	8.6	8.7	8.8	8.9	9.0	9.1	9.2	9.3	9.4	9.5	9.6	9.7	9.8	9.9	10.0	10.1	10.1	10.2	10.3	10.4	10.5	10.6	10.7	10.8	10.9	11.0	11.0	11.1	11.2	11.2	11.3	11.3	11.3
51	9.1	9.2	9.3	9.4	9.5	9.6	9.7	9.8	9.8	9.9	10.0	10.1	10.2	10.3	10.4	10.5	10.5	10.6	10.7	10.8	10.9	11.0	11.1	11.2	11.2	11.3	11.4	11.5	11.6	11.7	11.7	11.8	11.9	12.0	12.0	12.1	12.1	12.1	12.1
50	10.1	10.2	10.2	10.3	10.4	10.5	10.6	10.6	10.7	10.8	10.9	11.0	11.0	11.1	11.2	11.3	11.4	11.4	11.5	11.6	11.7	11.8	11.8	11.9	12.0	12.1	12.1	12.2	12.3	12.4	12.4	12.5	12.6	12.6	12.7	12.8	12.8	12.8	12.8
49	11.1	11.2	11.2	11.3	11.4	11.5	11.5	11.6	11.7	11.7	11.8	11.9	12.0	12.0	12.1	12.2	12.2	12.3	12.4	12.5	12.5	12.6	12.7	12.8	12.8	12.9	13.0	13.0	13.1	13.2	13.2	13.3	13.4	13.4	13.5	13.6	13.6	13.6	13.6
48	12.1	12.2	12.2	12.3	12.4	12.4	12.5	12.6	12.6	12.7	12.7	12.8	12.9	12.9	13.0	13.1	13.1	13.2	13.3	13.3	13.4	13.5	13.5	13.6	13.6	13.7	13.8	13.8	13.9	14.0	14.0	14.1	14.1	14.2	14.2	14.3	14.3	14.3	14.3
47	13.1	13.2	13.2	13.3	13.3	13.4	13.5	13.5	13.6	13.6	13.7	13.7	13.8	13.9	13.9	14.0	14.0	14.1	14.2	14.2	14.3	14.3	14.4	14.4	14.5	14.5	14.6	14.7	14.7	14.8	14.8	14.9	14.9	15.0	15.0	15.1	15.1	15.1	15.1
46	14.1	14.1	14.2	14.2	14.3	14.3	14.4	14.4	14.5	14.5	14.6	14.6	14.7	14.7	14.8	14.8	14.9	14.9	15.0	15.0	15.1	15.1	15.2	15.2	15.3	15.3	15.4	15.4	15.5	15.5	15.6	15.6	15.6	15.7	15.7	15.8	15.8	15.8	15.8
45	15.0	15.1	15.1	15.2	15.2	15.3	15.3	15.4	15.4	15.4	15.5	15.5	15.6	15.6	15.7	15.7	15.8	15.8	15.9	15.9	16.0	16.0	16.1	16.1	16.1	16.2	16.2	16.3	16.3	16.4	16.4	16.4	16.5	16.5	16.6	16.6	16.6	16.6	16.6
44	16.0	16.1	16.1	16.1	16.2	16.2	16.3	16.3	16.3	16.4	16.4	16.4	16.5	16.5	16.6	16.6	16.6	16.7	16.7	16.7	16.8	16.8	16.9	16.9	16.9	17.0	17.0	17.0	17.1	17.1	17.1	17.2	17.2	17.3	17.3	17.3	17.4	17.4	17.4
43	17.0	17.1	17.1	17.1	17.1	17.2	17.2	17.2	17.3	17.3	17.3	17.4	17.4	17.4	17.4	17.5	17.5	17.5	17.6	17.6	17.6	17.6	17.7	17.7	17.7	17.8	17.8	17.8	17.8	17.9	17.9	17.9	18.0	18.0	18.0	18.0	18.1	18.1	18.1
42	18.0	18.0	18.1	18.1	18.1	18.1	18.1	18.2	18.2	18.2	18.2	18.3	18.3	18.3	18.3	18.3	18.4	18.4	18.4	18.4	18.4	18.5	18.5	18.5	18.5	18.6	18.6	18.6	18.6	18.6	18.7	18.7	18.7	18.7	18.7	18.8	18.8	18.8	18.8

LISTED PUT OPTION PRICE WHEN EXERCISE PRICE IS 70

NUMBER OF WEEKS BEFORE THE OPTION EXPIRES

Common Stock Price	1	2	3	4	5	6	7	8	9	10	11	12	13	14	15	16	17	18	19	20	21	22	23	24	25	26	27	28	29	30	31	32	33	34	35	36	37	38	39
91	0.0	0.0	0.0	0.0	0.0	0.0	0.0	0.0	0.0	0.0	0.0	0.0	0.0	0.0	0.0	0.0	0.0	0.0	0.0	0.0	0.0	0.0	0.0	0.0	0.0	0.0	0.0	0.0	0.1	0.2	0.3	0.4	0.5	0.6	0.7	0.8	0.9	1.0	1.1
90	0.0	0.0	0.0	0.0	0.0	0.0	0.0	0.0	0.0	0.0	0.0	0.0	0.0	0.0	0.0	0.0	0.0	0.0	0.0	0.0	0.0	0.0	0.0	0.0	0.0	0.0	0.0	0.1	0.2	0.3	0.4	0.5	0.6	0.7	0.8	0.9	1.0	1.1	1.2
89	0.0	0.0	0.0	0.0	0.0	0.0	0.0	0.0	0.0	0.0	0.0	0.0	0.0	0.0	0.0	0.0	0.0	0.0	0.0	0.0	0.0	0.0	0.0	0.0	0.0	0.0	0.1	0.2	0.3	0.4	0.5	0.6	0.7	0.8	0.9	1.0	1.1	1.2	1.3
88	0.0	0.0	0.0	0.0	0.0	0.0	0.0	0.0	0.0	0.0	0.0	0.0	0.0	0.0	0.0	0.0	0.0	0.0	0.0	0.0	0.0	0.0	0.0	0.0	0.0	0.1	0.2	0.3	0.4	0.5	0.6	0.7	0.8	0.9	1.0	1.1	1.2	1.3	1.4
87	0.0	0.0	0.0	0.0	0.0	0.0	0.0	0.0	0.0	0.0	0.0	0.0	0.0	0.0	0.0	0.0	0.0	0.0	0.0	0.0	0.0	0.0	0.0	0.0	0.1	0.2	0.3	0.4	0.5	0.6	0.7	0.8	0.9	1.0	1.1	1.2	1.3	1.4	1.5
86	0.0	0.0	0.0	0.0	0.0	0.0	0.0	0.0	0.0	0.0	0.0	0.0	0.0	0.0	0.0	0.0	0.0	0.0	0.0	0.0	0.0	0.0	0.0	0.1	0.2	0.3	0.4	0.5	0.6	0.7	0.8	0.9	1.0	1.1	1.2	1.3	1.4	1.5	1.6
85	0.0	0.0	0.0	0.0	0.0	0.0	0.0	0.0	0.0	0.0	0.0	0.0	0.0	0.0	0.0	0.0	0.0	0.0	0.0	0.0	0.0	0.0	0.1	0.2	0.3	0.4	0.5	0.6	0.7	0.8	0.9	1.0	1.1	1.2	1.3	1.4	1.5	1.6	1.7
84	0.0	0.0	0.0	0.0	0.0	0.0	0.0	0.0	0.0	0.0	0.0	0.0	0.0	0.0	0.0	0.0	0.0	0.0	0.0	0.0	0.0	0.1	0.2	0.3	0.4	0.5	0.6	0.7	0.8	0.9	1.0	1.1	1.2	1.3	1.4	1.5	1.6	1.7	1.8
83	0.0	0.0	0.0	0.0	0.0	0.0	0.0	0.0	0.0	0.0	0.0	0.0	0.0	0.0	0.0	0.0	0.0	0.0	0.0	0.1	0.2	0.3	0.4	0.5	0.6	0.7	0.8	0.9	1.0	1.1	1.2	1.3	1.4	1.5	1.6	1.7	1.8	1.9	2.0
82	0.0	0.0	0.0	0.0	0.0	0.0	0.0	0.0	0.0	0.0	0.0	0.0	0.0	0.0	0.0	0.0	0.0	0.1	0.2	0.3	0.4	0.5	0.6	0.7	0.8	0.9	1.0	1.1	1.2	1.3	1.4	1.5	1.6	1.7	1.8	1.9	2.0	2.1	2.2
81	0.0	0.0	0.0	0.0	0.0	0.0	0.0	0.0	0.0	0.0	0.0	0.0	0.0	0.0	0.0	0.1	0.2	0.3	0.4	0.5	0.6	0.7	0.8	0.9	1.0	1.1	1.2	1.3	1.4	1.5	1.6	1.7	1.8	1.9	2.0	2.1	2.2	2.3	2.4
80	0.0	0.0	0.0	0.0	0.0	0.0	0.0	0.0	0.0	0.0	0.0	0.0	0.1	0.2	0.3	0.4	0.5	0.6	0.7	0.8	0.9	1.0	1.1	1.2	1.3	1.4	1.5	1.6	1.7	1.8	1.9	2.0	2.1	2.2	2.3	2.4	2.5	2.6	2.7
79	0.0	0.0	0.0	0.0	0.0	0.0	0.0	0.1	0.2	0.3	0.4	0.5	0.6	0.7	0.8	0.9	1.0	1.1	1.2	1.3	1.4	1.5	1.6	1.7	1.8	1.9	2.0	2.1	2.2	2.3	2.4	2.5	2.6	2.7	2.8	2.9	3.0	3.1	3.2
78	0.0	0.0	0.1	0.2	0.3	0.4	0.5	0.6	0.7	0.8	0.9	1.0	1.1	1.2	1.3	1.4	1.5	1.6	1.7	1.8	1.9	2.0	2.1	2.2	2.3	2.4	2.5	2.6	2.7	2.8	2.9	3.0	3.1	3.2	3.3	3.4	3.5	3.6	3.7
77	0.0	0.1	0.2	0.3	0.4	0.6	0.7	0.8	0.9	1.0	1.1	1.2	1.3	1.4	1.5	1.7	1.8	1.9	2.0	2.1	2.2	2.3	2.4	2.5	2.7	2.8	2.9	3.0	3.1	3.2	3.3	3.4	3.5	3.7	3.8	3.9	4.0	4.1	4.2
76	0.0	0.1	0.2	0.4	0.5	0.6	0.7	0.9	1.0	1.1	1.2	1.4	1.5	1.6	1.7	1.9	2.0	2.1	2.2	2.4	2.5	2.6	2.7	2.9	3.0	3.1	3.2	3.3	3.5	3.6	3.7	3.8	4.0	4.1	4.2	4.3	4.5	4.6	4.7
75	0.0	0.1	0.3	0.4	0.6	0.7	0.8	1.0	1.1	1.3	1.4	1.5	1.7	1.8	2.0	2.1	2.2	2.4	2.5	2.7	2.8	2.9	3.1	3.2	3.4	3.5	3.6	3.8	3.9	4.1	4.2	4.3	4.5	4.6	4.8	4.9	5.0	5.2	5.3
74	0.0	0.2	0.3	0.5	0.6	0.8	0.9	1.1	1.2	1.4	1.6	1.7	1.9	2.0	2.2	2.3	2.5	2.6	2.8	2.9	3.1	3.3	3.4	3.6	3.7	3.9	4.0	4.2	4.3	4.5	4.6	4.8	4.9	5.1	5.3	5.4	5.6	5.7	5.9
73	0.1	0.3	0.4	0.6	0.8	0.9	1.1	1.3	1.4	1.6	1.8	1.9	2.1	2.3	2.4	2.6	2.8	2.9	3.1	3.3	3.4	3.6	3.8	3.9	4.1	4.3	4.4	4.6	4.8	4.9	5.1	5.3	5.4	5.6	5.8	5.9	6.1	6.3	6.5
72	0.2	0.4	0.6	0.7	0.9	1.1	1.3	1.5	1.6	1.8	2.0	2.2	2.4	2.5	2.7	2.9	3.1	3.3	3.4	3.6	3.8	4.0	4.2	4.3	4.5	4.7	4.9	5.1	5.2	5.4	5.6	5.8	6.0	6.1	6.3	6.5	6.7	6.9	7.1
71	0.4	0.6	0.8	1.0	1.2	1.3	1.5	1.7	1.9	2.1	2.3	2.5	2.7	2.9	3.1	3.2	3.4	3.6	3.8	4.0	4.2	4.4	4.6	4.8	4.9	5.1	5.3	5.5	5.7	5.9	6.1	6.3	6.5	6.6	6.8	7.0	7.2	7.4	7.7
70	0.7	0.9	1.1	1.3	1.5	1.7	1.9	2.1	2.3	2.5	2.7	2.9	3.1	3.3	3.5	3.7	3.9	4.1	4.3	4.5	4.7	4.9	5.1	5.3	5.5	5.7	5.9	6.1	6.3	6.5	6.7	6.9	7.1	7.3	7.5	7.7	7.9	8.1	8.3
69	1.2	1.4	1.6	1.8	2.0	2.2	2.4	2.6	2.8	3.0	3.2	3.4	3.6	3.8	4.0	4.2	4.4	4.6	4.8	5.0	5.2	5.4	5.6	5.8	6.0	6.2	6.4	6.6	6.8	7.0	7.2	7.4	7.6	7.8	8.0	8.2	8.4	8.6	8.8
68	2.2	2.4	2.6	2.8	3.0	3.1	3.3	3.5	3.7	3.9	4.1	4.3	4.5	4.6	4.8	5.0	5.2	5.4	5.6	5.7	5.9	6.1	6.3	6.5	6.7	6.8	7.0	7.2	7.4	7.6	7.8	7.9	8.1	8.3	8.5	8.7	8.9	9.1	9.3
67	3.2	3.4	3.5	3.7	3.9	4.1	4.2	4.4	4.6	4.8	4.9	5.1	5.3	5.5	5.6	5.8	6.0	6.2	6.3	6.5	6.7	6.9	7.0	7.2	7.4	7.6	7.7	7.9	8.1	8.3	8.4	8.6	8.8	9.0	9.1	9.3	9.5	9.7	9.8
66	4.1	4.3	4.4	4.6	4.8	4.9	5.1	5.3	5.4	5.6	5.7	5.9	6.1	6.2	6.4	6.6	6.7	6.9	7.1	7.2	7.4	7.6	7.7	7.9	8.0	8.2	8.4	8.5	8.7	8.9	9.0	9.2	9.4	9.5	9.7	9.9	10.0	10.2	10.4
65	5.1	5.3	5.4	5.6	5.7	5.9	6.0	6.2	6.3	6.5	6.7	6.8	7.0	7.1	7.3	7.4	7.6	7.8	7.9	8.1	8.2	8.4	8.5	8.7	8.8	9.0	9.2	9.3	9.5	9.6	9.8	9.9	10.1	10.3	10.4	10.6	10.7	10.9	11.0
64	6.1	6.2	6.4	6.5	6.7	6.8	7.0	7.1	7.3	7.4	7.5	7.7	7.8	8.0	8.1	8.3	8.4	8.6	8.7	8.9	9.0	9.1	9.3	9.4	9.6	9.7	9.9	10.0	10.2	10.3	10.5	10.6	10.7	10.9	11.0	11.2	11.3	11.5	11.6
63	7.1	7.2	7.4	7.5	7.6	7.8	7.9	8.0	8.2	8.3	8.5	8.6	8.7	8.9	9.0	9.1	9.3	9.4	9.5	9.7	9.8	10.0	10.1	10.2	10.4	10.5	10.6	10.8	10.9	11.0	11.2	11.3	11.4	11.6	11.7	11.8	12.0	12.1	12.2
62	8.1	8.2	8.4	8.5	8.6	8.7	8.9	9.0	9.1	9.2	9.4	9.5	9.6	9.7	9.9	10.0	10.1	10.2	10.4	10.5	10.6	10.8	10.9	11.0	11.1	11.3	11.4	11.5	11.6	11.8	11.9	12.0	12.1	12.3	12.4	12.5	12.6	12.8	12.9
61	9.1	9.2	9.3	9.5	9.6	9.7	9.8	9.9	10.0	10.2	10.3	10.4	10.5	10.6	10.8	10.9	11.0	11.1	11.2	11.4	11.5	11.6	11.7	11.8	11.9	12.1	12.2	12.3	12.4	12.5	12.7	12.8	12.9	13.0	13.1	13.3	13.4	13.5	13.6
60	10.1	10.2	10.3	10.4	10.5	10.7	10.8	10.9	11.0	11.1	11.2	11.3	11.4	11.6	11.7	11.8	11.9	12.0	12.1	12.2	12.3	12.5	12.6	12.7	12.8	12.9	13.0	13.1	13.2	13.4	13.5	13.6	13.7	13.8	13.9	14.0	14.1	14.2	14.3
59	11.1	11.2	11.3	11.4	11.5	11.6	11.7	11.8	11.9	12.0	12.1	12.2	12.3	12.5	12.6	12.7	12.8	12.9	13.0	13.1	13.2	13.3	13.4	13.5	13.6	13.7	13.8	13.9	14.0	14.1	14.2	14.3	14.5	14.6	14.7	14.8	14.9	15.0	15.0
58	12.1	12.2	12.3	12.4	12.5	12.6	12.7	12.7	12.8	12.9	13.0	13.1	13.2	13.3	13.4	13.5	13.6	13.7	13.8	13.9	14.0	14.1	14.2	14.3	14.4	14.5	14.5	14.6	14.7	14.8	14.9	15.0	15.1	15.2	15.3	15.4	15.5	15.6	15.7
57	13.1	13.2	13.3	13.4	13.4	13.5	13.6	13.7	13.8	13.9	14.0	14.0	14.1	14.2	14.3	14.4	14.5	14.6	14.6	14.7	14.8	14.9	15.0	15.1	15.2	15.2	15.3	15.4	15.5	15.6	15.7	15.8	15.8	15.9	16.0	16.1	16.2	16.3	16.4
56	14.1	14.2	14.3	14.3	14.4	14.5	14.6	14.7	14.7	14.8	14.9	15.0	15.0	15.1	15.2	15.3	15.4	15.4	15.5	15.6	15.7	15.8	15.8	15.9	16.0	16.1	16.2	16.2	16.3	16.4	16.5	16.5	16.6	16.7	16.8	16.9	16.9	17.0	17.1
55	15.1	15.2	15.2	15.3	15.4	15.5	15.5	15.6	15.7	15.7	15.8	15.9	16.0	16.0	16.1	16.2	16.2	16.3	16.4	16.5	16.5	16.6	16.7	16.7	16.8	16.9	17.0	17.0	17.1	17.2	17.2	17.3	17.4	17.5	17.5	17.6	17.7	17.7	17.8
54	16.1	16.2	16.2	16.3	16.3	16.4	16.5	16.5	16.6	16.7	16.7	16.8	16.8	16.9	17.0	17.0	17.1	17.2	17.2	17.3	17.3	17.4	17.5	17.5	17.6	17.6	17.7	17.8	17.8	17.9	18.0	18.0	18.1	18.1	18.2	18.3	18.3	18.4	18.5
53	17.0	17.1	17.1	17.2	17.2	17.3	17.4	17.4	17.5	17.5	17.6	17.7	17.7	17.8	17.8	17.9	17.9	18.0	18.1	18.1	18.2	18.2	18.3	18.4	18.4	18.5	18.5	18.6	18.6	18.7	18.8	18.8	18.9	18.9	19.0	19.1	19.1	19.2	19.2
52	18.0	18.0	18.1	18.2	18.2	18.3	18.3	18.4	18.4	18.5	18.5	18.6	18.6	18.7	18.7	18.8	18.8	18.9	18.9	19.0	19.0	19.1	19.1	19.2	19.2	19.3	19.3	19.4	19.4	19.5	19.5	19.6	19.6	19.7	19.7	19.8	19.8	19.9	19.9
51	19.0	19.0	19.1	19.1	19.2	19.2	19.3	19.3	19.4	19.4	19.5	19.5	19.6	19.6	19.7	19.7	19.7	19.8	19.8	19.9	19.9	20.0	20.0	20.1	20.1	20.2	20.2	20.2	20.3	20.3	20.4	20.4	20.5	20.5	20.5	20.6	20.6	20.6	20.6
50	20.0	20.0	20.1	20.1	20.2	20.2	20.2	20.3	20.3	20.4	20.4	20.4	20.5	20.5	20.5	20.6	20.6	20.7	20.7	20.7	20.8	20.8	20.8	20.9	20.9	21.0	21.0	21.0	21.1	21.1	21.1	21.2	21.2	21.2	21.2	21.3	21.3	21.3	21.3
49	21.0	21.0	21.1	21.1	21.1	21.1	21.2	21.2	21.2	21.3	21.3	21.3	21.3	21.3	21.4	21.4	21.4	21.4	21.5	21.5	21.5	21.5	21.6	21.6	21.6	21.6	21.7	21.7	21.7	21.7	21.8	21.8	21.8	21.8	21.9	21.9	21.9	21.9	22.0

LISTED PUT OPTION PRICE WHEN EXERCISE PRICE IS 80

Common Stock Price

NUMBER OF WEEKS BEFORE THE OPTION EXPIRES

Stock Price	1	2	3	4	5	6	7	8	9	10	11	12	13	14	15	16	17	18	19	20	21	22	23	24	25	26	27	28	29	30	31	32	33	34	35	36	37	38	39
104	0.0	0.0	0.0	0.0	0.0	0.0	0.0	0.0	0.0	0.0	0.0	0.0	0.0	0.0	0.0	0.0	0.0	0.0	0.0	0.0	0.0	0.0	0.0	0.0	0.0	0.0	0.1	0.1	0.2	0.3	0.4	0.5	0.6	0.7	0.8	0.9	1.0	1.1	1.2
102	0.0	0.0	0.0	0.0	0.0	0.0	0.0	0.0	0.0	0.0	0.0	0.0	0.0	0.0	0.0	0.0	0.0	0.0	0.0	0.0	0.1	0.2	0.3	0.5	0.6	0.7	0.8	0.9	1.0	1.1	1.2	1.3	1.4	1.5	1.6	1.7	1.8	1.9	1.6
100	0.0	0.0	0.0	0.0	0.0	0.0	0.0	0.0	0.0	0.0	0.0	0.0	0.0	0.0	0.0	0.0	0.0	0.0	0.0	0.2	0.3	0.4	0.5	0.7	0.7	0.8	0.9	1.1	1.0	1.1	1.2	1.3	1.4	1.6	1.6	1.7	1.8	1.9	2.0
99	0.0	0.0	0.0	0.0	0.0	0.0	0.0	0.0	0.0	0.0	0.0	0.0	0.0	0.0	0.0	0.0	0.1	0.1	0.3	0.4	0.5	0.6	0.8	0.9	1.0	1.1	1.2	1.3	1.4	1.5	1.6	1.7	1.8	1.9	2.0	2.1	2.2	2.3	2.2
98	0.0	0.0	0.0	0.0	0.0	0.0	0.0	0.0	0.0	0.0	0.0	0.0	0.0	0.0	0.0	0.1	0.3	0.3	0.5	0.6	0.7	0.9	1.0	1.1	1.2	1.3	1.4	1.5	1.6	1.7	1.9	2.0	2.1	2.2	2.3	2.3	2.4	2.4	2.4
97	0.0	0.0	0.0	0.0	0.0	0.0	0.0	0.0	0.0	0.0	0.0	0.0	0.1	0.2	0.3	0.4	0.5	0.6	0.8	0.9	1.0	1.2	1.3	1.4	1.5	1.6	1.7	1.8	1.9	2.0	2.1	2.2	2.3	2.4	2.5	2.5	2.6	2.6	2.6
96	0.0	0.0	0.0	0.0	0.0	0.0	0.0	0.0	0.0	0.0	0.0	0.1	0.3	0.4	0.5	0.7	0.8	0.9	1.0	1.2	1.3	1.4	1.5	1.6	1.7	1.8	1.9	2.0	2.1	2.2	2.3	2.4	2.5	2.6	2.7	2.7	2.8	2.8	2.8
95	0.0	0.0	0.0	0.0	0.0	0.0	0.0	0.0	0.1	0.3	0.4	0.4	0.6	0.7	0.8	1.0	1.1	1.3	1.4	1.5	1.6	1.7	1.8	1.9	2.0	2.2	2.3	2.4	2.5	2.6	2.7	2.7	2.8	2.9	3.0	3.0	3.1	3.1	3.1
94	0.0	0.0	0.0	0.0	0.0	0.0	0.0	0.1	0.3	0.5	0.6	0.7	0.8	1.0	1.1	1.2	1.4	1.5	1.6	1.8	1.9	2.0	2.1	2.2	2.3	2.4	2.5	2.6	2.7	2.8	2.9	3.0	3.1	3.1	3.2	3.3	3.3	3.3	3.3
93	0.0	0.0	0.0	0.0	0.0	0.0	0.2	0.3	0.5	0.7	0.8	0.9	1.0	1.2	1.3	1.4	1.6	1.7	1.8	2.0	2.1	2.2	2.4	2.5	2.6	2.6	2.8	2.9	3.0	3.1	3.2	3.3	3.4	3.3	3.4	3.5	3.5	3.4	3.5
92	0.0	0.0	0.0	0.0	0.0	0.2	0.5	0.5	0.8	1.0	1.2	1.1	1.3	1.4	1.5	1.7	1.9	2.0	2.1	2.3	2.4	2.5	2.6	2.7	2.8	3.0	3.1	3.2	3.3	3.4	3.5	3.6	3.7	3.5	3.6	3.7	3.8	3.7	3.8
91	0.0	0.0	0.0	0.0	0.1	0.4	0.7	0.8	1.0	1.3	1.4	1.4	1.5	1.7	1.8	2.0	2.1	2.2	2.4	2.5	2.6	2.7	2.9	3.0	3.1	3.2	3.3	3.4	3.5	3.6	3.7	3.8	3.9	3.8	3.9	4.0	4.1	4.0	4.0
90	0.0	0.0	0.0	0.2	0.4	0.7	1.0	1.1	1.4	1.6	1.7	1.6	1.8	1.9	2.0	2.2	2.3	2.5	2.6	2.7	2.9	3.0	3.1	3.3	3.3	3.5	3.6	3.7	3.8	3.9	4.0	4.1	4.2	4.0	4.1	4.2	4.3	4.2	4.3
89	0.0	0.0	0.2	0.5	0.8	1.1	1.3	1.4	1.7	2.0	2.1	2.1	2.2	2.4	2.5	2.7	2.8	3.0	3.0	3.2	3.3	3.4	3.6	3.5	3.6	3.7	3.8	3.9	4.1	4.2	4.3	4.4	4.5	4.3	4.4	4.5	4.6	4.4	4.5
88	0.0	0.1	0.5	0.8	1.1	1.3	1.6	1.7	2.0	2.3	2.4	2.4	2.6	2.8	2.9	3.0	3.1	3.3	3.4	3.5	3.7	3.8	3.9	4.1	4.0	4.3	4.4	4.5	4.6	4.5	4.6	4.7	4.8	4.6	4.7	4.8	4.9	4.7	4.8
87	0.0	0.4	0.8	1.0	1.4	1.7	2.0	2.1	2.4	2.7	2.8	2.9	3.0	3.2	3.3	3.5	3.6	3.8	3.9	4.0	4.2	4.3	4.5	4.4	4.3	4.4	4.5	4.7	4.8	4.9	5.0	5.1	5.2	5.0	5.1	5.2	5.3	5.1	5.1
86	0.2	0.7	1.0	1.4	1.8	2.0	2.3	2.4	2.7	3.0	3.1	3.2	3.4	3.5	3.6	3.9	4.0	4.2	4.2	4.4	4.6	4.8	4.9	5.0	4.9	5.2	5.3	5.4	4.6	4.7	4.8	4.9	5.0	5.1	5.2	5.3	4.9	5.2	5.1
85	0.5	1.0	1.4	1.8	2.1	2.4	2.7	2.8	3.1	3.4	3.5	3.6	3.8	3.9	4.0	4.2	4.3	4.5	4.6	4.8	4.9	5.0	5.1	5.3	5.2	5.4	5.5	5.6	4.9	5.0	5.1	4.9	4.9	5.1	5.2	5.3	5.4	5.5	5.3
84	0.8	1.3	1.8	2.1	2.5	2.8	3.0	3.2	3.5	3.8	3.8	3.9	4.1	4.2	4.4	4.6	4.7	4.9	5.0	5.1	5.3	5.5	5.6	5.7	5.4	5.7	5.8	5.9	5.2	5.3	5.4	5.5	5.6	5.7	5.8	5.9	5.7	5.5	5.6
83	1.1	1.7	2.1	2.5	2.9	3.2	3.4	3.6	3.9	4.2	4.2	4.4	4.5	4.7	4.8	5.0	5.2	5.3	5.5	5.6	5.8	5.8	6.0	6.1	5.8	6.0	6.1	6.2	5.5	5.6	5.7	5.8	5.9	6.0	6.1	5.9	6.0	6.1	6.2
82	1.6	2.0	2.5	2.9	3.3	3.6	3.9	4.1	4.4	4.7	4.8	4.9	5.1	5.2	5.4	5.6	5.7	5.9	6.0	6.1	6.3	6.4	6.5	6.6	5.2	5.4	5.5	5.7	5.8	5.9	6.0	6.1	6.2	6.0	6.1	6.5	6.3	6.4	6.5
81	2.1	2.5	3.0	3.4	3.8	4.1	4.3	4.5	4.8	5.1	5.2	5.3	5.5	5.7	5.8	5.9	6.1	6.3	6.4	6.6	6.8	6.8	6.9	5.6	5.7	5.8	5.9	6.0	6.1	6.3	6.4	6.5	6.3	6.4	6.7	6.5	6.6	6.7	6.8
80	2.6	3.0	3.4	3.8	4.2	4.5	4.8	5.0	5.3	5.6	5.8	5.9	6.1	6.2	6.4	6.6	6.7	6.9	7.0	7.1	7.2	5.5	5.5	5.6	5.7	5.8	6.0	6.0	6.1	6.2	7.2	6.1	6.7	6.8	6.7	7.0	6.9	6.7	6.8
79	3.2	3.6	4.0	4.4	4.9	5.1	5.3	5.5	5.8	6.2	6.3	6.4	6.6	6.8	6.9	7.1	7.3	7.5	7.5	7.7	5.1	5.2	5.3	5.4	5.4	5.8	5.9	6.0	6.1	7.1	7.2	7.4	7.4	7.5	6.7	6.8	7.8	6.7	7.1
78	4.2	4.4	4.7	5.1	5.5	5.8	6.0	6.2	6.5	6.8	6.9	7.1	7.2	7.4	7.6	7.8	7.9	8.1	8.1	8.3	6.2	6.4	6.6	6.8	7.0	7.2	7.4	7.6	7.8	8.0	8.1	8.2	8.3	8.4	8.5	8.6	8.7	8.8	8.9
77	5.2	5.4	5.6	6.0	6.1	6.5	6.9	7.1	7.4	7.8	7.9	8.0	8.2	8.4	8.5	8.7	8.8	9.0	9.0	6.9	7.1	7.4	7.4	7.6	7.8	8.0	8.2	8.4	8.6	8.0	8.1	8.2	8.3	9.3	9.4	9.5	9.6	9.7	9.8
76	6.2	6.3	6.4	6.8	7.0	7.4	7.8	8.0	8.3	8.6	8.8	8.9	9.1	9.3	9.4	9.6	9.7	9.9	10.1	7.7	8.1	8.5	8.3	8.6	8.8	8.8	9.0	9.2	9.4	9.6	9.7	9.9	10.1	10.2	10.4	10.4	10.5	10.6	10.7
75	7.2	7.5	7.5	7.8	8.4	8.4	8.7	9.2	9.3	9.5	9.7	9.9	10.0	10.3	10.5	10.7	10.9	11.1	8.4	8.5	10.4	8.7	9.1	9.4	9.6	9.6	9.8	9.9	10.9	11.1	11.3	10.7	10.8	11.0	11.2	11.3	11.4	11.5	11.6
74	8.2	8.5	8.6	8.8	9.2	9.9	10.0	10.2	10.5	10.8	11.0	11.1	11.3	11.5	11.7	11.9	12.1	12.3	11.8	11.9	11.2	11.4	11.5	11.7	12.0	12.0	12.2	12.3	11.7	12.0	12.1	12.2	12.3	12.5	12.7	12.8	12.3	12.1	12.5
73	9.1	9.4	9.5	9.6	10.8	10.8	11.1	11.1	11.8	12.0	12.2	12.4	12.6	12.8	13.0	13.2	13.3	12.5	12.6	13.6	12.9	13.0	13.2	13.3	13.5	13.6	13.7	13.9	13.2	13.4	13.5	13.7	13.8	14.0	14.2	13.5	13.0	13.1	13.3
72	10.1	10.3	10.4	10.6	11.7	11.8	12.0	12.1	12.5	13.2	13.2	13.5	13.7	13.9	14.1	12.2	12.3	13.5	13.8	14.4	13.7	13.9	14.0	14.1	14.3	14.4	14.6	14.7	14.0	14.1	14.3	14.4	14.6	14.7	13.4	13.5	13.7	13.9	14.0
71	11.1	11.3	11.4	11.5	12.6	12.7	13.0	13.0	13.8	14.1	14.3	14.5	14.7	14.9	13.0	13.1	12.8	13.3	14.3	15.3	14.6	14.7	14.9	15.0	15.1	15.2	15.4	15.5	14.8	15.0	15.1	15.3	15.5	15.7	14.3	14.5	14.4	14.5	15.4
70	12.1	12.2	12.4	12.5	14.4	14.6	14.7	14.9	14.9	15.1	15.2	14.7	14.5	15.6	13.9	14.0	14.1	14.2	14.4	16.1	15.4	15.5	15.6	15.8	15.9	16.0	16.2	16.2	15.5	15.7	15.8	16.0	16.2	14.7	15.0	15.0	14.4	14.5	14.7
69	13.1	13.4	13.3	13.6	14.5	15.6	15.7	16.0	16.0	16.4	16.5	16.6	16.7	16.9	14.7	15.4	14.9	15.2	15.4	16.9	16.2	16.3	16.5	16.6	16.8	16.8	16.9	17.0	16.3	16.4	16.6	16.7	16.9	15.4	15.6	15.6	15.8	15.9	15.4
68	14.1	14.2	14.3	14.4	15.5	16.5	16.6	16.7	17.0	16.9	17.0	17.2	17.4	18.0	15.6	14.0	14.1	17.6	17.7	17.8	17.0	17.2	17.3	17.4	17.5	17.6	17.7	17.8	17.1	17.2	17.3	17.4	16.0	16.2	16.3	16.4	16.5	16.7	16.1
67	15.1	15.3	15.3	15.4	16.5	17.5	17.6	17.7	18.0	16.9	17.9	18.0	18.1	18.6	16.5	15.7	15.8	18.4	18.5	18.7	17.9	18.0	18.1	18.2	18.3	18.4	16.9	17.0	17.1	17.4	17.5	17.4	16.0	16.9	16.3	17.1	17.2	17.4	16.8
66	14.1	16.2	16.3	16.6	17.4	18.5	17.6	17.7	18.6	16.8	18.9	19.0	18.1	17.2	15.7	16.6	16.7	17.6	16.0	18.6	18.7	16.2	16.6	16.6	17.5	16.8	16.8	17.0	17.1	17.2	17.4	17.4	17.5	17.6	17.7	17.8	17.8	17.9	17.5
65	15.1	15.2	15.3	15.4	16.5	15.6	15.7	15.8	16.9	10.1	16.1	16.2	16.2	16.4	16.5	16.6	16.7	16.8	16.9	16.1	17.1	17.2	17.3	17.4	17.5	18.0	18.9	18.6	17.9	18.0	18.1	18.2	18.3	18.4	18.5	18.6	18.7	18.8	18.2
64	16.1	16.2	16.3	16.4	16.5	16.5	15.6	16.7	16.8	16.9	17.0	17.1	17.2	18.0	17.4	16.6	16.7	17.6	16.9	18.6	18.7	16.8	16.9	18.2	18.3	18.4	18.4	18.6	17.9	18.0	18.8	19.0	19.1	19.1	19.3	19.4	19.4	18.8	16.1
63	17.1	17.2	17.2	17.3	17.4	17.5	16.6	17.7	17.7	17.8	17.9	18.0	18.1	18.2	18.2	18.3	18.4	18.5	18.6	18.7	18.7	18.8	18.9	19.0	19.1	19.2	19.2	19.3	19.4	19.5	19.6	19.7	19.7	19.8	19.9	19.9	20.1	18.8	19.6
62	18.1	18.1	18.2	18.2	18.4	18.5	18.5	18.6	18.7	18.8	17.9	18.9	18.9	19.0	19.1	19.2	19.2	19.4	18.6	20.4	19.6	18.8	19.7	20.6	20.7	19.2	20.8	20.1	21.0	20.3	21.1	21.2	20.5	20.6	20.7	20.7	20.8	20.2	20.2
61	19.1	19.1	19.2	19.3	19.3	19.4	19.5	19.5	19.6	19.7	19.7	19.8	18.9	19.9	20.0	20.1	20.1	20.2	20.3	20.4	20.4	20.5	20.6	20.6	20.7	20.8	20.8	20.9	21.0	21.0	21.1	20.9	21.6	20.6	20.9	20.7	20.8	20.9	20.9
60	20.1	20.1	20.2	20.2	20.3	20.4	20.4	20.5	20.5	20.6	20.7	20.7	20.8	20.8	20.9	21.0	21.0	21.1	21.1	21.2	21.3	21.3	21.4	21.4	21.5	21.6	21.6	22.5	21.7	21.8	21.9	21.9	22.0	22.0	22.1	22.2	22.2	22.3	21.6
59	21.1	21.2	21.2	21.3	21.3	21.4	21.4	21.4	21.5	21.6	21.6	21.7	21.7	21.7	21.8	21.8	21.9	21.9	22.0	22.0	22.1	22.2	22.2	22.2	22.3	22.3	22.6	22.5	22.6	22.6	22.6	22.7	22.7	22.8	22.1	22.2	22.9	23.0	23.0
58	22.0	22.1	22.1	22.2	22.2	22.3	22.3	22.4	22.4	22.4	22.5	22.5	22.6	22.6	22.7	22.7	22.7	22.8	22.8	22.9	22.9	23.0	23.0	23.1	23.1	23.1	23.2	23.2	23.3	23.3	23.4	23.4	23.5	23.5	23.5	23.6	23.6	23.7	23.7
57	23.0	23.1	23.1	23.1	23.2	23.2	23.3	23.3	23.3	23.4	23.4	23.4	23.5	23.5	23.5	23.6	23.6	23.7	23.7	23.7	23.8	23.8	23.8	23.9	23.9	23.9	24.0	24.0	24.1	24.1	24.1	24.2	24.2	24.2	24.3	24.3	24.3	24.4	24.4

LISTED PUT OPTION PRICE WHEN EXERCISE PRICE IS 90

NUMBER OF WEEKS BEFORE THE OPTION EXPIRES

Common Stock Price	1	2	3	4	5	6	7	8	9	10	11	12	13	14	15	16	17	18	19	20	21	22	23	24	25	26	27	28	29	30	31	32	33	34	35	36	37	38	39
118	0.0	0.0	0.0	0.0	0.0	0.0	0.0	0.0	0.0	0.0	0.0	0.0	0.0	0.0	0.0	0.0	0.0	0.0	0.0	0.0	0.0	0.0	0.0	0.0	0.0	0.0	0.0	0.0	0.1	0.2	0.3	0.4	0.5	0.6	0.7	0.9	1.0	1.1	1.2
116	0.0	0.0	0.0	0.0	0.0	0.0	0.0	0.0	0.0	0.0	0.0	0.0	0.0	0.0	0.0	0.0	0.0	0.0	0.0	0.0	0.0	0.0	0.0	0.0	0.0	0.1	0.2	0.3	0.4	0.6	0.7	0.8	0.9	1.0	1.1	1.2	1.3	1.4	1.5
114	0.0	0.0	0.0	0.0	0.0	0.0	0.0	0.0	0.0	0.0	0.0	0.0	0.0	0.0	0.0	0.0	0.0	0.0	0.0	0.0	0.0	0.0	0.1	0.2	0.3	0.5	0.6	0.7	0.8	1.0	1.1	1.2	1.3	1.4	1.5	1.6	1.7	1.8	1.9
112	0.0	0.0	0.0	0.0	0.0	0.0	0.0	0.0	0.0	0.0	0.0	0.0	0.0	0.0	0.0	0.0	0.0	0.0	0.0	0.1	0.2	0.4	0.5	0.6	0.7	0.9	1.0	1.1	1.2	1.4	1.5	1.6	1.7	1.8	1.9	2.0	2.1	2.2	2.3
110	0.0	0.0	0.0	0.0	0.0	0.0	0.0	0.0	0.0	0.0	0.0	0.0	0.0	0.0	0.0	0.0	0.0	0.2	0.3	0.5	0.6	0.8	0.9	1.0	1.2	1.3	1.4	1.5	1.7	1.8	1.9	2.0	2.1	2.2	2.3	2.4	2.6	2.7	2.8
108	0.0	0.0	0.0	0.0	0.0	0.0	0.0	0.0	0.0	0.0	0.0	0.0	0.0	0.0	0.2	0.3	0.5	0.6	0.8	0.9	1.1	1.2	1.3	1.5	1.6	1.7	1.9	2.0	2.1	2.2	2.3	2.4	2.6	2.7	2.8	2.9	3.0	3.1	3.2
106	0.0	0.0	0.0	0.0	0.0	0.0	0.0	0.0	0.0	0.0	0.0	0.1	0.3	0.4	0.6	0.8	0.9	1.1	1.2	1.4	1.5	1.7	1.8	1.9	2.1	2.2	2.3	2.4	2.6	2.7	2.8	2.9	3.0	3.1	3.2	3.3	3.4	3.5	3.7
104	0.0	0.0	0.0	0.0	0.0	0.0	0.0	0.0	0.0	0.2	0.4	0.6	0.7	0.9	1.1	1.2	1.4	1.6	1.7	1.9	2.0	2.1	2.3	2.4	2.5	2.7	2.8	2.9	3.0	3.1	3.3	3.4	3.5	3.6	3.7	3.8	3.9	4.0	4.1
102	0.0	0.0	0.0	0.0	0.0	0.0	0.0	0.2	0.5	0.7	0.9	1.0	1.2	1.4	1.6	1.7	1.9	2.0	2.2	2.3	2.5	2.6	2.8	2.9	3.0	3.1	3.3	3.4	3.5	3.6	3.7	3.9	4.0	4.1	4.2	4.3	4.4	4.5	4.6
100	0.0	0.0	0.0	0.0	0.0	0.3	0.5	0.7	1.0	1.2	1.4	1.6	1.7	1.9	2.1	2.2	2.4	2.6	2.7	2.8	3.0	3.1	3.3	3.4	3.5	3.7	3.8	3.9	4.0	4.1	4.3	4.4	4.5	4.6	4.7	4.8	4.9	5.0	5.1
99	0.0	0.0	0.0	0.0	0.2	0.5	0.8	1.0	1.2	1.4	1.6	1.8	2.0	2.2	2.3	2.5	2.7	2.8	3.0	3.1	3.3	3.4	3.5	3.7	3.8	3.9	4.0	4.2	4.3	4.4	4.5	4.6	4.7	4.9	5.0	5.1	5.2	5.3	5.4
98	0.0	0.0	0.0	0.2	0.5	0.8	1.0	1.3	1.5	1.7	1.9	2.1	2.3	2.4	2.6	2.8	2.9	3.1	3.2	3.4	3.5	3.7	3.8	3.9	4.1	4.2	4.3	4.4	4.5	4.7	4.8	4.9	5.0	5.1	5.2	5.3	5.4	5.5	5.6
97	0.0	0.0	0.1	0.5	0.8	1.1	1.3	1.5	1.8	2.0	2.2	2.4	2.5	2.7	2.9	3.0	3.2	3.4	3.5	3.6	3.8	3.9	4.1	4.2	4.3	4.5	4.6	4.7	4.8	4.9	5.1	5.2	5.3	5.4	5.5	5.6	5.7	5.8	5.9
96	0.0	0.0	0.4	0.8	1.1	1.3	1.6	1.8	2.0	2.3	2.4	2.6	2.8	3.0	3.2	3.3	3.5	3.6	3.8	3.9	4.1	4.2	4.3	4.5	4.6	4.7	4.9	5.0	5.1	5.2	5.3	5.4	5.6	5.7	5.8	5.9	6.0	6.1	6.2
95	0.0	0.3	0.7	1.0	1.3	1.6	1.9	2.1	2.3	2.5	2.7	2.9	3.1	3.3	3.4	3.6	3.8	3.9	4.1	4.2	4.4	4.5	4.6	4.8	4.9	5.0	5.1	5.3	5.4	5.5	5.6	5.7	5.8	6.0	6.1	6.2	6.3	6.4	6.5
94	0.1	0.6	1.0	1.3	1.6	1.9	2.2	2.4	2.6	2.8	3.0	3.2	3.4	3.6	3.7	3.9	4.1	4.2	4.4	4.5	4.6	4.8	4.9	5.0	5.2	5.3	5.4	5.6	5.7	5.8	5.9	6.0	6.1	6.2	6.4	6.5	6.6	6.7	6.8
93	0.4	0.9	1.3	1.6	1.9	2.2	2.5	2.7	2.9	3.1	3.3	3.5	3.7	3.9	4.0	4.2	4.4	4.5	4.7	4.8	4.9	5.1	5.2	5.3	5.5	5.6	5.7	5.8	6.0	6.1	6.2	6.3	6.4	6.5	6.6	6.8	6.9	7.0	7.1
92	0.7	1.2	1.6	1.9	2.2	2.5	2.8	3.0	3.2	3.4	3.6	3.8	4.0	4.2	4.3	4.5	4.7	4.8	5.0	5.1	5.2	5.4	5.5	5.6	5.8	5.9	6.0	6.2	6.3	6.4	6.5	6.6	6.7	6.8	7.0	7.1	7.2	7.3	7.4
91	1.0	1.5	1.9	2.2	2.5	2.8	3.1	3.3	3.5	3.7	3.9	4.1	4.3	4.5	4.6	4.8	5.0	5.1	5.3	5.4	5.6	5.7	5.8	6.0	6.1	6.2	6.3	6.5	6.6	6.7	6.8	6.9	7.0	7.2	7.3	7.4	7.5	7.6	7.7
90	1.3	1.8	2.2	2.6	2.9	3.1	3.4	3.6	3.8	4.1	4.2	4.4	4.6	4.8	5.0	5.1	5.3	5.4	5.6	5.7	5.9	6.0	6.1	6.3	6.4	6.5	6.7	6.8	6.9	7.0	7.1	7.2	7.4	7.5	7.6	7.7	7.8	7.9	8.0
89	1.5	1.6	2.0	2.4	2.7	3.2	3.5	3.7	4.0	4.2	4.4	4.6	4.8	5.0	5.2	5.3	5.6	5.7	5.9	6.1	6.3	6.4	6.5	6.7	6.9	7.1	7.4	7.6	7.8	7.9	8.0	8.1	8.3	8.4	8.5	8.6	8.7	8.8	8.9
88	2.2	2.5	2.7	2.9	3.1	3.4	3.6	3.8	4.1	4.3	4.5	4.7	5.0	5.2	5.4	5.6	5.9	6.1	6.3	6.6	6.8	7.0	7.2	7.5	7.7	7.9	8.2	8.4	8.6	8.8	8.9	9.0	9.2	9.3	9.4	9.5	9.6	9.7	9.8
87	3.2	3.4	3.7	3.9	4.1	4.3	4.5	4.8	5.0	5.2	5.4	5.6	5.9	6.1	6.3	6.5	6.7	7.0	7.2	7.4	7.6	7.8	8.1	8.3	8.5	8.7	8.9	9.2	9.4	9.6	9.8	9.9	10.1	10.2	10.3	10.4	10.5	10.6	10.7
86	4.2	4.4	4.6	4.8	5.1	5.3	5.5	5.7	5.9	6.1	6.3	6.5	6.8	7.0	7.2	7.4	7.6	7.8	8.0	8.2	8.5	8.7	8.9	9.1	9.3	9.5	9.7	9.9	10.2	10.4	10.6	10.8	11.0	11.1	11.2	11.3	11.4	11.5	11.6
85	5.2	5.4	5.6	5.8	6.0	6.2	6.4	6.6	6.8	7.0	7.2	7.5	7.7	7.9	8.1	8.3	8.5	8.7	8.9	9.1	9.3	9.5	9.7	9.9	10.1	10.3	10.5	10.7	10.9	11.1	11.3	11.5	11.7	11.9	12.1	10.2	12.3	12.4	12.5
84	6.2	6.4	6.6	6.8	7.0	7.2	7.4	7.6	7.8	8.0	8.2	8.4	8.6	8.8	8.9	9.1	9.3	9.5	9.7	9.9	10.1	10.3	10.5	10.7	10.9	11.1	11.3	11.5	11.7	11.9	12.1	12.3	12.5	12.7	12.9	13.1	13.2	13.3	13.4
83	7.2	7.4	7.6	7.8	7.9	8.1	8.3	8.5	8.7	8.9	9.1	9.3	9.5	9.6	9.8	10.0	10.2	10.4	10.6	10.8	11.0	11.1	11.3	11.5	11.7	11.9	12.1	12.3	12.5	12.7	12.8	13.0	13.2	13.4	13.6	13.8	14.0	14.2	14.3
82	8.2	8.4	8.5	8.7	8.9	9.1	9.3	9.4	9.6	9.8	9.9	10.2	10.4	10.5	10.7	10.9	11.1	11.3	11.4	11.6	11.8	12.0	12.2	12.3	12.5	12.7	12.9	13.1	13.2	13.4	13.6	13.8	14.0	14.1	14.3	14.5	14.7	14.9	15.1
81	9.2	9.3	9.5	9.7	9.9	10.0	10.2	10.4	10.6	10.7	10.9	11.1	11.2	11.4	11.6	11.8	11.9	12.1	12.3	12.5	12.6	12.8	13.0	13.2	13.3	13.5	13.7	13.8	14.0	14.2	14.4	14.5	14.7	14.9	15.1	15.2	15.4	15.6	15.7
80	10.2	10.3	10.5	10.7	10.8	11.0	11.2	11.3	11.5	11.7	11.8	12.0	12.1	12.3	12.5	12.6	12.8	13.0	13.1	13.3	13.5	13.6	13.8	14.0	14.1	14.3	14.5	14.6	14.8	15.0	15.1	15.3	15.4	15.6	15.8	15.9	16.1	16.3	16.4
79	11.2	11.3	11.5	11.6	11.8	11.9	12.1	12.3	12.4	12.6	12.7	12.9	13.0	13.2	13.4	13.5	13.7	13.8	14.0	14.1	14.3	14.5	14.6	14.8	14.9	15.1	15.2	15.4	15.6	15.7	15.9	16.0	16.2	16.3	16.5	16.7	16.8	17.0	17.1
78	12.1	12.3	12.4	12.6	12.7	12.9	13.0	13.2	13.3	13.5	13.6	13.8	13.9	14.1	14.2	14.4	14.5	14.7	14.8	15.0	15.1	15.3	15.4	15.6	15.7	15.9	16.0	16.2	16.3	16.5	16.6	16.8	16.9	17.1	17.2	17.4	17.5	17.7	17.8
77	13.1	13.3	13.4	13.6	13.7	13.8	14.0	14.1	14.3	14.4	14.6	14.7	14.8	15.0	15.1	15.3	15.4	15.5	15.7	15.8	16.0	16.1	16.3	16.4	16.5	16.7	16.8	17.0	17.1	17.2	17.4	17.5	17.7	17.8	18.0	18.1	18.2	18.4	18.5
76	14.1	14.3	14.4	14.5	14.7	14.8	14.9	15.1	15.2	15.3	15.5	15.6	15.7	15.9	16.0	16.1	16.3	16.4	16.5	16.7	16.8	16.9	17.1	17.2	17.3	17.5	17.6	17.7	17.9	18.0	18.1	18.3	18.4	18.5	18.7	18.8	19.0	19.1	19.2
75	15.1	15.3	15.4	15.5	15.6	15.8	15.9	16.0	16.1	16.3	16.4	16.5	16.6	16.8	16.9	17.0	17.1	17.3	17.4	17.5	17.6	17.8	17.9	18.0	18.1	18.3	18.4	18.5	18.7	18.8	18.9	19.0	19.2	19.3	19.4	19.5	19.7	19.8	19.9
74	16.1	16.2	16.4	16.5	16.6	16.7	16.8	16.9	17.1	17.2	17.3	17.4	17.5	17.7	17.8	17.9	18.0	18.1	18.2	18.4	18.5	18.6	18.7	18.8	19.0	19.1	19.2	19.3	19.4	19.5	19.7	19.8	19.9	20.0	20.1	20.3	20.4	20.5	20.6
73	17.1	17.2	17.3	17.4	17.6	17.7	17.8	17.9	18.0	18.1	18.2	18.3	18.4	18.5	18.7	18.8	18.9	19.0	19.1	19.2	19.3	19.4	19.5	19.6	19.8	19.9	19.9	20.1	20.2	20.3	20.4	20.5	20.6	20.8	20.9	21.0	21.1	21.2	21.3
72	18.1	18.2	18.3	18.4	18.5	18.6	18.7	18.8	18.9	19.0	19.1	19.2	19.3	19.4	19.5	19.6	19.7	19.8	19.9	20.0	20.2	20.3	20.4	20.5	20.6	20.7	20.8	20.9	21.0	21.1	21.2	21.3	21.4	21.5	21.6	21.7	21.8	21.9	22.0
71	19.1	19.2	19.3	19.4	19.5	19.6	19.7	19.8	19.9	19.9	20.0	20.1	20.2	20.3	20.4	20.5	20.6	20.7	20.8	20.9	21.0	21.1	21.2	21.3	21.4	21.5	21.6	21.6	21.7	21.8	21.9	22.0	22.1	22.2	22.3	22.4	22.5	22.6	22.7
70	20.1	20.2	20.3	20.3	20.4	20.5	20.6	20.7	20.8	20.9	21.0	21.0	21.1	21.2	21.3	21.4	21.5	21.6	21.6	21.7	21.8	21.9	22.0	22.1	22.2	22.3	22.3	22.4	22.5	22.6	22.7	22.8	22.9	23.0	23.0	23.1	23.2	23.3	23.4
69	21.1	21.2	21.2	21.3	21.4	21.5	21.6	21.6	21.7	21.8	21.9	21.9	22.0	22.1	22.2	22.3	22.3	22.4	22.5	22.6	22.7	22.7	22.8	22.9	23.0	23.1	23.1	23.2	23.3	23.4	23.4	23.5	23.6	23.7	23.8	23.8	23.9	24.0	24.1
68	22.1	22.1	22.2	22.3	22.4	22.4	22.5	22.6	22.6	22.7	22.8	22.9	22.9	23.0	23.1	23.1	23.2	23.3	23.4	23.4	23.5	23.6	23.6	23.7	23.8	23.8	23.9	24.0	24.1	24.1	24.2	24.3	24.3	24.4	24.5	24.6	24.6	24.7	24.8
67	23.1	23.1	23.2	23.3	23.3	23.4	23.4	23.5	23.6	23.6	23.7	23.8	23.8	23.9	23.9	24.0	24.1	24.1	24.2	24.3	24.3	24.4	24.5	24.5	24.6	24.6	24.7	24.8	24.8	24.9	25.0	25.0	25.1	25.2	25.2	25.3	25.3	25.4	25.5
66	24.1	24.1	24.2	24.2	24.3	24.3	24.4	24.4	24.5	24.6	24.6	24.7	24.7	24.8	24.8	24.9	24.9	25.0	25.1	25.1	25.2	25.2	25.3	25.3	25.4	25.4	25.5	25.6	25.6	25.7	25.7	25.8	25.8	25.9	25.9	26.0	26.1	26.1	26.2
65	25.0	25.1	25.1	25.2	25.2	25.3	25.3	25.4	25.4	25.5	25.5	25.6	25.6	25.7	25.7	25.8	25.8	25.9	25.9	26.0	26.0	26.0	26.1	26.1	26.2	26.2	26.3	26.3	26.4	26.4	26.5	26.5	26.6	26.6	26.7	26.7	26.8	26.8	26.9
64	26.0	26.1	26.1	26.2	26.2	26.2	26.3	26.3	26.4	26.4	26.4	26.5	26.5	26.6	26.6	26.6	26.7	26.7	26.8	26.8	26.8	26.9	26.9	27.0	27.0	27.0	27.1	27.1	27.2	27.2	27.2	27.3	27.3	27.4	27.4	27.4	27.5	27.5	27.6

LISTED PUT OPTION PRICE WHEN EXERCISE PRICE IS 100

NUMBER OF WEEKS BEFORE THE OPTION EXPIRES

Common Stock Price	1	2	3	4	5	6	7	8	9	10	11	12	13	14	15	16	17	18	19	20	21	22	23	24	25	26	27	28	29	30	31	32	33	34	35	36	37	38	39
130	0.0	0.0	0.0	0.0	0.0	0.0	0.0	0.0	0.0	0.0	0.0	0.0	0.0	0.0	0.0	0.0	0.0	0.0	0.0	0.0	0.0	0.0	0.0	0.0	0.0	0.0	0.0	0.1	0.3	0.4	0.5	0.7	0.8	0.9	1.0	1.2	1.3	1.4	1.5
128	0.0	0.0	0.0	0.0	0.0	0.0	0.0	0.0	0.0	0.0	0.0	0.0	0.0	0.0	0.0	0.0	0.0	0.0	0.0	0.0	0.0	0.0	0.0	0.0	0.1	0.3	0.4	0.5	0.7	0.8	0.9	1.1	1.2	1.3	1.4	1.5	1.7	1.8	1.9
126	0.0	0.0	0.0	0.0	0.0	0.0	0.0	0.0	0.0	0.0	0.0	0.0	0.0	0.0	0.0	0.0	0.0	0.0	0.0	0.0	0.0	0.1	0.2	0.4	0.5	0.7	0.8	0.9	1.1	1.2	1.3	1.4	1.6	1.7	1.8	1.9	2.1	2.2	2.3
124	0.0	0.0	0.0	0.0	0.0	0.0	0.0	0.0	0.0	0.0	0.0	0.0	0.0	0.0	0.0	0.0	0.0	0.0	0.0	0.2	0.3	0.5	0.6	0.8	0.9	1.1	1.2	1.3	1.5	1.6	1.7	1.9	2.0	2.1	2.2	2.3	2.5	2.6	2.7
122	0.0	0.0	0.0	0.0	0.0	0.0	0.0	0.0	0.0	0.0	0.0	0.0	0.0	0.0	0.0	0.0	0.1	0.3	0.4	0.6	0.8	0.9	1.1	1.2	1.3	1.5	1.6	1.8	1.9	2.0	2.2	2.3	2.4	2.5	2.6	2.8	2.9	3.0	3.1
120	0.0	0.0	0.0	0.0	0.0	0.0	0.0	0.0	0.0	0.0	0.0	0.0	0.0	0.0	0.2	0.4	0.5	0.7	0.9	1.0	1.2	1.3	1.5	1.6	1.8	1.9	2.1	2.2	2.3	2.5	2.6	2.7	2.8	3.0	3.1	3.2	3.3	3.4	3.6
118	0.0	0.0	0.0	0.0	0.0	0.0	0.0	0.0	0.0	0.0	0.0	0.0	0.3	0.4	0.6	0.8	1.0	1.2	1.3	1.5	1.6	1.8	1.9	2.1	2.2	2.4	2.5	2.6	2.8	2.9	3.0	3.2	3.3	3.4	3.5	3.7	3.8	3.9	4.0
116	0.0	0.0	0.0	0.0	0.0	0.0	0.0	0.0	0.0	0.1	0.3	0.5	0.7	0.9	1.1	1.3	1.5	1.6	1.8	2.0	2.1	2.3	2.4	2.6	2.7	2.8	3.0	3.1	3.3	3.4	3.5	3.6	3.8	3.9	4.0	4.1	4.2	4.4	4.5
114	0.0	0.0	0.0	0.0	0.0	0.0	0.0	0.1	0.3	0.6	0.8	1.0	1.2	1.4	1.6	1.8	1.9	2.1	2.3	2.4	2.6	2.7	2.9	3.0	3.2	3.3	3.5	3.6	3.7	3.9	4.0	4.1	4.2	4.4	4.5	4.6	4.7	4.8	5.0
112	0.0	0.0	0.0	0.0	0.0	0.1	0.3	0.6	0.8	1.1	1.3	1.5	1.7	1.9	2.1	2.3	2.4	2.6	2.8	2.9	3.1	3.2	3.4	3.5	3.7	3.8	4.0	4.1	4.2	4.4	4.5	4.6	4.7	4.9	5.0	5.1	5.2	5.3	5.5
110	0.0	0.0	0.0	0.0	0.3	0.6	0.9	1.1	1.4	1.6	1.8	2.0	2.2	2.4	2.6	2.8	3.0	3.1	3.3	3.5	3.6	3.8	3.9	4.1	4.2	4.3	4.5	4.6	4.8	4.9	5.0	5.1	5.3	5.4	5.5	5.6	5.7	5.9	6.0
108	0.0	0.0	0.1	0.5	0.8	1.1	1.4	1.7	1.9	2.1	2.3	2.6	2.8	3.0	3.1	3.3	3.5	3.7	3.8	4.0	4.2	4.3	4.5	4.6	4.7	4.9	5.0	5.2	5.3	5.4	5.6	5.7	5.8	5.9	6.0	6.2	6.3	6.4	6.5
106	0.0	0.2	0.7	1.0	1.4	1.7	2.0	2.2	2.5	2.7	2.9	3.1	3.3	3.5	3.7	3.9	4.1	4.2	4.4	4.6	4.7	4.9	5.0	5.2	5.3	5.4	5.6	5.7	5.9	6.0	6.1	6.2	6.4	6.5	6.6	6.7	6.8	7.0	7.1
104	0.2	0.8	1.2	1.6	2.0	2.3	2.5	2.8	3.0	3.3	3.5	3.7	3.9	4.1	4.3	4.5	4.6	4.8	5.0	5.1	5.3	5.4	5.6	5.7	5.9	6.0	6.2	6.3	6.4	6.6	6.7	6.8	6.9	7.1	7.2	7.3	7.4	7.5	7.7
102	0.8	1.4	1.8	2.2	2.6	2.9	3.1	3.4	3.6	3.9	4.1	4.3	4.5	4.7	4.9	5.1	5.2	5.4	5.6	5.7	5.9	6.0	6.2	6.3	6.5	6.6	6.8	6.9	7.0	7.2	7.3	7.4	7.5	7.7	7.8	7.9	8.0	8.1	8.3
100	1.4	2.0	2.5	2.8	3.2	3.5	3.8	4.0	4.3	4.5	4.7	4.9	5.1	5.3	5.5	5.7	5.9	6.0	6.2	6.4	6.5	6.7	6.8	7.0	7.1	7.3	7.4	7.5	7.7	7.8	7.9	8.1	8.2	8.3	8.4	8.5	8.7	8.8	8.9
99	1.6	2.2	2.7	2.9	3.3	3.6	4.0	4.2	4.5	4.8	5.0	5.1	5.4	5.6	5.8	6.0	6.2	6.4	6.6	6.8	6.9	7.1	7.2	7.3	7.6	7.8	8.1	8.4	8.6	8.7	8.8	9.0	9.1	9.2	9.3	9.4	9.6	9.7	9.8
98	2.3	2.5	2.8	3.0	3.4	3.8	4.2	4.4	4.7	5.1	5.3	5.5	5.8	6.0	6.2	6.4	6.6	6.8	7.0	7.1	7.4	7.6	7.9	8.1	8.4	8.6	8.9	9.1	9.4	9.6	9.7	9.9	10.0	10.1	10.2	10.3	10.5	10.6	10.7
97	3.2	3.5	3.7	4.0	4.2	4.5	4.7	5.0	5.2	5.5	5.7	6.0	6.2	6.5	6.7	7.0	7.2	7.4	7.7	7.9	8.2	8.4	8.7	8.9	9.2	9.4	9.7	9.9	10.2	10.4	10.6	10.8	10.9	11.0	11.1	11.2	11.4	11.5	11.6
96	4.2	4.5	4.7	5.0	5.2	5.4	5.7	5.9	6.2	6.4	6.6	6.9	7.1	7.3	7.6	7.8	8.1	8.3	8.5	8.8	9.0	9.3	9.5	9.7	9.9	10.2	10.5	10.7	10.9	11.2	11.4	11.7	11.8	11.9	12.0	12.1	12.3	12.4	12.5
95	5.2	5.5	5.7	5.9	6.2	6.4	6.6	6.9	7.1	7.3	7.5	7.8	8.0	8.2	8.5	8.7	8.9	9.2	9.4	9.6	9.9	10.1	10.3	10.6	10.8	11.0	11.2	11.5	11.7	11.9	12.2	12.4	12.6	12.8	12.9	13.0	13.2	13.3	13.4
94	6.2	6.4	6.7	6.9	7.1	7.3	7.6	7.8	8.0	8.2	8.5	8.7	8.9	9.1	9.4	9.6	9.8	10.0	10.2	10.5	10.7	10.9	11.1	11.4	11.6	11.8	12.0	12.3	12.5	12.7	12.9	13.2	13.4	13.6	13.8	14.1	14.1	14.2	14.3
93	7.2	7.4	7.6	7.9	8.1	8.3	8.5	8.7	8.9	9.2	9.4	9.6	9.8	10.0	10.2	10.5	10.7	10.9	11.1	11.3	11.5	11.7	12.0	12.2	12.4	12.6	12.8	13.0	13.3	13.5	13.7	13.9	14.1	14.3	14.5	14.8	15.0	15.1	15.2
92	8.2	8.4	8.6	8.8	9.0	9.2	9.5	9.7	9.9	10.1	10.3	10.5	10.7	10.9	11.1	11.3	11.5	11.7	11.9	12.2	12.4	12.6	12.8	13.0	13.2	13.4	13.6	13.8	14.0	14.2	14.4	14.7	14.9	15.1	15.3	15.5	15.7	15.9	16.1
91	9.2	9.4	9.6	9.8	10.0	10.2	10.4	10.6	10.8	11.0	11.2	11.4	11.6	11.8	12.0	12.2	12.4	12.6	12.8	13.0	13.2	13.4	13.6	13.8	14.0	14.2	14.4	14.6	14.8	15.0	15.2	15.4	15.6	15.8	16.0	16.2	16.4	16.6	16.8
90	10.2	10.4	10.6	10.8	11.0	11.2	11.3	11.5	11.7	11.9	12.1	12.3	12.5	12.7	12.9	13.1	13.3	13.5	13.7	13.8	14.0	14.2	14.4	14.6	14.8	15.0	15.2	15.4	15.6	15.8	16.0	16.1	16.3	16.5	16.7	16.9	17.1	17.3	17.5
89	11.2	11.4	11.6	11.7	11.9	12.1	12.3	12.5	12.7	12.8	13.0	13.2	13.4	13.6	13.8	13.9	14.1	14.3	14.5	14.7	14.9	15.1	15.2	15.4	15.6	15.8	16.0	16.2	16.3	16.5	16.7	16.9	17.1	17.3	17.5	17.6	17.8	18.0	18.2
88	12.2	12.4	12.5	12.7	12.9	13.1	13.2	13.4	13.6	13.8	13.9	14.1	14.3	14.5	14.6	14.8	15.0	15.2	15.4	15.5	15.7	15.9	16.1	16.2	16.4	16.6	16.8	16.9	17.1	17.3	17.5	17.6	17.8	18.0	18.2	18.4	18.5	18.7	18.9
87	13.2	13.3	13.5	13.7	13.8	14.0	14.2	14.3	14.5	14.7	14.9	15.0	15.2	15.4	15.5	15.7	15.9	16.0	16.2	16.4	16.5	16.7	16.9	17.0	17.2	17.4	17.6	17.7	17.9	18.1	18.2	18.4	18.6	18.7	18.9	19.1	19.2	19.4	19.6
86	14.2	14.3	14.5	14.6	14.8	15.0	15.1	15.3	15.4	15.6	15.8	15.9	16.1	16.3	16.4	16.6	16.7	16.9	17.1	17.2	17.4	17.5	17.7	17.9	18.0	18.2	18.3	18.5	19.7	18.8	19.0	19.1	19.3	19.5	19.6	19.8	19.9	20.1	20.3
85	15.2	15.3	15.5	15.6	15.8	15.9	16.1	16.2	16.4	16.5	16.7	16.8	17.0	17.1	17.3	17.4	17.6	17.8	17.9	18.1	18.2	18.4	18.5	18.7	18.8	19.0	19.1	19.3	19.4	19.6	19.7	19.9	20.0	20.2	20.4	20.5	20.7	20.8	21.0
84	16.1	16.3	16.4	16.6	16.7	16.9	17.0	17.2	71.3	17.5	17.6	17.7	17.9	18.0	18.2	18.3	18.5	18.6	18.8	18.9	19.0	19.2	19.3	19.5	19.6	19.8	19.9	20.1	20.2	20.4	20.5	20.6	20.8	20.9	21.1	21.2	21.4	21.5	21.7
83	17.1	17.3	17.4	17.5	17.7	17.8	18.0	18.1	18.2	18.4	18.5	18.6	18.8	18.9	19.1	19.2	19.3	19.5	19.6	19.7	19.9	20.0	20.2	20.3	20.4	20.6	20.7	20.8	21.0	21.1	21.3	21.4	21.5	21.7	21.8	21.9	22.1	22.2	22.4
82	18.1	18.3	18.4	18.5	18.6	18.8	18.9	19.0	19.2	19.3	19.4	19.6	19.7	19.8	19.9	20.1	20.2	20.3	20.5	20.6	20.7	20.8	21.0	21.1	21.2	21.4	21.5	21.6	21.8	21.9	22.0	22.1	22.3	22.4	22.5	22.7	22.8	22.9	23.1
81	19.1	19.2	19.4	19.5	19.6	19.7	19.9	19.9	20.1	20.2	20.3	20.5	20.6	20.7	20.8	20.9	21.1	21.2	21.3	21.4	21.6	21.7	21.8	21.9	22.0	22.2	22.3	22.4	22.5	22.7	22.8	22.9	23.0	23.1	23.3	23.4	23.5	23.6	23.7
80	20.1	20.2	20.3	20.5	20.6	20.7	20.8	20.9	21.0	21.1	21.3	21.4	21.5	21.6	21.7	21.8	21.9	22.0	22.2	22.3	22.4	22.5	22.6	22.7	22.8	23.0	23.1	23.2	23.3	23.4	23.5	23.6	23.8	23.9	24.0	24.1	24.2	24.3	24.4
79	21.1	21.2	21.3	21.4	21.5	21.6	21.7	21.8	22.0	22.1	22.2	22.3	22.4	22.5	22.6	22.7	22.8	22.9	23.0	23.1	23.2	23.3	23.4	23.5	23.7	23.8	23.9	24.0	24.1	24.2	24.3	24.4	24.5	24.6	24.7	24.8	24.9	25.0	25.1
78	22.1	22.2	22.3	22.4	22.5	22.6	22.7	22.8	22.9	23.0	23.1	23.2	23.3	23.4	23.5	23.6	23.7	23.8	23.9	24.0	24.1	24.2	24.3	24.4	24.5	24.6	24.7	24.7	24.8	24.9	25.0	25.2	25.2	25.3	25.4	25.5	25.6	25.7	25.8
77	23.1	23.2	23.3	23.4	23.5	23.5	23.6	23.7	23.8	23.9	24.0	24.1	24.2	24.3	24.4	24.4	24.5	24.6	24.7	24.8	24.9	25.0	25.1	25.2	25.3	25.3	25.4	25.5	25.6	25.7	25.8	25.9	26.0	26.1	26.2	26.3	26.3	26.4	26.5
76	24.1	24.2	24.2	24.3	24.4	24.5	24.6	24.7	24.7	24.8	24.9	25.0	25.1	25.2	25.2	25.3	25.4	25.5	25.6	25.7	25.7	25.8	25.9	26.0	26.1	26.1	26.2	26.3	26.4	26.5	26.6	26.6	26.7	26.8	26.9	27.0	27.1	27.1	27.2
75	25.1	25.1	25.2	25.3	25.4	25.4	25.5	25.6	25.7	25.7	25.8	25.9	26.0	26.0	26.1	26.2	26.3	26.3	26.4	26.5	26.6	26.6	26.7	26.8	26.9	26.9	27.0	27.1	27.2	27.2	27.3	27.4	27.5	27.5	27.6	27.7	27.8	27.8	27.9
74	26.1	26.1	26.2	26.3	26.3	26.4	26.5	26.5	26.6	26.7	26.7	26.8	26.9	26.9	27.0	27.1	27.1	27.2	27.3	27.3	27.6	27.5	27.5	27.6	27.7	27.7	27.8	27.9	27.9	28.0	28.1	28.1	28.2	28.3	28.3	28.4	28.5	28.5	28.6
73	27.1	27.1	27.2	27.2	27.3	27.4	27.4	27.5	27.5	27.6	27.6	27.7	27.8	27.8	27.9	27.9	28.0	28.1	28.1	28.2	28.2	28.3	28.4	28.4	28.5	28.5	28.6	28.7	28.7	28.8	28.8	28.9	28.9	29.0	29.1	29.1	29.2	29.2	29.3
72	28.1	28.1	28.2	28.2	28.3	28.3	28.4	28.4	28.5	28.5	28.6	28.6	28.7	28.7	28.8	28.8	28.9	28.9	29.0	29.0	29.1	29.1	29.2	29.2	29.3	29.3	29.4	29.4	29.5	29.5	29.6	29.6	29.7	29.7	29.8	29.8	29.9	29.9	29.9
71	29.0	29.1	29.1	29.2	29.2	29.3	29.3	29.3	29.4	29.4	29.5	29.5	29.6	29.6	29.7	29.7	29.7	29.8	29.8	29.9	29.9	29.9	29.9	30.0	30.1	30.1	30.2	30.2	30.3	30.3	30.3	30.4	30.4	30.5	30.5	30.6	30.6	30.6	30.7
70	30.0	30.1	30.1	30.1	30.2	30.2	30.2	30.3	30.3	30.4	30.4	30.4	30.5	30.5	30.5	30.6	30.6	30.6	30.7	30.7	30.7	30.8	30.8	30.9	30.9	30.9	31.0	31.0	31.0	31.1	31.1	31.1	31.2	31.2	31.2	31.3	31.3	31.3	31.4

LISTED PUT OPTION PRICE WHEN EXERCISE PRICE IS 110

NUMBER OF WEEKS BEFORE THE OPTION EXPIRES

Common Stock Price	1	2	3	4	5	6	7	8	9	10	11	12	13	14	15	16	17	18	19	20	21	22	23	24	25	26	27	28	29	30	31	32	33	34	35	36	37	38	39
144	0.0	0.0	0.0	0.0	0.0	0.0	0.0	0.0	0.0	0.0	0.0	0.0	0.0	0.0	0.0	0.0	0.0	0.0	0.0	0.0	0.0	0.0	0.0	0.0	0.0	0.0	0.0	0.0	0.1	0.3	0.4	0.5	0.7	0.8	1.0	1.1	1.2	1.3	1.5
142	0.0	0.0	0.0	0.0	0.0	0.0	0.0	0.0	0.0	0.0	0.0	0.0	0.0	0.0	0.0	0.0	0.0	0.0	0.0	0.0	0.0	0.0	0.0	0.0	0.0	0.1	0.2	0.4	0.5	0.6	0.8	0.9	1.1	1.2	1.3	1.5	1.6	1.7	1.8
140	0.0	0.0	0.0	0.0	0.0	0.0	0.0	0.0	0.0	0.0	0.0	0.0	0.0	0.0	0.0	0.0	0.0	0.0	0.0	0.0	0.0	0.0	0.0	0.1	0.3	0.4	0.6	0.7	0.9	1.0	1.2	1.3	1.5	1.6	1.7	1.9	2.0	2.1	2.2
138	0.0	0.0	0.0	0.0	0.0	0.0	0.0	0.0	0.0	0.0	0.0	0.0	0.0	0.0	0.0	0.0	0.0	0.0	0.0	0.0	0.0	0.2	0.4	0.5	0.7	0.8	1.0	1.1	1.3	1.4	1.6	1.7	1.9	2.0	2.1	2.3	2.4	2.5	2.6
136	0.0	0.0	0.0	0.0	0.0	0.0	0.0	0.0	0.0	0.0	0.0	0.0	0.0	0.0	0.0	0.0	0.0	0.0	0.1	0.3	0.4	0.6	0.8	0.9	1.1	1.3	1.4	1.6	1.7	1.8	2.0	2.1	2.3	2.4	2.5	2.7	2.8	2.9	3.0
134	0.0	0.0	0.0	0.0	0.0	0.0	0.0	0.0	0.0	0.0	0.0	0.0	0.0	0.0	0.0	0.0	0.2	0.3	0.5	0.7	0.9	1.0	1.2	1.4	1.5	1.7	1.8	2.0	2.1	2.3	2.4	2.6	2.7	2.8	3.0	3.1	3.2	3.3	3.5
132	0.0	0.0	0.0	0.0	0.0	0.0	0.0	0.0	0.0	0.0	0.0	0.0	0.0	0.0	0.2	0.4	0.6	0.8	1.0	1.1	1.3	1.5	1.6	1.8	2.0	2.1	2.3	2.4	2.6	2.7	2.8	3.0	3.1	3.3	3.4	3.5	3.7	3.8	3.9
130	0.0	0.0	0.0	0.0	0.0	0.0	0.0	0.0	0.0	0.0	0.0	0.0	0.2	0.4	0.6	0.8	1.0	1.2	1.4	1.6	1.8	1.9	2.1	2.3	2.4	2.6	2.7	2.9	3.0	3.2	3.3	3.4	3.6	3.7	3.8	4.0	4.1	4.2	4.4
128	0.0	0.0	0.0	0.0	0.0	0.0	0.0	0.0	0.0	0.0	0.2	0.5	0.7	0.9	1.1	1.3	1.5	1.7	1.9	2.1	2.2	2.4	2.6	2.7	2.9	3.0	3.2	3.3	3.5	3.6	3.8	3.9	4.0	4.2	4.3	4.4	4.6	4.7	4.8
126	0.0	0.0	0.0	0.0	0.0	0.0	0.0	0.0	0.2	0.5	0.7	1.0	1.2	1.4	1.6	1.8	2.0	2.2	2.4	2.5	2.7	2.9	3.0	3.2	3.4	3.5	3.7	3.8	4.0	4.1	4.2	4.4	4.5	4.7	4.8	4.9	5.1	5.2	5.3
124	0.0	0.0	0.0	0.0	0.0	0.0	0.2	0.5	0.7	1.0	1.2	1.4	1.7	1.9	2.1	2.3	2.5	2.7	2.8	3.0	3.2	3.4	3.5	3.7	3.9	4.0	4.2	4.3	4.5	4.6	4.7	4.9	5.0	5.2	5.3	5.4	5.5	5.7	5.8
122	0.0	0.0	0.0	0.0	0.0	0.4	0.7	1.0	1.2	1.5	1.7	2.0	2.2	2.4	2.6	2.8	3.0	3.2	3.4	3.5	3.7	3.9	4.0	4.2	4.4	4.5	4.7	4.8	5.0	5.1	5.3	5.4	5.5	5.7	5.8	5.9	6.1	6.2	6.3
120	0.0	0.0	0.0	0.2	0.6	0.9	1.2	1.5	1.8	2.0	2.3	2.5	2.7	2.9	3.1	3.3	3.5	3.7	3.9	4.1	4.2	4.4	4.6	4.7	4.9	5.0	5.2	5.4	5.5	5.6	5.8	5.9	6.1	6.2	6.3	6.5	6.6	6.7	6.8
118	0.0	0.0	0.3	0.7	1.1	1.4	1.8	2.0	2.3	2.6	2.8	3.0	3.3	3.5	3.7	3.9	4.1	4.3	4.4	4.6	4.8	5.0	5.1	5.3	5.4	5.6	5.7	5.9	6.0	6.2	6.3	6.5	6.6	6.7	6.9	7.0	7.1	7.3	7.4
116	0.0	0.4	0.9	1.3	1.7	2.0	2.3	2.6	2.9	3.1	3.4	3.6	3.8	4.0	4.2	4.4	4.6	4.8	5.0	5.2	5.4	5.5	5.7	5.8	6.0	6.2	6.3	6.5	6.6	6.8	6.9	7.0	7.2	7.3	7.4	7.6	7.7	7.8	8.0
114	0.3	1.0	1.5	1.9	2.3	2.6	2.9	3.2	3.5	3.7	4.0	4.2	4.4	4.6	4.8	5.0	5.2	5.4	5.6	5.8	5.9	6.1	6.3	6.4	6.6	6.7	6.9	7.0	7.2	7.3	7.5	7.6	7.8	7.9	8.0	8.2	8.3	8.4	8.5
112	0.9	1.6	2.1	2.5	2.9	3.2	3.5	3.8	4.1	4.3	4.6	4.8	5.0	5.2	5.4	5.6	5.8	6.0	6.2	6.4	6.5	6.7	6.9	7.0	7.2	7.4	7.5	7.7	7.8	7.9	8.1	8.2	8.4	8.5	8.6	8.8	8.9	9.0	9.1
110	1.6	2.2	2.7	3.1	3.5	3.8	4.1	4.4	4.7	5.0	5.2	5.4	5.6	5.9	6.1	6.3	6.5	6.6	6.8	7.0	7.2	7.3	7.5	7.7	7.8	8.0	8.1	8.3	8.4	8.6	8.7	8.9	9.0	9.1	9.3	9.4	9.5	9.7	9.8
108	2.3	2.6	3.0	3.3	3.7	4.0	4.3	4.6	4.9	5.2	5.5	5.7	6.0	6.4	6.6	6.8	7.0	7.2	7.4	7.6	7.9	8.2	8.5	8.8	9.0	9.3	9.6	9.9	10.2	10.4	10.5	10.7	10.8	10.9	11.1	11.2	11.3	11.5	11.6
106	4.3	4.5	4.8	5.1	5.3	5.6	5.9	6.1	6.4	6.7	6.9	7.2	7.5	7.7	8.0	8.3	8.5	8.8	9.1	9.3	9.6	9.9	10.1	10.4	10.7	10.9	11.2	11.5	11.7	12.0	12.3	12.5	12.6	12.7	12.8	12.9	13.1	13.3	13.4
104	6.3	6.5	6.8	7.0	7.3	7.5	7.8	8.0	8.3	8.5	8.8	9.0	9.3	9.5	9.8	10.0	10.3	10.5	10.8	11.0	11.3	11.5	11.8	12.0	12.3	12.5	12.8	13.0	13.3	13.5	13.8	14.0	14.3	14.5	14.6	14.7	14.9	15.1	15.2
102	8.2	8.5	8.7	8.9	9.2	9.4	9.6	9.9	10.1	10.3	10.6	10.8	11.1	11.3	11.5	11.8	12.0	12.2	12.5	12.7	12.9	13.2	13.4	13.6	13.9	14.1	14.3	14.6	14.8	15.0	15.3	15.5	15.8	16.0	16.2	16.5	16.7	16.9	17.0
100	10.2	10.4	10.7	10.9	11.1	11.3	11.5	11.8	12.0	12.2	12.4	12.6	12.8	13.1	13.3	13.5	13.7	13.9	14.2	14.4	14.6	14.8	15.0	15.3	15.5	15.7	15.9	16.1	16.4	16.6	16.8	17.0	17.2	17.5	17.7	17.9	18.1	18.3	18.5
99	11.2	11.4	11.6	11.8	12.1	12.3	12.5	12.7	12.9	13.1	13.3	13.5	13.7	14.0	14.2	14.4	14.6	14.8	15.0	15.2	15.4	15.7	15.9	16.1	16.3	16.5	16.7	16.9	17.1	17.3	17.6	17.8	18.0	18.2	18.4	18.6	18.8	19.0	19.2
98	12.2	12.4	12.6	12.8	13.0	13.2	13.4	13.6	13.8	14.0	14.2	14.4	14.6	14.8	15.1	15.3	15.5	15.7	15.9	16.1	16.3	16.5	16.7	16.9	17.1	17.3	17.5	17.7	17.9	18.1	18.3	18.5	18.7	18.9	19.1	19.3	19.5	19.7	19.9
97	13.2	13.4	13.6	13.8	14.0	14.2	14.4	14.6	14.8	15.0	15.2	15.3	15.5	15.7	15.9	16.1	16.3	16.5	16.7	16.9	17.1	17.3	17.5	17.7	17.9	18.1	18.3	18.5	18.7	18.9	19.1	19.3	19.5	19.7	19.9	20.0	20.2	20.4	20.6
96	14.2	14.4	14.6	14.8	14.9	15.1	15.3	15.5	15.7	15.9	16.1	16.3	16.4	16.6	16.8	17.0	17.2	17.4	17.6	17.8	17.9	18.1	18.3	18.5	18.7	18.9	19.1	19.3	19.4	19.6	19.8	20.0	20.2	20.4	20.6	20.8	21.0	21.1	21.3
95	15.2	15.4	15.5	15.7	15.9	16.1	16.3	16.4	16.6	16.8	17.0	17.2	17.3	17.5	17.7	17.9	18.1	18.2	18.4	18.6	18.8	19.0	19.1	19.3	19.5	19.7	19.9	20.0	20.2	20.4	20.6	20.8	20.9	21.1	21.3	21.5	21.7	21.8	22.0
94	16.2	16.3	16.5	16.7	16.9	17.0	17.2	17.4	17.6	17.7	17.9	18.1	18.2	18.4	18.6	18.8	18.9	19.1	19.3	19.4	19.6	19.8	19.9	20.1	20.3	20.5	20.7	20.8	21.0	21.2	21.3	21.5	21.7	21.9	22.0	22.2	22.4	22.5	22.7
93	17.2	17.3	17.5	17.7	17.8	18.0	18.2	18.3	18.5	18.6	18.8	19.0	19.1	19.3	19.5	19.6	19.8	19.9	20.1	20.3	20.5	20.6	20.8	20.9	21.1	21.3	21.4	21.6	21.8	21.9	22.1	22.3	22.6	22.6	22.8	22.9	23.1	23.2	23.4
92	18.2	18.3	18.5	18.6	18.8	18.9	19.1	19.3	19.4	19.6	19.7	19.9	20.0	20.2	20.3	20.5	20.7	20.8	21.0	21.1	21.3	21.4	21.6	21.8	21.9	22.1	22.2	22.4	22.5	22.7	22.9	23.0	23.2	23.3	23.5	23.6	23.8	23.9	24.1
91	19.1	19.3	19.4	19.6	19.7	19.9	20.0	20.2	20.3	20.5	20.6	20.8	20.9	21.1	21.2	21.4	21.5	21.7	21.8	22.0	22.1	22.3	22.4	22.6	22.7	22.9	23.0	23.2	23.3	23.5	23.6	23.8	23.9	24.1	24.0	24.4	24.5	24.7	24.8
90	20.1	20.3	20.4	20.6	20.7	20.8	21.0	21.1	21.3	21.4	21.5	21.7	21.8	22.0	22.1	22.3	22.4	22.5	22.7	22.8	23.0	23.1	23.2	23.4	23.5	23.7	23.8	23.9	24.1	24.2	24.4	24.5	24.6	24.8	24.9	25.1	25.2	25.4	25.5
89	21.1	21.3	21.4	21.5	21.7	21.8	21.9	22.1	22.2	22.3	22.5	22.6	22.7	22.9	23.0	23.1	23.3	23.4	23.5	23.7	23.8	23.9	24.1	24.2	24.3	24.5	24.6	24.7	24.9	25.0	25.1	25.3	25.4	25.5	25.7	25.8	25.9	26.1	26.2
88	22.1	22.3	22.4	22.5	22.6	22.8	22.9	23.0	23.1	23.3	23.4	23.5	23.6	23.8	23.9	24.0	24.1	24.3	24.4	24.5	24.6	24.8	24.9	25.0	25.1	25.3	25.4	25.5	25.6	25.8	25.9	26.0	26.1	26.3	26.4	26.5	26.6	26.8	26.9
87	23.1	23.2	23.4	23.5	23.6	23.7	23.8	23.9	24.1	24.2	24.3	24.4	24.5	24.6	24.8	24.9	25.0	25.1	25.2	25.3	25.5	25.6	25.7	25.8	25.9	26.1	26.2	26.3	26.4	26.5	26.6	26.8	26.9	27.0	27.1	27.2	27.3	27.5	27.6
86	24.1	24.2	24.3	24.4	24.5	24.7	24.8	24.9	25.0	25.1	25.2	25.3	25.4	25.5	25.6	25.8	25.9	26.0	26.1	26.2	26.3	26.4	26.5	26.6	26.7	26.8	27.0	27.1	27.2	27.3	27.4	27.5	27.6	27.7	27.8	27.9	28.1	28.2	28.3
85	25.1	25.2	25.3	25.4	25.5	25.6	25.7	25.8	25.9	26.0	26.1	26.2	26.3	26.4	26.5	26.6	26.7	26.8	26.9	27.0	27.1	27.2	27.3	27.4	27.5	27.6	27.7	27.8	28.0	28.1	28.2	28.3	28.4	28.5	28.6	28.7	28.8	28.9	29.0
84	26.1	26.2	26.3	26.4	26.5	26.6	26.7	26.8	26.8	26.9	27.0	27.1	27.2	27.3	27.4	27.5	27.6	27.7	27.8	27.9	28.0	28.1	28.2	28.3	28.3	28.4	28.5	28.6	28.7	28.8	28.9	29.0	29.1	29.2	29.3	29.4	29.5	29.6	29.7
83	27.1	27.2	27.3	27.3	27.4	27.5	27.6	27.7	27.8	27.9	27.9	28.0	28.1	28.2	28.3	28.4	28.5	28.5	28.6	28.7	28.8	28.9	29.0	29.1	29.2	29.2	29.3	29.4	29.5	29.6	29.7	29.8	29.8	29.9	30.0	30.1	30.2	30.3	30.4
82	28.1	28.2	28.2	28.3	28.4	28.5	28.5	28.6	28.7	28.8	28.9	28.9	29.0	29.1	29.2	29.3	29.3	29.4	29.5	29.6	29.6	29.7	29.8	29.9	29.9	30.0	30.1	30.2	30.3	30.3	30.4	30.5	30.6	30.7	30.8	30.9	30.9	31.0	31.1
81	29.1	29.1	29.2	29.3	29.4	29.4	29.5	29.6	29.6	29.7	29.8	29.8	29.9	29.9	30.1	30.1	30.2	30.3	30.3	30.4	30.5	30.5	30.6	30.7	30.8	30.8	30.9	31.0	31.0	31.1	31.2	31.3	31.3	31.4	31.5	31.5	31.6	31.7	31.7
80	30.1	30.1	30.2	30.3	30.3	30.4	30.4	30.5	30.6	30.6	30.7	30.8	30.8	30.9	30.9	31.0	31.1	31.1	31.0	31.3	31.3	31.4	31.4	31.5	31.6	31.6	31.7	31.8	31.8	31.9	31.9	32.0	32.1	32.1	32.2	32.3	32.3	32.4	32.4
79	31.1	31.1	31.2	31.2	31.3	31.3	31.4	31.4	31.5	31.5	31.6	31.7	31.7	31.8	31.8	31.9	31.9	32.0	32.0	32.1	32.1	32.2	32.3	32.3	32.4	32.4	32.5	32.5	32.6	32.6	32.7	32.8	32.8	32.9	32.9	33.0	33.0	33.1	33.1
78	32.0	32.1	32.1	32.2	32.2	32.3	32.3	32.4	32.4	32.5	32.5	32.6	32.6	32.7	32.7	32.8	32.8	32.8	32.9	32.9	33.0	33.0	33.1	33.1	33.2	33.2	33.3	33.3	33.4	33.4	33.5	33.5	33.5	33.6	33.6	33.7	33.7	33.8	33.8
77	33.0	33.1	33.1	33.2	33.2	33.2	33.3	33.3	33.4	33.4	33.4	33.5	33.5	33.5	33.6	33.6	33.7	33.7	33.7	33.8	33.8	33.9	33.9	33.9	34.0	34.0	34.1	34.1	34.1	34.2	34.2	34.3	34.3	34.3	34.4	34.4	34.4	34.5	34.5

LISTED PUT OPTION PRICE WHEN EXERCISE PRICE IS 120

Common Stock Price	NUMBER OF WEEKS BEFORE THE OPTION EXPIRES																																						
	1	2	3	4	5	6	7	8	9	10	11	12	13	14	15	16	17	18	19	20	21	22	23	24	25	26	27	28	29	30	31	32	33	34	35	36	37	38	39
156	0.0	0.0	0.0	0.0	0.0	0.0	0.0	0.0	0.0	0.0	0.0	0.0	0.0	0.0	0.0	0.0	0.0	0.0	0.0	0.0	0.0	0.0	0.0	0.0	0.0	0.0	0.0	0.2	0.3	0.5	0.6	0.8	0.9	1.1	1.2	1.4	1.5	1.7	1.8
154	0.0	0.0	0.0	0.0	0.0	0.0	0.0	0.0	0.0	0.0	0.0	0.0	0.0	0.0	0.0	0.0	0.0	0.0	0.0	0.0	0.0	0.0	0.0	0.0	0.1	0.2	0.4	0.6	0.7	0.9	1.0	1.2	1.3	1.5	1.6	1.8	1.9	2.1	2.2
152	0.0	0.0	0.0	0.0	0.0	0.0	0.0	0.0	0.0	0.0	0.0	0.0	0.0	0.0	0.0	0.0	0.0	0.0	0.0	0.0	0.0	0.0	0.1	0.3	0.5	0.6	0.8	1.0	1.1	1.3	1.4	1.6	1.7	1.9	2.0	2.2	2.3	2.4	2.6
150	0.0	0.0	0.0	0.0	0.0	0.0	0.0	0.0	0.0	0.0	0.0	0.0	0.0	0.0	0.0	0.0	0.0	0.0	0.0	0.0	0.1	0.3	0.5	0.7	0.9	1.0	1.2	1.4	1.5	1.7	1.8	2.0	2.1	2.3	2.4	2.6	2.7	2.8	3.0
148	0.0	0.0	0.0	0.0	0.0	0.0	0.0	0.0	0.0	0.0	0.0	0.0	0.0	0.0	0.0	0.0	0.0	0.0	0.2	0.4	0.6	0.7	0.9	1.1	1.3	1.4	1.6	1.8	1.9	2.1	2.2	2.4	2.5	2.7	2.8	3.0	3.1	3.3	3.4
146	0.0	0.0	0.0	0.0	0.0	0.0	0.0	0.0	0.0	0.0	0.0	0.0	0.0	0.0	0.0	0.0	0.2	0.4	0.6	0.8	1.0	1.2	1.4	1.5	1.7	1.9	2.0	2.2	2.4	2.5	2.7	2.8	3.0	3.1	3.3	3.4	3.6	3.7	3.8
144	0.0	0.0	0.0	0.0	0.0	0.0	0.0	0.0	0.0	0.0	0.0	0.0	0.0	0.0	0.2	0.4	0.6	0.8	1.0	1.2	1.4	1.6	1.8	2.0	2.1	2.3	2.5	2.6	2.8	3.0	3.1	3.3	3.4	3.6	3.7	3.8	4.0	4.1	4.3
142	0.0	0.0	0.0	0.0	0.0.	0.0	0.0	0.0	0.0	0.0	0.0	0.0	0.2	0.4	0.7	0.9	1.1	1.3	1.5	1.7	1.9	2.1	2.2	2.4	2.6	2.8	2.9	3.1	3.2	3.4	3.6	3.7	3.9	4.0	4.2	4.3	4.4	4.6	4.7
140	0.0	0.0	0.0	0.0	0.0	0.0	0.0	0.0	0.0	0.0	0.2	0.4	0.7	0.9	1.1	1.3	1.6	1.8	2.0	2.2	2.3	2.5	2.7	2.9	3.1	3.2	3.4	3.6	3.7	3.9	4.0	4.2	4.3	4.5	4.6	4.8	4.9	5.0	5.2
138	0.0	0.0	0.0	0.0	0.0	0.0	0.0	0.0	0.1	0.4	0.7	0.9	1.1	1.4	1.6	1.8	2.0	2.2	2.4	2.6	2.8	3.0	3.2	3.4	3.5	3.7	3.9	4.0	4.2	4.3	4.5	4.7	4.8	4.9	5.1	5.2	5.4	5.5	5.7
136	0.0	0.0	0.0	0.0	0.0	0.0	0.0	0.3	0.6	0.9	1.1	1.4	1.6	1.9	2.1	2.3	2.5	2.7	2.9	3.1	3.3	3.5	3.7	3.8	4.0	4.2	4.4	4.5	4.7	4.8	5.0	5.1	5.3	5.4	5.6	5.7	5.9	6.0	6.1
134	0.0	0.0	0.0	0.0	0.0	0.2	0.5	0.8	1.1	1.4	1.7	1.9	2.1	2.4	2.6	2.8	3.0	3.2	3.4	3.6	3.8	4.0	4.2	4.4	4.5	4.7	4.9	5.0	5.2	5.3	5.5	5.6	5.8	5.9	6.1	6.2	6.4	6.5	6.7
132	0.0	0.0	0.0	0.0	0.3	0.7	1.0	1.3	1.6	1.9	2.2	2.4	2.7	2.9	3.1	3.3	3.6	3.8	4.0	4.1	4.3	4.5	4.7	4.9	5.0	5.2	5.4	5.5	5.7	5.9	6.0	6.2	6.3	6.5	6.6	6.8	6.9	7.0	7.2
130	0.0	0.0	0.0	0.5	0.9	1.2	1.6	1.9	2.2	2.4	2.7	3.0	3.2	3.4	3.7	3.9	4.1	4.3	4.5	4.7	4.9	5.1	5.2	5.4	5.6	5.8	5.9	6.1	6.2	6.4	6.6	6.7	6.9	7.0	7.2	7.3	7.4	7.6	7.7
128	0.0	0.0	0.6	1.0	1.4	1.8	2.1	2.4	2.7	3.0	3.3	3.5	3.8	4.0	4.2	4.4	4.6	4.8	5.0	5.2	5.4	5.6	5.8	6.0	6.1	6.3	6.5	6.6	6.8	7.0	7.1	7.3	7.4	7.6	7.7	7.8	8.0	8.1	8.3
126	0.0	0.6	1.1	1.6	2.0	2.4	2.7	3.0	3.3	3.6	3.8	4.1	4.3	4.6	4.8	5.0	5.2	5.4	5.6	5.8	6.0	6.2	6.4	6.5	6.7	6.9	7.0	7.2	7.4	7.5	7.7	7.8	8.0	8.1	8.3	8.4	8.6	8.7	8.8
124	0.5	1.2	1.7	2.2	2.6	2.9	3.3	3.6	3.9	4.2	4.4	4.7	4.9	5.2	5.4	5.6	5.8	6.0	6.2	6.4	6.6	6.8	7.0	7.1	7.3	7.5	7.6	7.8	8.0	8.1	8.3	8.4	8.6	8.7	8.9	9.0	9.1	9.3	9.4
122	1.1	1.8	2.3	2.8	3.2	3.6	3.9	4.2	4.5	4.8	5.0	5.3	5.5	5.8	6.0	6.2	6.4	6.6	6.8	7.0	7.2	7.4	7.6	7.7	7.9	8.1	8.2	8.4	8.6	8.7	8.9	9.0	9.2	9.3	9.5	9.6	9.8	9.9	10.0
120	1.7	2.4	3.0	3.4	3.8	4.2	4.5	4.8	5.1	5.4	5.7	5.9	6.2	6.4	6.6	6.8	7.0	7.2	7.4	7.6	7.8	8.0	8.2	8.4	8.5	8.7	8.9	9.0	9.2	9.4	9.5	9.7	9.8	9.9	10.1	10.2	10.4	10.5	10.7
118	2.3	2.7	3.2	3.7	4.2	4.4	4.7	5.0	5.4	5.7	6.1	6.3	6.7	6.9	7.1	7.3	7.5	7.7	7.9	8.2	8.5	8.8	9.1	9.4	9.7	10.0	10.3	10.7	11.0	11.2	11.3	11.5	11.6	11.7	11.9	12.0	12.2	12.3	12.4
116	4.3	4.6	4.9	5.2	5.5	5.8	6.1	6.3	6.6	6.9	7.2	7.5	7.8	8.1	8.4	8.7	9.0	9.3	9.6	9.9	10.2	10.5	10.7	11.0	11.3	11.6	11.9	12.2	12.5	12.8	13.1	13.3	13.4	13.5	13.7	13.8	14.0	14.1	14.2
114	6.3	6.6	6.8	7.1	7.4	7.7	7.9	8.2	8.5	8.8	9.1	9.3	9.6	9.9	10.2	10.4	10.7	11.0	11.3	11.6	11.8	12.1	12.4	12.7	12.9	13.2	13.5	13.8	14.1	14.3	14.6	14.9	15.2	15.3	15.5	15.6	15.8	15.9	16.0
112	8.3	8.5	8.8	9.0	9.3	9.6	9.8	10.1	10.4	10.6	10.9	11.1	11.4	11.7	11.9	12.2	12.5	12.7	13.0	13.2	13.5	13.8	14.0	14.3	14.5	14.8	15.1	15.3	15.6	15.9	16.1	16.4	16.6	16.9	17.2	17.4	17.6	17.7	17.8
110	10.2	10.5	10.7	11.0	11.2	11.5	11.7	12.0	12.2	12.5	12.7	13.0	13.2	13.4	13.7	13.9	14.2	14.4	14.7	14.9	15.2	15.4	15.7	15.9	16.2	16.4	16.6	16.9	17.1	17.4	17.6	17.9	18.1	18.4	18.6	18.9	18.8	18.9	19.0
108	12.2	12.5	12.7	12.9	13.2	13.4	13.6	13.8	14.1	14.3	14.5	14.8	15.0	15.2	15.5	15.7	15.9	16.2	16.4	16.6	16.8	17.1	17.3	17.5	17.8	18.0	18.2	18.5	18.7	18.9	19.1	19.4	19.6	19.8	20.1	20.3	20.5	20.7	20.8
106	14.2	14.4	14.6	14.9	15.1	15.3	15.5	15.7	15.9	16.1	16.4	16.6	16.8	17.0	17.2	17.4	17.7	17.9	18.1	18.3	18.5	18.7	18.9	19.2	19.4	19.6	19.8	20.0	20.2	20.4	20.7	20.9	21.1	21.3	21.5	21.7	22.0	22.2	22.4
104	16.2	16.4	16.6	16.8	17.0	17.2	17.4	17.6	17.8	18.0	18.2	18.4	18.6	18.8	19.0	19.2	19.4	19.6	19.8	19.9	20.2	20.4	20.6	20.8	21.0	21.2	21.4	21.6	21.8	22.0	22.2	22.4	22.6	22.8	23.0	23.2	23.4	23.6	23.8
102	18.2	18.4	18.6	18.7	18.9	19.1	19.3	19.5	19.7	19.8	20.0	20.2	20.4	20.6	20.8	20.9	21.1	21.3	21.5	21.7	21.9	22.0	22.2	22.4	22.6	22.8	23.0	23.1	23.3	23.5	23.7	23.9	24.1	24.2	24.4	24.6	24.8	25.0	25.2
100	20.2	20.3	20.5	20.7	20.8	21.0	21.2	21.3	21.5	21.7	21.8	22.0	22.2	22.4	22.5	22.7	22.9	23.0	23.2	23.4	23.5	23.7	23.9	24.0	24.2	24.4	24.5	24.7	24.9	25.0	25.2	25.4	25.5	25.7	25.9	26.0	26.2	26.4	26.6
99	21.2	21.3	21.5	21.6	21.8	22.0	22.1	22.3	22.4	22.6	22.8	22.9	23.1	23.2	23.4	23.6	23.7	23.9	24.0	24.2	24.4	24.5	24.7	24.8	25.0	25.2	25.3	25.5	25.6	25.8	26.0	26.1	26.3	26.4	26.6	26.8	26.9	27.1	27.2
98	22.2	22.3	22.5	22.6	22.8	22.9	23.1	23.2	23.4	23.5	23.7	23.8	24.0	24.1	24.3	24.4	24.6	24.7	24.9	25.0	25.2	25.4	25.5	25.7	25.8	26.0	26.1	26.3	26.4	26.6	26.7	26.9	27.0	27.2	27.3	27.5	27.6	27.8	27.9
97	23.1	23.3	23.4	23.6	23.7	23.9	24.0	24.2	24.3	24.4	24.6	24.7	24.9	25.0	25.2	25.3	25.5	25.6	25.7	25.9	26.0	26.2	26.3	26.5	26.6	26.8	26.9	27.0	27.2	27.3	27.5	27.6	27.8	27.9	28.1	28.2	28.3	28.5	28.6
96	24.1	24.3	24.4	24.5	24.7	24.8	25.0	25.1	25.2	25.4	25.5	25.6	25.8	25.9	26.0	26.2	26.3	26.5	26.6	26.7	26.9	27.0	27.1	27.3	27.4	27.6	27.7	27.8	28.0	28.1	28.2	28.4	28.5	28.6	28.8	28.9	29.1	29.2	29.3
95	25.1	25.3	25.4	25.5	25.6	25.8	25.9	26.0	26.2	26.3	26.4	26.5	26.7	26.8	26.9	27.1	27.2	27.3	27.4	27.6	27.7	27.8	28.0	28.1	28.2	28.3	28.5	28.6	28.7	28.9	29.0	29.1	29.2	29.4	29.5	29.6	29.8	29.9	30.0
94	26.1	26.2	26.4	26.5	26.6	26.7	26.8	27.0	27.1	27.2	27.3	27.5	27.6	27.7	27.8	27.9	28.1	28.2	28.3	28.4	28.5	28.7	28.8	28.9	29.0	29.1	29.3	29.4	29.5	29.6	29.7	29.9	29.9	30.1	30.2	30.4	30.5	30.6	30.7
93	27.1	27.2	27.3	27.5	27.6	27.7	27.8	27.9	28.0	28.1	28.2	28.4	28.5	28.6	28.7	28.8	28.9	29.0	29.1	29.3	29.4	29.5	29.6	29.7	29.8	29.9	30.1	30.2	30.3	30.4	30.5	30.6	30.7	30.8	31.0	31.1	31.2	31.3	31.4
92	28.1	28.2	28.3	28.4	28.5	28.6	28.7	28.8	28.9	29.1	29.2	29.3	29.4	29.5	29.6	29.7	29.8	29.9	30.0	30.1	30.2	30.3	30.4	30.5	30.6	30.7	30.8	30.9	31.1	31.2	31.3	31.4	31.5	31.6	31.7	31.8	31.9	32.0	32.1
91	29.1	29.2	29.3	29.4	29.5	29.6	29.7	29.8	29.9	29.9	30.1	30.2	30.3	30.4	30.5	30.6	30.7	30.8	30.9	30.9	31.0	31.1	31.2	31.3	31.4	31.5	31.6	31.7	31.8	31.9	32.0	32.1	32.2	32.3	32.4	32.5	32.6	32.7	32.8
90	30.1	30.2	30.3	30.4	30.4	30.5	30.6	30.7	30.8	30.9	31.0	31.1	31.2	31.3	31.3	31.4	31.5	31.6	31.7	31.8	31.9	32.0	32.1	32.2	32.2	32.3	32.4	32.5	32.6	32.7	32.8	32.9	33.0	33.0	33.1	33.2	33.3	33.4	33.5
89	31.1	31.2	31.2	31.3	31.4	31.5	31.6	31.7	31.7	31.8	31.9	32.0	32.1	32.1	32.2	32.3	32.4	32.5	32.6	32.6	32.7	32.8	32.9	33.0	33.0	33.1	33.2	33.3	33.4	33.5	33.5	33.6	33.7	33.8	33.9	33.9	34.0	34.1	34.2
88	32.1	32.1	32.2	32.3	32.4	32.4	32.5	32.6	32.7	32.7	32.8	32.9	33.0	33.0	33.1	33.2	33.3	33.3	33.4	33.5	33.6	33.6	33.7	33.8	33.8	33.9	34.0	34.1	34.1	34.2	34.3	34.4	34.4	34.5	34.6	34.7	34.7	34.8	34.9
87	33.1	33.1	33.2	33.3	33.3	33.4	33.5	33.5	33.6	33.7	33.7	33.8	33.9	33.9	34.0	34.1	34.1	34.2	34.3	34.3	34.4	34.5	34.5	34.6	34.7	34.7	34.8	34.9	34.9	35.0	35.0	35.1	35.2	35.2	35.3	35.4	35.4	35.5	35.6
86	34.1	34.1	34.2	34.2	34.3	34.3	34.4	34.5	34.5	34.6	34.6	34.7	34.8	34.8	34.9	34.9	35.0	35.0	35.1	35.2	35.2	35.3	35.3	35.4	35.5	35.5	35.6	35.6	35.7	35.7	35.8	35.9	35.9	36.0	36.0	36.1	36.2	36.2	36.3
85	35.1	35.1	35.2	35.2	35.3	35.3	35.4	35.4	35.5	35.5	35.6	35.6	35.7	35.7	35.8	35.8	35.9	35.9	36.0	36.0	36.1	36.1	36.2	36.2	36.3	36.3	36.4	36.4	36.5	36.5	36.6	36.6	36.7	36.7	36.8	36.8	36.9	36.9	37.0
84	36.0	36.1	36.1	36.2	36.2	36.3	36.3	36.3	36.4	36.4	36.5	36.5	36.6	36.6	36.6	36.7	36.7	36.8	36.8	36.9	36.9	36.9	37.0	37.0	37.1	37.1	37.2	37.2	37.2	37.3	37.3	37.4	37.4	37.4	37.5	37.5	37.6	37.6	37.7

LISTED PUT OPTION PRICE WHEN EXERCISE PRICE IS 130

Common Stock Price	NUMBER OF WEEKS BEFORE THE OPTION EXPIRES 1	2	3	4	5	6	7	8	9	10	11	12	13	14	15	16	17	18	19	20	21	22	23	24	25	26	27	28	29	30	31	32	33	34	35	36	37	38	39
170	0.0	0.0	0.0	0.0	0.0	0.0	0.0	0.0	0.0	0.0	0.0	0.0	0.0	0.0	0.0	0.0	0.0	0.0	0.0	0.0	0.0	0.0	0.0	0.0	0.0	0.0	0.0	0.0	0.2	0.3	0.5	0.7	0.8	1.0	1.2	1.3	1.5	1.6	1.8
168	0.0	0.0	0.0	0.0	0.0	0.0	0.0	0.0	0.0	0.0	0.0	0.0	0.0	0.0	0.0	0.0	0.0	0.0	0.0	0.0	0.0	0.0	0.0	0.0	0.0	0.0	0.2	0.4	0.6	0.7	0.9	1.1	1.2	1.4	1.5	1.7	1.8	2.0	2.1
166	0.0	0.0	0.0	0.0	0.0	0.0	0.0	0.0	0.0	0.0	0.0	0.0	0.0	0.0	0.0	0.0	0.0	0.0	0.0	0.0	0.0	0.0	0.0	0.0	0.2	0.4	0.6	0.8	0.9	1.1	1.3	1.4	1.6	1.8	1.9	2.1	2.2	2.4	2.5
164	0.0	0.0	0.0	0.0	0.0	0.0	0.0	0.0	0.0	0.0	0.0	0.0	0.0	0.0	0.0	0.0	0.0	0.0	0.0	0.0	0.0	0.1	0.2	0.4	0.6	0.8	1.0	1.2	1.3	1.5	1.7	1.8	2.0	2.2	2.3	2.5	2.6	2.8	2.9
162	0.0	0.0	0.0	0.0	0.0	0.0	0.0	0.0	0.0	0.0	0.0	0.0	0.0	0.0	0.0	0.0	0.0	0.0	0.0	0.1	0.3	0.5	0.7	0.8	1.0	1.2	1.4	1.6	1.7	1.9	2.1	2.2	2.4	2.6	2.7	2.9	3.0	3.2	3.3
160	0.0	0.0	0.0	0.0	0.0	0.0	0.0	0.0	0.0	0.0	0.0	0.0	0.0	0.0	0.0	0.0	0.0	0.0	0.3	0.5	0.7	0.9	1.1	1.3	1.5	1.6	1.8	2.0	2.2	2.3	2.5	2.7	2.8	3.0	3.1	3.3	3.5	3.6	3.8
158	0.0	0.0	0.0	0.0	0.0	0.0	0.0	0.0	0.0	0.0	0.0	0.0	0.0	0.0	0.0	0.0	0.3	0.5	0.7	0.9	1.1	1.3	1.5	1.7	1.9	2.1	2.2	2.4	2.6	2.8	2.9	3.1	3.3	3.4	3.6	3.7	3.9	4.0	4.2
156	0.0	0.0	0.0	0.0	0.0	0.0	0.0	0.0	0.0	0.0	0.0	0.0	0.0	0.0	0.2	0.5	0.7	0.9	1.1	1.3	1.5	1.7	1.9	2.1	2.3	2.5	2.7	2.9	3.0	3.2	3.4	3.5	3.7	3.9	4.0	4.2	4.3	4.5	4.6
154	0.0	0.0	0.0	0.0	0.0	0.0	0.0	0.0	0.0	0.0	0.0	0.0	0.2	0.4	0.7	0.9	1.1	1.4	1.6	1.8	2.0	2.2	2.4	2.6	2.8	3.0	3.1	3.3	3.5	3.7	3.8	4.0	4.1	4.3	4.5	4.6	4.8	4.9	5.1
152	0.0	0.0	0.0	0.0	0.0	0.0	0.0	0.0	0.0	0.0	0.1	0.4	0.6	0.9	1.1	1.4	1.6	1.8	2.0	2.3	2.5	2.7	2.9	3.0	3.2	3.4	3.6	3.8	3.9	4.1	4.3	4.4	4.6	4.8	4.9	5.1	5.2	5.4	5.5
150	0.0	0.0	0.0	0.0	0.0	0.0	0.0	0.0	0.0	0.3	0.6	0.9	1.1	1.4	1.6	1.9	2.1	2.3	2.5	2.7	2.9	3.1	3.3	3.5	3.7	3.9	4.1	4.2	4.4	4.6	4.8	4.9	5.1	5.2	5.4	5.6	5.7	5.9	6.0
148	0.0	0.0	0.0	0.0	0.0	0.0	0.0	0.2	0.5	0.8	1.1	1.3	1.6	1.9	2.1	2.3	2.6	2.8	3.0	3.2	3.4	3.6	3.8	4.0	4.2	4.4	4.6	4.7	4.9	5.1	5.2	5.4	5.6	5.7	5.9	6.0	6.2	6.3	6.5
146	0.0	0.0	0.0	0.0	0.0	0.0	0.3	0.7	1.0	1.3	1.6	1.9	2.1	2.4	2.6	2.8	3.1	3.3	3.5	3.7	3.9	4.1	4.3	4.5	4.7	4.9	5.1	5.2	5.4	5.6	5.7	5.3	6.1	6.2	6.4	6.5	6.7	6.8	7.0
144	0.0	0.0	0.0	0.0	0.1	0.5	0.9	1.2	1.5	1.8	2.1	2.4	2.6	2.9	3.1	3.4	3.6	3.8	4.0	4.2	4.4	4.6	4.8	5.0	5.2	5.4	5.6	5.7	5.9	6.1	6.3	6.4	6.6	6.7	6.9	7.1	7.2	7.4	7.5
142	0.0	0.0	0.0	0.2	0.6	1.0	1.4	1.7	2.0	2.3	2.6	2.9	3.2	3.4	3.7	3.9	4.1	4.3	4.5	4.8	5.0	5.2	5.4	5.5	5.7	5.9	6.1	6.3	6.4	6.6	6.8	7.0	7.1	7.3	7.4	7.6	7.7	7.9	8.0
140	0.0	0.0	0.2	0.7	1.2	1.6	1.9	2.3	2.6	2.9	3.2	3.4	3.7	4.0	4.2	4.4	4.7	4.9	5.1	5.3	5.5	5.7	5.9	6.1	6.3	6.5	6.6	6.8	7.0	7.2	7.3	7.5	7.7	7.8	8.0	8.1	8.3	8.4	8.6
138	0.0	0.2	0.8	1.3	1.7	2.1	2.5	2.8	3.1	3.4	3.7	4.0	4.3	4.5	4.8	5.0	5.2	5.4	5.7	5.9	6.1	6.3	6.5	6.7	6.8	7.0	7.2	7.4	7.6	7.7	7.9	8.1	8.2	8.4	8.5	8.7	8.8	9.0	9.1
136	0.0	0.8	1.4	1.9	2.3	2.7	3.1	3.4	3.7	4.0	4.3	4.6	4.8	5.1	5.3	5.6	5.8	6.0	6.2	6.4	6.6	6.8	7.0	7.2	7.4	7.6	7.8	8.0	8.1	8.3	8.5	8.6	8.8	9.0	9.1	9.3	9.4	9.6	9.7
134	0.6	1.4	2.0	2.5	2.9	3.3	3.7	4.0	4.3	4.6	4.9	5.2	5.4	5.7	5.9	6.2	6.4	6.6	6.8	7.0	7.2	7.4	7.6	7.8	8.0	8.2	8.4	8.5	8.7	8.9	9.1	9.2	9.4	9.5	9.7	9.9	10.0	10.2	10.3
132	1.2	2.0	2.6	3.1	3.5	3.9	4.3	4.6	4.9	5.2	5.5	5.8	6.0	6.3	6.5	6.8	7.0	7.2	7.4	7.6	7.8	8.0	8.2	8.4	8.6	8.8	9.0	9.2	9.3	9.5	9.7	9.8	9.9	10.2	10.3	10.5	10.6	10.8	10.9
130	1.9	2.6	3.2	3.7	4.1	4.5	4.9	5.2	5.6	5.9	6.1	6.4	6.7	6.9	7.2	7.4	7.6	7.8	8.1	8.3	8.5	8.7	8.9	9.1	9.3	9.4	9.6	9.8	9.9	10.1	10.3	10.5	10.6	10.8	10.9	11.1	11.3	11.4	11.6
128	2.5	2.8	3.4	3.9	4.4	4.8	5.2	5.5	5.9	6.2	6.4	6.7	7.1	7.3	7.6	7.8	8.0	8.2	8.5	8.7	9.1	9.4	9.7	10.1	10.4	10.7	11.1	11.4	11.7	11.9	12.1	12.3	12.4	12.6	12.7	12.9	13.1	13.2	13.4
126	4.3	4.6	5.0	5.3	5.6	5.9	6.2	6.6	6.9	7.2	7.5	7.8	8.2	8.5	8.8	9.1	9.4	9.8	10.1	10.4	10.7	11.0	11.4	11.7	12.0	12.3	12.6	13.0	13.3	13.6	13.9	14.1	14.2	14.4	14.5	14.7	14.9	15.0	15.2
124	6.3	6.6	6.9	7.2	7.5	7.8	8.1	8.4	8.7	9.0	9.4	9.7	9.9	10.3	10.6	10.9	11.2	11.5	11.8	12.1	12.4	12.7	13.0	13.3	13.6	13.9	14.2	14.5	14.8	15.1	15.4	15.7	16.0	16.2	16.3	16.5	16.7	16.8	17.0
122	8.3	8.6	8.9	9.2	9.4	9.7	10.0	10.3	10.6	10.9	11.2	11.5	11.8	12.0	12.3	12.6	12.9	13.2	13.5	13.8	14.1	14.4	14.6	14.9	15.2	15.5	15.8	16.1	16.4	16.7	17.0	17.2	17.5	17.8	18.1	18.3	18.5	18.6	18.8
120	10.3	10.5	10.8	11.1	11.4	11.6	11.9	12.2	12.5	12.7	13.0	13.3	13.6	13.8	14.1	14.4	14.6	14.9	15.2	15.5	15.7	16.0	16.3	16.6	16.8	17.1	17.4	17.7	17.9	18.2	18.5	18.7	19.0	19.3	19.6	19.8	20.1	20.4	20.6
118	12.3	12.5	12.8	13.0	13.3	13.5	13.8	14.1	14.3	14.6	14.8	15.1	15.3	15.6	15.9	16.1	16.4	16.6	16.9	17.2	17.4	17.7	17.9	18.2	18.4	18.7	19.0	19.2	19.5	19.7	19.9	20.2	20.5	20.8	21.0	21.3	21.5	21.8	22.0
116	14.2	14.5	14.7	15.0	15.2	15.5	15.7	15.9	16.2	16.4	16.7	16.9	17.1	17.4	17.6	17.9	18.1	18.4	18.6	18.8	19.1	19.3	19.6	19.8	20.0	20.3	20.5	20.8	21.0	21.3	21.5	21.7	22.0	22.2	22.5	22.7	23.0	23.2	23.4
114	16.2	16.5	16.7	16.9	17.1	17.4	17.6	17.8	18.0	18.3	18.5	18.7	18.9	19.2	19.4	19.6	19.8	20.1	20.3	20.5	20.8	21.0	21.2	21.4	21.7	21.9	22.1	22.3	22.6	22.8	23.0	23.2	23.5	23.7	23.9	24.1	24.4	24.6	24.8
112	18.2	18.4	18.6	18.8	19.1	19.3	19.5	19.7	19.9	20.1	20.3	20.5	20.7	20.9	21.2	21.4	21.6	21.8	22.0	22.2	22.4	22.6	22.8	23.1	23.3	23.5	23.7	23.9	24.1	24.3	24.5	24.7	25.0	25.2	25.4	25.6	25.8	26.0	26.2
110	20.2	20.4	20.6	20.8	21.0	21.2	21.4	21.6	21.8	22.0	22.1	22.3	22.5	22.7	22.9	23.1	23.3	23.5	23.7	23.9	24.1	24.3	24.5	24.7	24.9	25.1	25.3	25.5	25.7	25.9	26.0	26.2	26.4	26.6	26.8	27.0	27.2	27.4	27.6
108	22.2	22.4	22.5	22.7	22.9	23.1	23.3	23.4	23.6	23.8	24.0	24.2	24.3	24.5	24.7	24.9	25.0	25.2	25.4	25.6	25.8	25.9	26.1	26.3	26.5	26.7	26.8	27.0	27.2	27.4	27.6	27.7	27.9	28.1	28.3	28.5	28.6	28.8	29.0
106	24.2	24.3	24.5	24.7	24.8	25.0	25.1	25.3	25.5	25.6	25.8	26.0	26.1	26.3	26.5	26.6	26.8	26.9	27.1	27.3	27.4	27.6	27.8	27.9	28.1	28.3	28.4	28.6	28.7	28.9	29.1	29.2	29.4	29.6	29.7	29.9	30.1	30.2	30.4
104	26.1	26.3	26.4	26.6	26.7	26.9	27.0	27.2	27.3	27.5	27.6	27.8	27.9	28.1	28.2	28.4	28.5	28.7	28.8	29.0	29.1	29.3	29.4	29.6	29.7	29.8	29.9	30.1	30.3	30.4	30.6	30.7	30.9	31.0	31.2	31.3	31.5	31.6	31.8
102	28.1	28.3	28.4	28.5	28.7	28.8	28.9	29.1	29.2	29.3	29.5	29.6	29.7	29.9	29.9	30.1	30.2	30.4	30.5	30.6	30.8	30.9	31.0	31.2	31.3	31.4	31.6	31.7	31.8	32.0	32.1	32.2	32.4	32.5	32.6	32.8	32.9	33.0	33.2
100	30.1	30.2	30.3	30.5	30.6	30.7	30.8	30.9	31.0	31.2	31.3	31.4	31.5	31.6	31.8	31.9	32.0	32.1	32.2	32.3	32.4	32.6	32.7	32.8	32.9	33.0	33.2	33.3	33.4	33.5	33.6	33.7	33.8	34.0	34.1	34.2	34.3	34.4	34.6
99	31.1	31.2	31.3	31.4	31.5	31.7	31.8	31.9	32.0	32.1	32.2	32.3	32.4	32.5	32.6	32.7	32.9	33.0	33.1	33.2	33.3	33.4	33.5	33.6	33.7	33.8	33.9	34.0	34.2	34.3	34.4	34.5	34.6	34.7	34.8	34.9	35.0	35.1	35.2
98	32.1	32.2	32.3	32.4	32.5	32.6	32.7	32.8	32.9	33.0	33.1	33.2	33.3	33.4	33.5	33.6	33.7	33.8	33.9	34.0	34.1	34.2	34.3	34.4	34.5	34.6	34.7	34.8	34.9	35.0	35.1	35.2	35.3	35.4	35.5	35.6	35.7	35.8	35.9
97	33.1	33.2	33.3	33.4	33.5	33.6	33.7	33.7	33.8	33.9	34.0	34.1	34.2	34.3	34.4	34.5	34.6	34.7	34.8	34.9	35.0	35.0	35.1	35.2	35.3	35.4	35.5	35.6	35.7	35.8	35.9	36.0	36.1	36.2	36.3	36.4	36.4	36.5	36.6
96	34.1	34.2	34.3	34.3	34.4	34.5	34.6	34.7	34.8	34.9	34.9	35.0	35.1	35.2	35.3	35.4	35.5	35.5	35.6	35.7	35.8	35.9	36.0	36.0	36.1	36.2	36.3	36.4	36.5	36.6	36.6	36.7	36.8	36.9	37.0	37.1	37.2	37.2	37.3
95	35.1	35.2	35.2	35.3	35.4	35.5	35.5	35.6	35.7	35.8	35.9	35.9	36.0	36.1	36.2	36.2	36.3	36.4	36.5	36.6	36.6	36.7	36.8	36.9	36.9	37.0	37.1	37.2	37.2	37.3	37.4	37.5	37.6	37.6	37.7	37.8	37.9	37.9	38.0
94	36.1	36.1	36.2	36.3	36.3	36.4	36.5	36.6	36.6	36.7	36.8	36.8	36.9	37.0	37.0	37.1	37.2	37.3	37.3	37.4	37.5	37.5	37.6	37.7	37.7	37.8	37.9	38.0	38.0	38.1	38.2	38.2	38.3	38.4	38.4	38.5	38.6	38.6	38.7
93	37.1	37.1	37.2	37.2	37.3	37.4	37.4	37.5	37.6	37.6	37.7	37.7	37.8	37.9	37.9	38.0	38.1	38.1	38.2	38.2	38.3	38.4	38.4	38.5	38.5	38.6	38.7	38.7	38.8	38.9	38.9	39.0	39.0	39.1	39.2	39.2	39.3	39.3	39.4
92	38.1	38.1	38.2	38.2	38.3	38.3	38.4	38.4	38.5	38.5	38.6	38.6	38.7	38.8	38.8	38.9	38.9	39.0	39.0	39.1	39.1	39.2	39.2	39.3	39.4	39.4	39.5	39.5	39.6	39.6	39.7	39.7	39.8	39.8	39.9	39.9	39.9	40.1	40.1
91	39.0	39.1	39.1	39.2	39.2	39.3	39.3	39.4	39.4	39.5	39.5	39.6	39.6	39.6	39.7	39.7	39.8	39.8	39.9	39.9	39.9	40.0	40.1	40.1	40.2	40.2	40.2	40.3	40.3	40.4	40.4	40.5	40.5	40.6	40.6	40.7	40.7	40.8	40.8

LISTED PUT OPTION PRICE WHEN EXERCISE PRICE IS 140

NUMBER OF WEEKS BEFORE THE OPTION EXPIRES

Common Stock Price	1	2	3	4	5	6	7	8	9	10	11	12	13	14	15	16	17	18	19	20	21	22	23	24	25	26	27	28	29	30	31	32	33	34	35	36	37	38	39
182	0.0	0.0	0.0	0.0	0.0	0.0	0.0	0.0	0.0	0.0	0.0	0.0	0.0	0.0	0.0	0.0	0.0	0.0	0.0	0.0	0.0	0.0	0.0	0.0	0.0	0.0	0.0	0.2	0.4	0.6	0.8	0.9	1.1	1.3	1.4	1.6	1.8	1.9	2.1
180	0.0	0.0	0.0	0.0	0.0	0.0	0.0	0.0	0.0	0.0	0.0	0.0	0.0	0.0	0.0	0.0	0.0	0.0	0.0	0.0	0.0	0.0	0.0	0.0	0.0	0.2	0.4	0.6	0.8	1.0	1.1	1.3	1.5	1.7	1.8	2.0	2.2	2.3	2.5
178	0.0	0.0	0.0	0.0	0.0	0.0	0.0	0.0	0.0	0.0	0.0	0.0	0.0	0.0	0.0	0.0	0.0	0.0	0.0	0.0	0.0	0.0	0.0	0.2	0.4	0.6	0.8	1.0	1.2	1.3	1.5	1.7	1.9	2.1	2.2	2.4	2.6	2.7	2.9
176	0.0	0.0	0.0	0.0	0.0	0.0	0.0	0.0	0.0	0.0	0.0	0.0	0.0	0.0	0.0	0.0	0.0	0.0	0.0	0.0	0.0	0.2	0.4	0.6	0.8	1.0	1.2	1.4	1.6	1.7	1.9	2.1	2.3	2.5	2.6	2.8	3.0	3.1	3.3
174	0.0	0.0	0.0	0.0	0.0	0.0	0.0	0.0	0.0	0.0	0.0	0.0	0.0	0.0	0.0	0.0	0.0	0.0	0.0	0.2	0.4	0.6	0.8	1.0	1.2	1.4	1.6	1.8	2.0	2.2	2.3	2.5	2.7	2.9	3.0	3.2	3.4	3.5	3.7
172	0.0	0.0	0.0	0.0	0.0	0.0	0.0	0.0	0.0	0.0	0.0	0.0	0.0	0.0	0.0	0.0	0.0	0.1	0.4	0.6	0.8	1.0	1.2	1.4	1.6	1.8	2.0	2.2	2.4	2.6	2.8	2.9	3.1	3.3	3.5	3.6	3.8	3.9	4.1
170	0.0	0.0	0.0	0.0	0.0	0.0	0.0	0.0	0.0	0.0	0.0	0.0	0.0	0.0	0.0	0.1	0.3	0.5	0.8	1.0	1.2	1.4	1.6	1.9	2.1	2.3	2.4	2.6	2.8	3.0	3.2	3.4	3.5	3.7	3.9	4.0	4.2	4.4	4.5
168	0.0	0.0	0.0	0.0	0.0	0.0	0.0	0.0	0.0	0.0	0.0	0.0	0.0	0.0	0.3	0.5	0.7	1.0	1.2	1.4	1.7	1.9	2.1	2.3	2.5	2.7	2.9	3.1	3.3	3.4	3.6	3.8	4.0	4.2	4.3	4.5	4.7	4.8	5.0
166	0.0	0.0	0.0	0.0	0.0	0.0	0.0	0.0	0.0	0.0	0.0	0.0	0.2	0.4	0.7	1.0	1.2	1.4	1.7	1.9	2.1	2.3	2.5	2.7	2.9	3.1	3.3	3.5	3.7	3.9	4.1	4.3	4.4	4.6	4.8	4.9	5.1	5.3	5.4
164	0.0	0.0	0.0	0.0	0.0	0.0	0.0	0.0	0.0	0.0	0.1	0.3	0.6	0.9	1.2	1.4	1.7	1.9	2.1	2.4	2.6	2.8	3.0	3.2	3.4	3.6	3.8	4.0	4.2	4.4	4.5	4.7	4.9	5.1	5.2	5.4	5.6	5.7	5.9
162	0.0	0.0	0.0	0.0	0.0	0.0	0.0	0.0	0.0	0.2	0.5	0.8	1.1	1.4	1.6	1.9	2.1	2.4	2.6	2.8	3.0	3.3	3.5	3.7	3.9	4.1	4.3	4.5	4.6	4.8	5.0	5.2	5.4	5.5	5.7	5.9	6.0	6.2	6.4
160	0.0	0.0	0.0	0.0	0.0	0.0	0.0	0.0	0.4	0.7	1.0	1.3	1.6	1.9	2.1	2.4	2.6	2.9	3.1	3.3	3.5	3.7	4.0	4.2	4.4	4.6	4.8	4.9	5.1	5.3	5.5	5.7	5.8	6.0	6.2	6.4	6.5	6.7	6.8
158	0.0	0.0	0.0	0.0	0.0	0.0	0.2	0.5	0.9	1.2	1.5	1.8	2.1	2.4	2.6	2.9	3.1	3.3	3.6	3.8	4.0	4.2	4.5	4.7	4.9	5.1	5.2	5.4	5.6	5.8	6.0	6.2	6.3	6.5	6.7	6.9	7.0	7.2	7.3
156	0.0	0.0	0.0	0.0	0.0	0.3	0.7	1.0	1.4	1.7	2.0	2.3	2.6	2.9	3.1	3.4	3.6	3.9	4.1	4.3	4.5	4.8	5.0	5.2	5.4	5.6	5.8	5.9	6.1	6.3	6.5	6.7	6.9	7.0	7.2	7.4	7.5	7.7	7.8
154	0.0	0.0	0.0	0.0	0.4	0.8	1.2	1.6	1.9	2.2	2.5	2.8	3.1	3.4	3.6	3.9	4.1	4.4	4.6	4.8	5.1	5.3	5.5	5.7	5.9	6.1	6.3	6.5	6.7	6.8	7.0	7.2	7.4	7.5	7.7	7.9	8.0	8.2	8.4
152	0.0	0.0	0.0	0.4	0.9	1.3	1.7	2.1	2.4	2.8	3.1	3.4	3.6	3.9	4.2	4.4	4.7	4.9	5.1	5.4	5.6	5.8	6.0	6.2	6.4	6.6	6.8	7.0	7.2	7.4	7.6	7.7	7.9	8.1	8.3	8.4	8.6	8.7	8.9
150	0.0	0.0	0.5	1.0	1.5	1.9	2.3	2.6	3.0	3.3	3.6	3.9	4.2	4.5	4.7	5.0	5.2	5.5	5.7	5.9	6.1	6.4	6.6	6.8	7.0	7.2	7.4	7.6	7.7	7.9	8.1	8.3	8.5	8.6	8.8	9.0	9.1	9.3	9.5
148	0.0	0.4	1.0	1.6	2.0	2.5	2.9	3.2	3.6	3.9	4.2	4.5	4.8	5.0	5.3	5.5	5.8	6.0	6.3	6.5	6.7	6.9	7.1	7.3	7.5	7.7	7.9	8.1	8.3	8.5	8.7	8.8	9.0	9.2	9.4	9.5	9.7	9.9	10.0
146	0.2	1.0	1.6	2.1	2.6	3.0	3.4	3.8	4.1	4.5	4.8	5.1	5.3	5.6	5.9	6.1	6.4	6.6	6.8	7.1	7.3	7.5	7.7	7.9	8.1	8.3	8.5	8.7	8.9	9.1	9.3	9.4	9.6	9.8	9.9	10.1	10.3	10.4	10.6
144	0.7	1.6	2.2	2.7	3.2	3.6	4.0	4.4	4.7	5.1	5.4	5.7	5.9	6.2	6.5	6.7	7.0	7.2	7.4	7.7	7.9	8.1	8.3	8.5	8.7	8.9	9.1	9.3	9.5	9.7	9.8	10.0	10.2	10.4	10.5	10.7	10.9	11.0	11.2
142	1.4	2.2	2.8	3.4	3.8	4.2	4.6	5.0	5.3	5.7	6.0	6.3	6.6	6.8	7.1	7.3	7.6	7.8	8.1	8.3	8.5	8.7	8.9	9.1	9.3	9.5	9.7	9.9	10.1	10.3	10.5	10.6	10.8	11.0	11.2	11.3	11.5	11.7	11.8
140	2.0	2.8	3.5	4.0	4.5	4.9	5.3	5.6	6.0	6.3	6.6	6.9	7.2	7.5	7.7	8.0	8.2	8.5	8.7	8.9	9.1	9.3	9.6	9.8	9.9	10.2	10.4	10.5	10.7	10.9	11.1	11.3	11.4	11.6	11.8	12.0	12.1	12.3	12.4
138	2.6	2.9	3.7	4.2	4.7	5.1	5.5	5.9	6.3	6.6	6.9	7.2	7.5	7.9	8.1	8.4	8.6	8.9	9.1	9.3	9.6	9.9	10.4	10.7	11.1	11.4	11.8	12.2	12.5	12.7	12.9	13.1	13.2	13.4	13.6	13.8	13.9	14.1	14.2
136	4.3	4.7	5.0	5.4	5.7	6.1	6.4	6.8	7.1	7.5	7.8	8.2	8.5	8.9	9.2	9.6	9.9	10.3	10.6	10.9	11.3	11.6	12.0	12.3	12.7	13.0	13.4	13.7	14.1	14.4	14.7	14.9	15.0	15.2	15.4	15.6	15.7	15.9	16.0
134	6.3	6.7	7.0	7.3	7.7	8.0	8.3	8.7	9.0	9.3	9.6	9.9	10.3	10.6	11.0	11.3	11.6	12.0	12.3	12.6	13.0	13.3	13.6	14.0	14.3	14.6	15.0	15.3	15.6	16.0	16.3	16.6	16.8	17.0	17.2	17.4	17.5	17.7	17.8
132	8.3	8.6	8.9	9.3	9.6	9.9	10.2	10.5	10.8	11.2	11.5	11.8	12.1	12.4	12.7	13.1	13.4	13.7	14.0	14.3	14.6	15.0	15.3	15.6	15.9	16.2	16.5	16.8	17.2	17.5	17.8	18.1	18.4	18.7	19.0	19.2	19.3	19.5	19.6
130	10.3	10.6	10.9	11.2	11.5	11.8	12.1	12.4	12.7	13.0	13.3	13.6	13.9	14.2	14.5	14.8	15.1	15.4	15.7	16.0	16.3	16.6	16.9	17.2	17.5	17.8	18.1	18.4	18.7	19.0	19.3	19.6	19.9	20.2	20.5	20.8	21.1	21.3	21.4
128	12.3	12.6	12.9	13.1	13.4	13.7	14.0	14.3	14.6	14.8	15.1	15.4	15.7	16.0	16.3	16.6	16.8	17.1	17.4	17.7	18.0	18.3	18.5	18.8	19.1	19.4	19.7	19.9	20.3	20.5	20.8	21.1	21.4	21.7	22.0	22.2	22.5	22.8	23.1
126	14.3	14.5	14.8	15.1	15.3	15.6	15.9	16.2	16.4	16.7	17.0	17.2	17.5	17.8	18.0	18.3	18.6	18.8	19.1	19.4	19.7	19.9	20.2	20.5	20.7	21.0	21.3	21.5	21.8	22.1	22.3	22.6	22.9	23.1	23.4	23.7	24.0	24.2	24.5
124	16.3	16.5	16.8	17.0	17.3	17.5	17.8	18.0	18.3	18.5	18.8	19.0	19.3	19.5	19.8	20.1	20.3	20.6	20.8	21.1	21.3	21.6	21.8	22.1	22.3	22.6	22.8	23.1	23.3	23.6	23.9	24.1	24.4	24.6	24.9	25.1	25.4	25.6	25.9
122	18.2	18.5	18.7	19.0	19.2	19.4	19.7	19.9	20.1	20.4	20.6	20.9	21.1	21.3	21.6	21.8	22.0	22.3	22.5	22.8	23.0	23.2	23.5	23.7	23.9	24.2	24.4	24.7	24.9	25.1	25.4	25.6	25.8	26.1	26.3	26.6	26.8	27.0	27.3
120	20.2	20.4	20.7	20.9	21.1	21.3	21.6	21.8	22.0	22.2	22.4	22.7	22.9	23.1	23.3	23.6	23.8	24.0	24.2	24.4	24.7	24.9	25.1	25.3	25.6	25.8	26.0	26.2	26.4	26.7	26.9	27.1	27.3	27.5	27.8	28.0	28.2	28.4	28.7
118	22.2	22.4	22.6	22.8	23.0	23.2	23.4	23.7	23.9	24.1	24.3	24.5	24.7	24.9	25.1	25.3	25.5	25.7	25.9	26.1	26.3	26.5	26.7	27.0	27.2	27.4	27.6	27.8	28.0	28.2	28.4	28.6	28.8	29.0	29.2	29.4	29.6	29.8	30.0
116	24.2	24.4	24.6	24.8	25.0	25.1	25.3	25.5	25.7	25.9	26.1	26.3	26.5	26.7	26.9	27.1	27.2	27.4	27.6	27.8	28.0	28.2	28.4	28.6	28.8	29.0	29.1	29.3	29.5	29.7	29.9	30.1	30.3	30.5	30.7	30.9	31.1	31.2	31.4
114	26.2	26.4	26.5	26.7	26.9	27.1	27.2	27.4	27.6	27.8	27.9	28.1	28.3	28.5	28.6	28.8	29.0	29.2	29.3	29.5	29.7	29.9	30.0	30.2	30.4	30.6	30.7	30.9	31.1	31.3	31.4	31.6	31.8	32.0	32.1	32.3	32.5	32.7	32.8
112	28.2	28.3	28.5	28.6	28.8	29.0	29.1	29.3	29.4	29.6	29.8	29.9	30.1	30.2	30.4	30.6	30.7	30.9	31.0	31.2	31.3	31.5	31.7	31.8	32.0	32.1	32.3	32.5	32.6	32.8	32.9	33.1	33.3	33.4	33.6	33.7	33.9	34.1	34.2
110	30.1	30.3	30.4	30.6	30.7	30.9	31.0	31.1	31.3	31.4	31.6	31.7	31.9	32.0	32.2	32.3	32.4	32.6	32.7	32.9	33.0	33.2	33.3	33.4	33.6	33.7	33.9	34.0	34.2	34.3	34.5	34.6	34.7	34.9	35.0	35.2	35.3	35.5	35.6
108	32.1	32.3	32.4	32.5	32.6	32.8	32.9	33.0	33.2	33.3	33.4	33.5	33.7	33.8	33.9	34.0	34.2	34.3	34.4	34.6	34.7	34.8	34.9	35.1	35.2	35.3	35.5	35.6	35.7	35.8	36.0	36.1	36.2	36.4	36.5	36.6	36.7	36.9	37.0
106	34.1	34.2	34.3	34.4	34.6	34.7	34.8	34.9	35.0	35.1	35.2	35.3	35.5	35.6	35.7	35.8	35.9	36.0	36.1	36.2	36.4	36.5	36.6	36.7	36.8	36.9	37.0	37.1	37.3	37.4	37.5	37.6	37.7	37.8	37.9	38.0	38.2	38.3	38.4
104	36.1	36.2	36.3	36.4	36.5	36.6	36.7	36.8	36.9	37.0	37.1	37.2	37.3	37.4	37.5	37.5	37.6	37.7	37.8	37.9	38.0	38.1	38.2	38.3	38.4	38.5	38.6	38.7	38.8	38.9	39.0	39.1	39.2	39.3	39.4	39.5	39.6	39.7	39.8
102	38.1	38.2	38.2	38.3	38.4	38.5	38.6	38.6	38.7	38.8	38.9	39.0	39.1	39.1	39.2	39.3	39.4	39.5	39.5	39.6	39.7	39.8	39.9	39.9	40.0	40.1	40.2	40.3	40.4	40.4	40.5	40.6	40.7	40.8	40.8	40.9	41.0	41.1	41.2
100	40.1	40.1	40.2	40.3	40.3	40.4	40.5	40.5	40.6	40.7	40.7	40.8	40.9	40.9	41.0	41.0	41.1	41.2	41.2	41.3	41.4	41.4	41.5	41.6	41.6	41.7	41.8	41.8	41.9	42.0	42.0	42.1	42.2	42.2	42.3	42.4	42.4	42.5	42.6
99	41.1	41.1	41.2	41.2	41.3	41.3	41.4	41.5	41.5	41.6	41.6	41.7	41.7	41.8	41.9	41.9	42.0	42.0	42.1	42.2	42.2	42.3	42.3	42.4	42.4	42.5	42.6	42.6	42.7	42.7	42.8	42.8	42.9	43.0	43.0	43.1	43.1	43.2	43.2
98	42.0	42.1	42.1	42.2	42.2	42.3	42.3	42.4	42.4	42.5	42.5	42.6	42.6	42.7	42.7	42.8	42.8	42.9	42.9	43.0	43.0	43.1	43.1	43.2	43.2	43.3	43.3	43.4	43.4	43.5	43.5	43.6	43.6	43.7	43.7	43.8	43.8	43.9	43.9

LISTED PUT OPTION PRICE WHEN EXERCISE PRICE IS 150

Common Stock Price	NUMBER OF WEEKS BEFORE THE OPTION EXPIRES																																						
	1	2	3	4	5	6	7	8	9	10	11	12	13	14	15	16	17	18	19	20	21	22	23	24	25	26	27	28	29	30	31	32	33	34	35	36	37	38	39
196	0.0	0.0	0.0	0.0	0.0	0.0	0.0	0.0	0.0	0.0	0.0	0.0	0.0	0.0	0.0	0.0	0.0	0.0	0.0	0.0	0.0	0.0	0.0	0.0	0.0	0.0	0.0	0.0	0.2	0.4	0.6	0.8	1.0	1.2	1.4	1.5	1.7	1.9	2.1
194	0.0	0.0	0.0	0.0	0.0	0.0	0.0	0.0	0.0	0.0	0.0	0.0	0.0	0.0	0.0	0.0	0.0	0.0	0.0	0.0	0.0	0.0	0.0	0.0	0.0	0.0	0.2	0.4	0.6	0.8	1.0	1.2	1.4	1.6	1.7	1.9	2.1	2.3	2.4
192	0.0	0.0	0.0	0.0	0.0	0.0	0.0	0.0	0.0	0.0	0.0	0.0	0.0	0.0	0.0	0.0	0.0	0.0	0.0	0.0	0.0	0.0	0.0	0.0	0.2	0.4	0.6	0.8	1.0	1.2	1.4	1.6	1.8	1.9	2.1	2.3	2.5	2.7	2.8
190	0.0	0.0	0.0	0.0	0.0	0.0	0.0	0.0	0.0	0.0	0.0	0.0	0.0	0.0	0.0	0.0	0.0	0.0	0.0	0.0	0.0	0.0	0.1	0.4	0.6	0.8	1.0	1.2	1.4	1.6	1.8	2.0	2.2	2.3	2.5	2.7	2.9	3.1	3.2
188	0.0	0.0	0.0	0.0	0.0	0.0	0.0	0.0	0.0	0.0	0.0	0.0	0.0	0.0	0.0	0.0	0.0	0.0	0.0	0.0	0.1	0.3	0.5	0.8	1.0	1.2	1.4	1.6	1.8	2.0	2.2	2.4	2.6	2.7	2.9	3.1	3.3	3.5	3.6
186	0.0	0.0	0.0	0.0	0.0	0.0	0.0	0.0	0.0	0.0	0.0	0.0	0.0	0.0	0.0	0.0	0.0	0.0	0.0	0.3	0.5	0.7	0.9	1.2	1.4	1.6	1.8	2.0	2.2	2.4	2.6	2.8	3.0	3.2	3.3	3.5	3.7	3.9	4.0
184	0.0	0.0	0.0	0.0	0.0	0.0	0.0	0.0	0.0	0.0	0.0	0.0	0.0	0.0	0.0	0.0	0.0	0.2	0.4	0.7	0.9	1.1	1.4	1.6	1.8	2.0	2.2	2.4	2.6	2.8	3.0	3.2	3.4	3.6	3.8	3.9	4.1	4.3	4.5
182	0.0	0.0	0.0	0.0	0.0	0.0	0.0	0.0	0.0	0.0	0.0	0.0	0.0	0.0	0.0	0.1	0.4	0.6	0.9	1.1	1.3	1.6	1.8	2.0	2.2	2.4	2.7	2.9	3.1	3.3	3.4	3.6	3.8	4.0	4.2	4.4	4.5	4.7	4.9
180	0.0	0.0	0.0	0.0	0.0	0.0	0.0	0.0	0.0	0.0	0.0	0.0	0.0	0.0	0.3	0.5	0.8	1.1	1.3	1.5	1.8	2.0	2.2	2.5	2.7	2.9	3.1	3.3	3.5	3.7	3.9	4.1	4.3	4.4	4.6	4.8	5.0	5.2	5.3
178	0.0	0.0	0.0	0.0	0.0	0.0	0.0	0.0	0.0	0.0	0.0	0.0	0.1	0.4	0.7	1.0	1.3	1.5	1.8	2.0	2.2	2.5	2.7	2.9	3.1	3.3	3.5	3.7	3.9	4.1	4.3	4.5	4.7	4.9	5.1	5.3	5.4	5.6	5.8
176	0.0	0.0	0.0	0.0	0.0	0.0	0.0	0.0	0.0	0.0	0.0	0.3	0.6	0.9	1.2	1.4	1.7	2.0	2.2	2.5	2.7	2.9	3.1	3.4	3.6	3.8	4.0	4.2	4.4	4.6	4.8	5.0	5.2	5.4	5.5	5.7	5.9	6.1	6.2
174	0.0	0.0	0.0	0.0	0.0	0.0	0.0	0.0	0.0	0.1	0.5	0.8	1.1	1.4	1.6	1.9	2.2	2.4	2.7	2.9	3.2	3.4	3.6	3.8	4.1	4.3	4.5	4.7	4.9	5.1	5.3	5.5	5.6	5.8	6.0	6.2	6.4	6.5	6.7
172	0.0	0.0	0.0	0.0	0.0	0.0	0.0	0.0	0.3	0.6	0.9	1.3	1.6	1.8	2.1	2.4	2.7	2.9	3.2	3.4	3.6	3.9	4.1	4.3	4.5	4.7	5.0	5.2	5.4	5.6	5.7	5.9	6.1	6.3	6.5	6.7	6.8	7.0	7.2
170	0.0	0.0	0.0	0.0	0.0	0.0	0.0	0.4	0.8	1.1	1.4	1.7	2.1	2.3	2.6	2.9	3.2	3.4	3.7	3.9	4.1	4.4	4.6	4.8	5.0	5.2	5.4	5.6	5.8	6.0	6.2	6.4	6.6	6.8	7.0	7.2	7.3	7.5	7.7
168	0.0	0.0	0.0	0.0	0.0	0.1	0.5	0.9	1.3	1.6	1.9	2.3	2.6	2.8	3.1	3.4	3.7	3.9	4.2	4.4	4.6	4.9	5.1	5.3	5.5	5.7	6.0	6.2	6.4	6.6	6.7	6.9	7.1	7.3	7.5	7.7	7.8	8.0	8.2
166	0.0	0.0	0.0	0.0	0.1	0.6	1.0	1.4	1.8	2.1	2.5	2.8	3.1	3.4	3.6	3.9	4.2	4.4	4.7	4.9	5.2	5.4	5.6	5.8	6.0	6.3	6.5	6.7	6.9	7.1	7.3	7.4	7.6	7.8	8.0	8.2	8.4	8.5	8.7
164	0.0	0.0	0.0	0.2	0.7	1.1	1.6	1.9	2.3	2.7	3.0	3.3	3.6	3.9	4.2	4.4	4.7	5.0	5.2	5.4	5.7	5.9	6.1	6.4	6.6	6.8	7.0	7.2	7.4	7.6	7.8	8.0	8.2	8.4	8.5	8.7	8.9	9.1	9.2
162	0.0	0,0	0.1	0.7	1.2	1.7	2.1	2.5	2.8	3.2	3.5	3.8	4.1	4.4	4.7	5.0	5.2	5.5	5.7	6.0	6.2	6.5	6.7	6.9	7.1	7.3	7.5	7.7	7.9	8.1	8.3	8.5	8.7	8.9	9.1	9.3	9.4	9.6	9.8
160	0.0	0.0	0.7	1.3	1.8	2.2	2.6	3.0	3.4	3.8	4.1	4.4	4.7	5.0	5.3	5.5	5.8	6.1	6.3	6.5	6.8	7.0	7.2	7.5	7.7	7.9	8.1	8.3	8.5	8.7	8.9	9.1	9.3	9.4	9.6	9.8	9.9	10.2	10.3
158	0.0	0.6	1.3	1.8	2.3	2.8	3.2	3.6	4.0	4.3	4.7	5.0	5.3	5.6	5.8	6.1	6.4	6.6	6.9	7.1	7.4	7.6	7.8	8.0	8.2	8.5	8.7	8.9	9.1	9.3	9.5	9.6	9.8	10.0	10.2	10.4	10.6	10.7	10.9
156	0.3	1.2	1.9	2.4	2.9	3.4	3.8	4.2	4.6	4.9	5.2	5.5	5.9	6.1	6.4	6.7	7.0	7.2	7.5	7.7	7.9	8.2	8.4	8.6	8.8	9.0	9.2	9.5	9.7	9.8	10.0	10.2	10.4	10.6	10.8	11.0	11.1	11.3	11.5
154	0.9	1.8	2.5	3.0	3.5	4.0	4.4	4.8	5.2	5.5	5.8	6.1	6.5	6.7	7.0	7.3	7.6	7.8	8.1	8.3	8.5	8.8	9.0	9.2	9.4	9.6	9.8	10.0	10.2	10.4	10.6	10.8	11.0	11.2	11.4	11.6	11.7	11.9	12.1
152	1.5	2.4	3.1	3.6	4.1	4.6	5.0	5.4	5.8	6.1	6.4	6.8	7.1	7.4	7.6	7.9	8.2	8.4	8.7	8.9	9.2	9.4	9.6	9.8	10.0	10.3	10.5	10.7	10.9	11.1	11.3	11.4	11.6	11.8	12.0	12.2	12.4	12.5	12.7
150	2.1	3.0	3.7	4.3	4.8	5.2	5.6	6.0	6.4	6.8	7.1	7.4	7.7	8.0	8.3	8.5	8.8	9.1	9.3	9.5	9.8	10.0	10.2	10.5	10.7	10.9	11.1	11.3	11.5	11.7	11.9	12.1	12.3	12.4	12.6	12.8	13.0	13.2	13.3
148	2.7	3.2	3.9	4.5	5.0	5.4	5.8	6.3	6.7	7.1	7.4	7.7	8.0	8.3	8.7	8.9	9.2	9.5	9.7	9.9	10.2	10.6	11.0	11.4	11.8	12.1	12.5	12.9	13.3	13.5	13.7	13.9	14.1	14.2	14.4	14.6	14.8	15.0	15.1
146	4.4	4.7	5.1	5.5	5.9	6.2	6.6	7.0	7.4	7.7	8.1	8.5	8.9	9.2	9.6	9.9	10.4	10.7	11.1	11.5	11.9	12.2	12.6	13.0	13.4	13.7	14.1	14.5	14.9	15.2	15.5	15.7	15.9	16.0	16.2	16.4	16.6	16.8	16.9
144	6.4	6.7	7.1	7.4	7.8	8.2	8.5	8.9	9.2	9.6	9.9	10.3	10.7	11.0	11.4	11.7	12.1	12.5	12.8	13.2	13.5	13.9	14.3	14.6	15.0	15.3	15.7	16.0	16.4	16.8	17.1	17.5	17.7	17.8	18.0	18.2	18.4	18.6	18.7
142	8.3	8.7	9.0	9.4	9.7	10.1	10.4	10.7	11.1	11.4	11.8	12.1	12.5	12.8	13.1	13.5	13.8	14.2	14.5	14.9	15.2	15.5	15.9	16.2	16.6	16.9	17.3	17.6	17.9	18.3	18.6	19.0	19.3	19.6	19.8	20.0	20.2	20.4	20.5
140	10.3	10.7	11.0	11.3	11.6	12.0	12.3	12.6	12.9	13.3	13.6	13.9	14.3	14.6	14.9	15.2	15.6	15.9	16.2	16.5	16.9	17.2	17.5	17.9	18.2	18.5	18.8	19.2	19.5	19.8	20.2	20.5	20.8	21.1	21.5	21.8	22.0	22.1	22.3
138	12.3	12.6	12.9	13.2	13.6	13.9	14.2	14.5	14.8	15.1	15.4	15.7	16.1	16.4	16.7	17.0	17.3	17.6	17.9	18.2	18.5	18.9	19.2	19.5	19.8	20.1	20.4	20.7	21.0	21.4	21.7	22.0	22.3	22.6	22.9	23.2	23.5	23.8	24.1
136	14.3	14.6	14.9	15.2	15.5	15.8	16.1	16.4	16.7	17.0	17.3	17.6	17.8	18.1	18.4	18.7	19.0	19.3	19.6	19.9	20.2	20.5	20.8	21.1	21.4	21.7	22.0	22.3	22.6	22.9	23.2	23.5	23.8	24.1	24.4	24.7	25.0	25.3	25.5
134	16.3	16.6	16.8	17.1	17.4	17.7	18.0	18.2	18.5	18.8	19.1	19.4	19.6	19.9	20.2	20.5	20.8	21.0	21.3	21.6	21.9	22.2	22.5	22.7	23.0	23.3	23.6	23.9	24.1	24.4	24.7	25.0	25.3	25.5	25.8	26.1	26.4	26.7	26.9
132	18.3	18.5	18.8	19.1	19.3	19.6	19.9	20.1	20.4	20.6	20.9	21.2	21.4	21.7	22.0	22.2	22.5	22.8	23.0	23.3	23.6	23.8	24.1	24.4	24.6	24.9	25.1	25.4	25.7	25.9	26.2	26.5	26.7	27.0	27.3	27.5	27.8	28.1	28.3
130	20.2	20.5	20.7	21.0	21.2	21.5	21.7	22.0	22.2	22.5	22.7	23.0	23.2	23.5	23.7	24.0	24.2	24.5	24.7	25.0	25.2	25.5	25.7	26.0	26.2	26.5	26.7	27.0	27.2	27.5	27.7	28.0	28.2	28.5	28.7	29.0	29.2	29.5	29.7
128	22.2	22.5	22.7	22.9	23.2	23.4	23.6	23.9	24.1	24.3	24.6	24.8	25.0	25.3	25.5	25.7	26.0	26.2	26.4	26.7	26.9	27.1	27.4	27.6	27.8	28.1	28.3	28.5	28.8	29.0	29.2	29.5	29.7	29.9	30.2	30.4	30.6	30.9	31.1
126	24.2	24.4	24.7	24.9	25.1	25.3	25.5	25.7	26.0	26.2	26.4	26.6	26.8	27.0	27.3	27.5	27.7	27.9	28.1	28.4	28.6	28.8	29.0	29.2	29.4	29.7	29.9	30.1	30.3	30.5	30.8	31.0	31.2	31.4	31.6	31.8	32.1	32.3	32.5
124	26.2	26.4	26.6	26.8	27.0	27.2	27.4	27.6	27.8	28.0	28.2	28.4	28.6	28.8	29.0	29.2	29.4	29.6	29.8	30.0	30.2	30.4	30.6	30.9	31.1	31.3	31.5	31.7	31.9	32.1	32.3	32.5	32.7	32.9	33.1	33.3	33.5	33.7	33.9
122	28.2	28.4	28.6	28.7	28.9	29.1	29.3	29.5	29.7	29.9	30.1	30.2	30.4	30.6	30.8	31.0	31.2	31.4	31.5	31.7	31.9	32.1	32.3	32.5	32.7	32.8	33.0	33.2	33.4	33.6	33.8	34.0	34.2	34.3	34.5	34.7	34.9	35.1	35.3
120	30.2	30.3	30.5	30.7	30.9	31.0	31.2	31.4	31.5	31.7	31.9	32.0	32.2	32.4	32.6	32.7	32.9	33.1	33.2	33.4	33.6	33.8	33.9	34.1	34.3	34.4	34.6	34.8	35.0	35.1	35.3	35.5	35.6	35.8	36.0	36.1	36.3	36.5	36.7
118	32.2	32.3	32.5	32.6	32.8	32.9	33.1	33.2	33.4	33.6	33.7	33.9	34.0	34.2	34.3	34.5	34.6	34.8	34.9	35.1	35.3	35.4	35.6	35.7	35.9	36.0	36.2	36.3	36.5	36.7	36.8	37.0	37.1	37.3	37.4	37.6	37.7	37.9	38.0
116	34.1	34.3	34.4	34.6	34.7	34.8	35.0	35.1	35.3	35.4	35.5	35.7	35.8	36.0	36.1	36.2	36.4	36.5	36.6	36.8	36.9	37.1	37.2	37.3	37.5	37.6	37.8	37.9	38.0	38.2	38.3	38.5	38.6	38.7	38.9	39.0	39.2	39.3	39.4
114	36.1	36.2	36.4	36.5	36.6	36.7	36.9	37.0	37.1	37.2	37.4	37.5	37.6	37.7	37.9	38.0	38.1	38.2	38.4	38.5	38.6	38.7	38.8	39.0	39.1	39.2	39.3	39.5	39.6	39.7	39.8	39.9	40.1	40.2	40.3	40.5	40.6	40.7	40.8
112	38.1	38.2	38.3	38.4	38.5	38.6	38.8	38.9	39.0	39.1	39.2	39.3	39.4	39.5	39.6	39.7	39.8	39.9	40.1	40.2	40.3	40.4	40.5	40.6	40.7	40.8	40.9	41.0	41.1	41.2	41.4	41.5	41.6	41.7	41.8	41.9	42.0	42.1	42.2
110	40.1	40.2	40.3	40.4	40.5	40.6	40.6	40.7	40.8	40.9	41.0	41.1	41.2	41.3	41.4	41.5	41.6	41.7	41.8	41.8	41.9	42.0	42.1	42.2	42.3	42.4	42.5	42.6	42.7	42.8	42.9	43.0	43.1	43.1	43.2	43.3	43.4	43.5	43.6
108	42.1	42.2	42.2	42.3	42.4	42.5	42.5	42.6	42.7	42.8	42.8	42.9	43.0	43.1	43.2	43.2	43.3	43.4	43.5	43.5	43.6	43.7	43.8	43.8	43.9	44.0	44.1	44.1	44.2	44.3	44.4	44.5	44.5	44.6	44.7	44.8	44.8	44.9	45.0
106	44.1	44.1	44.2	44.2	44.3	44.4	44.4	44.5	44.5	44.6	44.7	44.7	44.8	44.9	44.9	45.0	45.0	45.1	45.2	45.2	45.3	45.3	45.4	45.5	45.5	45.6	45.6	45.7	45.8	45.8	45.9	46.0	46.0	46.1	46.1	46.2	46.3	46.3	46.4

INDEX

Arbitrage 269
American Options Exchange 195, 251, 265
Backspreads 169
Bail-out points 133, 140
Bear market 111, 112, 131, 136, 137
Bear spread 212
BEAT THE MARKET 3, 126, 159
Beta factor 275
Board broker 185, 187, 189-191, 195
Brokers 241, 243-246
Bull market 111, 131, 136, 137
Butterfly spread 169, 212
Buying options 52-63, 209
CBOE (Chicago Board Options Exchange) 4, 5, 12 16, 18, 22, 126, 129, 184-185, 225, 248, 251
Calendar spreads 171
Commissions 53, 62, 95, 112-113, 118, 152, 166, 168, 182, 203, 208-244, 249, 255, 259
Computers 249, 254, 268
Computer software 250
Congress 263, 270
Contingency orders 192-195, 197, 203
Conversion 269
Covered option writing 5, 88, 103-120, 210, 224, 236
Day trader 213

Deep-in-the-money options 96, 98, 117, 118, 188
Discount brokers 214-215
Downside risk 115
Executions 184, 194
Exercise 95-96, 204
  defined 93
Exercise price 264
Expiration date—definition 9
Far-out-of-the-money options 188
Floor broker 185, 189-192, 197, 266
THE GAME PLAN CHART 80
  how to use 79-81
Initial margin requirement 223-235
Institutions 42
Interpolation 275
In-the-money spreads 144
Intrinsic value 25-27, 29-30, 35
  definition 114
IRS 259, 263
Kassouf, Sheen T. 3, 4, 6 126, 159, 163
Legging in 193-194
Legging out 194, 198
Limit order 189-190, 193-194, 197-198
Liquidity 43, 188
Listed call option 4, 9-11
  definition 8
Listed put option 6, 14
  definition 12
Long term capital gain 263

INDEX

Malkiel, Burton G. 67, 126, 153

Maintenance margin requirement 223–224, 236–238

Margin 113, 129, 139, 206, 221–240, 248

Market declines 40–43

Market makers 40, 95, 185, 187–188, 192, 198, 266–267

Market order 136, 187–189, 193, 195, 198

Market rallies 40–42

Market trend 64–66

Naked option writing 5, 88, 90, 121–142, 158, 169, 209, 225, 236

Naked Option Writing Stategy Chart 141

Naked spread 143–152, 210, 227–228, 237–238

Naked straddle 152–153, 156, 229–230, 237–238

New exercise prices 21–22

New York Stock Exchange (NYSE) 130, 185, 187, 247

Normal value tables 252–253

Normal value tables how to use 274–276

On-the-money options 126, 165

One-on-one spread 169, 171, 178, 211

Options exchange, definition 16

Option premium 110, 113, 137

Options specialist 183, 205, 214, 216–217, 240–248, 250, 254,

Option traders 40

Option writing 86, 87, 90–92, 103

OTC options (over-the-counter) 5, 11–12, 125–126, 268

Out-of-the-money options 30, 37, 106, 138, 165, 171

Out-of-the-money spreads 144

Partially-in-the-money spreads 144

Playable Option Comparison Chart 73–74 how to use 72, 75–76

Premium 37, 152

Quandt, Richard E. 67, 126, 153

Ratio calendar spreads 5

Ratio hedge 158–166, 171, 197, 210, 231–232, 238

Ratio spreads 238

Ratio vertical spreads 5

Rollover 117–118

SEC (Securities & Exchange Commission) 129

Spreads 62, 167, 233–234, 238

Spread order 190–192, 194

Stock volatility 39, 66–68, 108, 111, 137, 148–149, 252, 254

Stop loss order 134–136, 166,

INDEX

Stop loss order *(cont.)*
195, 198
Straddles 55, 62
Straps 55, 62
Strategy design 99
Strategies & rational
decisions in the options
securities market 67, 126,
153
Striking price—definition 9
Strips 55, 62
Supply & demand 41–43
Taxes 259, 263–264
Tax Reform Act of 1976 263
Thorp, Edward O. 3–6, 126,
159, 163

Time value 26–27, 29–30, 35,
115, 137
defined 25
Trading 184
Traver, Jerry M. 5
Treasury bills 139, 222–224
Variable call spread 171
Variable put spread 171
Variable spread 169, 171, 211
Vertical spreads 169, 171
Volume of options traded 19,
21–22
Wall Street 265
Warrants 4–6, 126
Yield of stocks 44, 114

PLEASE SEND ME INFORMATION ON THE FOLLOWING PRODUCTS AND SERVICES:

Market Letters

☐ Trester Compleat Option Report
☐ Put & Call Tactician

Books

☐ The Compleat Option Player
☐ The Option Player's Advanced Guidebook
☐ The New Index Options Game

Software & Other Products

☐ Computer Software —
  Option Master
☐ Special Option Reports
☐ Options Home Study Course
☐ Introduction to Options —
  Video Tape

Name_____

Address _____

City, State, Zip_____

Mail to:
InvesTrek Publishing
419 Main St., Suite 160
Huntington Beach, CA 92648